The Woman Racket

Praise for Steve Moxon's previous book
'The Great Immigration Scandal'

"A slow-burn Molotov cocktail on immigration... the most serious indictment yet published. His revelations in The Sunday Times brought down a minister and confirmed voters' belief that the government's managed migration policy is anything but that." **Frank Field**, *Sunday Times*

"One of the hardest-hitting exposés of the UK's immigration and asylum system to appear in a long time...deserves to be welcomed as a signal contribution to a debate that has hitherto been characterised by more heat than light." **Venkat Iyer**, *The Commonwealth Lawyer*

"Moxon's book is a frightening description of a total failure of government. Its most important — if unintended — message is that if the Home Office Immigration Department is anything to go by, Britain is far advanced down the road to losing its independent civil service." **Myles Harris**, *Salisbury Review*

"An outspoken account of life in the front line of immigration control. It lifts the lid, not only on the chaos in the Home Office, but on what the author describes as its 'progressive institutional failure to apply the immigration rules'. Mr. Moxon, an intelligent and courageous man, put it squarely to his minister that 'the Home Office was not concerned with the proper management of cases but with the creation of statistics in the interests of the Labour government'. The reader may come to a similar conclusion." **Sir Andrew Green**, Chairman, Migrationwatch

"A fascinating insider's account of the immigration and asylum fiasco of 2004, which reveals how bad ideas with harmful human consequences can flourish amidst obsessive official secrecy." **David G. Green**, Director, CIVITAS

"The story Mr. Moxon tells is rewarding to read, and he has combined his anecdotes and rumination on diverse subjects with very well-researched material, especially on why the economic arguments for immigration do not stand up." **Derek Turner**, *American Renaissance*

"No short review can do this wise and witty book any justice other than to recommend most strongly that readers buy and circulate copies as soon and as widely as possible."**David Ashton**, *Right Now!*

"Moxon appears not so much a racist as a visionary." *Evening Standard*

. . . and brickbats

"a crude and inflammatory tract." **Boyd Tonkin**, *Independent* (this review mysteriously vanished from the Independent website.)

. . . and a wonderful example of the contempt of 'progressives' for white working-class males (the theme of the present book):

"The best thing about this book is that it saves you the cost of an evening in the pub. Just reading Moxon conjured up the filthy red carpet, the sticky counter, the smoky air and the swivel-eyed patron on the next stool, sharing his opinions. Mmm.. . . the book also demonstrates the pernicious effect of the new breed of immigration Jeremiahs: Antony Browne, David Coleman, Andrew Green." **Will Higham**, *Progress*

The Woman Racket

The new science explaining how
the sexes relate at work,
at play and in society

Steve Moxon

ia

imprint-academic.com

Published in the UK by Imprint Academic
PO Box 200, Exeter EX5 5HY, UK

Published in the USA by Imprint Academic
Philosophy Documentation Center
PO Box 7147, Charlottesville, VA 22906-7147, USA

ISBN 9 781845 401092 (cloth)
ISBN 9 781845 401504 (pbk.)

A CIP catalogue record for this book is available from the
British Library and US Library of Congress

imprint-academic.com/moxon

Contents

This book is dedicated to
Norman Kingsley Mailer
(1923–2007)

A fearless and fierce critic of what he christened
'the woman racket'

Foreword

If, like me, you turn to the very end of a book first, then you'll see that this one has been a full decade in the making. It's *not* a follow-up to my account of another racket that I encountered when working for the Home Office. That racket concerned immigration—the book being *The Great Immigration Scandal*—and my revelations led to the resignation of the government minister in charge, Beverley Hughes. The present book concerns a much bigger problem—in part a political scandal in which the Home Office is very much involved—but that's just a coincidence. And essentially this is more a popular science book than another exposé.

When I blew the whistle on the immigration scandal some four years ago, it provoked the predictable 'shoot the messenger' response from government and much of the 'liberal' media. However, within months—and certainly by the summer of 2006 (when the Home Office spectacularly imploded)—*The Great Immigration Scandal* was seen as somewhat prescient. If anything the problems were under-stated. The stories streaming out of the Home Office and from our so-called national 'borders' competed for the top prize in the 'you-couldn't-make-it-up' stakes.

Was this just a case of beginner's luck? Does foresight in one area mean that my arguments in another, unrelated, area should be taken any more seriously? In fact these matters are not unconnected. They are both similar facets of 'political correctness' (PC); albeit that how the sexes relate is important in a more perennial way than recent trends in migration. My decade of research into men–women helped me to see the wider damage caused by PC in the part of the Home Office where I was working.

The *Great Immigration Scandal* was a hot-off-the press affair: it had to be out in the shops as soon as possible after the Home Office officially parted company with me. By contrast, I've had plenty of time to get this one right. And a convoluted genesis it most certainly has had. My original conception was of a P.J. O'Rourke-style polemic; but that was before I came to realise the astonishing extent of the scientific findings that underpinned my arguments. The science more than the politics began to drive the project. I spent several years getting fully conversant with a range of biology and psychology disciplines (my own undergraduate subject was psychology, but that was a long time ago, when the discipline was still labouring under the behaviourist delusion), and the book dropped any pretence to humour. The subject is far too important to be treated in any other than a serious manner, and the original polemic has evolved beyond all recognition into a work of popular science exposition.

This book is, for reasons of accessibility, distilled from an original text that includes full explanations of research that can only be briefly mentioned here. I have also written a long, fully-referenced scientific paper on the function of dominance hierarchy and the male, that underpins the key strand running through this book.

The scientific paper is available on-line, along with supplementary notes to this book, for the benefit of those who wish to understand the exposition here in detail or who would question the provenance of some of the ideas that I develop (imprint-academic.com/moxon). This allows the book to flow more easily, uncluttered with digressions or excess references. Referencing (other than news items, which are well archived on-line and therefore highly accessible) has nonetheless been retained where the findings are pivotal, likely to be greeted with particular scepticism, or can be expected to arouse the very prejudice which it is my purpose here to expose.

Reductionism defended

The arguments in *The Woman Racket* are grounded in recent research undertaken in a range of scientific disciplines, including the new science of evolutionary psychology (EP). Some critics argue that a biologically-based perspective underplays distinctively human attributes, as opposed to those we share with other species. But our higher cognitive functions are no less products of evolution than are our more basic motivations, so they are not as 'in control' of our behaviour as our intuitions would suggest they are. Higher cognition is fine-tuning or making more flexible the ancient evolved motivations—especially those of becoming more attractive to the opposite sex, and competing with same-sex others to this end. This certainly does not exclude the ability to ideate, no matter how much it may appear to have 'a life of its own'. Our 'conscious reasoning' is never other than instrumental to the 'tree' of motivation that drives us. Even the high point of ideation, morality, is now analysed as evolutionary adaptation (eg; Ridley, 1997). Indeed, after the recent adaptationist turn in the humanities, even philosophers have joined in with the attempt to bring morality down to earth from the realm of Kantian abstraction (Katz, 2000).

Consequently, I make no apology for what might seem to some to be a form of reductionism. All science—on whatever level: physical, biological or social—is reductive. The opposing reductionist camp—the social constructivists, critical theorists, cultural anthropologists, feminists and

How the Leopard Got His Spots

An empty but oft repeated criticism of evolutionary psychology is that it is on a par with Kiplingesque 'just so' stories; but this is an elementary misunderstanding of science. Any theory or hypothesis in science must be testable. (Strictly speaking, a hypothesis must be refutable, and a theory must be able to predict, so I will use the term 'proposition'.) A scientific proposition generically is that, counter-intuitively, X causes Y; and by virtue of this it can be shown that Z (or W, or whatever) does not cause Y (rather than this being obvious through simple observation and deductive reasoning).

Freudian theory doesn't pass muster here: a proposition that we behave in some way because our ego needs boosting is indeed a 'just so' story. This is why psychoanalysis is a pseudoscience. This isn't true of real sciences, such as evolutionary psychology.

So, for example, the EP theory of sex difference in what elicits jealousy is a counter-intuitive proposal that an adaptation to increase fitness causes men to be jealous in response to a long-term partner's sexual infidelity, whereas a woman is similarly made jealous by her partner's emotional infidelity. (This reflects the different problems the sexes have: men are concerned that they really are the father of their supposed children, and women are concerned they and their children may be left to fend for themselves.) The standard view is that there can't be any sex difference in what elicits jealousy, because the sexes have exactly the same social psychology.

So here we have a proposition that is easy to test, and which faces an opposite standard view, so data that supports one will necessarily exclude the other. Surveys and experiments have been done using jealousy-inducing scenarios, and the EP proposition is supported. Methodological criticisms of the work have been answered by revised experiments. And a fall-back position of the opposing model that concedes a sex difference but that it is through reasoning, is countered by looking at spontaneous responses.

This sex difference in jealousy is apparent from simple observation, but the explanation of it is not; and distinguishing between rival explanations can't be decided without proper investigation.

their political allies—peddle their 'standard social science model' (SSSM), that the human neonate is a tabula rasa—a blank slate on which society engraves its story. Or to update the analogy, the status of the human subject is reduced to that of an empty computer memory, ready to be programmed. They've had it all their own way for over half a century, but the scientific community is now mostly united in the view that 'nature' is much more important than 'nurture'; the latter providing us not with the important things we have in common but some of our idiosyncrasies. Nevertheless, notwithstanding the overwhelming evidence against it, the 'nurture' form of reductionism has become so deeply entrenched in popular thinking that it requires an equally powerful antithesis to counter it.[1] You can only fight fire with fire.

This book is part of this counter-blast. No doubt one day a mature and synthetic understanding of how 'nature' and 'nurture' entwine will come to pass. In the meantime, this is an unashamedly campaigning text, written from the scientific position of the triumph of the 'nature' perspective. Most of my claims should be prefaced 'from an evolutionary bio-psycho-sociological perspective', but this would be a little tedious, so please take that as implied throughout. Don't say I didn't warn you.

And while we are dealing with philosophical issues let me acknowledge that my historical perspective is *sub specie aeternitatis*—history is viewed less as a series of random events and more as the expression of our underlying (biological) nature. (Although human nature may not be, strictly speaking, eternal, nevertheless the time-frame is long enough as to make no practical difference.) I'm aware that this puts me in uncomfortable company—Hegel is best known for viewing history as the unfolding of the universal *weltgeist* (world spirit); Marx just took the Hegelian perspective and secularised it. And a whole generation of positivist historians, such as Carl Hempel, attempted to explain (and predict) historical events in terms of universal 'covering laws'. This led to a historiographical backlash: under the influence of constructivist philosophers like Michael Oakeshott, historians are now only concerned with detailed historical events—'just one damn thing after another.' This led Oakeshott to deny that there was such a thing as human nature: human characteristics (and human cultures) being nothing more than a contingent response to circumstances. History, from a constructivist perspective, is not so much teleology as tragedy, with the gods interfering in human affairs in an entirely arbitrary and contingent matter.

But this is something of an over-reaction (Oakeshott was always a polemicist). How is it possible to explain, say, ubiquitous Islamic dress

---

[1] Upward (top-down) reductionism explains mental processes as derived from the social-discursive environment, whereas downward (bottom-up) reductionism explains the same in terms of biological endowments (Valsiner & van der Veer, 2000).

codes[2] without understanding that man will *always* have a wandering eye? Feminists argue that it is unfair that women have to cover themselves up as a consequence, but what's the alternative? Chemical castration? Putting out men's eyes? Similarly, my 'Historical Blindsight' chapter shows how much of our 'patriarchal' history is in fact an attempt to protect and *privilege* (sic) women. This is not seeking to deny (I'm no David Irving) that individual men did not use the law of coverture to exploit individual women. I'm just arguing that these seemingly Jurassic practices have to be seen in the context of their time (when the focus was firmly on the family unit rather than the individual) and that they did serve a necessary function from the point of view of society as a *whole*. Even Oakeshott acknowledges that individualism is a modern invention.

I should also point out that in this book about the sexes you will find barely a mention of 'gender'. When I do use the term, it's in scare quotes or followed by '(sic)'. This is because the word 'gender' implies that the sexes are 'socially constructed', rather than essentially different in their nature. My exposition is of the overwhelming evidence against this position, hence the abandonment of the loaded term 'gender' in favour of the (equally loaded) term 'sex'. This issue seems to me to eclipse the occasional usefulness of the term 'gender' to describe some quality of the sexes as distinct from the sexes themselves (or the sex act).

On Knowing Where to Draw the Line

This book has been ten years in preparation and has undergone extensive revision at proof stage. Inevitably, as is the case with any book that alludes to current affairs, it's hard to know when to stop—I was contemplating adding a section dealing with David Cameron's capitulation to the pressure groups over the rape conviction statistics but decided that transient political events were not worth chronicling.

One area that I avoided due to lack of space was the increasing feminisation of childhood and our education system. Our traditional all-or-nothing examination system has been replaced by a modular approach which favours girls' systematic study skills (but disadvantages the truly inspired student who fails to tick the right boxes). Boys are now three times as likely as girls to need extra help with reading at primary school—a statistic that is not unrelated to the lack of male role models at home (although the connection has been challenged) and the fact that 93% of primary school teachers are female. Competitive school team sports—along with any form of contest in which there are winners and losers—are frowned on, and our health and safety culture penalises boys' attraction to

---

[2] An adequate discussion of men–women in the Islamic and Hebraic traditions would require a whole book, so I limit myself here to one sentence (see also page 175, below): Islamic garb, like other phenomena such as foot-binding and female circumcision, is as much to do with female-female competition as it is with men jealously guarding their women.

risk taking and unsupervised play. When did you last see a group of boys climbing a tree? Deprived of these natural diversions it is not surprising that 75% of the children suffering from ADHD (attention deficit hyperactivity disorder) are male. Anyone wishing to examine the devastating effects of the feminisation of childhood and education should read James Tooley's *The Miseducation of Women* (2002), and Sue Palmer's *21st Century Boys* (forthcoming: September 2008).

Acknowledgements

First and foremost, I would like to thank Bruce Charlton, Reader in Evolutionary Psychiatry at Newcastle University, who has taken a close interest in shaping this book; being a diligent reader and commentator on all its sections, and provider of much encouragement and reassurance. Likewise Valerie Grant, Senior Lecturer in Health Sciences at the University of Auckland; and Margaret Jervis, a British legal academic: both of whom deserve special mention. Many thanks go to the following academics in their various fields who in some way significantly contributed, either by argument/making comments or by reading parts or the whole of this book: Catherine Hakim, Malcolm George, Helena Cronin, David Martin, Wirt Atmar, Nicola Graham-Kevan, Jay Feierman, Simon Baron-Cohen, Lionel Tiger and Sir Michael Marmot. In a category of his own for his knowledge and fearlessness regarding campaigning on men–women issues: appreciation goes to Robert Whiston. Then there are those who will not wish to be commended at all, but who provided catharsis through adorning my dartboard as photographs: Harriet Harman, Fiona Mac-Taggart and Vera Baird, with (on the bullseye) Jenni Murray and (on the treble twenty) Julie Bindel. (Germaine Greer resides not on my dartboard but above the loo, accompanied by quotes from her more recent writings railing against the idea that women could consider sex empowering.) Lastly, there's someone I am unable to avoid thanking: the man whose dartboard features a pic of me, my long-suffering editor and publisher Keith Sutherland, to whom I also owe the evolutionary perspective on the size-zero modelling controversy (see page 196) and some of the other panels.

Steve Moxon
Sheffield, November 2007

Progressing Backwards

The political and social foreground

W e're told that men and women are the same. Or, rather, some of the time we're told this. At other times we're told that men and women are essentially and irrevocably different. We're further told that although men and women are different, this is really just something to do with the way we are at the moment, albeit that we have been that way for a long time, living in the sort of society we do. In time, we keep being reminded, all will revert to how supposedly it should be and how it used to be in times of yore: i.e. men and women are the same after all. Even so, it's then insisted that actually, in the end, no matter what we do, men will never get to be *truly* the same as women: men and women are forever and totally different (except when it's more convenient to regard them as exactly the same).

We're also told that women are disadvantaged, and that they've got this way because of oppression by men. We're never told how or why this could be. We're not told why—especially if men and women are supposedly the same—there would be any point in one sex oppressing the other. We're not told how it can be—if indeed men are different to women and oppress them—that by most measures it is not women who are disadvantaged but men (or, at least, a large sub-group or even the majority of men). Nobody tells us why men are maligned as if they're at one with the very few at the top of the pile, whereas all women are championed irrespective of who they are, what they have done, or how they have lived their lives.

Confused? You certainly should be. The notion that males and females—or some essence of what is male or female—are the same or different, oppressed or actually advantaged, is like a juggler with two balls up in the air. He never gets hold of either of them but is constantly palming each upwards and across the path of the other. Eventually the whole spectacle has to come crashing to the ground. That's what is about to happen to what we currently think about men and women.

The contradictory madness about men and women in which we wallow is not shallow. As I will be explaining in depth, it arises from the most profound prejudices we have; prejudices that are currently denied, being invisible to us. We are too close to them, so we can't see the wood for the trees, even though they are the very basis of our politics. They are what the philosopher R.G. Collingwood called 'absolute' presuppositions. They come from the hidden heart of what we are, in the fundamental difference — and complementarity — between men and women. These hidden prejudices are *against men and in favour of women*. It is because of this that astonishing nonsense about men and women can hold sway, hanging unsupported from the political sky. The general consensus about human social behaviour — at least within the chattering classes — is the most plainly false in history. In no other culture — and at no other point in the history of our own culture — have people got things so spectacularly wrong.

The real story of men and women, that cuts through all of this, has only fully crystallised within the last few years with a deluge of new science. It will be a revelation to almost all, having been merely scratched on the surface in self-help pop titles like *Men are from Mars, Women are from Venus*. It is not merely that men and women are different. We all knew that. And ordinary people, at least, admit it. It is that they are different in ways far beyond what anyone had thought. Men and women are also unequal, but it is not women at all, but men — not all men, but the majority — who make up the biggest disadvantaged sub-group in every society. Women by contrast are universally and perennially privileged: *over*-privileged. This unconditional favour has no counterpart for men, who have to meet certain criteria even to be afforded the most basic consideration.

Even so, you won't find me suggesting adding men to the ever-expanding list of 'victims'. As it stands there's but a minority of people who aren't already on this list. It really would be the case that 'we're all victims now'. Instead, the real story of men and women is the key to tearing up the entire list and throwing it away.

The revolution that we are supposedly undergoing towards an androgynous, unisexual world is all but dead. Revolution has always been a case of 'meet the new boss, same as the old boss' (as The Who's Roger Daltrey sang back in 1971), and the revolution regarding men and women is very much a case in point. We've merely been chasing our own shadows, perpetuating the same old attitudes in disguise. The benign consequences of wising up to see this can hardly be over-stated. We're set now for what really *is* a revolution: a science-inspired revolution of understanding.

This is a book of popular science, intended to explain the psychology that underlies the prejudice that in turn reveals why politics manifests in the way that it does. Of necessity I tackle political issues, and I'm aware that this is an awkward mix, but such is the nature of the project. Thus the rest of this chapter sets the scene before the science proper starts. This may appear to distract from the science, but it's essential to outline the seriousness of the political issues from the off. Some readers will disagree with me on the politics, but that need not affect the science. If you're not interested in my analysis of the political and cultural developments that have led to our current problems then by all means skip the rest of this chapter.

Politics naturally comes up at regular junctures in the rest of the book because this is how so often what I'm discussing manifests. The penultimate chapter, on the position of men in family law, deals primarily with political developments—there being little science in this context to present. The point, of course, is that the family is very much the domain of women and an expression of their separate world, with men in effect included on sufferance. I could hardly ignore this area, given the controversy over child contact and divorce settlements that can't be understood other than by the prejudice towards men that the science in turn explains.

Politics is in the end a matter of conjecture, but its manifestation and the social psychology that underlies it can be informed by science. Never before has there been a time when political debate was more in need of this than today.

The Great Disruption

Even if there hasn't been a revolution proper in the relationship between the sexes, certainly we have experienced a major social shift, beginning in the 1960s and continuing apace. Opinion differs as to quite what this is and what factors led to it. It's an interesting question as to whether our current ideas about men–women are (or are in part) a product of this, or whether it was this broad social change that gave rise to our altered ideas. Whatever the answer, the two have become subsequently entwined.

What, in general, determines social change? Do ideas matter or is it more, as Marx insisted, a case of the economic and technological infrastructure? Callum Brown (2000) attributes the decline of Christianity in the West to the hedonistic philosophy of the 1960s, whereas older clergy have been known to claim that it was all down to the *Radio Times*. (A.J.P. Taylor's famously quipped that the cause of the Great War was railway timetables.) According to this Taylorite view, the death of Christian Britain was an accidental consequence of the BBC scheduling The Forsyte Saga at a time that clashed with Evensong.

So what gave rise to this great cultural change, or, as Francis Fukuyama put it, *The Great Disruption*? Most of this chapter is devoted to *ideational* factors—the reaction of Left-leaning intellectuals to their banishment from the commanding heights of economic theory. But first of all we need to take a quick look at more concrete factors. Was the key cause change in the workplace, or new education policy?

Well, both were significant, but they now look more like second-order factors: those that arrived in the wake of change to then drive it further, rather than the initial cause. Probably top of most people's list of prime causes is the advent of universal, near-infallible (and unobtrusive) contraception with, from 1961, the availability on general prescription of the Pill. Reproduction was now no longer inevitable.

The obvious impact of this is the removal of the constraint on women's options caused by repeated childbirth, and women henceforth not necessarily being defined in terms of child-rearing. But family size had long been in decline. The truth is that this wasn't the critical impact that the Pill had. It has now been largely forgotten that the Pill produced a profound shift of identity in *both* sexes. Before the Pill, by unspoken collective agreement, everyone's lives were mapped out before them as an inevitable consequence of the overriding necessity to form and sustain a family. Since time immemorial, the focus has been not on the individual but the family —the basic economic unit of society. (Economists view the division of labour as the principal generator of surplus wealth, and the division within the traditional social unit was inevitably based on sex.) With the removal of the obligation on everyone to prepare for reproduction, there has been a disengagement on the part of both sexes—in their different ways—from the age-old duties to household, family and community; instead to embrace the social abandon of individual freedom and rights.

Coincident with the invention of the Pill, which in a way deprived woman of her archetypal role as mother, other technological change made woman's role as a home-maker increasingly redundant—and correspondingly made the world of work much more woman-friendly. Was it the case then that women were 'liberated' into education and the workplace, or was it because they had no other place to go? If it was the latter, then women were understandably peeved when they arrived at university in the '60s and '70s to find that they were still expected to make the tea while the boys plotted the downfall of capitalism—and then went on to find similar attitudes in the world of work.

At the same time great increases in personal wealth drove expectation to wider horizons. But what most of all opened everyone's eyes to new possibilities was the extension of life itself. With life expectancy as it was a century ago, a woman would have spent all or almost all of her life within a family: first her natal family, and then (without any transition) into the one she created herself. She may well not have survived long enough to see her eldest child follow suit. By the late twentieth century, huge increases in longevity meant that a woman could expect to live fully half her adult life free of any sort of child rearing. This one factor alone, it has been argued, explains the rise of feminism (Davis, 1982).

Fukuyama gives centre stage to all of these factors to explain what he dubs the 'great disruption'; his 1999 book is to date the most comprehen-

But do we really want to?

sive investigation of the phenomenon. He's looking at a cluster of related changes, not least the massive rises in crime and the falls in some forms of 'social capital'; but he sees the core change as concerning the family, men and women.

Whether you can call all this a liberation of women or a change in women's lifestyle because they had nowhere else to go, is another interesting question. (It strikes me that the relative collapse of the raison d'etre of female life—motherhood and home-making—and the elevation of the male world of work to the be-all-and-end-all, can hardly be characterised as male redundancy, but so runs the standard line. It smacks of irrationally lashing out in frustration at what has been lost and the inadequacy of what was on offer by way of replacement.) Yet human beings are nothing if not adaptable, and we would expect that women would be quite able to adapt to the world of work, with or without somehow 'feminising' it. Sure enough, it's hard to think of any work that at least some women couldn't do. (As I will explain in chapter nine, that was never the issue.)

However, it is a different question altogether as to whether women would actually *want* to opt for what were not distinctively female roles unless they had little if any choice—wartime munitions factories may have demonstrated that women could do men's work, but many or even most women were glad to return home once the armistice was signed. The answer to this motivational question is complex and in the main what I'll be talking about when I come on to the science. But there were also ideological factors. The new set of contingencies through which women were obliged to see the story of their lives provided fertile ground for various strands of feminism. Neo-Marxism underwent a revival, and then morphed into a strange new way of thinking about disadvantage, and about men–women in particular. This, along with other varieties of feminism, had an impact on sustaining the 'great disruption'. This is the focus of the rest of this chapter.

The role of political ideology

"Our problem now is to do away with the household and to free women from the care of children."

Anatoly Lunacharsky
Soviet Commissar of Education in the early 1930s

Twenty-five or thirty years ago, the Left was beginning to look like it was out for the count. But in reality it was the beginning of a retrenchment that would have a much more pervasive influence on society than traditional (economic) socialism. For today, the Left looks like it's on a roll, taking hold of all major political parties in the wake of the compromise over market economics and the rapprochement between the socialist and liberal wings that had separated 100 years previously. Conservatives have largely abandoned their habitual realism in favour of Left-styled utopianism, under the influence of so-called neoconservatives (many of whom were formerly Trotskyites). How can this dramatic swing to the Left be explained and what has it to do with the topic of this book?

Over recent decades standards of living have improved beyond recognition, removing the problem of absolute poverty completely — even for the most wilfully feckless — thereby placating the mass of people and distracting them from their allotted role in the Left project. It looks like Marx was wrong in his choice of opiates — when given the choice the proles all trooped off to Ikea on Sunday, as shopping was a lot more fun than religion. The masses changed in the eyes of those in power, from downtrodden workers to be kept in their place, to an army of consumers that had to be appealed to. Margaret Thatcher understood her Marx much better than the Comrades and agreed with him that ideology was an epiphenomenon of material factors; so she concentrated on changing class consciousness by letting the masses buy their council houses (along with cheap shares in the gas board). As a result, perception of class and of conflict between the bosses and the workers faded. Thatcher's ousting of Labour in 1979 is now entrenched, and then the Soviet block spectacularly disintegrated in 1989.

The worldwide collapse of the Marxist/socialist experiment — both in practice and in theory — meant that the intelligentsia had to perform a dramatic rethink and they turned to academia for help. Since the turn of the twentieth century the dominant idea in the humanities and social sciences was that society itself was the most powerful force, influencing or even determining how we all behaved and thought. In earlier decades this took the form of the social-engineering projects of the behaviourists, as symbolised by B.F. Skinner's utopian vision *Walden Two*. During the flower-power generation — the 1960s — the idea was expressed in a very different (and far more anarchic) fashion, but the goals were equally utopian. However, by the end of that influential decade, the innocent 'we can change the

The double life of B.F. Skinner.

Skinner liked to view his work as scientific but he only entered psychology after failing as a stream-of-consciousness novelist. His utopian novel Walden Two *(1948), shows that his real passion was for top-down social engineering.*

world 'spirit had already gained a hard political edge — partly as a consequence of the anti-Vietnam war protests.

Yet it was already dawning on the Left that they had got the wrong end of the stick. As we've just seen, the real legacy of the '60s was a materialistic obsession with 'keeping up with the Joneses' and, against this 'sell-out', radical political philosophy was impotent. The 1960s gave rise not to a more socialist society but to Margaret Thatcher. The end of Marxist-Leninist class war came with the defeat of Arthur Scargill; whereas the demise of Derek Hatton's brand of Trotskyite entryism showed that an even deeper subterfuge would be needed, where people would not express their politics directly (and so be exposed as part of the 'loony Left'), but in a deeply encrypted fashion.

But the dream of the Left to engineer a better society, although mangled beyond recognition, was not going to die. In fact, Marx and Thatcher were both wrong: utopianism is very deep-seated. It's a near unshakeable mindset in the West, being the core remnant of Christianity (Gray, 2007). Something would have to be refashioned, because an entire new elite was still in a different frame of mind from the rest of society. Sizeable numbers of those with a Leftist mindset had found positions away from the commercial ('capitalist') world: in education, the media, social services and government. These people now collectively redrew the picture of 'oppressed' versus 'oppressors' according to a predictably self-serving rationale; spiced or kick- started by what had filtered down from a few key political philosophers such as Herbert Marcuse, Michel Foucault and Erich Fromm, building on the work of the 'Frankfurt School' of cultural Marxism (Jay, 1973).

A recapitulation of a previous political crisis

In the Britain of the 1980s a bigger and more influential elite, born of the 1960s expansion in higher eduction, was recapitulating what had happened in central Europe in the interwar years. It had become evident even

Max Horkheimer (front left), Theodor Adorno (front right), and Jürgen Habermas, luminaries of the Frankfurt school of cultural Marxism

then that the Soviet experiment was failing to compete economically with Western capitalism. Marxism had not brought about a widespread change of mindset at the time, so this was not a crisis for the man in the street. But it was indeed a crisis for intellectuals and those who were minded to put the theory to practical revolutionary test, because Marxism was an *economic* theory if it was anything. So an organisation was set up to develop a model of Marxism that could be applied to Germany and other European countries without encountering what had befallen the USSR. The Institute for Social Research opened at the University of Frankfurt in 1923. The name originally intended for it was the Institute for Marxism, to copy the Marx-Engels Institute in Moscow in dressing up Marxism as a science. But reference to Marx was expunged when it was decided that it served its purpose better if the Marxist inspiration was concealed.

The 1920s were spent fruitlessly trying to resurrect Marxism as a viable economic force to rival Western capitalism. From 1930, the Frankfurters gave up and turned from socio-economics to an examination of the culture from which socio-economics grows or into which it has to be bedded down. This is where the 'critical theory' that is taught today in university humanities departments was developed. It is an extension of the Marxist idea of a dialectical critique designed not to find truth (as in Hegel) but to engineer revolutionary change. For doctrinaire reasons it had to be maintained that Marxist theory was basically sound, so it must be something else that is found wanting. As Raymond Raehn noted:

> When these revolutionary opportunities presented themselves, however, the workers did not respond. The Marxist revolutionaries did not blame their theory for these failures. They blamed the Workers.

Now, although the theory was not found wanting (though very clearly it was, because the foundation of Marxism is the idea that it is historically inevitable) it was felt that capitalism must be in some way more insidious than previously thought. The reasoning went along the lines that if the people were to act according to the Marxist prescription, then somehow they would have to be provisionally liberated to allow them the freedom necessary to act according to what was (supposed to be) inevitable. The shift of ideological conflict from economic to social issues is an extension of the Marxist conception of all power being economic — itself a fundamental mistake — to the even more mistaken idea that all social interactions are invariably about 'power', and are therefore economic.

The whole enterprise exported itself to the USA in 1933 with the rise of Hitler, who was a direct competitor in that he had his own ideas about revolution that radically dispensed with the Marxist analysis of class warfare. There was no option other than exile, and here they could dedicate themselves in a comfortable if still more alienated ivory tower to indulge in the usual quest of thinkers in Western civilization: that of biting the hand that fed them. Now without any contact with reality, and a zest for revenging Nazism, the Frankfurters ascribed to Nazis a supposed distinct authoritarian personality that rendered all individual adherents psychologically unbalanced. This was then applied generally to people living in western civilization as the answer to why the workers weren't revolting.

They used the only tool then available — and now long comprehensively discredited — Freudian psychoanalysis. This was the work of Erich Fromm, who was the pivotal figure to have broken from Marxist orthodoxy to look instead to culture and inter-personal relations (Burston, 1991). They were his ideas that underpinned the subsequent trajectory of the whole Frankfurt School, for all that internecine conflict would see him largely written out of the history (McLaughlin, 1999). The idea was that everyone supposedly was suffering from the Freudian 'repression' of early family experiences in childhood. Whereas Freud saw repression as aberrant and requiring lengthy sessions on his couch as a patient, the Frankfurters saw repression as inherent in all families within capitalist society. They were taking their cue from Marx and Engels, who had both decried the pivotal function of the family in 'bourgeois' society. If the family itself was seen as intrinsic to capitalist society, then since the Marxist analysis is that capitalism is pathological, then so too must be the family. (Of course, not only is there no evidence for the unscientific concept of 'repression', but the family is the universal building block of human social grouping and will arise no matter what kind of society is imposed or attempted. You only have to stop and think of the various extant non-capitalist traditional societies right down to hunter-gatherers, and the invariable failure of any form of 'commune' that revoked the family, to realise that the family can hardly be some invention of early industrialism.)

The key publication by the Frankfurt School was the book that put the seal on the wedding of Marx and Freud: Herbert Marcuse's *Eros and Civilization*. This was the main conduit through which ideas passed to the 1960s student rebellion, and the origin of the notion of total rebellion to bring about a neo-Marxist nirvana of free sex and no work: 'a new civilization where work and productivity were unimportant'.

According to William Lind, *Eros and Civilization* was the book that 'put the match to the tinder'. University of Pennsylvania professor Alan Kors concurs that Marcuse was the key figure in the development of political correctness (Kors & Silvergate, 1999). He turned and returned consistently in his late writings to the subject of feminism, claiming that 'the Women's Liberation Movement is perhaps the most important and potentially the most radical political movement that we have.' Marcuse was a major inspiration to socialist feminism as he saw in it the promise of 'a socialism which could no longer be understood as a change in social institutions, but had to be deepened to include a vision of a change in consciousness and the very instinctual structures of human beings deformed by exploitation and domination' (Cerullo, 1979).

Meanwhile, Erich Fromm argued in his book, *Escape from Freedom,* that man's nature causes him to throw his freedom away and embrace fascism unless he 'masters society and subordinates the economic machine to the purposes of human happiness'; i.e., adopts socialism. In other words, man is intrinsically bad and needs a new society to make him good. No ideology with such a gloomy view has caused anything but grief.[1] Just how a good society is supposed to emanate from universally bad people is never explained. It's a denial of the fact that morality resides within individuals, having been produced by the evolutionary process (Ridley, 1997). It's a misplaced faith in society as a supra-organism in which somehow the organisation, intelligence and indeed morality of humanity is supposed to reside, rather than in human beings themselves. The foolishness that underpins 'cultural Marxism' is just as you might expect from a fusion of the wishful thinking (historicism) and pseudo-economics of Marx with the psychobabble of Freudian 'psychoanalysis' — the two great unscientific armchair theories of the twentieth century mutually accommodated as if two platforms of ungrounded speculation could make up for each other's deficiencies.

Fromm was perhaps the best known Freudian-Marxist, through his text beloved of students, *The Art of Loving* (and, for the younger generation in the 1950s and 1960s, his book *The Sane Society*). It was something of a bible for many students on the psychology degree I took in the late 1970s. They declared themselves to be Freudian-Marxists (in between vehemently denouncing the notion that intelligence is in any way heritable, in

---

[1]   In fact no ideology of any description has ever caused anything but grief, because an ideology is the elevation of at best a partial view of reality to the exclusion of all others, and is necessarily wrong. Science in its various forms is also as a partial view, but the all-important difference is that it is not only empirical but always open to test, and to challenge from other levels of analysis, which, if proving incongruent, then force modification of the theory.

Michel Foucault, who traded in the neo-Marxist cause in favour of a depressive and sarcastic nihilism

proto-PC style, or that inherent biological distinctions — especially sex — had any role at all to play in psychology). This unholy fusion aggressively assimilated the 'me–me' self-centredness that had grown out of the 1960s, and in the end developed into a form of extreme feminism. Fromm is one of the few members of the Frankfurt School who engaged directly with theorizing the problems of gender (sic) and the differences between men and women. Fromm anticipated later attempts to produce a feminist Marxism and poststructuralist analyses of the 'socially constructed nature of gender' (Kellner, n.d.).

Another notable Freudian-Marxist, who shared some common intellectual ground with the Frankfurt School, was Michel Foucault, who gave up the cause in profound disillusionment, developing the apathetic relativism with which we're all too familiar. Foucault was a depressive and sarcastic nihilist; his anti-humanism leading him to a theory of the insidiousness of 'capitalist' social 'power' that makes us control ourselves in the prison of our own minds. This he called 'micro-fascism'. He certainly captured the zeitgeist. Although Foucault made few references to women or to the issue of sex in his writings, his treatment of the relations between power, the body and sexuality stimulated extensive feminist interest. His idea that the body and sexuality are cultural constructs rather than natural phenomena made a significant contribution to the feminist critique of biological 'essentialism'.

The feminism derived from the ideas of these writers went beyond the idea of destroying the family, to destroying any separateness between the sexes, and promoting the displacement of men in favour of a 'matriarchy'. Once again this was taking a cue from Marx in his notion of 'a community of women' (as outlined in *The Communist Manifesto*). With the abandonment of the workers, the largest constituency of the supposedly oppressed was deemed to be women. As recently as 1993, Frankfurt School member Wilhelm Reich claimed (in his book, *The Mass Psychology of Fascism*) that matriarchy was the only 'natural society'. According to Raymond Raehn (Raehn, 1996):

> Critical Theory as applied mass psychology has led to the deconstruction of gender in the American culture. Following Critical Theory, the distinction between masculinity and femininity will disappear. The traditional roles of the mothers and fathers are to be dissolved so that patriarchy will be ended. Children are not to be raised according to their biological genders and gender roles according to their biological differences. This reflects the Frankfurt School rationale for the disintegration of the traditional family.

Writing about multiculturalism in 1994, Richard Bernstein agrees:

> The Marxist revolutionary process for the past several decades in America has centred on race and sex warfare rather than class warfare as in earlier times. This reflects a scheme more total than economics to restructure American society. As the social revolutionaries readily proclaim, their purpose is to destroy the hegemony of white males.

This revolutionary social programme, originating in the Frankfurt School of cultural Marxism, is now usually referred to as 'political correctness'.

'Political correctness gone mad'

The idea behind political correctness (PC) and the 'speech codes' which are a principal embodiment of it, is that even-handedness merely preferences the powerful, so that when there are competing claims between questions of liberty and social equality, there needs to be a re-balancing in favour of social equality. Enter the idea of dismissing the individual and championing the supposed disadvantaged group. It's in a sense an appeal to utilitarianism (an ethics based on the happiness of the greatest number) writ large and is diametrically opposed to the (original) Anglo-American liberal tradition (the word liberal is derived from *liber*, Latin for 'free'). This is before American liberalism became contaminated by cultural Marxism and ended up decidedly illiberal. (To a certain extent the rump of English liberalism was protected by the existence of an avowedly socialist party.)

Imagine there is at issue the liberty of an individual — who belongs to no sub-group deemed by PC to be disadvantaged — then no matter how serious the liberty issue may be, if competing against this is the social equality question regarding a disadvantaged sub-group of society (no matter how slight the disadvantage); then the sub-group is always championed and the individual is always undermined. The sub-group deemed disadvantaged by PC in any instance could be (and usually is) embodied as another individual. So it is just a contest between two individuals; but one will have PC on their side, and the other will have PC as an enemy. The outcome is automatically pre-judged.

This individual, victimised not by being deemed so by PC but actually made so by PC — that is, oppressed by PC — may be simply a guest speaker who is prevented from taking to a platform, or, more usually, self-censors what he/she was going to say. This is an issue of free speech, and important more in principle than in any dire impact personally. But it may be that the liberty question is much more serious, such as the proper examination of facts in a trial, where this individual faces the possibility of long-term incarceration. The principle is the same.

You can see why adherents of PC can use twisted logic to then consider this system beyond criticism. But it is one thing to adopt the absurd premise of treating competing claims to rights in the way that PC does; it is quite another to unquestioningly accept a list of forms of disadvantage that ensure status as disadvantage, which then automatically sorts all individuals within society into either someone PC must support or someone PC must 'decapitate' (the word often used). The crazy logic of PC's adherents completely falls apart as soon as there is any error here. In fact, the dire consequences of making an error is at the root of why all societies have the very checks and balances that PC purports to render obsolete. The point is that PC has made exactly such a profound error regarding men–women, as this book explains and details.

Political correctness seeped into the American university system, actually taking hold firmest in the more elite institutions, and by the time anyone saw that the pursuit of knowledge itself was being fundamentally undermined, it was past reversing. As T. Kenneth Cribb confirms (Cribb, 2004):

> Though some pundits have claimed that the prevalence of the ideological intolerance known as Political Correctness has been exaggerated, the opposite is closer to the truth....(the university environment is) dominated by suspicion that is far more intense than anything spawned by anti-Communist Senator Joseph McCarthy in the 1950s.

At root, PC is an attempt to bring about a political goal by pretending that it is already a *fait accompli* — the ultimate elision of 'ought' and 'is'. It involves lying about what pertains in the present in order to bring about what is supposed to be inevitable: it's what philosophers call 'teleology' masquerading as politics.

For example, because it's held to be axiomatic that men and women are identical in all respects, then the existence of any sex difference is denied. Inasmuch as the sexes are as yet not identical, it's presumed that they will soon be so; and it's therefore deemed important not to reinforce supposed stereotypes for fear of delaying the 'inevitable' change. Conversely, any sex difference must be amplified, to portray it as the supposed oppression of women that the making identical of men and women will erase. This is not just in the case of sex differences too apparent to disguise: anything that highlights the oppression of women must be exaggerated, however slight it may be. PC is nothing if not self-contradictory.

* * *

Most definitions of PC are more to do with how it presents itself on the surface. Anthony Browne's take in his book *The Retreat of Reason* is that it is: 'an ideology that classifies certain groups of people as victims in need of protection from criticism, and which makes believers feel that no dissent should be tolerated.' A liberal heresy whereby an argument is put forward not for its rationality but for its appeal to emotion (especially the feeling of virtue of those making the argument); it's at its strongest when this involves the suppression of any opinion that is at odds with PC. In a nutshell, it's 'the dictatorship of virtue'. This would be bad enough if the virtue was real, but—as the present book reveals—the supposed virtue PC promotes is itself far worse than a vice. The picture PC paints of disadvantage and oppression is not merely false, but regarding the sub-group that PC most despises (men) it's the diametric opposite of the reality.

In his book *Institutional Injustice*, Martin Mears, an ex-president of the Law Society, claims that political correctness is the mindset that has taken over most of the establishment, including the judiciary. PC is usually dismissed jokingly as some sort of irritating zealousness, but of little practical consequence. This is because the great majority of people still don't know what PC really is or where it came from. The term itself was inherited from Soviet Russia, where it dates back at least to the 1930s, and meant ensuring that the comrades kept to the party line. Indeed, Khrushchev employed it in his famous 'secret' speech to denounce Stalin. This reads very ironically today: 'Instead of proving his political correctness and mobilizing the masses, he often chose the path of repression.' (Khrushchev, 1956).

PC was picked up and used in earnest by the 'New Left', before being used sarcastically by some portions of the Left in the 1980s. It was only subsequently that it acquired a new lease of life as a term of derision by conservatives in the 1990s. So the notion that PC had a recent conservative origin—even the term, let alone the actual political philosophy it denotes—is clearly in error. The notion gets merely one-line mentions in oft-cited newspaper articles by Will Hutton and Polly Toynbee, and there is a distinct paucity of scholarship regarding this claim, even within the most extreme confines of academia (a handful of critically savaged or highly partisan articles and books in the previous decade that dismiss critics on the grounds that PC is beyond criticism: Wilson, 1995; Scatamburlo, 1998; Schultz, 1993; Messer-Davidow, 1993).

Such is the ignorance of the origins of political correctness, using the term PC is often portrayed as a *Daily Mail* backlash—'political correctness gone mad'—which is a deep irony, in that PC, as we have just seen, is itself a backlash against the failure of economic Marxism. And this is not simply a case of Left-leaning intellectuals trying to deny the depths to which their own philosophy has descended, because PC has evolved from the grass-roots as well as from intellectuals, to produce what is as much an emotional attitude as it is a documented creed.

Looking up from the pavement

The top-down analysis of Mears, Browne, Lind, Raehn and others is mirrored in the view from the bottom up. Those who grew up through the 1970s and '80s, will have matured in synchrony with the emergence of an acrimonious politics, that was 'personal' right down to the provincial pavement. Extreme feminism (along with virulent 'anti-racism') became an oppressive presence that could entail direct persecution of individuals by self-appointed bigots. There was a widespread flavour of frustration, but this seemed less to do with the reversal of extreme politics after the defeat of Labour (and, later on, the withdrawal of Labour patronage from extreme feminist and other movements), and more to do with a ferocious self-righteousness—a personal self-consciousness of membership of a sub-group that could claim to be oppressed.

The aspect of the intellectual polemic that many ordinary people picked up enthusiastically is that, whereas classical Marxism saw history as all to do with the ownership of the means of production, 'cultural Marxism' had a different one-dimensional account of history—i.e. which group has power over other groups. Any member of any group identified as a sub-group by virtue of 'gender', sexual orientation, ethnicity or disability, automatically had victim status. It was as if all social life and social history mirrored the experience of the black slave under the white slave-owner. This was the perfect excuse for failure, at the same time as it provided a passport to a new social life as a confirmed member of a new club, and even a focus for turning frustration and anger into a legitimated perpetration of abuse. Most could place themselves in a supposedly disadvantaged sub-group, but in particular could trumpet an 'I'm more egalitarian than you' moral supremacy on behalf of others. Starting in single-issue organizations, college clubs, local Labour Party ward and constituency associations etc., these people took their acquired prejudices into the workplace.

Until the end of the 1970s, asserting the interests of the ordinary working man was the cliché resolution of any pub argument about social justice. But the 'working man' seemed to be immune to change, even when spearheaded by a vaunted student elite. So now the attitude of the would-be revolutionaries transformed into a far wider phenomenon to give up as a hopeless cause the acquisitive and relatively affluent worker, who had consistently failed to 'rise up' when he had the chance. Now, in the eyes of an ever-broadening swathe of the politically minded, he would be lumped together with the bosses in the ranks of the oppressors.

The wannabe revolutionaries had, after all, come through the universities at the time when students were seen as the new vanguard that could prod the quiescent workers to wake up to their subjugation. At that time the workers were regarded in a not dissimilar way to how women used to be — and in many ways still are — seen: as being in a state of 'false consciousness'. They had to be liberated from themselves as much as from the system. At the same time, because so many like-minded people had taken refuge within the various organizations of the state, the state came to be seen as not the creation of the bosses that had to be replaced, but the new instrument of social change.

As this generation moved on to fill roles that were supposed to be those of 'oppressors' — albeit much less so, for some reason, than in the commercial sector — then the desire for self-justification demanded that the whole rationale had to be pushed still further. The complete jettisoning of 'the workers' from any consideration within the 'progressive project', left a vacuum where previously ordinary people had been thought of as victims of 'the system'. The vacuum came to be filled with easily identified subgroups in the wake of the American civil rights movement (that itself could trace its origins to the anti-slavery coalition), starting with blacks and other ethnic minorities. Then the focus shifted decisively to women. (This was a reprise of what happened in the nineteenth century in both Britain and America, when the anti-slavery campaign begat a women's rights movement.) Because women were half or more of the population, then the 'progressive project' thereby restored to majority status the 'oppressed'; albeit according to a new definition, and in respect of a completely different group of individuals. In former days, the main question would have been one of class; so middle-class women would not have been included. No more. The new perspective was very much *by* women of the middle class, so women had to be regarded as homogenous, even though conspicuously they are not.

In this roundabout way, the oppressed were redefined as non-male or non-white (or non-heterosexual, or non-able). By default, white male workers need not apply to join the ranks, no matter how low a class to which they belonged. (For a study of the jettisoning of the 'ordinary working man' by the politically-correct intelligentsia see Michael Collins, *The Likes of Us: A Biography of the White Working Class.*)

It is a testament to the emotionality of the shifts in intellectual analysis that a similar process had happened in the minds of ordinary if politically-minded people. Highfalutin' texts mirrored the gut feeling of those who would be the willing cogs in a new state machine. So it is that the political world in which we now live is a bizarre inversion of what it was only, say, three decades ago; with overt socialism now residing in a nostalgia zone akin to 'the summer of love'. The main body of the workforce, then as now, are men (because men work full-time and continuously, whereas women still typically work part-time and/or discontinuously, if at all). Instead of being handed the control of the means of production, as Marxism demanded and predicted (indeed purported to guarantee), working men have been falsely demonized as a mass of oppressors. The state has become a growing parasite on those who do the real commercial labour on which all prosperity depends. In a fantastic form of double-speak, the state's quack form of Marxism imposes an economics that does not merely 'oppress' workers, but now intervenes in private family life to the extent that the workers' own families have been effectively sequestered for the state's own use. And sexual life as well as male family life is subject to unwarranted intrusion in what is a quantum leap of oppression.

Social work is perhaps the pivotal area, because the staff here are at the interface between government, academia and people in families. This is not some articulate and powerful elite but mostly ordinary lowly professionals. The dire situation in social services has been documented from the inside by Ken McLaughlin (McLaughlin, 2004):

> Mirroring the demise of the political left, social work's move from a macro to a micro critique of social power meant that more and more attention was being paid to interpersonal relations. For radicals who had become disillusioned with the prospect of change in a wider political sense, the workplace provided an opportunity to continue their political mission and ease the radical conscience...Gradually there was a move away from seeing the State as problematic to seeing interpersonal relations as the site and source of conflict. The personal was very much political, and being 'anti-oppressive' had become a 24/7 job. You were either anti-oppressive or oppressive.
>
> For all its talk of empowerment, anti-oppressive theory betrays contempt for the masses, whose behaviour and thoughts do not match current middle-class ideals. Its conflation of words and action, public and private, political and personal in social work theory has provided the authorities with ever-increasing justification for intruding in people's lives.
>
> The extent of the backlash (against PC) is exaggerated....It is rare for the criticisms actually to be addressed—especially the charge that new forms of social work are illiberal and intolerant, in imposing speech codes or increasingly intruding in the private realm....Most importantly, talk of a PC backlash overlooks how these 'radical' theories and practices are now embraced by most sections of the British establishment. It is not only the social work profession that talks about endemic, institutional or unwitting racism—the police and judiciary are just as likely to use such language.

* * *

Post hoc attempts to justify the *real* backlash—the Marxist redefinition of 'class' in response to their defeat in the economic sphere—have failed to provide any tenable theoretical support. Men and women are separated by no criteria that fulfil sociological notions of class. Biologically, the idea that dominance is inter-sexual (men over women) is absurd, so there can be no such thing as male 'power' over the female—this is a major point at issue that I will be discussing in chapter three. What we suppose to be some historical glitch whereby a garden-of-Eden type sex equality has been temporarily usurped by—quite what, no-one seems to know—is a chimera.

The whole edifice rests on a vague imagining of an overarching description of masculinity, both within and without individual men, whereby somehow women are victimised. This is the ghost in the machine of society that somehow gave rise to 'patriarchy'. No mechanism for this has ever been tendered, let alone tested empirically, for the reason that researchers well know that nothing of the kind does or could exist.

This is a classic paradox. A man who ceases to be an ordinary pro-social man and descends into criminality is deemed himself to be a victim of 'patriarchy'.[2] He is deemed merely sick, and for reasons outside of his control. A criminal must not be viewed as being intrinsically wicked, or he will be impervious to the social engineering of the state (social engineering being, after all, the raison d'etre of the state). So we get the attitude that male criminals are essentially quite decent, whilst ordinary male citizens (the collective perpetrators of 'patriarchy') are the real criminals. This is what the psychiatrist Charles Krauthammer identified as: 'the vast social project of moral levelling'. He explains:

> It is not enough for the deviant to be normalised. The normal must be found to be deviant. Therefore, while for the criminals and the crazies deviancy has been defined down, for the ordinary deviancy has been defined up.

Normal, middle-class (male) life then stands exposed as the true home of violence, whilst regarding the places where it is actually rife—on the streets of damaged communities—excuses are made of social disadvantage.

There is also a more sophisticated take on this whereby men are thought of as simultaneously intrinsic agents of 'patriarchy' and passive victims of it at the same time—as part of some imagined cybernetic feedback loop. This is handy because, as soon as the faulty reasoning begins to be exposed, there is the flipside retreat to the position that it is not men themselves who are being attacked but the abstraction of 'patriarchy'. The notion of 'patriarchy' really is just a convenient fig-leaf to avoid the charge that the rhetoric is always directly attacking individual men and/or the mass of men. It's the perfect cerebral gulag. From the spirit of the 1960s that Ian MacDonald brilliantly analyzed as a *Revolution in the Head*, we have now come to the '*oppression* in the head' of our contemporary totalitarianism—a Foucauldian self-fulfilling prophecy.

What is not argued is that men are held to be incapable of transcending 'patriarchy', whilst the 'system' continues to be itself that of 'patriarchy'. So although it is their political duty to attempt this impossible feat, only

---

[2] Unless, of course his victims are female, or his crime is supposedly misogynist—sexual assault or domestic violence. In this case his crimes are considered to be patriarchy incarnate, so permanently placing him beyond the pale.

when the agents of political change — non-men (all women plus non-white or non-heterosexual or non-able-bodied men) — have fulfilled their supposed revolutionary destiny, can men begin to live their lives in a non-'patriarchal' manner.

* * *

So pervasively has PC penetrated the establishment that there is almost nobody prepared to gainsay it; most people see PC as just a problem of the political classes and the 'metropolitan elite' being completely out of touch through their own self-interest. Not understanding the origins of PC — in despising the masses for their apostasy — the complaint is that if only those who 'rule' us could get closer to the people, then all would be well.

Was ever a situation so set up for a fall? Perhaps there will be just a gradual dawning followed by a 'what was *that*?' inquisition, but could there be rapid implosion? Once the blindfolds with which the twentieth century has left us are wrenched off, there should be a distinct feeling of liberation. Though the political Left will be rightly held responsible for the new PC totalitarianism, its collapse may herald the resumption of a genuine 'progressive project': one based on a full acceptance of science, rather than a resort to Freudian Marxism, post-structuralism or other forms of discredited mumbo-jumbo. Even better, perhaps at long last we will abandon the adolescent notion of relentless progress that has had such a hold of us. This residue of Christian thought at the root of our Western utopianism leads not just to 'the personal is political' daftness in our own countries, but to politics as war in fruitless ventures in Afghanistan and Iraq. We might make most progress by rejecting 'the progressive project' in favour of a renewal of mature realism.

Anyway, enough of politics and philosophy; the rest of this book is devoted to the science. Here lies the most important and time-immemorial part of the explanation of our kooky notions about men and women.

Chapter 2

Why There Are Males

Men are humanity's essential genetic design and test lab

"Almost everything I ever did, even as a scientist, was in the hope of meeting a pretty girl."

James D. Watson, Nobel Laureate, author *The Double Helix*.

The sexes solve the problem sex itself failed to solve

The essential difference between a man and a woman? It's tied up with the mystery of sex.

Correction: the mystery of why there is such a thing as sex, in rough outline we know, and have known for some time. The real mystery is why we have the *sexes*. To understand the real root of sex difference, this has to be grasped; so what follows is an exposition — in as plain a language as possible — of the relevant science. The necessity for clarity and straightforwardness is bound to come across as a tad dry and didactic, but please do persevere, as you should find this focus worth it for the profound insight it leads to.

Just why are there males and females? After all, we could all be bisexual (hermaphrodites) — individuals each with both sets of sex organs, male and female. (On account of the primary association of the word 'bisexual' with sexual orientation, from now on I will use the term 'bi-sexed'). As long as we had sex with each other rather than with ourselves, then this would be perfectly valid sex according to what, supposedly, sex is for. This is the random swapping of all the genes between any and every two individuals when their mating makes offspring, so that all the genes in the gene pool get well mixed; thereby stopping us genetically getting set in our ways. It helps avoid a collective trip down some evolutionary blind alley, leading to eventual extinction. The point is that to achieve this, you don't need everyone to have only either the one or the other type of sex organs; male or female. Penises and vaginas don't need to be segregated between individuals.

We are not all bi-sexed for a very good reason, but before I can give you the reason — for it to make sense to you — I first have to explain, from a different but not unrelated angle, why there is such a thing as sex.

For a long time in the history of biological evolution there was no sex at all. All individuals of all species were *a*sexual reproducers, making simple duplicate copies of themselves, Xerox fashion. This was fine for simple creatures with simple genomes, because when they produced copies of themselves not much could go wrong. Even if it did, parthenogenesis (as asexual reproduction is called) is cheap, and the extended families of now unviable individuals could simply go to the wall. Quite a number of these dead-end lineages could bite the dust and the local population would just get on with it. But as new species evolved that had ever more complex genetic make-ups, this had to change, because their complexity meant that replication could turn out wrong in a vastly expanded range of ways. And the more sophisticated the genome, the more expensive they are to produce, and therefore the fewer of them there are. Consequently, allowing whole lineages to die was just too costly. So it was that sex arrived on the scene — and sure enough, at first these sexual species were hermaphrodites. Sex mixes up and dilutes genes damaged in replication (mutations), with the result that before they could do much damage to the reproducing group as a whole, they were lost from the gene pool. Or so it was supposed.

We now know that it was more complicated than that. The process of sex actually *exacerbates* the build-up of replication errors (Paland & Lynch, 2006). This is not least because whole lineages don't die off as in asexual reproduction, but also because the repeated mixing up of genes in sex dilutes any 'dodgy' genes, and then in their pairing up on chromosomes as alleles — two copies of the same gene that are not necessarily the same — defective genes can be hidden through being the 'recessive' (unexpressed) half of the gene pairing. The Xerox copy analogy of progressive degredation is more appropriate to describe sexual than asexual reproduction. Sex in itself still results in the genome in time accumulating malfunction to the point that it becomes unfeasible.

Paradoxically then, sex — the very process that evolved to deal with the problem of the building up of replication error — in itself actually contributes to this unwanted accumulation. How has Mother Nature solved this problem? By exploiting a consequence of the evolution of sex. Let me first explain this consequence and then how it was exploited.

Sex necessarily involves the fusion of two as yet undifferentiated cells (cells that have the potential to divide to make any cell type); one from each prospective parent, reserved for the purpose of sex. When sex first arrived on the evolutionary scene, these were identical; the gametes (as sex cells are called) were isogamous. There was no male and female because you could not tell them apart to so label them. Inevitably, though, ever so slight differences would emerge. One would be fractionally larger than the other: they became anisogamous. And once there was anisogamy, differences polarised, because there were advantages and disadvantages of being either the small or the large gamete that so-called 'selfish DNA' within the one or the other exploited to preserve the 'interests' of one gamete or the other after they fused in what is then called the zygote. The larger gamete took more energy to produce and so there were fewer of them, whereas the smaller gametes were relatively easy to make and consequently were made in larger numbers. The larger and consequently less-numerous gamete type represented a logjam in reproduction: the 'limiting factor' in the process. This necessarily places most selection pressure on the smaller gamete (Kodric-Brown & Brown, 1987; Parker et al., 1972).This logjam was thought to be the root of all the various sex differences we see across nature, and not least in men and women. So far as that goes, so it is. But a little more probing of this gets you to a much fuller explanation.

The smaller and more numerous gametes competed with each other to fuse with the rarer larger gametes. With the biological imperative always to reproduce as much as possible (within whatever constraints there were locally), the smaller, more numerous gametes became relatively disposable, and the larger gametes relatively more prized. As they polarised more and more, then this became an ever bigger problem.

It's not just that as the larger gamete gets still larger there are consequently fewer of them, but that sex is an inherently expensive way for individuals to replace themselves and for the population of genes in the gene pool to try to expand itself. One small and one large gamete together make just the one offspring, whereas asexually they would make two: one each. Then there is the problem of the build-up of replication error that sex itself exacerbates.

These long-known problems of the extra cost of sexual (over asexual) reproduction and the accumulation of replication error, were then together solved by the process of evolution taking advantage of anisogamy in a simple way.

The 'quarantining' of both 'good' and 'bad' genes in the male

The solution is really quite an obvious exploitation of the difference between the gametes—which we can usefully distinguish by giving them labels: the smaller and the larger gametes are, respectively, male and female, of course.

If lots of deleterious replication errors build up across the population, then why not simply keep it away from the gamete type that is already holding up reproduction as it is? We don't want females to be loaded down with genetic errors, that even if they don't kill the females, either slow or stop them reproducing altogether. They are, as I said, the logjam in reproduction and need to be left to get on with the job. The less valuable males, on the other hand, could act as a sort of quarantine quarters for all of the genetic dead wood (Atmar, 1991). Sure enough, many males will as a consequence die, or be damaged to the point that they're useless for reproduction; but they are in the majority or easier to produce in any case, so the population won't be affected in the overall rate of reproduction. The adult males that produce the smaller gametes can produce so many that if need be, a very few adult males could supply all of the necessary gametes to fertilise all of the adult females in the local population; and then to fertilise all of the females again as soon as they have finished producing the batch of offspring from the first fertilisation.

What goes for the gametes also goes for the adults they produce. Male adults work as the locus of this process just as male gametes do. But because the male adults are much more exposed to the wider environment and for much longer than are the male gametes, then adults are by far the main vehicle for the process.

The problem is solved.

A wider problem is solved, actually. The 'quarantining' is not just for genetic dead wood earmarked for purging, but also for genetic material that is beneficial and worth hanging on to. Mutations and new gene combinations are not always injurious. Purging deleterious and retaining enhancing genetic material are respectively the negative and the positive parts of the same process that explains why sex, as well as the sexes, have evolved; or rather, why they have been retained as useful adaptations.

This explanation subsumes the various theories that challenged the original view that has held sway for nigh on a century: that sex was necessary to produce sufficient genetic variation. Debate has become complicated (Agrawal, 2006; Misevic, Ofria & Lenski, 2005; Otto & Gerstein, 2006; de Visser & Elena, 2007; Jaffe, 2002) but it had already resolved to a 'pluralist' approach (West et al., 1999; Birky, 1999); the theories all being related. Having not sex per se, but the sexes, equips the reproducing population not just to avoid sinking under the weight of its own accumulated gene-replication error, but to more quickly adjust to any changes in the environment and to thereby out-compete other lineages (and other species), thus avoiding extinction. For simplicity, I'll refer just to the side of the process that gets rid of faulty genes; but please take it as read that I mean both the 'negative' (purging) and 'positive' (retaining) aspects.

Although the reproductive logjam may be the fundamental root cause of sex difference, it is the direct consequence of this 'quarantining' effect that is most illuminating of the sex differences we see in the more complicated organisms, not least in ourselves. So how is this 'quarantining' done? The problem is that if sex is random shuffling of genes, then it's just pot luck which genes end up in male offspring, just as it is for female offspring.

To answer this question we need to get a little technical. I have been putting the word 'quarantining' in scare quotes, because I've been using it as shorthand for what generally happens. Yes, there *are* kinds of actual quarantining in some species; and this can be very marked in certain lowly animals. Plus there are other, more widespread, apparent instances that are as yet disputable—notably 'achiasmate meiosis' (Atmar, personal communication, 2007). These are beyond the scope of discussion here and I will instead stick with the bigger picture. More generally, the defective genetic material *is* indeed purged from the whole lineage through the male; but it's not necessary to actually place the material in the male more than in the female. Instead, the material is either somehow expressed more in the male than in the female, or it's expressed no more and no less than it is in the female but otherwise rendered much more exposed. I mean, of course, that genetic material is subject to natural selection. The result is the same as actual quarantining: the unwanted genetic material ends up in dead or non-reproducing (or less prolifically reproducing) males.

The male 'filter' at work

One way in which genetic material is more expressed in the male than in the female is by putting a lot of the more crucial genes in chromosomes that only pair up in females. Most chromosomes come in similar pairs, so that a single gene is made up of two alleles, with one on each chromosome. An allele may be either 'dominant' or 'recessive', and if the latter it will not be expressed (function) if it is paired with a 'dominant' partner. The sex chromosomes are different in that there are two very different types: X and Y. In females there are two Xs, but in males there is a single X (plus a Y). This means that genes that are 'recessive' and usually disguised in females through being paired with a 'dominant' counterpart gene or allele, in the male are instead naked, as it were. What they code for is actually expressed in the male, although unexpressed in the female. This means that natural selection will act much more on the genes of male sex chromosomes than it does on the genes of female sex chromosomes. The X chromosomes are by far the largest of the two sex chromosomes, and in the genomes of some species they may make up a quarter or a third of all genetic material.

The Y, whilst it may be considerably smaller, is peculiar to the male, so here we do have some actual quarantining of genetic material in the male. And very recent research has shown that there is far more, and more important, genetic material on the Y chromosome than had been thought. In more primitive species, it's much bigger than it is in humans and other higher animals, so this quarantining evidently had more importance earlier in the evolutionary timescale.

The father of the 'genetic filter'

Wirt Atmar is the originator of the idea of a genetic 'filter', whereby males of most species in effect 'quarantine' deleterious genetic material away from females and eliminate it from the whole lineage (conversely allowing males to become the 'laboratory' for new genetic mutations or combinations). More narrowly conceived, it had occurred independently to several researchers over the years that something of this sort must be happening in species with an XX/X (denoted XX/XO) sex chromosome system ('haplodiploidy'). Here the genes on the male's single X chromosome necessarily are more exposed to natural selection than they would be in females with their pair. Atmar saw that a lesser but still very significant difference in exposure to natural selection would occur in common XX/XY sex chromosome systems, and then further realised that there were other mechanisms of effectively forcing more exposure to natural selection in the male of all genetic material; not just re genes on sex chromosomes. In particular, he recognised that the more vigorous and competitive behaviour of males was to this end.

Though he's renowned as a computer engineering professor, Wirt Atmar has always also worked in biology research, showing that a fresh perspective from the world of man-made information processing proves useful in understanding the processing of biological code.

What about the bulk of the chromosomes though? Those other than sex chromosomes — the autosomes — are the same in both males and females. If there is to be more exposure of genes in the male, then there will have to be some other way of doing this than having unpaired chromosomes peculiar to the male.

Enter the second way that males in effect quarantine genetic material without actually doing so: by rendering it more exposed. How? *By males behaving differently to females so that they come up against the environment in all sorts of ways that lead to natural selection.* If males can be driven to behave in ways that expose just how well-functioning or not are their genes, then natural selection will act more on males than on females, even though the sexes are equally likely to have some of the genes that the lineage needs to get shot of.

This contrast is evident in the gametes, which we know are subject to selection and much more so on the male (Lenormand & Dutheil, 2005; Jaffe, 2004). Compared to the single large egg lazily descending a woman's

Woody Allen experiences life as a male gamete in Everything You Always
Wanted to Know About Sex (But Were Afraid to Ask), *1972*

fallopian tube just once a month, there are tens or hundreds of millions of
sperm that a man ejaculates in a brief instant—possibly several times in
just a single evening. Huge quantities of individual male sex cells then
have to compete with each other as they negotiate the various stages of the
female genital tract before in the end either none of them get near the egg,
or one may be fortunate enough to actually attach itself to the egg and fuse
with it. All of the others have fallen by the wayside and thereby taken what
may be their (relatively) faulty genetic make-up with them.

   We all start and end as gametes, you could say; but just as the male and
female gametes are very different, so male and female adults continue in
the same vein. The male is subject to the underlying rules that it is the
female that is the 'limiting factor' in reproduction, and the male that is the
vehicle for purging the whole lineage of deleterious genetic material.
These factors conspire to compel the male to compete fiercely with others
of his own sex.

   Our fertilised egg may be assigned male, and will then grow, in our
human case, into a boy, who soon starts behaving not unlike one of those
sperm that produced him. Research has revealed that by as early as just
eighteen months of age, a boy is competing with his same-sex peers for a
place in the all-male 'pecking order' or—as it's properly called in biology—dominance hierarchy: henceforth DH. This is built up by individual
boys non-consciously registering the outcomes of any contests with other
boys they are party to and self-calibrating their rank amongst all the boys
in their social group. (Not every permutation of pairs of males need fight,
because the 'gaps' can be mentally filled in, by inference: a facility that has
evolved for this very purpose: 'transitive reasoning'.) No individual needs
to comprehend the overall DH, which is merely an epiphenomenon of the

The dominance hierarchy is   *...and present in every species*
usually and most fiercely male ...

whole process (Moxon, 2007). Without these ritualised fights and the resulting DH, males would try to establish who was 'boss' each time they met. So the DH saves a lot of pointless confrontation. It also helps females find males of equivalent 'mate value' to reproduce with, and this makes sexual reproduction far more efficient, and is a major reason why sexual rather that asexual reproduction has been retained generally throughout the animal kingdom (Ochoa & Jaffe, 2006). What is even more crucial about the DH though, is not that it does away with the need for constant contest, but what the contest is over and for.

The human male, just as the male in any other animal species, is challenged in various ways that test aspects of what you could generically call vigour. By pushing systems to an extreme, any genes he is carrying that are not working properly are revealed. Through taunts and fights that get ever more prone to serious escalation as he gets older, if he lives in a hunter-gatherer (or certain other types of 'primitive' society), he is very likely to be killed—a 50/50 chance or more in some societies. In the 'first world' of today, he is unlikely even to get seriously injured, but nevertheless more likely than not to attain only a lowly rank in the DH of his peer group. This will set him up for difficulty when he comes to vie for a place in subsequent peer-group DHs, which in turn will set him up for difficulty in reproducing. His rank is as all-important when it comes to women choosing him as a sexual partner, as to him is the youth and beauty of girls/women when it comes to his own sexual choices. Male rank is the basis of female sexual choice in all species where there is a DH, including the human (albeit, in the latter case, mediated through higher-level cognitive and emotional processes, along with cultural factors).

Women may appear to choose men simply according to how 'good looking' they are, but this is still choice according to status. The qualities that make men handsome are the very ones that particularly predispose to gaining male rank. Height is the single most important physical determinate of status, and correspondingly is the principal physical attribute a man has for attracting the opposite sex (the research on this is so clear that none has been done in recent decades, but recent work does show that height is the main source of discrimination for men in job interviews). As well as height, there is stature — build and muscularity — and facial attractiveness, which is a matter of the symmetry that indicates good health, together with certain features like the 'chisel jaw' that betray high testosterone levels. All of these are obviously key to a male gaining status, from toddler age onwards. Status is still what is being considered when it comes to aspects of personality, and I don't mean just obviously competitive qualities like determination, though this in its various guises is very important. For example, a sense of humour shows self-confidence and social intelligence.

There is lots of research showing that status (male dominance rank) is the basis of mate choice by females generally (Klinkova et al., 2005; Cowlishaw & Dunbar, 1991; Di Fiore, 2003; De Ruiter & van Hooff, 1993); and that this is the case in humans in particular has been well reviewed (Buss, 2003; Okami & Shackelford, 2001). The finding would be even more pronounced if it were not for the drawing of some false distinctions. For example, Todd Shackelford and others found across many dozens of cultures that women choose men according to status, but also because of education and/or intelligence, and if they are dependable and/or stable (Shackelford et al., 2005). Yet intelligence is obviously an attribute key to gaining status, and it translates into educational attainment. Likewise, status translates into calm dependability and an established lifestyle. Having said that, dependability and reliability are best viewed as indicators of how long the male is likely to stay around to help to look after and provision children. So, yes, female mate choice is not just about status, but it is mainly so.

Another confusion is the notion that it is resources that women are after and not a man's status per se. You can't really separate the two, but clearly money is an excellent proxy for status, so that men will often pursue it seemingly as an end in itself. Yet when men discuss income, they talk of 'K' in terms of bands according to which they themselves are valued, rather than what such a level of income could buy. We know that even the highest of women 'high-flyers' still choose men with even higher incomes than their own, when clearly they have no need at all for a male partner as a provider. Research shows that having an income above remarkably low amounts has a negligible impact on happiness. Resources indicate status much more than status indicates resources. As Dawkins might say, resources are part of the male's 'extended phenotype'. There is no evidence to suppose that we are different from animals in that a male's rank in the male dominance hierarchy is central to female mate choice.

The reason that a male instinctively starts vying with his same-sex peers from when he is a toddler is for the very purpose of calibrating to what extent he will be able to reproduce. That women may be interested in him if he is the winner in a male–male contest is no mere by-product: it's the very thing he is competing for. DH rank is purposeless until it translates into mating opportunity and success.

Attaining only a lowly rank, even in societies where this does not seriously affect survival, will certainly mean difficulty in passing on to the next generation what have been judged to be a set of genes that have a degree of build-up of deleterious material that the population is best off without. Here the male comes up against the environment and may be selected against; though the environment in this case is the rather special one of other individuals: those of the opposite sex, that is. Here, instead of natural selection, he is subject to *sexual* selection. It's all the same though. They are both forms of evolutionary selection, and they both drive the working of the male 'filter'.

Self-suppression of reproduction

A lowly rank in the DH will most likely hinder a male in a more direct way. It's becoming increasingly apparent that part and parcel of the biological phenomenon of relative dominance, is the way that it triggers a hormonal damping down of fertility and sex drive (Moxon, 2007). Physiological 'reproductive suppression' has been revealed in all sorts of species, and to what extent it is evident in an individual is apparently linked with and determined by that individual's dominance rank. (The correspondence may be only a rough one, because there are costs to any adaptation that cancel benefits beyond the point at which 'expensive' fine-tuning is required.) Individuals seem simply to automatically suppress themselves, either entirely autonomously or in response to a signal from the top-ranked individual — by a non-conscious mechanism, of course. If you are high ranking, then you are not reproductively suppressed, or only to a small degree. But if — as is more likely — you are lower ranked, then you are reproductively suppressed to a greater degree; possibly completely so. In many species, the suppression is total for all but a sole breeder, the alpha male, with all other individuals acting as alloparents. These are the 'co-operative breeding species' (Creel, 2001). In most species, it appears that it must be a gradient of some kind.

Why would a male literally suppress his own fertility and sexual behaviour? For the same reason that he acquiesces to whatever is his rank in the DH; to which in any case reproductive suppression appears to be inextricably linked. It's for self-interest and — as if that doesn't seem strange enough — in the collective interest of everyone: all males and all females.

No matter what rank a male occupies, he has a strategic interest in being in the DH. There is usually no survivable alternative of being outside the DH, which includes all male individuals of a reproducing group, bar any that have been specifically excluded for trying to subvert it. Within it there is 'policing' through the evolution of psychological 'cheater detection' mechanisms to stop any individual from trying tactical subversion — anything that is directly or indirectly an attempt to gain sexual access other than through entitlement by rank (I'll have much more to say about 'cheater detection' in later chapters). At worst, a lowly rank offers a refuge. It may enable an individual to bide his time until he is better equipped to ascend the ranks. Any position is a platform offering the potential to climb the hierarchy, which a male will eagerly grasp because being the producer of the smaller gamete — and the victim of the polarisation between male and female this has driven — he has the potential to be a prodigious reproducer (though risks being consigned to reproductive oblivion).

For all the evident self-interest, however, the self-suppression of fertility and sexual behaviour is primarily driven by the biological imperative of gene replication itself, that in effect makes the male behave in the interests of the reproducing group as a whole. A 'population genetics' perspective is to study genes as they behave in the ecological reality of a whole finite reproducing population, rather than in what are merely their 'vehicles' (as Richard Dawkins called them) of individuals. It's in this local total gene population that maximisation of replication is achieved, and this is not simply by making many more 'vehicles', but also by making higher quality 'vehicles' that are not themselves going to fail to reproduce and take out all of the genes they are carrying with them.[1]

As the female is the 'limiting factor' in reproduction, it's important that all females reproduce, almost irrespective of their own quality. For males, on the other hand, it's very different. Given that potentially just a few of the males can provide all of the required male gametes for the whole reproducing group, then it makes sense that only the very fittest of them are allowed to do this, because they make the offspring that are most likely to reproduce themselves and thus maximise gene replication. Within the reproducing group, setting physiological reproductive suppression so

---

[1] This generally-accepted contemporary position transcends the stale old debate about whether there is 'group selection', that Richard Dawkins' over-emphasis on the individual gene level of analysis spawned (Keller, 1999). Lineage selection serves to favour long-term over short-term benefits, in any case (Nunney, 1999). It is now agreed that to understand natural/sexual selection you have to look simultaneously at the individual gene and the whole gene pool.

that it eases off the higher the male's DH ranking achieves this beautifully. Though paradoxical it may seem, the 'selfish gene' here drives in most males quintessentially *un*selfish behaviour.

It may well be that this variable physiological reproductive suppression is what dominance first evolved for. It may be that the way females use the male DH to select which males to mate with was something that evolved subsequently. We don't know. It would make sense, because it's a fairly simple process for the brain, after it has registered its owner's own rank, to simply trigger a roughly-corresponding level of release of a hormone that would in turn adjust fertility and/or sex drive to an appropriate level. It requires less sophisticated brain circuitry than that involved in working out the goings on in the alien society of the opposite sex; and we know we have to do this, so as to make choices about which individuals are worth having sex with.

The upshot of the male 'filter'

Individual males are selectively disadvantaged so that they can fulfil their collective function of acting as what we might call the 'genetic filter' on behalf of everyone (Atmar, 1991). There is no objective criteria to this. The evolutionary process runs away with itself, being blind and quite capable of producing all kinds of absurd adaptations, such as the peacock's crazily unwieldy tail—a case in point.

Male life is set up to produce disadvantage that is relative but nonetheless all too real; and this not for the minority but for the majority. So it is with men as it is with males of any species. The actual differences between males can be large or insignificant, or starting from a low or a high base; it makes no odds. Even if all or most men had as their common platform attributes sufficient to make them all a combination of the best qualities of, say, David Beckham and Albert Einstein. Given an elite that is still better endowed, however marginally, then the glut of Beckham-cum-Einsteins will be consigned to relative or even total reproductive oblivion. The reality is that by any objective measure, almost all men alive today *are* Beckham-cum-Einsteins. This perennial relativity, together with the drive to reproduce being fundamental to what we all are, means that males are trapped. To avoid social denigration, they are obliged to fulfil the biological role of acting as 'genetic filter' on behalf of the whole local reproducing community and, in effect, ultimately for the species as a whole.

This stark truth, and the contrast with the female, is behind the whole tree of motivation and behaviour common to each and across all species, and how this is dichotomized according to sex. Human social psychology must be attuned to and support this state of affairs. Evolutionary science would predict that, lurking beneath the veneer of our supposedly equitable and egalitarian modern societies, there must be profound prejudice against the male sex: by men and women alike. In fact it's startlingly obvious on the surface once you know where to look, as I will be demonstrating. It's apparent in every scenario where men and women come up against each other, so to speak. The way that prejudice against men is evident throws light on our social psychology, that has built on the essential difference between the sexes, and to make matters ever worse for the male sex.

This won't essentially change, but even though we can't ameliorate it in any essential way, we can do so in some respects. We can make ourselves aware that we are playing a game that artificially stretches out the men we know in our communities so that most falsely appear in some respects as losers, nitwits, weaklings, or devils beyond the pale. In our supposedly equitable societies we champion the 'socially excluded', but we have been unfairly excluding huge numbers of people — the vast majority of ordinary males — all along. Then, to outrageously compound the offence, we expressly exclude them from the consideration normally afforded to those socially excluded and in need of support.

Instead of ameliorating this most profound source of unfairness in all societies, we have been doing very much the opposite. Not understanding that our psychology is literally to 'do down' males, we have rationalised this into thinking that there must be something wrong with them all — we assume that our generic 'doing down' must be for good reason. This 'folk prejudice' has been ridden piggy-back by the politics of feminism that claims to identify just what it is that males supposedly are doing wrong: that they 'do down' females!

Males of all species do anything but. They *prize* females, for the essential biological reason that females represent the logjam in reproduction. Will the proponents of PC and extreme feminism continue to congratulate themselves when they find out that the notion that men somehow 'oppress' women is the biggest howler in history?

Once we get this inversion of reality right-side-up, then at least we can stop that part of our biological predisposition from turning into a political perversion. This is not to claim victim status for men. Not only are some men startlingly successful, but most if not almost all men are anything but deficient by any objective criteria. What is important to further social justice is *not to give victim status to men but to revoke it for women*. The entire 'victimocracy' that PC has created needs to be shown the door if we are to have any proper perspective on the reality of disadvantage, and thereby arrive at social justice. The linchpin of the 'victimocracy' though, is its major sub-group, and majority of the population: all of the non-men.

Summary

We knew, roughly, why there is such a thing as sex, but we didn't know why there are the sexes. The reason we're not all bi-sexed is not because of a problem that sex itself evolved to solve. Sex, strangely, made the problem worse.

To get shot of genes made faulty in copying, they are in effect 'quarantined' away from the female half of the reproducing group, because this is where there is already a logjam. So the males act as 'genetic filter' for the whole lineage.

Most 'quarantining' is not actually placing faulty genes in males and away from females, but making them more apparent in males, on whom selection can then operate. Males are driven to behave in ways that expose any genetic defects they have, and females then choose the better of them. In this way females augment natural selection to help the male 'filter' to work.

The male 'filter' function is still further entrenched by a male's rank in the dominance hierarchy directly impacting on his fertility. A male literally suppresses his own reproduction to a degree in line with how useful he is to the local reproductive pool.

Inevitably the female is valued and the male devalued. This evolved prejudice is now bolstered by a politically-motivated misreading that has got it all entirely back to front. Widespread understanding of this will be for the good of us all.

Chapter 3

The Real 'Power'

Intra-sex dominance and female privilege

'Power' and 'dominance'

Our mistaken beliefs about the sexes are derived from a false idea about 'power'. Men supposedly exercise some sort of 'power' over women. But it is never properly explained what exactly this 'power' is. It alternates between being either some *essence* of man, or something that is not inherent in men but instead is to do with a *historical invention* of what men are, or supposedly should be. The latter is the idea that somehow masculinity is not natural, but results from contamination by a cultural virus, and to such an extent that men have become the embodiment of it. The opposing and simultaneously-held position is that masculinity is natural. The point is that these two mutually-contradictory views have to be held together, because masculinity can hardly be *universally* inculcated in men by society if the basis of it is not in man in the first place. Society is only the representation of human social psychology, after all. The notion falls at this very first hurdle, but nevertheless it currently holds sway to underpin all discussion about the sexes, virtually unquestioned. This supposed cultural and psychological 'patriarchy' is reckoned to be the basis of our current social ills, albeit that some day, sociologists and ideologues tell us, it will fall away.

When the prejudicial attacking of men is pointed out for what it is, the ideologues then try to excuse this as not the targeting of men as such but an abstraction called 'masculinity'. It doesn't phase them that masculinity is inextricably bound up with men, and the goal of eliminating it apparently recedes ever further into the distance. This is put down to the insidiousness of this unnatural historical thought crime. It merely requires still more effort, we're told, and the link between men and masculinity in the end will be destroyed. The harm this does to men individually and collectively is deemed at worst collateral damage, necessary in the pursuit of a worthwhile goal.

What is lost sight of is that like all phenomena, human social behaviour is natural and cannot just fall out of the sky. Apart from the 'power' that arises from being the 'limiting factor' in reproduction—an entirely female 'power' base—the 'power' that exists in nature derives from dominance hierarchy (DH). And this cannot be the basis of a claimed 'power' of men over women, because dominance/DH never exists between the sexes; *it's only ever amongst same-sex individuals.*

Throughout the animal kingdom, as I explained in the last chapter, the fact that the female is the 'limiting factor' in reproduction explains the use of the male as a genetic 'filter'; which in turn explains why males are organised into a DH. It would hardly make sense for females to compete with males in this. The whole point of 'quarantining'—for the purpose of purging genetic material on the male side of the lineage—is to allow females to get on with reproduction. In joining males to be tested in various ways for vigour, not least in combat, females would risk injury or worse. This would be senseless for the sex that is the 'limiting factor' in reproduction, which is otherwise almost guaranteed to reproduce. For the very reason that males have to exhibit vigour in contest for DH rank to fulfil their role as genetic 'filter', they have evolved to be on average significantly larger than females, so if there were any contest in earnest between the sexes, males would win the overwhelming number of encounters.

Although a unisex DH would be absurd, there *is* a scenario where females and DH makes sense. This is if females take after males and 'battle' only with each other; only with other females to make a DH all of their own. 'Battle' is not really the word though, because there would be no sense in females proving their vigour. They have only to be fertile. This is the criteria of male sexual choice. In human terms, this is youth and beauty, because the most fertile women are those who are young and beautiful—beauty being simply facial symmetry and aspects of body shape that demonstrate healthy functioning or more directly fertility, such as hip-to-waist ratio (all of which we near instantaneously and non-consciously assess). This is a 'given' that can't be fought over or demonstrated by any action. So females wouldn't be risking their virtual guarantee to be able to reproduce. What then would be the point of females vying with each other over their relative fertility?

We have to look at the benefit to the whole reproducing group; to the whole gene pool. The male DH benefits the gene pool because the fittest and therefore higher ranking males are more likely to be chosen as mates, and these individuals are less reproductively suppressed. More of the genes that are best at replicating themselves are replicated, in a benign circle. But with females, the more fertile amongst them are going to be preferentially chosen by males anyway, so a female DH won't benefit the gene pool in this way. And don't all females need to be and will be mated? Yes, in an ideal world where there are no constraints on reproduction. In ecological reality, however, all reproducing groups most of the time cannot hope for all offspring of all matings to survive the various problems that

The dominance hierarchy is an intra-sex (usually male) phenomenon

arise, such as food scarcity. It makes sense, therefore, to give preference to the females that are most fertile and so of highest 'mate value', together with their correspondingly higher-ranking male mates. Consequently, a role for a female DH presents itself. As with males, the less-fit females could be reproductively suppressed. This would likewise benefit the gene pool. Not as much as does reproductive suppression in the male, but a benefit nonetheless. We should expect this, but for it to be not as pronounced as it is in the male.

So how does a female DH form if it does not involve physical contest? Mostly it's simply by inheritance—including in primates and human societies. The physical attributes of females that are attractive to males in signalling fertility of youth and beauty are predominantly genetically based, so are well conserved from one generation to the next (but see panel on facing page). Attractive women will tend to have attractive daughters. The key attribute of youth is an even more pronounced 'given', in that older age cohorts are simply not 'in the game'.

* * *

I've given a simple general account here: one that squares with what is going on in our own species. There is considerable variation according to species, especially looking far back down the evolutionary tree—DH being evident in insects and even more primitive forms. There may be:

- a female DH only (usually when there is no male sociality at all);
- a DH of very few individuals, or even the alpha pair only (usually where the environmental niche is extremely harsh and others are alloparents in a co-operative breeding system);

The Female DH

In traditional societies a woman's position in the DH is largely a product of nature, as youth and beauty are the main factors. However the existence in modern societies of multi-billion dollar cosmetics, fashion and plastic surgery industries shows that beauty can be enhanced and the ravages of age can at least be postponed. The rocketing sales of celebrity and beauty magazines shows that women are indeed keen to rank themselves according to a uniquely female DH; but the great difficulty involved in attempting to overcome the limitations of nature has manifested itself in the form of modern female epidemics such as anorexia nervosa and bulimia (see panel on page 196) — slimming disorders being rare in males.

Perhaps the sheer difficulty of the task of climbing the female DH (males simply have to work harder or take extra risks) explains the fascination of Victoria Beckham to a female audience — her strange elfish

features and cyborg-style cartoon body are more frequently found on the front cover of women's magazines than anyone else. If such an odd-looking creature is attractive to an uber-alpha male like her husband David, then women are understandably eager to reassess their *own* DH ranking in the light of this.

Females also tend to compete by doing down other females in terms of sexual propriety — hence the common playground 'ho' and 'slag' derogations. This alerts men to a woman's propensity to indulge in extra-pair sex, and consequently might well put them off considering her as a long-term partner.

There is in fact a growing interest in feminist evolutionary theory among a number of authors (Hurley, n.d.; Ingo, Mize and Pratarelli, 2007).

Is there an evolutionary explanation for women's fascination with the increasingly bizarre looking Victoria Beckham?

- no DH of one or even both sexes (usually when there is dispersal from the reproducing group before sexual maturity);
- or a DH amongst only a subset of individuals of one sex (usually those who are not natal to the group).

Through all this variation, however, two general rules seem to be evident. Where there is a DH there is physiological reproductive suppression that varies with rank, and vice-versa; and the male and female DHs are entirely separate (Moxon, 2007).

It is sometimes supposed, even by biologists, that there is just one DH that includes both sexes, but that all male individuals rank above all female individuals. As I outlined at the outset of this book, this is a *political* dogma that has been falsely imported into biology. A classic anthropomorphism. It is a false understanding because if the sexes were contesting in earnest then, albeit that most females would lose to males, not all of them would. In most species — not least our own — there are always some females who are bigger and/or feistier than some of the males. That males supposedly are invariably dominant 100% over females shows that something other than dominance is at issue. This is even clearer in the rare species where there is the reversed case of supposed 'female dominance'. Here, all female individuals are thought to be dominant to all male individuals, even though males tend to be the physically larger sex. Usually though, the 'dominance' is apparent exclusively in feeding, where (for example, in the ring-tailed and grey mouse lemurs) the female will just take food from the hands of males, who carry on as if nothing had happened (Radespiel & Zimmerman, 2001). There is not even yielding; just a non-interaction. This is not submission in the sense of sub-dominance. It's altogether different — it's deference. This happens because it's essential that the sex which is the 'limiting factor' in reproduction has feeding priority. This appears to explain all instances of supposed 'female dominance' (Kappeler, 1993). Much more usually, mechanisms of 'resource partitioning' between the sexes have evolved, and these may be behaviours or actual physical adaptation. For example, many bird species have different beak types for males and females so that they are bound to seek different foods or to do so in different habitats. Giraffes use a behavioural adaptation: males stretching their tall necks to feed on high tree branches, whereas females effortlessly put out their necks more horizontally to feed more easily at normal body height.

There may be seeming or actual aggression between the sexes in many species, but none of it is a contest over dominance. It's sometimes said that male youngsters (eg, chimpanzees) fight with adult females until they have bested all the females, and only then vie with males. It seems though that they're just playing; rehearsal for when the male youngsters have adult males to properly contend with. Females may snap at males and vice-versa, but this is likely to do with preventing a mate from straying ('mate guarding'). Females with newborn will often act aggressively to males if they approach, but this is maternal protection. There is always a better explanation than dominance whenever there is occasional mild aggression between the sexes.

What clinches it is that there is a clear-cut genetic basis ruling out dominance between the sexes. Amazingly, a single gene has been found in mammals that allows males to engage dominance behaviour when they encounter another male. It is possible to experimentally 'knock out' this one gene, called 'TRP2' or 'Trip2', to see the difference in behaviour. This has been done in mice (Stowers et al., 2002). Male mice with their 'Trip2' gene 'knocked out', stop using dominance behaviour to other male mice altogether, and instead behave to them exactly as they do towards females. Instead of trying to repel them from their cage, they try to mate with them. This shows that default male behaviour is to treat all others of the same species as females. Only if there are signals that the other individual is not female is dominance behaviour triggered. Presumably, if this is the case in mice, it is also the case in all mammals; primates included.

'Knocking out' the same gene in female mice likewise prevents them from identifying the sex of others, so that they treat males and females identically (Kimchi et al., 2007). Not only do the females stop being maternally aggressive, but they lose all of their sex-typical behaviour, even including female sexual behaviour! Just like the males, they try to mount other mice. Instead of the female copulatory position of a receptive arched back, they become sexually agentic.

This all makes good evolutionary sense. Reproduction is key, and the agentic sexual behaviour of the male is the most crucial behaviour – the female will conceive even if she does nothing. Certainly the male had better know when the other he meets is not female, but even more important is to be sexually agentic if indeed the other *is* a female. Females would do best to over-ride this default behaviour to become sexually receptive, but it's not so crucial. The most parsimonious mechanism is to evolve an algorithm whereby there is the facility in all individuals to behave with sexual agency, and then to build refinement on top of that by dichotomising to produce different behaviour in certain contexts according to sex.

What this neat research demonstrates is profound. There is a default sociality in both sexes of sexual, not dominance behaviour. It must be that the first event in any social encounter is to sex the other individual. It's important to do this before even considering engaging dominance behaviour. Yet I'm not aware of any research that shows this. I'm left with just an anecdote that may be revealing.

I recall when I was in my school library one day. A fair few other pupils were about, sitting or browsing the shelves. Mainly boys but some girls too; all in our mid-teens. Then someone entered the room and at once everything froze. It seemed like a long time, but I imagine it was just for a few seconds: all of us were struck by the same realisation that this new person suddenly in our company was somehow neither a boy nor a girl. For a few moments she was an intersex, and nobody could do anything but freeze and stare. Then everyone realised together: it was a girl. There was instant communication around the whole library as if by telepathy, followed by audible relaxation of tension. We all instinctively knew that we had all been stunned by exactly the same thing; had all taken the same length of time to finally sex this individual; and all felt precisely the same strange relief that the problem had been solved.

* * *

The same separation between the sexes that I've been discussing is apparent in ourselves, as I have previously mentioned. The male child who competes for a place in his peer-group DH from toddler age does so only with other boys; not with girls. Four-year-old boys can tell you all about the DH of which they are a part. Who is tougher than whom in their school playground, and where they themselves fit in to the scheme of things. In other words, they can rank everyone including themselves. They never include girls in this.

It might be thought that this is simply a case of childhood being a recapitulation of our evolutionary past, just as it's apparent that 'ontogeny recapitulates phylogeny' in human development in the embryo. No doubt childhood social life is a primitive forerunner of how we relate to each other as adults, but this does not mean that the underlying essentials of our behaviour suddenly disappear. Adult male social life can be envisaged as complicated by sometimes hugely extensive, multiple and overlapping DHs that fall across age cohorts, geographical location, etc; rather than the usual single DH of those in the same tight age cohort in the immediate neighbourhood that is all a young child has to contend with. The way that position in the DH is contested is also more complicated. The brute force of childhood encounters is usually replaced with far more subtle and wider-ranging modes of trying to win. There is more sophisticated coalition formation, where it seems that rather than dominance per se, there are attempts to attract others, and to do this via the group rather than in iterated one-to-one fashion. This can be seen as just an extension of 'transitive inference' of rank, but some posit the evolution of a new type of dominance sometimes dubbed 'hedonic' or 'prestige' dominance (rather than 'agonic' or 'agonistic'). But it's all more of the same: competition for status. Some argue that 'counter-dominance' has evolved, but this is simply dominance contest by another name, albeit that it may sometimes involve changing the grounds of contest — to be liked rather than feared; as if this is some innovation that our ancestors had not discovered. This cannot be: we know other primates had beaten them to it. It evolved further back in time.

A few have claimed that status in society can be on the basis of evident merit, as if this is somehow divorced from status to make not a hierarchy but a 'heterarchy'. Pretending that status can be conferred in a way that doesn't make it a rank is a nicely self-serving rationale for cultural anthropology professors, I don't doubt; but truly silly. It just goes to show how easy it is to fail to recognise the various manifestation of dominance and/or behaviour that is instrumental to it.

Many will object that there is something unique in humans that entirely supersedes what motivates animals, but this is not to understand that higher animal species are merely more sophisticated variants of lower animal species — essentially functioning in the same way. Seen from an evolutionary perspective, they are just better at doing the same things; often more subtly or flexibly so as to take account of more information from the environment, and to use delay or deception. They do not somehow transcend their biology, no matter how it may seem that they do. Behavioural flexibility to satiate the motivational set is often mistakenly confused with empty debate about determinism — rooted in a confusion about what determinism is. Indeed, the more successful at self-actualisation are higher animal species, in no matter how roundabout a manner, then the *more* faithful is their adherence to their biological blueprint.

In their male aspect, all human societies — in common with those of animals — are hierarchical. Our mega societies stretch the evolved social psychology that we all as humans share, but you can discern DH in adult human male groups easily enough, either as an onlooker or as a participant, just as young boys can. To help with coping in unwieldy social structures — and to support higher-order manifestation of DH — we give labels to positions in organisational hierarchies. Nevertheless, men may not be necessarily more than vaguely aware of what drives them; rarely reflecting on how their lives are bound up with hierarchy, even though most of what they do only makes sense in these terms.

Psychological salience:
The more important the behaviour, the less we're aware of it

Men are not directly aware of their behaviour within the DH, just as we're all not aware of any but a tiny proportion of everything else that goes on in our own minds. And even this tiny proportion is often not at all to do with our most important motivation and cognition. (I'm using the word 'cognition' here as a catch-all for 'thought', whether conscious or non-conscious: all of the processing and inter-connective neural activity that goes on within the brain). The vast majority of our brain processes are non-conscious, despite evolution having made humans the pinnacle of evolved motivational and behavioural flexibility. Consciousness is not unique to humanity, being simply the integration of brain processes, shiftingly focussing to link salient aspects with the bigger picture, enabling us to make an informed choice about how to behave in a certain situation. The more levels of sophistication that evolution provides, then the more that basic function is obscured underneath it—obscured but very much still there and pulling the strings.

Humans are like all life forms in that we are machines to reproduce; vehicles for constellations of genes that are designed to replicate. The higher the life form, the better placed it is to manage replication within whatever environment it finds itself. Nevertheless, the individual vehicle for all this is built economically on a 'need to know' basis; and the more important is the behaviour, then the more likely we are *not* to be conscious of it. This is a paradox but it makes obvious sense. For example, for you to be able to deal with accidentally placing your hand in a flame or being bitten on the hand by an animal, it would be no good for the evolutionary process to have left you with the one option of engaging a conscious focus and interlinking various centres of the brain to come up with an action plan and then to work out how to implement it. Cognition takes time. What is needed is immediate damage limitation: a rapid withdrawal of the hand. It doesn't matter where the hand is withdrawn to, or in what fashion it's withdrawn. Hence the reflexes that we all have. Reflexes are universal because we all need them, and we all need them to work without any interference from any other part of the brain. We know nothing about them other than to see the behaviour that utilises them when it happens.

This applies not just to immediate survival situations, but also more generally to all kinds of much more complicated behaviour concerning the most fundamental job of any and every individual living thing: to reproduce. There is all of the behaviour that leads immediately to reproduction—having sex—and there is all of the behaviour that is instrumental to having sex—what to do to get chosen by the opposite sex in preference to others. For all males, this is acquiring, maintaining and displaying rank in a DH. Sex itself is the easy part, and the flirting and courtship leading up to it is also fairly straightforward; it's getting to the situation where sex may be in the offing that is the difficulty. This is not at all to say that some aspects of 'dominance' behaviour are not subject to conscious scrutiny. Indeed, men spend much time focussing on what they can do to 'climb the greasy pole' of a work organisation. The more mundane nuts and bolts of the various behaviours concerning 'dominance' are, however, 'second nature'; and not only do we not need to be aware of them, but it's in our interests not to be aware of them. So we aren't. If we were, then we might mess up. Like the reflex to withdraw any part of the body from adverse stimuli such as a flame or an animal bite, 'dominance' behaviours are so important that an individual needs to get them right all of the time. And, as with the reflex, the possibility of interference by other considerations

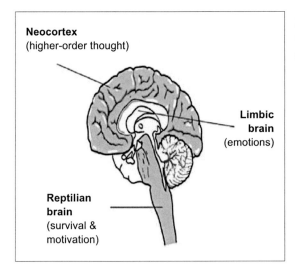

Neocortex
(higher-order thought)

**Limbic
brain**
(emotions)

**Reptilian
brain**
(survival &
motivation)

Figure 3.1:
The Triune Brain
(Mclean, 1959)

needs to be excluded, and this has become 'fixed' by the evolutionary process very far back in time.

This is how we end up with the seeming paradox that in any particular situation we can be unaware of what is actually most psychologically salient. We know that behaviour concerned with hierarchy is generated in an oldest parts of the brain (see Figure 3.1). The brain has evolved in layers: the ancient centre is concerned with essential body regulation, and motivations for survival and reproduction. These functions are located in what is sometimes referred to as the reptilian brain, which is the type of brain possessed by the now extinct ancestor common to ourselves and the current range of reptile species. This is the first of three major evolutionary stages of the brain, and the one reptiles today retain, and which we retain buried beneath the subsequent layers of development. Our brains are in some respects a map of evolution, with the tissues hosting activity concerned with more nuanced behaviour progressively nearer the brain surface.

The problem of our profound lack of awareness of our own mental processes is, after all, why we need a science of psychology. You cannot rely at all on what people tell you about their behaviour, because usually they have little insight into it, and are very likely to completely misconstrue what actually is motivating them to behave in a certain way in a certain situation. Likewise, it's very difficult to infer motivation simply from looking at someone's behaviour. Before there was an evolutionary perspective —linking human behaviour and the psychology which underlies it with that of animals—psychology wasn't really a science at all. It was just a cluster of various schools of thought that vied with each other to provide the most seemingly believable take on any particular topic within the subject. The completely non-scientific and now shown to be erroneous theory of Freud held sway in this climate, as did the view that the brain is a 'black box', interesting only regarding the behavioural responses it generates to stimuli. With an evolutionary underpinning that has progressively gained ground, psychology has begun at last to be relevant to discussion about what makes us all tick. It's been a revolution exposing the whole spectrum of social sciences as inadequate without an evolutionary base.

The importance of what I've called psychological salience is evident when you look at the workplace, for example. Although very many people work in single-sex environments, most work alongside the opposite sex. This is a recent phenomenon that took some getting used to for many of those accustomed to single-sex workplaces. It doesn't seem strange to many of us because we know no different. People can adapt to all kinds of unnatural conditions if they have to. Most are then not actually averse to the requirement that they both co-operate with and compete against men and women equally. But this is not the same as actually experiencing the workplace as cross-sexual co-operation and competition in any other than a superficial way. You don't have to go deep down to find that what is important to each of us when we interact with the opposite sex is its essentially sexual nature. That's a profound contrast with the essentially competitive and (non-sexual) affiliative interactions we have with those of the same sex. The default behaviour we see evidence of in mice gene 'knock-out' experiments asserts itself.

With the apparent paradox of the most important aspects of our psychology being in many respects what we are least aware of, what seems to be the social reality in the workplace is an illusion. Our mega-societies with their large organisations, though perfectly natural — like all culture — in coming out of our biology, are unnatural in the sense that they have culturally evolved so fast in scale that we have been hard pushed to use our evolved psychological endowment to 'work around' what we are faced with. The world of work is an amorphous social construction where we go along with the required blandness of behaviour — treating men and women as if there is only a human unisex. We can perform in the ways that our employers require by adapting what we have for use in a new environment in order to get by. The intriguing question though, is how the workplace could be made much more conducive to those who work there if it was designed not in spite of our evolved psychology, but with it in mind. The same goes for all the other scenarios where the sexes interact. I'll have a lot more to say about the nature of same-sex (intra-sexual) as opposed to between-sex (inter-sexual) behaviour, and notably in the world of work.

How the male hierarchy works without our being conscious of it: Assessing and signalling status

It's now beginning to be understood how men interact dominance-wise with other men, using deep-seated non-conscious mechanisms. Men who

Getting all in a muddle over motivation

The most highly influential—and hardly ever challenged—model of human motivation is Abraham Maslow's 'hierarchy of needs'. (The figure of it included here shows how it has been extended.) Maslow's premise is that the more basic the motivation the more we wish to get the satiation of it out of the way, so that we can free ourselves to aspire to finer things. The idea therefore is that we have to respond to and satiate a given layer of motivation before we can try to respond to and satiate the next layer above it. So to be in a position to aspire to 'the higher things in life' we have to go through a staged process of dealing with the various layers lower down the pyramid.

The model has a fatal problem: a basic failure to understand motivation (caused by Maslow's 'humanistic' philosophical beliefs). What he misses is that our more rarefied behaviours have evolved for the purpose of progressively fine-tuning the way that we respond to our essential motivations. They are not removed from them to live some sort of life of their own. Why otherwise would we have them? The pyramidal model should in effect have sex/reproduction at both its base and its apex, because all that we do has to be in some way instrumental to this function; however far away, and however much it may seem to have 'short-circuited' into its own positive feedback loop. All that we do in the end is successful in terms of how it furthers sex/reproduction over some timescale. Motivation necessarily is an interconnected tree, not a series of separate levels. It is impossible to get a handle on any biological system (including the human animal) without an evolutionary understanding.

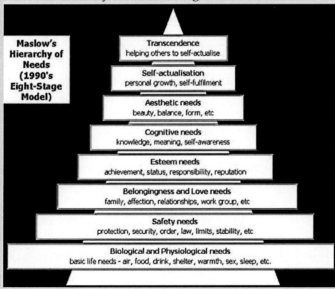

have never met need nothing more than a mutual glance and some non-verbal communication to automatically decide who ranks over whom, even before a word is spoken (Kalma, 1991). And when words *are* spoken, they don't change the already-decided ranking. Men also monitor relative dominance constantly and unconsciously by registering each other's vocal sounds, but this is not referring to speech. The ranking signals in the human voice are a low-pitched and segmented hum at frequencies below 50Hz, which is beneath the range of sounds used in speech within the fundamental frequency of phonation. Men use this information to then adjust their pattern of communication according to whether they are interacting with a man of higher or lower social status than themselves (Gregory et al., 1993; Gregory & Webster, 1996; Gregory et al., 1997; Gregory, 2005). Being lower status than the other man means accommodating patterns of speech, from use of words, phrasing, intonation, accent and tone — right down to complex wavelength and amplitude forms — to be similar to that of the other man. If instead the other man is of lower status, then it's a question of monitoring the other's accommodation of speech patterns to see if he is abiding by the social norm of sub-dominance. The importance of this interaction becomes clear if you run an experiment to filter out the low frequencies and so eliminate the vocal status signals. When this is done, men find social encounters very difficult, or even impossible, to handle (Gregory et al., 1997). And the signals are not just regarding status but also deference — which is not sub-dominance, but non-engagement in terms of dominance. This is to signal 'I'm not competing with you', which is likely also to be a feature of how the sexes signal to each other. As with everything else here, the parties are not conscious of what they are doing, of course. The deference to women showed up in data of interactions between host and guests on the Larry King show, though the authors missed its significance (Gregory & Gallagher, 2002).

For a man to behave otherwise to women would have a major negative impact on his status. Women don't have to be so careful, but social psychologists have observed that a woman tends to defer to a man if there is a task at hand demanding leadership, especially if it's not obviously in a female domain, and in which she feels herself to have no expertise. As is evident in experiments where the sexes are set up in what you might expect to be competitive situations (see chapter four), it seems that it is in a woman's interest to provide space for men to demonstrate abilities which indicate their status, or are likely to have status consequences. This is the better for her to be able to make accurate sexual selection (either directly or indirectly; it's important to make a social assessment of every man in the social group because — apart from potential partners — other men are possible conduits to associating with potential partners). She can also use the opportunity for sexual display. A man is interested in female youth and beauty, so no performance, physical or verbal, is required.

Whilst female voices activate the brain's auditory region in both female and male listeners — as you would expect, since voices are sounds — when men listen to other men's voices, a completely different brain region is involved (Hunter et al., 2005). This is the area right at the back of the brain known as 'the mind's eye'; so called because it's here where people compare other individuals and things to themselves. How men and women listen to the voices of those of the same sex is 'hard-wired' differently, and for men it would appear to be part of or key to the mechanism that works out relative dominance in the male status hierarchy. (We don't know, but this may be also how *women* listen to men's voices, so that they can work out which males are dominant, to help them in sexual selection.)

The 'folk prejudice' against men

With their deftness at 'relational aggression', women have the skills to indirectly influence male–male behaviour. With their strong interest in stable social order (to aid their sexual choice) as against the interests of most men in overturning it, women are active in 'policing' the male DH using psychological 'cheater detection' mechanisms. These have evolved, as I previously mentioned, to prevent tactical subversion of the DH, principally (as I explain shortly) regarding the basis of rank difference in males. This means that the usual situation in social groups is that low-status men are unfairly assessed and so treated by women, both directly and indirectly through other men. This is in addition to the strong 'policing' of the male DH by males themselves, of course. Men have no reason to judge women in such a way. The normal reaction is simply deference. This leaves only other women for a woman to contend with, and although women do 'police' their own social world, it seems they do so in terms of 'cheater detection', not in the same way or to the same degree as is reserved for men. This is because women live in what is more like a network than a DH (as I outline in chapter four), and have further social-psychological mechanisms peculiar to women that favour other women over men, to the extent that women tend to function collectively as a permanently salient collective (an 'in-group') as against the 'out-group' of men; a phenomenon that has no parallel in men. (But of this too I will defer consideration, until I look at the very separate worlds of the sexes in the next chapter.) The upshot is that in humans, as in animals generally, the most socially-disadvantaged sub-group is always that of relatively low-status males.

This naturally-evolved prejudice against men can be shown experimentally if you arbitrarily label or describe individuals to distinguish between them according to social status, and then get strangers to look at and assess their behaviour. They will underestimate and 'do down' the lower-ranked individuals, and even elevate those of higher status. If on top of this you similarly play around with the status of the assessors themselves, then as the status disparity between them and those they are observing widens, the assessors look much harder to try to find violations (Cummins, 1999). People also more easily remember individuals who are lowly ranked (Yamagashi et al., 2003; Oda, 1997; Mealey, Daood & Krage, 1996), because we associate low rank with violating social norms, and so think that they have 'cheated' in some way. (For summaries of all this research see Cummins, 2000, 1998, 1996a). It seems also that those who are most concerned about low-status 'cheaters' are those of lower status themselves (Fiddick & Cummins, 2001). The potential cheaters apparently do a good job of 'policing' themselves.

All this sets up a profound prejudice against the great majority of males, because status is how men (but not women, as I will explain) are judged. Those who are already relatively socially disadvantaged — males who are not of high status — are treated harshly in exactly the sort of ways that will ensure that their social status will fall still further. At the same time, those who enjoy elevated social status are not only excused reprimand but are actually perceived to be behaving in a more pro-social fashion than in fact they are. Their social status consequently will tend to rise still further. This serves to emphasise, indeed effectively further polarise the male DH and so make it easier for women to select men, and therefore for males to fulfil their role as 'genetic filter'.

In line with this, human ethological studies show that people seek to associate with and give more attention to those of higher status than themselves, and to withdraw attention and association from those of lower status. Brain mechanisms have been discovered that provide us with 'reward' hormones, and depress levels of stress hormones when we deal harshly with others perceived to be of lower status. If, on the other hand, we attempt to retaliate against a person we regard as higher status, then stress levels are maintained or rise. The same thing is found in various primate species.

Another series of social-psychology experiments by Denise Cummins (Cummins, 1996, 1996c) reveals a related way that the male DH is 'policed'. This is to do with how we reason. Although we distort and hone our reasoning when what is at issue are social concerns, otherwise we reason in a much more relaxed way. In situations where social status is not salient, we just look for any single piece of evidence to confirm what we already think is going on, and that settles the issue. This contrasts with reasoning about situations where social status *is* salient. Here we use a completely different approach. We now look for anything which appears not to fit; and even if all other evidence squares with what ostensibly is going on, just one piece of evidence against is enough to change our minds. This way of assessing evidence is far more sensitive. We use it for 'violation detection' against individuals of lower status where there is a suspicion that they will behave in ways not permitted for someone given such a position in the hierarchy. It's a way of reasoning where the default conclusion asserts itself: 'he's cheating!' It's so important to our social psychology to 'police' the male DH, that children aged just three think in this way. We know that it can't have evolved for any other purpose, because we are incapable of applying this 'violation detection' mode in any other context where such rigorous scrutiny would be appropriate. After training we can use it where it's essential, in science; but it's a formal use and never effortless, which is why people can't spot the fallacy of, say, astrology or the MMR vaccine scare.

The insight that there must be adaptive ways of reasoning that are specifically employed to detect violation of social norms is now a burgeoning experimental field (eg; Sugiyama et al., 2002; Fiddick et al., 2000; Cosmides, 1989). Other researchers have gone looking for and found the relevant brain structures (Adolphs, 1999; Stone et al., 2002).

* * *

When social psychologists talk about status, they really mean male status. So 'male status tags' are simply 'status tags': there can't really be 'female status tags'. You can give status tags to females and in some sense mimic what is going on with males in that females thereby become surrogate males, but it's incongruous, and not just cross-sexually; for to label as status how women hold different rank amongst each other would be strange, other than as a reflection of the rank of their male partners. We know that there's an essential difference here, but it awaits research—Cummins used individuals of both sexes and doesn't distinguish. We should not talk, for example, of the 'status' of the housewife. If, nevertheless, you do include the housewife in a comparison of the prestige in which various jobs are held, then you get interesting results. Unexpectedly, she comes in at fully half-way up the rankings (Bose, 1985; Tyree & Hicks, 1998). This is way above any equivalent to the job if it was paid employment; and the house*husband* is rated considerably lower still: the same as a laundry worker. This anomaly is what you might expect by the non-applicability of the male status hierarchy to women. Trying to think of the housewife in this way is as meaningless as asking people to assess the relative job status of gestation and childbirth.

To distinguish between male ranking and its female equivalent, to correspond to male status it's perhaps best to refer to female *privilege*. And rather than talk about rank in either or both sexes—since the female social world is more like a network than a strict hierarchy (as I will explain in the next chapter)—a more appropriate generic term would be either male or female 'mate value'. It's apposite because reproductive potential is what both status and privilege translate into, for males and females respectively.

Female rank is privilege in the sense that youth/beauty is simply bestowed and cannot be taken away—other than by advancing years, obviously—whereas a man's rank is much more fluid: his status can fall even from a very low base, or rise to dizzying heights; and this through his own efforts, or lack thereof. He can fall beneath the floor and become in effect a non-person, whereas a woman can never do so. Merely being female is a privilege. Any attributes just extend this further. Even when age destroys any vestige of sexual allure, a woman will still retain consideration as being a woman, and will have a major family role never guaranteed for a man.

Rank for women appears not as privilege but equivalent to male status when it comes to the workplace, but this is an illusion. Status per se would be useless to women. When women battle each other at work,[1] then yes, they are battling for social position amongst themselves (and as with men, though to a lesser extent, women may behave as if in a short-circuited tight-feedback loop in seeing the job as an end in itself); but beyond this they are trying to place themselves in situations where they are more likely to be encountered by high-status men — both reliable high-status men who can be trusted to invest heavily in offspring, and also high-status 'philanderers' (see below, chapter eleven). We similarly misunderstand as female 'status' the reflection on a woman of the status of her husband. This is simply ignoring the rank of the woman, which will be a female near-equivalent of her husband's—similar ranks tending to assort. We take the husband's rank as his wife's by proxy, and then mistakenly refer to the wife as having status.

How 'power' really plays out

How does all this square up with the notion we have today of 'power' and how it plays between the sexes? It doesn't.

The ultimate locus of 'power' is what we might call self-actualisation: the ability an individual has to capitalise on and realise what he/she is. If we add up the motivations we have to do things and the capacity to do them, we have the full picture of what we are. First and foremost, at the apex of our motivational set, is the imperative to reproduce. (I should qualify this, because aside from the possibility of 'broodiness', which strangely remains un-researched, individuals seem motivated not to reproduce per se, but to have sex, and also to have regard for their children. Sex usually leads to reproduction, or it does after a sufficient number of copulations. So it is that we say that we are motivated *ultimately* to reproduce but *proximally* to have sex.) All else—including even survival

---

[1]   See also *The Apprentice* panel on page 146.

itself — is merely instrumental to this. It's not the other way round, as some insist — nature is full of examples of males who sacrifice themselves in the very act of insemination.

'Power' in these most essential terms is vividly apparent in all societies, though notably in primitive human ones, which are not unlike how all human society must have been prior to the advent of historical civilisations. Those individuals with least 'power' are the majority of males, who either fail even to reach adulthood or, if they do so, then fail to reproduce. In extant hunter-gatherer societies, a large proportion — if not half or more of males — lose their lives, principally at the hands of other males, before they reach full adulthood. Of those surviving to full reproductive age, there is then a large proportion who are denied the chance of ever having sex at all. There is no corresponding situation for women.

This is the underlying pattern in all human society, albeit that this can be ameliorated by a cultural superstructure enabling ever-larger assemblages of people to cohere, albeit minimally. A large minority of males suffer reproductive oblivion, having no sex at all, or very little. This would be the majority were it not that in complex societies there is ostensibly monogamy — though the serial monogamy practiced by the minority of males is actually clandestine polygyny. A majority of males have no option of sex outside of marriage, and their marriages themselves may well be sexless. These men belong to an even wider strata of men who can hardly be said to be advantaged.

Many men succeed in reproducing only by convincing a woman of their reliability in staying around to help look after children. Women to an extent will trade off what they are ideally looking for in a man — in the end, his sheer ability to successfully mate with females — for reliability. This includes provisioning, which is why the primary breadwinner in households has always been and remains the man. Men sacrifice their own natural 'numbers game' reproductive strategy to fall in line with the female mode of raising a small number of quality offspring. Men thereby allow themselves to be exploited as the principal generators of income, that is then mainly disposed of by their wives or on their wives' behalf.

Even if we look at the very apex of the male DH, our current notions of 'power' are still mistaken. Here men certainly do have 'power' in terms of realising their core 'motivation' of reproducing/having sex, because they are attractive to women for extra-pair sex, as well as being highly eligible as husbands. Yet usually they have had to make an enormous effort to achieve this position. The risk-taking and heavy competition with other males that will for most males lead to low success if not reproductive oblivion, has for them paid off handsomely, but it will have been hardly cost-free. As well as the huge effort and sacrifices required, there are possible adverse consequences in terms of health or of retribution from the many others that a male necessarily must have trodden down on the way to the top. The reality of male reproductive skew is that all males carry scars from trying to realise what they are motivated to do, with no comparable cost sustained by females. This is completely at odds with how currently we are led to believe 'power' is distributed amongst people.

We've been duped and dupe ourselves for reasons that are at root the same fundamental inequality — consequent from the female being the 'limiting factor' in reproduction. The fierce competitive world of males hardly allows them to in any way complain about their lot, because this would immediately expose weaknesses that other males could exploit. Simultaneously, it would destroy female interest in them for the same reason. For females, the effect of complaining is the very opposite. It draws male attention and gives males a handle on how to display their strengths to enable a female to choose between them. Indeed, it's a guide to males of what particular criteria females are judging them by. These can be quite arbitrary, as in the case of peahens obliging peacocks to evolve ever more elaborate tail-feather displays despite the extra predators this inevitably attracts (the increased chance of being eaten is more than offset by the extra chances of reproduction). The very fact that a peacock can escape predation despite his cumbersome, enormous and bright plumage, intrinsically demonstrates his genetic fitness overall, which helps him to get chosen by peahens. This is why 'sexual selection' is so effective and can easily run away with itself down a (seemingly) crazy blind alley.

There is no limit to female demand for changes in the way that males compete against each other. Females can direct male–male competition to produce behaviour that is directly beneficial to them; such as parental care, provisioning, nest building, etc. It's easy to see how this can become a meta-development in human society along a political dimension. Feminist polemic is a variously-conceived systemisation of female complaint running away with itself and turning reality on its head to make out that it's the male that imposes on the female. There could be no more perfect cover for an ever-more outlandish capitalisation on being the sex that is the 'limiting factor' in reproduction. This is in the interests of women (though as we shall see, only a minority of women, and it seriously backfires even on this minority), but also in the interests of the small minority of males in a 'winner-takes-all' position, because it helps to ensure that other males don't dislodge them from their exalted perch. Also, inasmuch as women are propelled into the male world, it provides males at the top of the tree with a wider range of prospective partners.

Extreme feminism is therefore a disguised re-branding of the perennial conspiracy of the elite, and a natural doctrine for rapidly-changing times where new economic conditions make established chivalrous habits appear out-of-date. To get round the fact that what is being railed against is a chimera, feminism has developed into progressively more extreme forms that argue simultaneously mutually-exclusive viewpoints. Ostensibly a politics of liberation, it's the ultimate anti-democratic movement. Anything but a radical conception, it's an ultra-conservative extension of what has always been the male–female dynamic, and the pivot of a wider political fraud in the wake of the collapse of Marxist theory into what we know as 'political correctness', as I explained in chapter one. Still further politicisation of the inverse of the real sexual inequality and male disadvantage, is facilitated by this misconception of 'power' ever more effectively hiding its origins. There is seemingly no limit to what must be the greatest confidence trick in political history.

That not women but men are the disadvantaged in any human society, can at best be only ameliorated by an egalitarian ethos; even if the actual social reality is fully recognised. Folk feminism, as it were, as well as feminism per se, will always push us into acting on a false sense of social reality. Not merely negating the positive social benefits of egalitarianism, this will turn egalitarianism into a negative, oppressive force.

We live in a society that is based on a particularly bad combination: a rigorous ethos of egalitarianism, but one which inverts the truth of the most fundamental social structures and interactions. This provides a wide range of support for the very people who are already over-privileged, directly at the expense of those other very people who are under-privileged. Compounding this is that it's naturally in cahoots with the conservative view of allowing the unsuccessful to fail, on the grounds that their lack of success is just desserts for their supposed objective lack of qualities.

Sexual selection finds differences between people that are barely apparent and may be quite arbitrary, and then tries to magnify them or to beget new ones. Hardly of great benefit to society, if indeed it's not seriously deleterious. And all for the purpose of reproduction (currently manifesting more as sex) which is an ambiguous benefit to contemporary highly overpopulated societies in any case. Men driven in fact by women, cutting corners in pursuit of ever more wealth, is of dubious social benefit in itself; but especially when you consider that it merely ups the ante for the rest of us. This drives social inequality, so that society's costs are disproportionately borne by those who not only do not reproduce, but are excluded from male-female relationships altogether.

Increasingly unsustainable social injustice eventually creates social breakdown. It's in everyone's interests that men should not be routinely disparaged, penalised and abandoned, simply for not being women.

Summary

The mistake is to see the 'dominance' contests apparent between males of all species (and between females of many species) as being also across the sexes. This is the case neither for animals nor for humans. The idea that 'power' is exerted by men over women is nonsense, biologically speaking.

We don't see our intra-sexual dominance behaviours, just as we don't see any of our other key behaviours. A tiny proportion only of brain processes are apparent to us consciously; our most essential functions are buried underneath successive layers of evolved neural architecture, and left inaccessible so that we can't subvert our key motivations. So it is that the most important male behaviour that is instrumental to acquiring sex partners, of male–male dominance, is hidden by the 'need to know' 'design' of our brains.

The reality of the non-conscious separate male world is becoming apparent with the uncovering in experiments of mechanisms for mutually communicating relative status information.

Prejudice against (lower status) men is exacerbated by psychological 'cheater detection' mechanisms that 'police' the male DH. This is by both men and women, and applies only to men because it's in respect of status and not the equivalent measure of rank in women.

The majority of men are, of necessity and quite literally, *losers*, being disadvantaged in the most real sense living things can be. Females can exploit their power of sexual choice to get males to compete in ways that do things for them, and to respond to complaints, however manufactured. Unlike females, males cannot complain, however legitimately, without reducing both their social standing and appeal to females. This facilitates politicisation to insist that female privilege is disadvantage.

Chapter 4

Separate Worlds

The self-segregation of the sexes, and how they compete and affiliate differently

G iven that 'dominance' or 'power' is not what is going on between men and women, then in an important sense, apart from the necessary coming together in flirting, courtship, pair-bonding and child-support, there is no point in the sexes coming together—at least from a biological perspective. We should expect that below the surface, as it were, the sexes effectively should live in separate social worlds, where male–male, female–female and male–female interactions are always essentially different. Looking more closely at the self-segregation of the sexes in childhood, and how this develops into adulthood, ought to be revealing in this regard.

The self-segregation of the sexes

Self-segregation of the sexes, where boys choose other boys as playmates and likewise girls seek other girls, is a progressive affair. First apparent at a surprisingly very early age (certainly in infants of two to three years, though some researchers claim as early as eighteen months), it becomes so pronounced that for the great majority of children there is little contact with the other sex outside of any forced contact in school. By the age of six, children are eleven times more likely to interact with same-sex peers (Maccoby & Jacklin, 1987; Etaugh & Liss, 1992). The overwhelming predominance of same-sex play is the most obvious and well-documented aspect of child development. Even strenuous efforts by parents and teachers always fails to reduce same-sex preference for playmates (Rubin & Coplan, 1993), nor does it even reduce the time spent in same-sex play. Any enforced cross-sex togetherness is made up for by extra same-sex play away from direct adult control (Segal et al., 1987). This separation of the sexes is a cross-cultural universal (Omark, Omark, & Edelman, 1975), and is apparent in a range of mammals (Bernstein, Judge, & Ruehlmann, 1993). It has all the hallmarks of behaviour that has evolved to be universal.

What's more, the kind of association is different in the respective sex groupings. The boys are in a DH that is so quickly established that it's stable and rigid by the time they are just three years old, and by a year later the boys themselves can precisely report and describe it. The groupings of girls by contrast are far more fluid, less stable and smaller (Benenson, 1993). They play in places that are less public than do boys, preferring adults to be close by, and activity that is adult-structured rather than the collectively self- organised team games of the boys.

Self-segregation by sex starts at an age before the child can have any kind of meaningful social interaction, because he/she at this stage does not grasp that other people have thought processes. A child doesn't have even the sense of the constancy of its own sex until aged three. Same-sex interaction is the first kind of interaction that leads to socialisation. As I have pointed out, not only is sex-segregation spontaneous, but it happens regardless of what adults try to get children to do. As has been shown, mixed-sex play at this time does not do likewise (Fabes, Martin & Hanish, 2004). If very young children could be socialised, then there should be some socialisation effects of mixed-sex as well as of same-sex play. So same-sex play must be a pre-programmed emergent quality. Social behaviour appears to be a consequence of self-segregation by sex, not its cause. Marilyn Brewer concludes that both 'gender awareness' and 'gender constancy' post-date the actual behaviour which it was previously thought required these very cognitive leaps (Brewer, 2001).

The creation of different worlds for the sexes was presumed to be due to the different kind of play that boys go in for compared to that of girls. The 'play styles' explanation of sex segregation is shown to be wrong by letting children either choose a play activity but without knowing the sex of the playmate they would be given; or to select a boy or girl playmate without knowing what sort of play they would be allowed to do. Provided with these alternatives, children don't bother to choose a sex-typical play activity, and instead opt for a playmate, and one that is of the same sex (Hoffman & Powlishta, 2001). If the difference between boys' and girls' play was simply the activity itself, then boys' predilection for 'rough-and-tumble' would mean that they should enjoy muscling in on the play of girls and disrupting it. Not only does this not happen, but in later childhood it is boys rather than girls who become the 'gender police', as it were, keeping boys within their same-sex grouping.

The alternative assumption was that parents socialise the sexes differently, but this has it backwards. Parents behave differently to baby boys and girls because they are in fact reacting to how babies themselves behave differently according to sex. It's true that adults respond differently according to quite arbitrary cues as to a baby's sex, such as the colour of clothing they themselves provide a child. In fact, you can alter a parent's behaviour to a baby simply by changing the colour of its nappy from blue

Self-segregation by the sexes is apparent from an early age. Girls form personal networks, whereas boys rapidly establish a competitive dominance hierarchy.

to pink. Nevertheless, any *effect* of different behaviour by carers on babies according to whether they're boy or girl has not been found. And that's not for the want of looking.

We know that much is different about the sexes from the very start. Behavioural sex differences are evident to researchers even on the first day after birth (Connellan et al., 2001), with fully sex-typical behaviour apparent before the first birthday (Lutchmaya et al., 2002). Any parent will tell you that boys and girls gravitate towards different activities before they are two-and-a-half years old, and also that boys and girls are markedly different in how they try to get their way. There is a vast array of measurable sex differences that emerge at progressive trigger points and which are too difficult to account for other than that they must have been present at birth. For ethical reasons we can't prove this by keeping babies from birth in solitary confinement until adolescence and then at last introducing them to other children to see if they behave sex-typically. But this very experiment has been done with rhesus monkeys, and they do indeed reliably exhibit sex-typical behaviour when eventually they are for the first time given access to others.

Even if any kind of influence on the child could be shown, it would still be necessary (and very difficult) to show that stereotypical parental behaviour was socially conditioned rather than itself an innate response we're just not conscious of. Social conditioning is useless as an explanation because it just begs the question: what is it about the person doing the social conditioning that makes him try to instil what it is he is trying to instil. If, as the theory must insist, it too has been socially conditioned, then it begs the same question about the person who had in turn socially conditioned the social conditioner … and so on, ad infinitum. Ultimately there has to be a real reason, and there are none other than those that are merely description without explanatory power, until we end up in biology.

Although it's difficult to tease apart the relative contributions of 'nature' and 'nurture'; nevertheless researchers now conclude that it's mostly down to 'nature' (Ridley, 2003). More to the point, 'nurture' tends not to contribute anything uniform but instead idiosyncrasy; environmental factors being inherently unpredictable. This is just as we would expect, because with behaviour as important as this, the evolutionary process will fully code for the behaviour rather than leaving it to be contingent on conditions in the environment that would allow a large leeway either side of the optimum. It means that the standard social science model (SSSM) of socialisation used to explain phenomena such as sex differences is not feasible even in theory (referenced in debate as 'the gloomy prospect'). The whole notion that what is sex-typical is a social construct is scientifically dead (Turkheimer, 2000; Turkheimer & Waldron, 2000; Plomin & Daniels, 1987).

It is far from the case that children are socialised by both parents and peers, and inconsequentially separated by their sex. In fact sex—that is, peer group formation of same-sex individuals—turns out to be the force through which children socialise themselves (Harris, 1998). Same-sex grouping is not the platform on which sex-typical behaviour then develops, but an arena where what was pre-established as sex-typical is acted out in preparation for, and as part of early behaviour within the adult world.

Self-segregation is apparent through all social structures; only mixed-sex grouping breaks down

Self-segregation by sex in producing a different social world for boys compared to girls is evident in what has been found of childhood and adolescent grouping—although there is surprisingly little research about this, clouded as it is by sticking to the political line (necessary for acquiring funding) that the sexes are interchangeable. I'll summarise and cut across what has been found by those few who have ventured, such as Kathryn Urberg (Urberg, 1992; Urberg et al., 1995; Urberg et al.,2000; Degirmenci-oglu et al., 1998), Peter & Patricia Adler (Adler & Adler, 1998), Bradford Brown (Brown & Clute, 2003) and Dexter Dunphy (Dunphy, 1963).

As younger children, boys naturally take to team sports, etc., to furnish competition opportunities; and for this they gather in quite large but fluid groupings. Girls go around in twosomes and threesomes as they build more co-operative relationships. As they get older, essentially girls get together in large cliques and their friendships are much more embedded in the peer structure, whereas boys are part of a pyramid of status but are otherwise more floating interactors. This is not to say that girls are not also hierarchical, but they are so really only at the apex of the top clique, and in the aspiration that girls (sometimes dubbed 'wannabes') have to join this

The clique – life for girls at the top gets more like a DH

Rosaline Wiseman's *Queen Bees and Wannabees*, a non-fiction account of how female American high school cliques operate – 'Girl World' – has spurred a book series and a film. *Mean Girls* (2004), starring Lindsay Lohan, was based on Wiseman's research. While adults find it funny, young girls watch *Mean Girls* like it's a reality TV show, being far too close for comfort – especially the drop-dead gorgeous and ostensibly sweet character (who is really supremely manipulative, two-faced, vindictive, arrogant, and all-round nasty).

The titles of the 'Clique' series of books by Lisi Harrison say it all: *Best Friends for Never, Revenge of the Wannabes, The Invasion of the Boy Snatchers, The Pretty Committee Strikes Back, Dial L For Loser, It's Not Easy Being Mean,* and *Sealed with a Diss.*

Harrison's website is captioned 'the only thing harder than getting in is staying in'. Such is the world of the top clique, run by 'the pretty committee' of four stunners, one of whom, Massie Block, is 'queen bee'.

The plot summaries for *Best Friends for Never* and (the first in the series), *Clique*, are au fait with adolescent female social psychology:

> To keep her spot at the top, Massie throws a boy/girl Halloween party. But she's not sure what's scarier – that her parents are making her invite the entire grade or that they are forcing her to co-host with Claire, who by the way, accidentally steals Cam Fisher, Massie's ah-dorable crush. But all of that will seem minor once Massie realizes Alicia has stabbed her in the back and humiliated her in front of the entire school.

> Claire Lyons, the new girl from Orland-ew, Florida has the nerve to show up at OCD wearing Keds and two-year old GAP overalls. She is clearly not Pretty Committee material and Massie, Alicia, Dylan and Kristen have no problem letting everyone know it. Claire's future looks worse than Prada knockoff. But with a little luck and a lot of scheming, she might just stand a chance.

Mean Girls has a convoluted plot of scheming and deception, and friendlessness turned to popularity and back again. The top clique contains the 'queen bee' of the whole school, appropriately named Regina. She's hated by one girl in particular for spreading rumours about her sexuality – a classic form of female 'relational aggression'.

The 'clique' novel *Sealed with a Diss* has an ultimate plotline in the alpha female having a 'secret weapon' that 'shows them exactly how boys' brains work'.

stratum from the rather narrower social life outside of it. It's only boys who can be altogether excluded from their same-sex social organisation. When boys do have friendships, they are part of the status organisation, whereas girls' friendships are much more independent of it. Higher-status boys are far more likely to be part of larger groups, whereas most girls have this advantage.

In a nutshell, whereas boys live in a social pyramid, girls are together in a personal network. This makes respective sense for both sexes in terms of preparation for the sexual choice preceding reproduction. Males need to assort themselves by rank, and females need to exchange information with each other to identify the relative ranks of the males.

The sexes for some time through childhood actively avoid each other, typically ascribing a kind of supernatural disease ('lurgy', 'icky', etc) to the other which it's imagined could be caught on contact. This doesn't stop sexual interest from a distance, nor the occasional 'kiss-chase' game; but such cross-sex behaviour has nothing to do with hierarchy and dominance.

Adolescent life seems to be a development in stages, the speed of which varies markedly from one person to the next. It begins with very much self-contained same-sex mutual interest groups comprising a handful or more. If these groups get together, it's still a same-sex affair. Later, the separate boy and girl organisations begin to rub along at the boundaries as individuals dip their toes in the water of the opposite sex in the secure environment of their same-sex peers. Soon the high 'mate value' individuals in some of the groupings come together to form a super-group of boys and girls who date considerably earlier than everyone else, have more romantic attachments, and have sex at a younger age. This elite is to an extent imitated by the rest, and the old groupings give way to much larger crowds, albeit mostly of one sex. Then pairing off really gathers pace and the crowds disintegrate. All that remains is a very loose assembly of couples as people no longer need a group structure.

The sexes are now in adult society and the boundaries to the effective same-sex competitive arena have stretched to the point of being limitless, confined only by whatever limits an individual perceives and imposes for himself/herself. In the absence of group structures, the overall male status hierarchy and female personal network by default reassert themselves. Not only are people less inclined to group, but with sexual coupling, making and maintaining cross-sex friendships becomes harder. The number of cross-sex friendships continues to decline with age until in old age it reaches near zero, but the dynamics evident in adolescent peer groups resurface in future dealings with same-sex and opposite-sex peers and groups when again pair formation is on the cards. For some, the adolescent social world is never eclipsed: the full transitions seem either not to take place or are seriously delayed or incomplete. This must be especially true for many of the lowest-status males.

Within their same-sex and then adolescent cross-sex groupings, for males especially there is apparently a race to reproduce, which is won by a vanguard of winners who mate early. This tends to increase lifetime reproduction of the fittest individuals, but more importantly in our evolutionary past it would be often the difference between reproducing at all and being barren. Natural male mortality and morbidity rates were extraordinarily high—up to or even exceeding a 50% chance of early death at the hands of other men, as is still the case today in some hunter-gatherer societies. Consequently, to have sex as soon as possible after puberty would be imperative. From the perspective of gene replication and the whole reproducing group, this might be critical in times of extreme environmental stress.

One thing is obvious. The sexes don't come together to compete against each other or to be sexlessly interchangeable; but only so as to pair off. Essentially they are together for no longer than it takes to bond as couples and then they move apart again. The staged cross-sex group socialisation process had served to point up, further tease out and itself manufacture status difference amongst the males, the better to facilitate female choice. Female choice is also aided by the female personal network being put in closer touch with the male world. It seems that regarding what is most salient to us all psychologically, it is mixed-sex group structure that is ephemeral, with the separate social worlds of the sexes being the default condition.

The separate worlds can be most apparent in adults: prisoners

If the separate worlds never break down, are there scenarios in adult life where this underlying reality comes to the fore?

Most commonly it's apparent in the workplace. There is very strong evidence that people naturally gravitate to job segregation according to sex, just as people tend to choose same-sex friends. And far from this being a predilection of older workers who may be thought to cling to the ways of former times, the younger the workers the more they are likely to choose sex-typical occupations. Those who have felt quite uncomfortable working in a sex-atypical job frequently become aware of problems and may well leave their jobs because of them. It would seem that it's not any aspect of the job itself that is the issue, but the sex of work colleagues. (I will have much more to say about this in chapter nine.)

The urban 'underclass' phenomenon of street gangs is a very strict adult self-sex segregation, and there are several all-girl gangs in London just as there are in Los Angeles. Albeit always much fewer in number than the male gangs, they are just as sex-segregated. There are also girls attached to male gangs — as 'honey traps', or followers — but they are not in the gang per se.

Most starkly though, the separate worlds are apparent when people are *compelled* to live only with those of the same sex. This is most complete in prison. In this protracted opposite-sex-free environment, men form clear, rigid DHs, and women — as well as almost ubiquitous homosexual pairing — form strong friendships and a diffusely-led, co-operative pseudo family network with women expected to and willingly taking on the various different roles just as you would find in an extended family (Colarelli, Spranger & Hechanova, 2006; Giallombardo, 1966; Ward & Kassebaum, 1965; Ireland, 1999; Onojeharho & Bloom, 1986).

This is a striking reprise of pre-adult behaviour particularly revealing of the same-sex social world of women; but more than that, it's revealing of the underlying reality of social life according to sex. The non-hierarchical but integrated female world apparent in childhood and adolescence looks like the nascent women's gossip network that helps women with deciding which men are desirable. But in the light of what we see in women's prisons, we can see something else as well. The twosomes and threesomes of female adolescents look like role-playing relations: mother–father, mother–daughter–sibling — i.e. preparation for family life.

Albeit that prison is an extreme environment, and the inmates are hardly a representative cross-section of society; nevertheless, here is evidence that the natural tendency towards same-sex social organisations so clear in childhood and adolescence persists into adulthood. Despite the interlude of adult life, the very different worlds of men and women are default conditions under the surface. The even bigger contrast between pyramidal male hierarchy and the female network apparent here in adult prisoners — compared to how it was in childhood and adolescence — shows just how distinct they truly are.

Males and females don't compete against each other, competition being essentially between males

That males and females live in separate worlds should mean that the sexes do not compete against each other in any real sense. Superficially, of course, it appears that they do. But experiments (Gneezy & Rustichini, 2004; Gneezy, Niederle & Rustichini, 2003) show that when boys or men ostensibly compete against girls or women, the males apparently win not because they are being competitive with the females, but because females are backing off from competing with them. Consciously or unconsciously displaying their youth/beauty to the men, women pull back from contest. This mirrors even quite young girls radically changing their behaviour in the school playground when boys are around; resuming usual play as soon as the boys leave. The same is found even if girls/women are just pitting themselves against their own previous performance, as long as there is a male audience. Boys show the opposite: they crank *up* their efforts, but this too is for reasons of displaying to the opposite sex; athleticism being, after all, the obvious male display. They are effectively competing against their own previous performances to present themselves in the best light. The sexes would much rather display to than compete against each other (Niederle & Vesterlund, 2005; Larson, 2005).

We know that the essentially competitive nature of men is opposed to the networking behaviour of women as a fundamental sex difference. This is because there are profound physiological differences according to sex that attend contest situations. The same differences have been found time and again in all kinds of competitive tasks (Mazur et al., 1997; Booth et al., 2006). When men compete, their testosterone levels increase before the competition proper begins, and this is in response to how they rate the chances of their opponent winning. Then after the competition, winning males have heightened levels of testosterone and losers have lower levels. This disparity in levels continues long afterwards. Nothing like this is apparent in women. In males, testosterone appears to act as part of a mechanism that 'memorises' outcomes that are carried over to future contests. Testosterone levels of females indeed do rise before a contest, and markedly so, but only in relation to how difficult they perceive the *task*; not according to how difficult they regard their opponent. Then afterwards, the levels of the female winners and losers do not significantly differ (Bateup et al., 2002).

There are other hormones involved in the 'competition memory' mechanism in men. It's known that before contests, men's cortisol levels differ according to status or having the relevant skill: markedly-higher resting levels of cortisol are the result of the persistent losing of contests experienced by lower-status males. This is also peculiar to men (Ennis, Kelly & Lambert, 2001; Kirschbaum, Wust & Hellhammer, 1992). If you set both men and women two different sorts of challenges; one that entails possible achievement and the other possible social rejection; then whereas the men show marked cortisol response to the achievement challenge, women show it regarding the challenge that risks social rejection (Stroud, Salovey & Epel, 2002). Women seem to have a fear of failure as their motivation, whereas for men it's more like hope of success. (The central importance of cortisol in understanding DH and the separation of men from women will become apparent in the chapter on health.)

Clearly, the hormonal mediation of competition is strikingly different according to sex, and in the case of men there is a contribution to the machinery of establishing and maintaining status hierarchies. Just how testosterone, cortisol, and another hormone associated with dominance — serotonin — interact in males is as yet a confusing picture. (Serotonin is concerned with a more permanent registering by an individual of his/her relative rank, and the lack of serotonin is associated with depression in both sexes.) What is not confusing is that there is something going on in men that has no counterpart in women.

The profound contrast between men's and women' affiliation

There are 'chalk and cheese' distinctions between the sexes: not just when it comes to competition, but also in respect of co-operation. Just as men and women compete in different ways, and men compete much more strongly than do women; so men and women group together dissimilarly, and women in some respects do so more readily than do men.

It's long been established that an individual distinguishes in quite profound ways between those people perceived to be in the same group as him/herself and those who are outside it. A fair presumption would be that originally this was the community which for most of human evolution was no larger than one hundred and fifty people (or merely fifty, as some authorities maintain). For a man, this would be the extent of the male DH of which he was a member, plus all of the opposite sex and child members of the community. Just as in our mega societies our notion of DH has vastly expanded and become more flexible, so must our sense of the 'in-group'. It's stretched to apply to all kinds of social contexts, such as the workplace. For a woman though, the sense of 'in-group' is *not* her community — her natal personal network plus the associated men and children — but her family and friends, plus in turn their family and friends.

Instead of a straight identification with her own community, this is to (potentially) cut across communities. This has been studied in the context of the university student community (Maddox & Brewer, 2005). A male sees his fellow students as his 'in-group', but his female counterpart includes students in another college altogether; many of whom she may not even have met, but with whom she has a mere potential relationship. She can feel as much trust in the as yet unmet friend of someone she knows in another university as she does in one of her co-students. By contrast, men would always feel more trust in someone from their own college, even if they were a stranger. Men look to their club or their firm, etc,, which is made up of others with whom they have a symbolic connection. Women look to find others who can fill spaces in their ever-expandable personal network.

This is an astonishingly different social outlook; and it's even more so when on top of this there is a massive sex difference in preference for same-sex versus opposite-sex 'in-group' members (Goodwin & Rudman, 2004). Women show same-sex favouritism *four times* greater than do men, who don't have a preference for either sex. Women very much prefer other women, whereas men like either men or women in equal measure. This difference is so great that it suggests that the female 'in-group' might well have originated as a form of all-female affiliation. This would make perfect sense because humans have evolved female dispersal from the natal community — that is, women marry male outsiders and leave to go and live with them — so women must have the facility to make a completely new personal network amongst the women in a foreign husband's community. Men tend not to disperse (unless it's to set up an entirely new community), so the sense of 'in-group' they have, of their natal community, likewise makes perfect sense.

As we shall see, this sex difference has profound effects in the workplace.

Summary

The phenomenon of self-initiated segregation is real and profound, and not some unimportant cultural phenomenon that may recede in time. The assumption usually has been that any difference in behaviour between the sexes is due to 'social conditioning', yet not only has no mechanism been demonstrated but it is not feasible even in theory. Such crucial behaviour is clearly fixed in the genes and not left to the vagaries of the environment.

A picture has emerged of separate and different worlds of the sexes in childhood and adolescent social structure. Boys form a tight hierarchical pyramid but to which they are not strongly attached through other grouping. In contrast, girls are members of large groups, and additionally form strong twosomes and threesomes. Single-sex cliques merge for the purpose of pairing off, but these mixed-sex pools have only this function, so after pairing they dissolve, leaving same-sex social structures as before.

The separate same-sex social worlds are not so apparent because unavoidably we all live in a mixed-sex environment. But same-sex behaviour can be shown to be a default when either sex is forcibly placed in a total single-sex setting for a long period. In prison, women form a profoundly pseudo-family structure, whereas men form a rigid status hierarchy.

The disengagement of the sexes (females especially) from cross-sex competition in favour of displaying to each other, is shown by controlled experiment. Proof that competition is a male and not a female preoccupation is that it is mediated hormonally in a completely different way according to sex. In men there is reaction to the perceived difficulty regarding the opponent, but in women it is only concerning the task; and only in men is there hormonal 'memory' of competition outcome – essential in the assembly of a DH.

Social psychology is split along the divide of sex: not just regarding competition, but also with respect to affiliation. Men automatically conceive of their 'in-group' as their work colleagues or community, whereas for women the 'in-group' is those belonging to their personal network, however tenuous is the connection with any one other individual. Women preferentially choose their own sex four times more often than men, whereas men have no sex preference at all.

Chapter 5

Difference Incarnate

Sex-typical variation – men's focus and women's connectedness

Many claim that sex difference is not as profound as it seems. It's one of those often-said supposed truisms that the range of differences between individuals of either sex exceeds the range of differences across the sexes. This is of course true of some things, but in regard to what is important it isn't true, and in many cases where it might seem to be true, it's fundamentally misleading.

Men's competitive status-seeking and women's personal networking appear to be chalk and cheese—profoundly different motivated behaviours that underlie most of what people do. These are related to, or the product of, the different mating strategies of the sexes: males being sexually selected by females for status and parental reliability, in complete contrast to the sexual selection of females by males simply for their fertility. This is in turn rooted in the female being the 'limiting factor' in reproduction, and the male functioning as 'genetic filter' (see chapter two, above).

The effort males make in trying to climb the status hierarchy, given the potential pay-off in prodigious reproduction, is well worth the risk—even though, as will be the case for most male individuals, it turns out to be futile. Bear in mind that prior to institutionally monogamous societies, most males ended up consigned to reproductive oblivion in what was much more like a winner-takes-all scenario. All men retain the mentality that has evolved to cope with that, and all kinds of seemingly blind-alley behaviour that can often be the most distinguishing feature of men's lives is explained by this, including lots of actual or apparent foolhardiness.

Not only are men and women intrinsically chalk and cheese in how they behave, but how they are treated by others is an even more dichotomous distinction. No matter how unusual nor even how many sex-typically *female* traits he may exhibit, a man will always be treated as a man; and vice versa. There is no grey area in how we treat others: they are either men or women. This mutually reinforces intrinsic sex difference, ensuring that the behaviour that marks out the sexes always polarises and never converges.

How sex and offspring invariably impact differently on males and females of all animal species led to profound sex differences in the course of evolution. These have been further elaborated in the hominid line, so that now there are big differences distinguishing the behaviour of men from those of women, but not all of these may be obvious on the surface. There is an enormous second-order impact on other aspects of life which drives men and women still further apart, to produce all kinds of specific sex differences in abilities (Geary, 1998; Mealey, 2000). Many of these cannot be measured directly, being inevitably confounded with other characteristics, so that they are apparent as statistical rather than 'black and white' differences. Then there are differences that are indeed statistical — the sexes differing merely by degree — that are evident only because of the distinctly male motivation to compete. This makes for a characteristic spread of all kinds of attributes that is quite different in males to what it is in females. So even when attributes are shared by the sexes, the way that they are distributed amongst the individuals of one sex is itself a sex-specific signature.

It's this way in which the global male–female dichotomy cuts across just about any attribute you could think of, that I want to focus on here. The upshot is that both pre-eminence and abject failure are typically male territories, whilst mediocrity tends to be the female lot (with exceptions, of course: nurturance certainly being one). This difference cuts across everything and is rooted in male–male competition. This *motivational* divide is the greatest sex difference of all (Baumeister, 2007); the most direct manifestation of the fact that the female is the 'limiting factor' in reproduction. Interestingly, looking at the range of sex differences and their sex-typical spread, leads to various but related takes on what is the general distinction in orientation between the sexes: to what is the 'essential difference', as Simon Baron-Cohen would characterise it. In his book of that title, Baron-Cohen's central point is that male and female are distinguished by a general approach to life that he sums up as respectively 'systemising' and 'empathising'(Baron-Cohen, 2003). I will outline this and how it complements other takes on global distinctions between the sexes later on.

Encapsulating what the sexes are about by contrasting their general attitudes and ways of behaving inevitably leads us to the contrast between male status-seeking and female personal networking.

Sex-typical spread

Because men compete with each other for sex indirectly through status, then anything that can translate into status will be contested by men in a different way to women. Few things cannot be so translated. This transforms and amplifies what would otherwise be less significant differences between men and women. The amplification is at both extremes, because male effort tends to be all-or-nothing. If it's something that a male individual is good at, then he competes in earnest; if not, then he does so less than half-heartedly and he puts his real effort elsewhere. This explains why in an area of creativity, like musical ability for example, where although there is evidence of an inherent greater ability on average in women, it's almost always men who are found at the pinnacle of achievement (as well as at its foot).

I'm going to take music as a case study, but first I need to elaborate on the different typical distribution of attributes according to sex.

Across any population comprising two distinct types — such as women (X) and men (Y), a preponderance of one type at the top end of the distribution of performance (such as musical achievement) does not imply that this type overall is weighted more towards the top end of the distribution than is the other type. Not even if at the apex of distribution there is exclusively Y; no individual of the other type, X, being present. Certainly we would *expect* that a preponderance of Y at the top would be reflected in a gradation from top to bottom, so that at the very bottom there would be the very smallest proportion of Y compared to what it would be at any other point in the distribution. However, this expectation is confounded by what is sometimes found in the real world. It seems that often one type has some quality that means that what enabled it to out-compete other types to become preponderant at the top end, also makes it more likely than other types to fall to the bottom. Here the preponderance at the top end of a distribution would be mirrored by a similar preponderance at the bottom end, leaving fewer than you would expect in the middle range. So Y is in such high proportion as to pretty well exclude X at both extremes. The type is *polarised*, and it's what is usually found in respect of male performance, more or less regardless of whatever is being measured. By contrast, the other type within the population may be poorly represented at both extremes but crowded in the middle. Having been crowded out of the extremes by Y, X is left dominating the average values. This is what is usually found in respect of female performance; the opposite of polarisation.

The way that male performance across the board is distributed is not a form of distribution that we intuit. This is central to why we falsely perceive men as advantaged. Because women crowd the middle and men crowd the extremes, it's the contrast between the men at the top end and the women in the middle that registers, and not that between the women in the middle and the men at the bottom end. The exclusive male occupancy of the apex makes us falsely imagine that males must be scarce at the base of the distribution, and even that there must be an inverted pyramid. The mirror at the bottom of what is happening at the top we tend not to see.

The preponderance of men at the bottom is made even more invisible by the reinforcement of this misperception by our predilection to look at and prefer high-status over low-status men. This is the tendency of both sexes

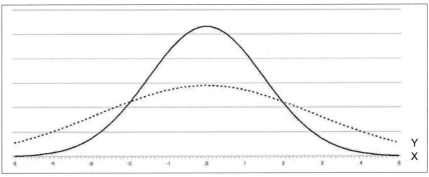

Figure 5.1: Sex-typical distribution (X = women, Y = men)

to 'police' the male DH. And on top of this is the focus by women on successful men (and ignoring the 'losers') in the process of sexual choice. It's a
fundamental insight that feminism has always ignored, or misused as and
when convenient. Men are seen as unfairly successful, or as hopeless failures, according to what suits the line of argument.

The different sex-typical distributions are not just overlapping normal
distribution curves that differ only in their position on the horizontal axis,
but different *shaped* curves (see Figure 5.1). The female curve is more
peaked in the middle, whilst the male curve by contrast is flatter and lower
in the central region, and progressively decreases less than does the female
curve as it extends in both directions beyond where the female curve disappears. This reflects the more 'strung out' variation of the men, with
extreme high flyers as well as extreme no-hopers, and consequently fewer
in the neutral centre.

Why this systematic difference between the sexes exists pretty much
across the board of whatever you test for comparison, stems from the high
degree of between-male competition that has no female counterpart. Competitive urgency can produce both positive and negative results. The high-
testosterone racing driver can be propelled to victory just as he can also be
propelled to push too hard and spin off at the corner into the gravel and
out of the race. If the field was a mix of men and women, even if they were
drivers of equal skill, you would end up with all males on the podium, and
those taking an early bath would also all be male. All of the females likely
would be in the middle of the field, and progressively nearer the tail end of
this middle region rather than the low end of the distribution as more of
the men spun, crashed or wore out their cars in their long-shot attempt at
success. This is why Formula One racing is an all-male sport and will
remain so bar the very rare exception of a woman who unusually has male
'brain patterning'—when a male-style focus can perhaps make up for
some of the shortfall in drive.

The implications of the contrast between the male polarised and female
centralised distribution forms are highlighted in considering overall intel-

ligence. There is an additional factor here though: men are measured as being more intelligent than women by about five IQ points on average (Irwing & Lynn, 2005 – this being also an average of all of the other recent studies), making them better suited for highly complex tasks. This is a relatively small difference in itself, but because of the male- typical distribution compared to the female, this average difference is greatly amplified towards the top end. The proportion of men increases as intelligence levels rise, so that there are twice as many men compared to women with IQ scores of 125 – which is the sort of IQ level typical for first- class degree holders – and at the 'genius' level of 155, men outnumber women sixfold.

What we have with IQ is a combination of the distribution patterns that distinguish men and women, and a sex difference. There is an overlap of normal distribution curves so that the male curve is further along the bottom axis, *and* the different kinds of 'bell curves' of polarisation and centralisation; with the males distributed more at either end and less bunched in the middle, and the female distributed with few at either end but predominantly in the central portion.

It's anathema in some academic circles to challenge the dogma that IQ must be the same for both sexes: either as an absolute difference or in its spread. Yet the difference in spread is incontrovertible, and the absolute difference has been long known. Up until the mid-1920s women lagged behind men by a similar point spread, and the tests were redesigned to be 'unbiased'. Given that there are various significant sex differences in cognitive function in different areas, then it would be surprising if everything evened up to give an overall equal cognitive ability. Indeed, the question is whether the difference has any real meaning, because different cognitive styles are qualitatively rather than quantitatively distinct.

There are two obvious reasons for the male superiority. Men have a four percent faster nerve-conduction speed (Reed, Vernon & Johnson, 2004; Silverman, 2006; Deary & Der, 2005; Jensen, 2006); this being a direct measure of processing rate, meaning that men can perform tasks faster than women, or more/more complex tasks in a given time. Men also have proportionately bigger brains than women: even adjusting for the overall larger body size of men, their brains are ten percent bigger (Falk et al., 1999). There are in fact far more substantial differences between the brains of the sexes, and I will come on to these later on in this chapter.

Men excel in music and the arts although overall women may be the more artistic

Bearing all this in mind, I now consider as an example the preponderance of men at the top end of achievement in music; music being an ability that on average is more apparent in females. I won't take the higher, more abstract art of classical composition, where male pre-eminence is indisputable; but instead make life harder for my argument by looking at 'lower' musical life, as it were.

If there is an accessible art form that gladly opens its arms to women, it's the world of the singer/songwriter: a world I have been closely involved with for twenty-five years. In the city where I used to live, there was quite a home-grown singer/songwriter tradition: several outstanding male artists but *not one* outstanding female tune- and word-smith. Good women singers yes, but with middling song-writing abilities. Behind them were a large number of fairly good males and by comparison only a handful of females. The same was true, if less so, when I ran the principal 'new acoustic' venue in central London in the early 1990s, but the proportion of women is no higher today in a university open-performance slot such as that which currently runs weekly at Sheffield University students' union.

Given the significant average loading in women's favour, why should this be? Is it because of lack of opportunity? Anything but. At every turn now it's much easier for a woman to get a platform than a man. Scarcity value alone means a relatively talentless woman will get a spot or a gig over a more talented man, and that's before woman's sexual power comes into play. The stuff of song is the interpersonal: the very thing that is surely the reason why women have made good novelists. Women are also, on average, more gifted in language than men. Add this to their head-start in music, and the singer/songwriter should be a genre where women, compared to men, are a runaway success. Sure enough, of the crop of women singer/songwriters there are some apparently up with the men. Yet of the ones at the very top in the eye of the mass media very few, if any, are of the best. Still the men outnumber the women and their dominance increases the closer you get to the apex of excellence. Too many commercially-successful women are run-of-the-mill.

That the women do not have to try so hard is evidenced by the plethora of American country-based female singer/songwriters too numerous to name and mostly too talentless as writers to recall or too formulaic and constricted by genre. All of these, I suggest, are good examples of those who have made some career out of being a singer/songwriter in spite of unexceptional talent and no special inspiration, but with the protection from competition that the accidental status of womanhood confers.

Look honestly at the songs of female singer/songwriters from the past two decades or so: Tracy Chapman, Tanita Tikarum, Michelle Shocked, Jewel, Beth Orton, Tori Amos, Alanis Morrissette, Dido (whose brother writes the music in any case), Kathryn Williams, P.J. Harvey … I'm struggling to come up with the very recently emerged because they turn out to be singers who either don't write their own material (like Katie Melua, who is merely the vehicle for the hit factory that is Mike Batt), or very little of it (Norah Jones, for instance). The most recently conspicuously-successful new female artist, KT Tunstall, mostly co-writes songs with more seasoned professionals. Tunstall shows that the current chart fling with the singer/songwriter can be manufactured almost as cynically as are boy and girl bands. Her debut album is less singer/songwriter than mid-tempo AOR with lacklustre lyrics and vocal nuance providing much of the musical interest—not to mention a soulful voice. Her follow-up release is remarkably anodyne. Once again what we have here is a singer rather than a writer. The most notable and most recently emerged of all, Kate Walsh, makes beautiful contemplative music that is mesmerising in live performance, but as either melodist or lyricist, 'great' she is not.

Ask yourself how on earth these women got where they are with largely the veneer of slick arrangement disguising lacklustre songs (assuming the songs were theirs in the first place). There has always been a crop plucked from nowhere that have no male counterparts who disappear as fast as they have risen when they're 'found out'. Lisa Loeb was the classic instance of a girl plucked from obscurity—by a record producer who lived in the same block, on the strength of just one song. The song was shaped musically by a band got together by the producer. *Stay*—a good song to be sure—made the top ten, but the album of a year later turned out to be unrelenting juvenile embarrassment. Can you imagine a man being given the same fairytale break without having first to convince squads of A&R men, execs and pubs, clubs and then halls full of punters?

There has been hardly a glut of convincing male singer-songwriters of late. Men do not see this as a prime arena of competition. But certainly they did see it in this way thirty or forty years ago. This is why there was the flowering of the singer-songwriter era in the 1960s and '70s. Where were the great women then? So almost non-existent that it's sometimes said that women have lacked 'role models'. Well, almost every female singer/songwriter cites one of the truly great singer/songwriters of the modern period, woman or man: Joni Mitchell. Definitive uniquely female singing style; distinctive writing bridging old and new world with an eclectic mix of American folk and German *lieder*; new rhythms and ideas on guitar; oozing with things to say from a female perspective. You could even argue that no single male figure is as successfully innovative but clearly imitable in every department as is Mitchell. There are several enduring male models an aspirant could try to copy, though their very success in breaking new ground and developing an original niche makes them largely *in*imitable. Bob Dylan, for example.

There is a string of men to accompany Dylan who have revolutionised singer/songwriting from the mid-1960s. Tim Buckley, David Crosby, Leonard Cohen, Richard Thompson, Roy Harper, Nick Drake, Paul Simon. There are also those of the likes of James Taylor, who may not so much innovate as simply display the peak of their craft with supremely memorable songs. A female counterpart of Taylor would be Carol King. But what about pre-eminent female innovators? After Mitchell, only rela-

Joni Mitchell —
The exception that proves the rule

tively minor figures come to mind, along with the cult of the weird female voice, beginning with Kate Bush. One good collection of songs (her debut album *The Kick Inside)*, but her legacy is merely the search for ever stranger vocalists. Hence Sinead O'Connor, Tori Amos and Bjork. Singers rather than songwriters; relative failures as writers, with little to say either lyrically or musically. They all required pop-arrangement clothing to cover what would be insubstantial if it was pared down to just voice and guitar or piano. Joni Mitchell is the exception that proves the rule.

In interview, Mitchell once confessed that she's always been a 'surrogate man'. She is, one suspects, a rare example of a woman possessing the embryological accident of a 'male-patterned' brain (which I will shortly explain). The lack of great female singer/songwriters, bar Mitchell, begs a question. Do you have to be, if not a man then in some way male in the way you think, to not just want to be a singer/songwriter but to achieve greatness in this art? Is this why most of the best and the most numerous singer/songwriters are, or have been, men?

So far, I have made the line of argument difficult for myself through deliberately choosing an artistic field where the gap between the sexes is not at first glance so apparent — or where superficially it may seem that women are actually in the ascendant. It may or may not be sufficiently convincing, not least because disagreements that are partly to do with taste cloud the discussion. But even if the supremacy of men at the very top is merely debateable rather than certain, this would still betray a considerable difference between the sexes, given the various head starts that women enjoy in the field of music generally and in the genre of the singer/songwriter in particular. There is a much more clear-cut separation in achievement according to sex in music of a more formal, or abstract nature — and we can include progressive rock and jazz along with classical composition. Here women are almost non-existent.

This is to be expected given the new research conclusions of the afore-mentioned Simon Baron-Cohen, with the analysis of what he terms 'the essential difference' as that between the male patterned 'systemising' brain and the 'empathising' brain of the female. Music is a system, and the more so the further you move away from simple song to anything more complex, and especially so with extended pieces of polyphonic develop-ment. Again, and as Baron-Cohen emphasises, we are dealing with the dif-ferences *on average,* but this means that at the apex of achievement everyone, or almost everyone, is likely to be male; with the rare exception being down to the accident of a genetic female developing a 'male pat-terned' brain in the embryonic stage, as may be the case with Joni Mitchell.

Feminists have tried to dig up long-lost female classical composers but struggle to break the duck. Not one who could hold a candle to the ranks of pre-eminent men. Victorian ladies, like their less-numerous Georgian pre-decessors, had endless spare time and no responsibilities. An average middle-class, let alone upper-class woman had servants galore to relieve her of all work and childcare duties. Never before or since has there been such a large sub-group of people with unlimited time to do as they chose. Struggling with a choice of what's not too unfashionable to do in your own drawing room comes bottom of anybody's list of life's great hindrances. These women could spend all day playing the drawing room piano, which they would have been encouraged to do from an early age as part of the usual education to be a lady. In period novels the after-dinner pianist was invariably a woman. If such a lady became a good pianist and sight reader, then why should she not then go on to compose? The truth seems to be that she was often quite a good pianist, but had little inclination to put in the enormous effort and discipline and to summon up the inspiration to go beyond good playing to actually create the sort of polyphonic notated music she readily learned how to read and play. Some women must have tried, but failed to be better than plain good. The great majority were con-tent playing the well-groomed lady without venturing into composition.

To find women of real achievement we would need to travel to artistic areas that move away from 'system' and take on board 'empathy' (as Baron-Cohen would argue). To really stack things in women's favour, the art form that best utilises female strengths is novel writing. As well as requiring verbal ability, this is largely 'psychologising' a few individual main characters, which is precisely what women do socially. Plotting and character development also utilise the supposed female strength of hold-ing several things simultaneously in mind. Yet women don't dominate in the novelist's art. The very best women novelists have been merely 'literary' romance fiction writers: notably the Brontes and Jane Austen (Fay Weldon describes *Pride & Prejudice* as 'not Dostoyevksy for sure; more like Mills & Boon'.) Women have lacked both innovation and the ambition to paint on the large canvasses tackled by men. This is despite the

famous early figures having the advantage over men of completely lei-
sured lives with no distractions of any kind. Is there even a single instance
of the truly panoramic and visionary novel that has been written by
women? Women writers—even George Eliot—fail in capturing the male
outlook, whereas men have succeeded in the reverse. It may be that
women are in a sense just too close to the stuff of the novel to write a particularly good one; for the similar reason that good poetry comes from the
power of life's mystery which is fully and truly felt only at the extra distance experienced by men.

Some claim that there would have been more of them were it not for
novel writing being so frowned upon that the likes of the Brontes only succeeded by employing the ruse of male pseudonyms; yet nobody has con-
vincingly explained that being Curer Bell or George Eliot in print was
anything more than mere decorum. It is not true that creativity lauded in
the gentlemen was dismissed as trivia in the ladies: women in considerable numbers found little difficulty in getting into print and selling in commercial quantities. Major biographies of Mary Anne Evans (George Eliot)
and the Brontes appeared in 1995 and both argued that the famous pseudonyms were not necessary, that their use was more a case of playfulness
than prudence. And don't base your judgement on whether Jane Austen
experienced difficulty in having her work published on *Becoming Jane*—an
entirely fictional piece of feminist propaganda.

Shifting across the literary continuum, what about poetry as perhaps
where female pre-eminence can be found? On the surface at least it seems
potentially the quintessential feminine art form. However, if Robert
Graves is to be believed, it is an essentially masculine invocation of the
'earth mother' muse. Graves talked much nonsense in his prose, but perhaps he is on to something with the idea that good poetry comes from the
power of life's mystery which is fully and truly felt only at the extra distance experienced by men. Poetry is man's way of achieving a wholeness
that woman is perhaps more inclined to take for granted. By this reckoning, women's poetry is narcissistic or merely sentimental and a woman
can be a true poet only by being, essentially, a man. It is an irony that the
'earth mother' (the bogus elevation of whom was partly down to Graves'
gobbledegook about a bogus matriarchal prehistory in his book, *The White
Goddess*) can be cited to put clothes on male striving and how it eludes
woman. Is it all fancy?

Help is on hand from feminism's early queen (and professor of English
literature), Germaine Greer. 'It was sinfully easy to get published ... they
[female poets] got too much recognition for the wrong work for the wrong
reasons ... it's time they were judged by the highest standards' she said,
debating with Melvyn Bragg on Radio 4 in 1995 in the wake of her book,
The Slipshod Sibyls. In taking to task female poetry throughout the ages, she
includes even major twentieth-century figures like Sylvia Plath: 'a sort of

Pseuds Corner

Elizabeth Gaskell

Mary Elizabeth Braddon

A minority of female Victorian authors adopted male pseudonyms, the most famous being 'Curer Bell' (Charlotte Bronte) and 'George Eliot' (Mary Anne Evans). Because women were privileged and could expect protection in just about every circumstance — including an apparent endorsement of low morals — most women writers stuck with their own names. These included Mrs Gaskell, who was unafraid to publish daring social novels like *Mary Barton* and *North and South,* and Mary Elizabeth Braddon, who wrote of illicit affairs in so-called 'sensation novels' like *Lady Audleys' Secret.*

Many women authors, just as famous in their day, were so slight as now to be entirely forgotten, even by historians, but few of them bothered with the cover of a male alias — and though some did write anonymously, their sex was the one thing they *did* reveal. That Gaskell's and Braddon's books were almost exactly contemporaneous with those of 'Curer Bell' and 'George Eliot' dispatches the argument that novelists were somehow prevented from making their mark simply on account of being women.

parody of half understood male literature...still pleasing daddy'. Most women's poetry she dismisses on the grounds that you have to take yourself seriously to do poetry, and women either couldn't manage that at all or assumed a levity that became mere self-importance. She continued: 'Second-rate, dishonest, fake poetry is worse than no poetry at all. '

Plath has long been championed as a great figure held back through her betrayal by her partner, the much more substantial poet, Ted Hughes. The record has now been set straight. Hughes did much to help Plath in her writing, but she was very much in the shadow of a far greater artist. A classic instance of an artist who in the end failed to connect the inner and the outer, Plath imploded. Perhaps Graves was right that males and not females have the right tension between inner and outer, and his insight, if that's what it is, may be what Greer is trying to express when she writes of women not taking themselves seriously.

The evidence is all around us that there *is* something in men that makes them want to create in the purest, most abstract art forms. We should exclude here the recent capitulation of art into the thinly-disguised grab for (celebrity) status — at root certainly what art is *for*, but not what it *is*. That would risk granting admission to such charlatans as Tracy Emin and others whose 'conceptual' work not only substitutes what art is for for what it should be; but does no more than lamely ape what rebellious men did nearly a century before them. We have plenty of serious music, large-canvas poetry, and truly evocative (not merely decorous) painting. These are all artistic endeavours from which women have been completely or at least largely absent, and still are. Feminist-led resurrections of supposedly lost greats are all damp squibs: the composer Clara Schumann is remembered only as a pianist, Angelica Kaufman's paintings are rarely exhibited, and Aphra Benn's plays can't hold the stage today.

Is another way of looking at art — other than (male) striving for status and expression of systemising skills — that it's the male means of 'making whole' that which is available to women by a more natural and direct route? Is it that women don't *need* to make art — which explains why they are so mediocre compared to pre-eminent men?

Two complementary models of the basis of sex difference

There are two overarching categories of sex-typical 'cognitive style', as could be described, that are normally distributed and overlap each other, and this has spawned a theory as to their essence. I've been alluding to the Cambridge psychologist Simon Baron-Cohen's general theory of sex difference based on two types of 'brain patterning' — 'systemising' and 'empathising'. Everyone has some of both, but in different proportions, so that typically boys and men have much more 'brain patterning' that is systemising than empathising, and girls and women vice-versa. As you get closer to the extremes of distribution, those individuals who have the highest skew towards systemisation are all male, and conversely 'brain patterning' that is maximally empathising at the expense of systemising is the exclusive preserve of females. By 'systemising', Baron-Cohen means simply the ability and predilection for perceiving mechanical systems and responding accordingly. So, for example, tool use and navigation are facilitated. 'Empathising' is self-explanatory. Clearly, these are respectively typical male and female modes of cognition. It's been pointed out that Baron-Cohen's conceptualisation is an extension of the notion, based on a range of observed sex differences, that there are distinct brain 'modules' of 'folk physics' and 'folk psychology' that are much stronger in men and women respectively. There is now voluminous evidence that these are not learned but genetically based, and relate at root to evolutionarily ancient distinctions.

What he means by 'brain patterning' Baron-Cohen does not detail, but in general, brain tissue is characterised by either its processing ability or connectivity with other areas. Self-evidently, empathising must concern taking multiple aspects into account that are mirrored in yourself, so more pronounced neural connectivity must be key in this respect. If there is more neural connectivity—necessarily at the expense of other neural structure—then there would be evident 'brain patterning' to facilitate empathising. In systemising, processing power is key. So if brain areas themselves rather than their interconnectedness is prioritised as the brain develops in the embryo, then systemising is facilitated in 'brain patterning'. Although brain function is spread across various loci, and loci tend to have multiple function, some loci are the main focus of particular function. So empathising ability will tend to be to do with activity across various loci, whilst systemising skills will rely crucially on major activity in certain key loci.

The theory came about through two quite different lines of research. Having a particular interest in autism, Baron-Cohen had noticed that individuals at the higher-performing end of the autistic spectrum (Asperger's syndrome) were sometimes up to what we might consider genius level at analytical tasks, but far less than of average competence at social interaction, if not pathologically inept. Autism afflicts males at the rate of eight times more than females, so he wondered if autism may be an extreme manifestation of the 'male brain'. Mathematical geniuses include a disproportionate number of people with Asperger's syndrome; the elephant in the room for social constructivists is the minuscule number of female participants in the International Mathematical Olympiads, as there is no inherent cultural reason for mathematics to be a quintissentially male pursuit. Baron-Cohen's team had also done a lot of investigation of the perceptual preferences of new-born babies, finding that girls preferred to look at faces, boys at mobiles (Connellan et al., 2001); suggesting from birth the empathising/systemizing sex difference.

* * *

Paralleling Baron-Cohen's conceptualisation is that of Irene Claremont de Castillejo, a Jungian psychoanalyst. In her outstanding 1973 book, *Knowing Woman: A Feminine Psychology*, de Castillejo sees the great sex difference as woman's retention of a diffuse awareness of nature, as against man's focused consciousness and his heroic quest to sharpen it still further. The man needs the woman's rootedness, and the woman needs man's bright focused light to help her to fully realise what would otherwise still be vague and unconscious, and to be able to make use of it. De Castillejo

talks about the danger facing woman of blindly accepting man's values as though they were her own:

There can be little doubt that with rare exceptions the masculine of woman is inferior in quality to that of a man. It is apt to be less original and less flexible. She tends to be impressed by organisation and theories which she frequently carries to excess because her masculine power to focus runs away with her. She then becomes hidebound by regulations and obsessed by detail. She is much less likely to be will-ing to make exceptions than a man, as the masculine side which runs away with her is wholly impersonal and disregards the human need of any particular man or woman.

But the same sort of thing applies to the feminine within man. It is less vital and dynamic than that of a woman. The feminine in women is not solely passive and receptive. It is also ruthless in its service of life, or rather those particular lives which personally concern her. She is as ruthless as nature. There are no lengths to which a woman will not go to fos-ter the welfare of her immediate family or those she loves. The feminine of man on the other hand is soft and gentle, lacking the ruthless service of life every bit as much as the masculine of woman lacks originality and flexibil-ity....

As man and woman have, throughout the ages, walked on either side of the river of life, there have always been bridges which have enabled them to meet. Mutual understanding may have been at a minimum but we have always been able to trust that devotion, passion and sexuality would throw bridges across the stream over and over again.

Today it is as though the banks were crumbling, narrowing the river bed until it can be jumped across. Already I see in my mind's eye the sands from either side mingling and mounting slowly till they form a terra-firma on which anyone can walk in easy companionship. But if this should happen, the dynamic river would have ceased to flow, dammed up by the mingling sands. Separation is the keynote of relating the opposites in life. Perhaps the greatest paradox in man's psyche is our longing for union, for peace, for solutions, though experience has taught us that it is our conflicts and our fail-ures which are in fact our points of growth.

This is a brilliant and poetic encapsulation of the tension and attraction between the sexes that may be just the author's personal spiritual insight. Yet despite hailing from the pseudoscience of psychoanalysis, the gong of truth is deafening. It's a clear warning against the spiritual emptiness of inappropriately or prematurely bridging the clear natural divide between the sexes in a delusion of sexlessness, instead of allowing the free play of this separation until the right times for them to come together as more than the sum of their parts. What the book is about, in essence, is that men and women don't know themselves, and still less do they know each other; but the complementarity of the sexes works so that both the partners can better know themselves *through* the other. Their mutual sexual attraction serves to bring them closer to then allow a mutual indirect self-discovery.

Looking for the basis of sex difference in the brain

Does neuroscience have anything to tell us that might reinforce in some way de Castillejo's insights and Baron-Cohen's 'essential difference', or the preponderance of the 'folk physics' module in males and that of 'folk psychology' in females?

It's not always appreciated that there are major sex differences in the brain. Women have nine times more intelligence-related *connectivity* brain tissue (white matter) in their brains than men do, whilst men have six times more intelligence-related *processing* tissue (grey matter) than women (Haier, 2005). This means that the information-processing power of men is greater, whilst co-ordination between centres is more evident in women. This last would explain the thicker bundles of nerves connecting the cerebral hemispheres (the corpus callosum) in women. Where the relevant structures are located in the brain also reveals sex differences. For men, their IQ- related grey matter is divided equally between the frontal lobes and (immediately behind) the parietal lobes, which deal with skills like maths, reading and perception. More than four-fifths of men's IQ-related white matter, on the other hand, is located in the temporal lobes, which among other tasks process memory and perceive sound. Women have a large proportion of their complement of both white and grey IQ-related brain matter in the frontal lobes, which is a brain area involved in speech, reasoning and judgement, as well as movement and emotions.

Although 'IQ-related' neural tissue is only a fraction of all neural tissue, it is highly important and means that there must be sex-distinct *kinds* of intellectual capacity. It was beyond anyone's expectation that there should be such a structural correspondence with theories of cognitive sex difference along the lines of 'systemising' versus 'empathising' (Baron-Cohen) or male focus and female diffusiveness (de Castillejo). Cohen's and de Castillejo's theories appear to be getting at something similar, and the contrast between male processing and female connectivity found by neuroscientific enquiry is pretty much what both theories would predict. Clearly this is a significant contribution to explaining the gap between the sexes in achievement.

Strong clues that major functional and structural differences separated the sexes had been in the air since scientists began to explain a difference according to the dominance of one half of the brain. The problem was finding which parts of the brain do what. Techniques of brain imaging were refined to partially solve this, though a clearly defined locus for any particular function is still elusive — because the brain is integrated, and sometimes other parts can take over functions in the event of damage. Apparently, female brains are better at this sort of recovery. No wonder, if female brains are less concerned with processing in various centres and more about connectivity. Earlier research had shown that female brains have less clear-cut separate function of the hemispheres — again presaging the new findings — and it was starting to be suggested that if the brains of men are more differentiated than those of women, then the inference could be that in one sense males have more complicated, developed minds.

It's a seeming paradox that boys and men are always seeking novelty, are highly distractable, have a short attention span, and even when they find an interest it's often a fickle one; yet once they find something that intrigues them, they become obsessed by it. This explains on the one hand the short attention span and on the other extreme obsession (Moir & Moir, 1998). This makes good sense for men. The male willingness to take long-shot gambles to try to acquire a high pay-off in terms of raised status explains the facility for extreme focus; but equally if there is nothing currently for him that makes sense to practice such focus upon, then it may be that a man is better employed sampling a wide range of what is happening in the environment to try to spot where intense effort might be well deployed. Short attention span and obsessive focus are both facets of the drive to status, and another take on why males tend either to be successful or failures and not a middling in-between.

Summary

That the sexes are in different worlds is underlined by chalk-and-cheese distinctions between men and women. It is not true, as is often claimed, that differences within the sexes exceed those across the sexes. And the differences diverge rather than converge. There are many differences that are merely statistical but often this is simply masking an underlying contrast by related but confounding measures.

Because of the intensive competitive nature of men with a 'winner takes all' attitude, for most attributes the way they are distributed amongst individuals is strikingly different according to sex. Men tend to occupy the extremes and women tend to aggregate in the middle range.

Even taking the art form of music, and specifically the singer- songwriter, where compared to men, women would be expected to excel, it is still mostly men who are pre-eminent. There is something within men that makes them excel that is lacking in women.

The distinction between male 'systemising' versus female 'empathising' is a scientific theory developed by Simon Baron-Cohen, but it is uncannily like the famous conception of male focus and female diffuse connection in the work of the Jungian psychoanalyst, Irene Claremont de Castillo.

Overall brain size, the extent of connections between the hemispheres, and the degree to which functions are in one as against both hemispheres: all are distinctive according to sex. Most of all is the huge contrast between the amount of IQ-related processing tissue as against IQ-related connective brain tissue, with several times more of the former in male brains and the latter in females.

Chapter 6

Sex In Care

Men's poor health stems from the 'status syndrome'

It follows from the fact that throughout biology the female is the 'limiting factor' in reproduction, and the male the dispensable 'genetic filter', that much more care for and protection of women than of men must be fully expected. By extension, care and protection is afforded women, and men are obliged to provide this, without it being reciprocal. So the biology would lead us to predict the likelihood of not mere indifference towards men, but even denial of care and protection. When it comes to the clearest way that care and protection is given— healthcare—a big sex difference in women's favour in inevitable.

This is evident across the board in the take-up of healthcare and most starkly in respect of the treatment of diseases that impact only on one sex. Budget constraints in the NHS are no barrier to over-resourcing for women. This was beautifully illustrated by the huge fuss over Herceptin: the incredibly expensive and remarkably ineffectual drug for treating breast cancer. Given that the drug helps only one out of twenty patients to which it's deemed suitable, it costs half a million pounds to keep just one patient alive for merely one year. In addition to Herceptin, Docetaxel and Paclitaxel were also earmarked for fast-tracked licensing—that's three out of just five drugs so prioritised in that year, all for the one disease of breast cancer. Correspondingly for men, the 'inequitable treatment' of prostate cancer patients—on every measure of healthcare—was exposed and excoriated by the Commons' Public Accounts Committee (January 2006). Whereas out of all types of cancer, breast cancer patients have the shortest wait to see a specialist, for prostate cancer the wait is by far the longest. Research into prostate cancer—which is sorely needed so as to get a reliable test and to distinguish between treatment methods—receives just four percent of the funding that research into breast cancer attracts, despite a difference in mortality rates of only one percent (and in fact prostate cancer may well be the bigger killer because often it is never detected, and the cause of death is recorded as cancer of another organ when this is actually the secondary disease through metastasis).

Regarding contraception, men's needs have been totally ignored. Still we await the introduction of the 'male pill' to replace the invasive surgery of vasectomy and/or the destruction of sexual pleasure in the use of the condom, yet the male sexual biochemistry such a pill is required to circumvent is far simpler than in the female. As for sexual health, chlamydia contracted by men is seen as a condition needing treatment because of its possible impact on the fertility of their female sexual partners, and there is no publicity about the problem of consequent infertility for the male patients themselves. Publicity about health when it is directed at men is presented as a joke, ostensibly because this is how best to get men to consume the message. But campaigning TV series with titles such as *The Trouble With Men* and *No Hard Feelings* betray an attitude simply that health provision for men is an add-on to the more important provision for women; that men are literally a joke.

The targeting of specifically female conditions backfires on women as it necessarily entails poorer outcomes for women (as well as for men) suffering more common serious illnesses not peculiar to their sex. This was clear in the scrapping of the planned screening for bowel cancer, yet pushing ahead with screening for the comparatively rare ovarian cancer. The rising expense of drugs such as Herceptin is cited as the reason — and this too is part of the boomerang effect on women, because rushing through the adoption of new treatments for women itself can be dangerous for them: Herceptin can have a fatal side effect on the heart. Screening by examining patients for early breast cancer tumours is useless if not actually counterproductive — and that's according to both of the UK's leading breast cancer experts, Michael Baum and Karol Sikora (Bosanquet & Sikora, 2006). But more importantly, it absorbs staff and equipment time, which then cannot be given over to diagnosis of other cancers in patients whose symptoms are already sufficiently advanced for them to have come forward. Consequently — as estimated by the Royal College of Radiologists in February 2002 — 10,000 people a year die unnecessarily. David Tulloch, an Edinburgh consultant urologist, has said that even allowing for the accuracy problems with the main test for prostate cancer, breast cancer screening was no more reliable than would be screening for prostate cancer, and either would be a better use of money than cervical cancer screening, which is not at all cost-effective. Yet it's another screening programme that, like breast cancer, the government is yet further extending; and for the one reason that it's specifically for women.

Real men don't go to the doctor

To hear the complaints on behalf of women in the media, you would think that it was women and not men who were being poorly treated. Men are also popularly supposed to be malingerers and 'wimps' regarding health, contrasting with women stoically enduring the maternity room. Yet even excluding everything maternity-related, men's use of the health service, from visiting the surgery upwards, is less than half that of women. That includes treatment for pain, which women popularly are supposed to endure, in contrast to the fuss men make over it. In fact it is women who have lower threshold and tolerance for pain (Fillingim & Maixner, 1995; Riley et al., 1998), and in pregnancy and childbirth, women produce natural pain suppressants (Komisaruk & Whipple, 2000). And it's hardly that physical trauma is more of a feature of women's lives than men's: injuries caused by others, or sustained in work and in play, are overwhelmingly male. This fact, clearly, explains the adaptive significance of the disparity between the sexes regarding pain tolerance.

It is both common knowledge and well researched, that many men simply dismiss symptoms of the early stages of serious conditions, refusing to seek treatment even in the face of persistent exhortations by those around them. This is not least their own fault, but it shows the bind that men are in. A man cannot complain without risking a fall in his personal status. Many men are afraid that going to the doctor will end with unwanted advice or to be told of a serious illness, either way leading to a compromise in their ability to provide (for a family), or in their ability to display an ability to provide (to prospective partners). A man with a family would fear concern being raised on his behalf by those he is providing for, because this itself undermines the relief from cares about the world that is part of what his providing for his family brings. A man feels that he has no permission to seek help that otherwise would go to women, children and old people.

None of this is an excuse for the health service not offering and encouraging men to seek healthcare; rather it is an indictment of it. Other than for heart disease, the NHS does not even publicise information about health problems to men in the way it has long been done for women, children and old people. The NHS should not be there to respond to the lobby groups that shout the loudest—not least because they are most likely to be advocates for groups already receiving disproportionate care—but to care for the patient groups most in clinical need, and which can best benefit from intervention. The women's lobby often goes to absurd lengths. The NHS came under attack regarding the supposed risk of thrombosis for women taking certain brands of birth-control pills, but the risk was actually only half the risk of acquiring the same condition in pregnancy.

Stark as these problems are, there is an even bigger problem for men than sex discrimination in treatment or the low propensity to seek it:

The major inequality in health is that men get seriously ill more than women do

The assumption is that the sexes have roughly equal healthcare needs, but there is a profound sex difference, with men suffering considerably greater health problems than women. What's more, this is an inherent result of the separate worlds of the sexes, as I will explain. The average male life expectancy at birth in the USA is seven years short of the female, and in Russia it's a staggering fifteen years. These are enormous disparities which cannot be accounted for by inequalities in treatment. Underlying factors that precipitate serious illness are far more significant. Early death for men comes mainly from a spectrum of diseases, notably coronary heart disease and a number of very different conditions, but all related. Why are men so much more prone to these than women?

This is the big question in health, and it has now been answered and on more than one level. The basic difference between the lives of men and those of women is, of course, that men have to compete with other men for status so as to be chosen by women; whereas women do not have to compete with other women, because what allows them to be accepted by the men they choose are their given attributes of youth and beauty. Overall, this creates a big difference between the sexes, with far more long-term physical and psychological stress experienced by males. (This difference is only slightly narrowed by the multi-billion dollar commodification of youth and beauty in modern Western societies that has led to a dramatic rise in illnesses like anorexia and bulimia—effectively diseases triggered by female intra-sex competition. It will be interesting to see if this trend continues and what the resulting effect on women's health will be).

But men do not suffer uniformly. Those males who have generally lost out through competition and are as a consequence of lower status, are the ones who suffer more stress. By contrast, for higher-status males, stress can be invigorating and actually contributes to better health.

The physiological mechanism for this is now understood. The body has a medium and long-term reaction mechanism to stress (in addition to the mechanism mediated by adrenalin), that uses the hormone cortisol to keep the body at a more sustained readiness for action by gearing it up to produce glucose from otherwise inaccessible stores of fat and protein.

It's known that there are consistent sex differences in cortisol responses to psychological stress (Kirschbaum, Wust & Hellhammer, 1992). In an experimental social evaluation task, men react with much higher levels, and these levels are maintained for much longer before falling back. Such is the preparedness of men (but not women) that their levels rise merely in anticipation of the psychological stress situation without actually having to perform the tasks. For a lower-status man, who by virtue of his status is much more likely to experience physically and psychologically stressful situations on various levels, his background cortisol level becomes permanently elevated.

Over time, this has a massive impact on health. High cortisol produces a corresponding excess of glucose, which is then stored as fat; while at the same time, fat cells become resistant to giving up glucose in response to

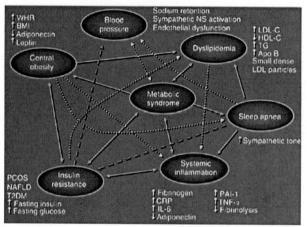

The metabolic syndrome. The six circles reflect the differing patho-physiological mechanisms that are implicated. Metabolic syndrome is at the centre of this diagram, which emphasizes that no one mechanism is responsible for explaining the syndrome and that each of these components is likely to have an impact on its prevalence and patho-physiology.

Key: *Apo, apolipoprotein; BMI, body mass index; CRP, C-reactive protein; HDL-C, high-density lipoprotein cholesterol; IL, interleukin; LDL-C, low-density lipoprotein cholesterol; NAFLD, non-alcoholic fatty liver disease; NS, nervous system; PAI-1, plasminogen-activating inhibitor-1; PCOS, polycystic ovarian syndrome; T2DM, type 2 diabetes mellitus; TG, triglyceride; TNF, tumor necrosis factor; WHR, waist–hip ratio.*

cortisol. The excess glucose generates a strong insulin response when its concentration in the blood gets too high, and this in turn stimulates storage of fat and proteins and prevents their breakdown. Inevitably, the man puts on the abdominal weight that is such a familiar part of getting older (the 'pot belly'). Over time, the brain and body cells are so often stimulated by insulin that they become resistant to it, so insulin levels rise further until the pancreas becomes worn out with the effort of having to produce it. This 'insulin resistance' progresses to a condition known as the metabolic syndrome (Sapolsky 2004, 2005; Kaufman et al., 2005) which is a combination of insulin resistance, elevated levels of cholesterol and certain sugars, and obesity. This in turn leads to heart disease, stroke, and several other major conditions afflicting the kidneys, liver, the gastro-intestinal tract and other organs; not least diabetes. It's estimated that as many as one in four adults have the metabolic syndrome, and given that these are overwhelmingly male, that means a majority and even a large majority of men. The metabolic syndrome is *the* health problem worldwide, completely dwarfing all others, and explains the huge 'gender' gap in life expectancy.

The 'status syndrome' in men

The impact of all this on men of differing status was uncovered in the massive 'Whitehall' study of male civil servants ('Whitehall I', 1967). Men in the lowest employment grades were much more likely to die prematurely than men in the higher grades. An even bigger and longer follow-up study ('Whitehall II', 1985) was then started to find what underlies this 'social gradient' (as it was dubbed) in death and disease, and to include women (Marmot et al., 1991). A striking 'social gradient' in mortality from most of the major causes of death—coronary heart disease, other cardiovascular disease, stroke, chronic lung disease, gastrointestinal disease, renal disease, accident and violence—collectively termed by epidemiologist Sir Michael Marmot the 'status syndrome', were thought to be related to the extent of the imbalance between the control that men felt over what they did in the job, what demands were stacked upon them, and what rewards accrued. Those jobs that combined high demands, low control, and poor rewards were experienced as stressful, and this combination was progressively more and more in evidence the further down the grading you look. Or so it was argued. But this mixes up cause and effect. Nobody considered how the men got into and failed to escape these lowly jobs. The status these men had and felt they had, would be long established and would usually be reflected in the level of education achieved and the sort of job they then went for. Also, there would be a very big difference between a man who had recently gone into the job with an expectation of a progressive rise through the grades, and a man who remained stuck in a lower grade, resigned to such a position until he retires. A job in itself for these reasons has a limited impact on male status. Being in a lowly position would most certainly impact on how women perceive a man, but those who are able to, not only can move on or up, but can express their status in other realms of life.

The mixing up of cause and effect in Marmot's interpretation of the findings was through some rethinking when the outcome was not as expected. Everyone had assumed that the high-status men would be more stressed because their top jobs were inherently stressful. What hadn't been anticipated is that although the top jobs are indeed inherently the more stressful, the experience of the high status that being in such a top job brings, means that it's less stressful for men than being in a lowly job.

The big surprise for the researchers was that the 'social gradient' *only applied to men* (Sacker et al., 2000). For women, it was not only far less pronounced, but it related not to their grade at work but to their situation at home, and only indirectly to their position at work (Chandola et al., 2004; Moser, Pugh & Goldblatt, 1988). The 'social gradient' at work was a male phenomenon only.

Why the home and not work is the factor for women is explained by the separation of the male DH from the female personal network, and the difference between male status competition and female privilege. A woman attracts a man of as high a status as corresponds to her own 'mate value' in terms of youth/beauty, so a woman's social standing is a combination of her own social circle (that may be particularly privileged if she is or was more than averagely attractive) and the position of her male partner (which is usually according to his job). If she doesn't feel good about her situation at home, this could indicate a perception of the fragility of her long-term partnership. She may be fearing her partner deserting her, or perhaps she is regretting her choice of partner. Perhaps she had opted for a partner who offered a trade-off between status and reliability that she now realises she should not have accepted. Alternatively, did she over-estimate her man's status, or underestimated her own 'mate value'? Either way, now she feels less happy to perform the homemaker role. Of course, it's most likely that she had ended up with a low-status male because she had a corresponding relative lack of youth/beauty, and she may up her efforts at homemaking, at least to try to assuage the fear she has of her man deserting her. This relatively low 'mate value' will have caused her health disadvantages through a cortisol stress response within the female peer group from childhood, with a depression of immune response as well as fertility caused by the stress induced by her low position; mild though this is compared to what a low-status male endures.

Any relation with the position at work can be explained in two ways. First, there is a correlation between the women's civil-service jobs and the jobs their partners did, because higher-status men tend to have more privileged women partners. The more privileged women, when they do work tend to have jobs that in male terms are higher status than the jobs that less privileged women tend to have. Second, women's interest in their own jobs is not a little to do with the status of the men around them. The higher a woman's position in an organisation, the more she is in the milieu of potential high-status partners within the workplace. This is at root her real motivation to get to where she has got (see chapter nine).

The problem of the serious impact of low rank on men, is made worse by the social incohesion of modern life, which reduces the effectiveness of the DH and so exacerbates the health impact. What I mean by the effectiveness of the DH, is that if the relative rank of men becomes less visible, then it becomes harder for women to assess and choose men. Consequently, men will be obliged to narrow the scope and nuance of male–male competition towards cruder and more prolonged conflict. This comes on top of another problem of life in our mega-societies. As the size of what people consider to be their social 'in-group' expands, DHs in effect stretch to near infinity and nest inside each other. This makes it almost impossible for males realistically to aspire to alpha status, and they are to all intents and purposes rendered sub-dominant to men they are not in any way in contact with. Men set themselves impossible goals and fail to discount downwards — that is, they do not realistically downplay in their minds their own competitive failure when imagining themselves pitted against almost impossibly successful individuals at the top of their profession. At the same time, when males do win through, then in their own minds they dismiss their own success as an empty achievement. So a budding footballer may well compare himself in an absolute ability sense with a premier division player, yet take little consolation from the fact that his talent is above that of his actual direct competitors; say, those players belonging to a rival school's second team. When you consider that the long-shot risk-taking typical of male behaviour does not take much to be pushed into hopeless delusional ambition, then it's not a healthy situation.

The modern world can easily be a grim one for the majority of men, even without care and protection being something they are obliged to provide yet considered ineligible to receive.

We're back, through another window, to what DH and males are for

A highly interesting aspect of the 'social gradient' in health is that prolonged high levels of cortisol lead to depressed fertility; both behaviourally — through burnout, depression, and fatigue — and most particularly, physiologically. It leads ultimately to impotence or failed ovulation. Cortisol causes reproductive suppression. And this is found through much of the animal kingdom, so it looks to be the likely hormone mediating reproductive suppression generically (Tilbrook, Turner & Clarke, 2000; Fernald et al., 2002; Burmeister, 2005; Russell et al., 2002).

Stress is dealt with by directing bodily resources to where they are most needed, and shutting down some functions. Over the longer term, there are wider effects, notably a depression of immune response … and reproductive suppression. The mechanism of reproductive suppression is not fully understood, but in addition to cortisol it involves another hormone, prolactin, which is also released through stress (Wilkinson, 2000; Bribiescas, 2006). But we are back where I started, with the idea of the male as 'genetic filter' and the consequent adaptation of DH: the reproductive suppression that DH directly facilitates. In the 'social gradient' of health we have found, albeit indirectly, the same phenomenon; and with full data, in the animal that is at the very apex of the evolutionary tree. Ourselves.

We know that low rank for both females and males in various species leads to serious loss of fertility, if not complete infertility. As I mentioned previously, in some species this is so pronounced that only the alpha pair ever gets to mate. There is complete physiological suppression of fertility of all individuals except the alpha male and female, neither of whom is affected at all. This is very like the breeding scenarios in eusocial insects, so it would appear to be an evolutionarily ancient mechanism. In most species, there is a less extreme balance between sterile and fertile individuals, so that several of the higher ranks mate and breed; if indeed not many, most or even almost all individuals do so. There is some sort of gradient of reproductive suppression in inverse proportion to 'mate value'. Just as there is a gradient in health. They appear to be related.

The mechanism makes sense in terms of maximising gene replication for the whole reproducing group, which is the essential rule in biology. In terms of all of the genes in a reproducing group, differential reproductive suppression skews reproduction to those individuals whose offspring are themselves most likely to reproduce well. This maximises gene replication by the reproducing group overall.

Bolstered by what we know of the physiology of the 'status syndrome', we now have another angle on DH; further evidence of what it's for, and another window on the male.

Summary

Better care for and protection of women in comparison to men is general, but especially apparent in institutions like the health service. There is blatant sex discrimination evident in treatment differentials.

The clear inequality in health-care to the disadvantage of men might at root be because men seek health-care less than half as much as women do. This seems to be at least in part down to men's sense of their care and protection role towards women and dependents, which does not give them the permission to seek help themselves. Health services can thereby discriminate against men with impunity. But is this the main factor underlying the relative poor health of men?

The most telling statistic in health is not to do with discrimination in treatment, but the profound disparity in the propensity to get seriously ill. This is revealed overall in the wide gap in life expectancy between the sexes, which is caused by the complex of diseases of middle age caused by the 'metabolic syndrome'. This in turn is caused by the sustained elevated cortisol levels through the failure in competition most men experience that produces the general long-term stress response that is more apparent in men.

The lower in the hierarchy a man stands, the more he suffers from the 'metabolic syndrome'. This was discovered in a major epidemiological study of the health of civil servants, in which it was also found that in the work context this applies only to men. Women were not only less affected: for them the relation was with their situation not at work but at home.

The relationship between poor health and low rank and its much more pronounced nature in men, is the same pattern as that of reproductive suppression. They are related mechanisms. The health impact of the 'status syndrome' is an indirect measure of reproductive suppression in humans. It's another window on the working of the male 'genetic filter' and the function this gives to DH.

Chapter 7

Historical Blindsight

Uncovering social justice in the past:
woman's perennial privilege

The position women are in today is so obviously a good one that those who argue men have 'power' over women usually resort to pointing out how clearly women were disadvantaged in the past. Mere mention of the vote or of marriage or child custody in times not so long ago, closes down debate. But it doesn't take much probing beneath the surface of what apparently used to be the lot of women, to see that very far from disadvantage, women enjoyed privilege. Here, I'll look at a number of what are often cited as litmus tests from history; before, in the next chapter, focusing on the key issue of the vote.

It's a mistake to view the past through the eyes of today. Our own perspectives imposed, anachronistically, on the behaviour and thinking of people in former times is unfair. It would be silly to take our notions of social justice in the late twentieth and early twenty-first centuries and, finding such principles not apparent in Victorian and earlier times, to then castigate society in earlier periods for unfairly disadvantaging women. Disadvantaged compared to whom? You have to make comparison with others at the same time, and take account of what was then feasible.

This is exactly the mistake we make though. We're blinded to the possibility that conceptions of social justice as they were at different periods in history may have secured the optimum benefits to women under the constraints that were then operating; and that in no sense were women 'oppressed', nor men unduly favoured. It turns out that, if we take the blindfolds off, it's apparent not just that people at the time perceived that women were not disadvantaged, but that indeed women were as privileged throughout history as they are today. The privilege that women enjoy is not contingent on any historical factors, but is biologically based.

* * *

Scholarship with a feminist bent is almost as inept when it comes to history as it is at selectively ignoring what is most relevant in science. This applies to very recent times as well as to the much touted fiction of a prehistoric social inversion where women filled the roles that men do today. This is interesting for its *denial* that women were disadvantaged. The natural order envisaged here is that woman is 'on top', and that the societies we see subsequently in recorded history are aberrant. A prehistoric female (but male-styled) political power base is now comprehensively debunked by historians and anthropologists, so I won't take up space here with analysis that can readily be found elsewhere. Suffice to say that the evidence for such societies boils down to archaeological finds of figurines taken to show that women held overall 'power' in society. But the consensus is that they are fertility symbols and as such don't indicate 'goddess worship'; and even if they did, that would be no evidence of an ancient 'matriarchy'. We know that the different social roles of the sexes is evolutionarily ancient, and that you have to look back along not historical but evolutionary timescales to understand the relationship between the sexes.

Moving forward into recorded history, a big issue has been made of the late medieval epidemic of witchcraft allegation. The feminist reading of this has grown into a false history, and this too has been comprehensively dismissed by scholars. Again, I don't need to go into this here, save for relaying the main points made by informed scholarship. Contrary to popular notions, far from the authorities being behind accusations, they attempted to diffuse the hysteria. Most of the accusers were not men but women, and it was the absence of a male protector that was the biggest problem for an accused woman. Women were particularly vulnerable to accusation because the areas of activity that lent themselves to suspicion were those over which women had jurisdiction. Nonetheless, a proportion (about a quarter) of those put to death were men ('warlocks'). The total number of supposed 'witches' and 'warlocks' who lost their lives is but a tiny fraction of the massively-inflated estimates—hundreds of thousands or even millions—that have been put about. The root of the centuries-long hysteria over the 'witch' was the classic phenomenon of female 'relational aggression', and it's therefore a great fraud to present it as some kind of 'patriarchal' tyranny. The witch-hunt, as far as the church was concerned, was more religious propaganda than serious sanction, which was hijacked from the authorities and transformed into a platform for community score settling. Sometimes this concerned property, because older (unmarriageable) women could hold property unproductively but, as with 'honour crime', the chief detractors were usually women acting nepotistically. 'Honour crime' is falsely thought to produce only female victimisation, but this is simply because we fail to see the male victimisation as being to do with 'honour', and in any case these victims would not be newsworthy. It is also falsely thought to be specifically male perpetrated. Many phenomena we decry in other cultures, such as female circumcision, the wearing of the veil, foot binding, etc; all stem from female intra-sexual competition, and have nothing to do with male oppression, as is usually supposed.

Social justice in terms of not the individual but the household

It's neither in pre-, nor late-medieval, but in recent history that supposed incontrovertible evidence exists that the lot of women was as the 'oppressed'. Flagship status goes to the issue of the vote, which is why I've given over a whole subsequent chapter to this subject. I'll just flag up the overall finding here: that it turns out that the real struggle for the franchise was that of ordinary men – who payed the taxes and were drafted into the armed forces to fight the wars their taxes paid for. These were the people who for centuries, millennia even, were denied democracy, not women. Where women had a direct interest, *they have always had the vote*. So it was that from time immemorial women have been enfranchised in their local communities, and when issues that concerned women moved up to the national level, then women were given the parliamentary ballot in an historical blink of the eye.

A key to understanding notions of democracy is that before the idea took hold of equal rights unconditionally for all on the basis of mere citizenship, rights were tied to responsibilities (especially the paying of taxes). 'No representation without taxation!' In the days prior to the notion that the individual reigns supreme, the functional component of society was the family household. This was underlined by the law of coverture that I explain below. The person who carried the can in the household (even though he did not reap the most benefits) was the husband, so naturally it was the man of the house who – if anyone could – voted on behalf of the whole household.

The concept of the family household as the unit in society rather than the individual, and of the sense of obligations as opposed to rights, is central to understanding the difference between attitudes concerning men–women in the past, compared to such attitudes nowadays. The sexes had different but complementary domains that couldn't be compared. In many respects the woman ran and ruled the household, and represented the household to the local community, whereas the man earned the money to make sure that the household could be run at all. For this effort he was granted admittance. From this perspective, it would be nonsense to compare the sexes in terms of rights, wrongs, privileges and duties.

A great feminist cause was the powerlessness of mothers when it came to custody of their children, together with the legal status of women in marriage. On the surface it's hard to believe that social justice could be served by such apparent legal one-sidedness, and once it became anachronistic the laws were changed. However, the notion that it was an expression of the subjugation of women unravels completely when you come to realise that the object was to prevent fathers from escaping their responsibility to provide for their children, thereby possibly condemning their offspring to penury and imposing a burden on the parish. It was by insisting that men be regarded in terms of their family household and not as individuals, that the doctrine of 'the best interests of the child' could be upheld. This is in distinct contrast to the perverse situation we have ended up with today, where 'the best interests of the child' has become a mantra that actually screens the self-interest of one individual—the mother. In reality, everyone else counts for very little; not least the children themselves. Such perversity is what happens when a false perspective is given to history to further misinform the present, so that instead of identifying disadvantage and remedying this, what was in fact a robust balance is set aside in favour of unfairly privileging one party. Out of past social justice misread comes social *in*justice.

The historical 'pay gap' was most beneficial not to men but to women

I will deal with marriage and custody in detail, but first I need to tackle an issue of seeming discrimination (absent the notion of family household). This is the 'pay gap'. Not the supposed 'pay gap' of around 20% today that is incorrectly put down to discrimination against women, when—as I fully explain in the section dealing with work—it's actually to do with inherent differences between men and women. I'm talking about the much wider historical 'pay gap', with women paid half or even a third of what men were paid, even for the same or similar job. The gap narrowed somewhat in the course of the industrial revolution, after full mechanisation eliminated or reduced many of the strength differentials between the sort of jobs that men and women performed, but a very large wage difference persisted. This continued into the twentieth century, though the 'gap' progressively shrank.

Neither strength differences nor an over-supply of women workers explain why women historically were always paid significantly less than men. A large 'pay gap' applied even in teaching; a professional job for which suitable applicants would be in short supply, and where female qualities would be appropriate—teaching being thought of as in some respects an extension of a mother's role. As a professional job, it would be chosen by single women as a means of supporting themselves. There seems to be no obvious reason why women teachers would have been paid substantially less than their male colleagues. A rationale there must have been, but one that today we are blind to.

The answer is very simple and demonstrates a very recent change in mindset. As we have just noted, historically people thought about themselves not as individuals but as part of a family household, because hardly anyone could get by on their own to combine earning an income with maintaining a home life. Wages from formal jobs tended to be low, house-work was heavily labour-intensive, and much important economic work was done informally, often from home and for payment in kind. Society was stable, with almost everyone living either in nuclear families or extended family households.

To a contemporary way of thinking, an officially-sanctioned policy of a 'pay gap' seems particularly unfair. But not from the perspective of pay-ment according to the differing inputs of men and women into the shared household, when the wealth available for distribution was so pitifully small that there had to be in effect some tough-minded rationing. Or looked at the other way: there had to be a system where there was one per-son at least in each household whose income could allow the household as a whole to subsist. (One of the effects of recent equal-pay policy has been to depress absolute pay levels to the extent that both partners now have to work in order to provide for a standard of living that would have been available from a single wage as recently as two decades ago. In 2006 real disposable income growth was zero.) Given that the person who always carried the can regarding the family was the husband, and he was far more available to go to work; then it made sense that he should be able to earn most if not all of the family income. The important issue for women was the total household income, not where it came from. The less of it they had to earn themselves, the better able they were to be home-makers and child-carers.

You would be stared at by dumbfounded wives and mothers if you could transport yourself back to, say, the early-nineteenth century, and ask why women were not up in arms about how little of their household income could be provided by themselves instead of by their husbands. Quite apart from the fact that being a housewife in the past was a full-time job in itself (even without allowing for rearing the large families then the norm), work was mostly very unpleasant, not to mention injurious to health and dangerous (not least because of the sheer amount you had to do to make any significant earnings). That work was a cost rather than a bene-fit was starkly obvious. It's a twisted logic we have today that presents work as a benefit. Why else do employers have to pay wages? The less work for money—the work that in the end you would rather delegate to someone else than perform yourself—that you have to do, the better off you are. Another consideration we have also lost sight of is that in tight-knit communities it was apparent to everyone that pay was a scarce resource, and if one family could have two good wages coming in with both wife and husband working, then some other household might well have nobody working at all. With little in the way of support for the desti-tute, that could have meant children and adults going sick and dying. From this perspective, it was immoral for there to be more than one major breadwinner per household. (This was one of the rationales behind the 'marriage bar', which I'll explain shortly.)

Obviously, as the one expected to be the main or sole breadwinner and the one unencumbered in direct care of a family (either his own nuclear family or the one from which he sprang), the man of the household would strive for and require the most income of all. His wife, if she was working, would be doing so to supplement the income of her husband as the family grew and household expenses multiplied. She might well have required more income than a typical single woman, notwithstanding that she had a husband bringing in a wage. (This is why in Ireland, historically there was a 'pay gap' in favour of married over single women, albeit much smaller than the one between the sexes.) There are in fact few if any losers in the system, including spinsters, because almost everyone lived in family households: if not their own, then that of others. Regarding the minority of women who were unmarried (and therefore hypothetically penalised) and the minority of men who were unmarried (and therefore hypothetically benefiting unfairly), they were still subject to the universal sexual dichotomy that men were seen as worthy in respect of their position within the outside, working world, and the money this brought in; whereas women were seen as worthy according to what they brought to life within the home. Men, then as now, were considered less than nobodies unless they were breadwinners. If they eschewed breadwinning, then men actually forfeited rights that women were afforded unconditionally. Up until the late 1970s, men — but not women — were imprisoned for relying on benefit payments if it was determined that they were making insufficient effort to secure a job. A mandatory six months for a first offence is still on the statute book. A woman risked social contempt, not by any failure in actively providing economically, but only by actively transgressing obvious social norms that all women in all societies are well aware of. This remains in the special treatment favouring single parents.

Taking everything together, it made sense in social justice terms that wages reflected the general category of person employed, instead of fixing them according to what should be 'the rate for the job' irrespective of who did the work. It was a social justice that dealt at source with what only later arose as a problem requiring redistribution. In a socially homogenous society, the systematic skewing of pay in favour of men benefited men and women collectively. This is to say that it benefited women especially, given that women controlled the home, and the home absorbed all available resources. (The minority of feckless husbands that spent their weekly wage in the tavern were the exception that proves the rule.) In working class communities — notably in steel-making and coal mining areas — the husband handed over his pay packet to his wife for her to have full control over. It was the fairest way of distributing wealth when wealth was scarce. It is anachronistic to regard this as being at the time unfair to women, from

Serving time for being unemployed

Up until the late 1970s, men — but not women — had been imprisoned by the National Assistance Board (NAB) for relying on benefit payments if it was determined that they were making insufficient effort to secure a job: it was a mandatory six months for a first offence. Many more men were sent for six months to centres up and down the country (some residential, some non-residential) to re-orientate them towards work. An Unemployment Re-establishment Centre was officially 'voluntary', but the only alternative was an automatic six months in jail. Jail and 'boot camps' had become law by an Act of 1948, and the facility to imprison men was never repealed.

Similarly in the USA draconian 'breadwinner regulation' laws had been enacted from the 1890s onwards in all states to tackle what were popularly referred to as 'home slackers'. Not just jail but jail with hard labour was the reward for indigence. As in Britain, women were exempted. Cases were processed in the family court, which was part criminal court, part 'social agency', staffed by psychiatrists, social workers and probation officers, as well as the usual court personnel. This system came about through pressure by women 'reformers', and in the very period (1890-1919) known as the Progressive Era.

On the receiving end of the NAB's attentions back in 1965 was Newcastle writer Tom Pickard, then aged just 20, but already married with a baby child whilst he was running, unpaid, a successful poetry venue:

> I started getting visits from National Assistance Board officers every other day to see if I was seeking work....I gambled that they wouldn't stop paying us the £9.10s per week, because there was a young child to feed. But, as an able bodied potential breadwinner, they told me, I had a duty to provide for my family, and refusing paid employment could certainly be seen as a failure to maintain them, which is illegal....

> Representatives of the disciplinary committee of the National Assistance Board were drawn from a range of institutions....The manager was looking at a file in front of him while the others studied me. What did they see? An unmarried unqualified labourer that wouldn't work to feed his bastard and common-law wife, and who insisted that his job was poetry....And they went on to say we want to give you another chance before we cut off your money; we want to send you to a Rehabilitation Centre where you'll get back into the habit of working. I refused and they offered the alternative of a Re-establishment Centre, which I again refused. There was silence for a moment, a conferring of bowed heads. Finally, they formally cautioned me that unless I accepted their offer of a place at a Re-Establishment Centre they would prosecute for failing to maintain my family and the current mandatory sentence for a first offence was six months in jail. The course at the Re-Establishment Centre was also six months and when I asked what the difference was they told me that the latter was voluntary (Pickard, 2000).

the perspective of a society that has become less formally homogenous and much wealthier. Not only was the system not unfair, but it was to some extent resistant to change, which shows it to have been well adapted to the times, contributing to social cohesion. What ensued was normal social inertia; nothing to do with some mythical 'patriarchy' dragging its heels. Quite the opposite. One system that benefited women in one set of circumstances, was replaced, because of a change in circumstances, with another system that likewise benefited women. The very driving force was that women were gainers, and to this end the systems of payment then and now actually contributed to this.

That the perception of society as a network of family households rather than of individuals was very strong and in many respects remains so, can be gauged by the continued currency of the expression 'a family wage' and 'a man's job'. Men and women routinely refer to jobs as unsuitable for men because they don't pay 'a family wage'. People express the idea, even if they don't use the phrase. Most people do think about work in this way. This is especially true in areas where heavy industry has collapsed and service-sector, light-assembly and low-skilled office jobs are all that are now available.

The 'marriage bar' was primarily an issue amongst women

Most intriguingly, there was a prominent official policy that persisted to within living memory: an *apparently* blatant sex discrimination—the 'marriage bar'. This was the rule whereby women who got married were given their cards or were refused promotion, and/or only single women were recruited. In Britain, America and Europe, this measure was brought in to combat mass unemployment in the cyclical economic depressions of the last century. Among the rank and file of the workforce, the common view was that the employment of married women was unfair to other family households that had no earner at all. In times of unemployment, there could be millions with no income for their starving families, while at the same time other households had two earners and luxuries.This was not at all an anti-woman sentiment, because single women were privileged in the workforce in being treated sympathetically. It was often (and usually wrongly) assumed that single women were essential earners for their family household. When the 'marriage bar' was investigated at General Electric in the USA, interestingly it was not men who voiced opinion in favour of the 'marriage bar' so much as women; notably single women who *did* have financial responsibilities at home. They saw themselves as competing for jobs with married women. And this was true. Most work was segregated sexually in some way, so that overwhelmingly a vacancy would be fought over by those of the same sex. Still today, male and female unemployment is very largely independent.

The 'marriage bar' was anything but sex discrimination against women. It was primarily a way of ensuring that the great majority of people — that is, the women and children in family households — had enough to get by. It was also a way to skew available work, not to men but to women who were likely most to be in need of it. It was with the need to help women and families, that the 'marriage bar' was introduced.

An instance where the 'marriage bar' worked alongside something similar that caught *men* proves that it was non-discriminatory. This was a wider net than one that caught married women, in catching any male who had reached the age of twenty-one. It was an '*age* bar' for men, and only for men. For example, Quaker-run firms like Cadburys and Huntley & Palmers separated the sexes in their factories; but as well as women being given their cards when they married, all young men were dismissed as soon as they reached the age of majority. This was because the factories could not compete using employees demanding full adult male wages, so the workforce was replenished with youths of both sexes, and adult unmarried women. The women at least had the choice of continued employment past the age of majority to support a single life instead of marriage, whereas men had no choice of any kind but were compelled to find work elsewhere; whether or not there was any available. Where, in any writing about men and women in the workplace, has this fact of blatant discrimination against men ever been mentioned? Of course, for most men and in normal times, they would have wanted to move on to better-paid work so as to support a family. In more desperate times, however, a wage of any kind would have been welcome; indeed necessary to avoid destitution — a situation almost unimaginable in the EU or North America today. A single man or a man with a family would be pushed below the poverty line, but a single woman would have remained in employment, and her married counterpart would have the support of her husband.

During boom times, reviews were undertaken to decide if the 'marriage bar' was to be kept, and then reasons would come to light in favour of the status quo. 'Marriage bars' were a particular feature of large employers and government, and a problem identified here was the large numbers employed in routine jobs. It was felt that the 'marriage bar' contributed to a healthy turnover of staff in basic grades. Removing it would lead to lengthier service in monotonous low-paid work, and this in turn would increase the turnover of men looking for something with better pay and prospects — men being the people the organisation wanted to hang on to for training up into management, as they were unlikely to cease work to become a home-maker. This was a latter-day rationale and did not eclipse the reasons for the 'marriage bar' being instituted in the first place.

The 'marriage bar' was not uniform in manufacturing — in some jobs where pay was tied to productivity rather than length of service, it made no economic sense to let go of experienced married women. In these cases, firms resisted popular calls for a bar. In clerical work, it was in just about every workplace. Teaching had long operated one, the civil service acquired one and, in 1932, so too did the BBC. The BBC and the civil service abandoned theirs in 1946, but in nursing—a near all-female profession, note—it was retained right up until 1973.

Married women workers were, to some degree, socially castigated and, even with the recession easing in the late 1930s, opposition was strong if the prospect of the bar's removal was raised. The Union of Post Office Workers, which had a high proportion of women in its ranks, not only supported the 'marriage bar', but even called for the end of female employment. London County Council staff voted two-to-one in favour of the status quo. A ballot of civil servants in 1930 had shown just *three percent of women* in favour of scrapping it.

The 'marriage bar' was not discrimination against women. It can never be understood in that way. It was discrimination in favour of the full set of family households: a fairer redistribution amongst them. It was the *progressive* policy of its times — an important measure to promote social justice in a period when real want was a problem for millions. Times changed and it was abolished, but that it persisted up until recent decades was partly or even largely at the behest of women—to prioritise women in the workplace who had no support from a husband. As soon as it ceased to be of use to women, it was rescinded.

Quota ceilings for female entry into professions was the best use of scarce resources

A barrier to women seemingly more difficult to explain, was that of entry into certain professions. This was certainly a practice of sex-discrimination against those few women who applied, but it was seen as anything but unjust at the time. The most notable example of a profession closed to women was medicine—as anything more than a nurse or in the nursing hierarchy, that is. Women at one time could not be doctors, until eventually a quota was introduced. Up until 1975 in Britain, only ten percent of a medical school's intake was open to women. In the USA a very similar unofficial system operated: a slightly lower post-war quota of between six and eight percent.

Access to medical treatment was a scarce resource, and it was imperative that the training of what supply of practitioners there was involved minimal if any attrition through training, and produced doctors who remained for their whole careers in the service of medicine. To this end, familiar as everyone was with the fact that it was only a small proportion of women who adopted lifelong careers, medical colleges regarded women collectively as liable to end their careers through marriage and child rearing. It was too big a risk to bet on them turning out to have a true vocation. It was therefore a disservice to the public to offer training places to would-be women doctors when there were plenty of suitably-qualified men competing for entrance. Another problem was that women tended to opt for one of only three areas: general practice, paediatrics or psychiatry (just as today women disproportionately still choose to be GPs—because of the potential flexibility of working, and the more rounded and straight-forwardly caring role compared to hospital work. It is because women GPs tend to want to work only part-time or leave altogether that the GP service is currently in crisis). All of these were peripheral fields, and not being at the forefront of medical practice, those who practised them were unlikely to contribute to the advancement of the profession and the college.

No doubt a further objection was the distraction that women would provide for the majority of male students, and that this might lead instead of competition between men for grades, to a problematic competition amongst them for the attentions of the women students. In place of a community of like-minded proto-professionals, a split would develop between those who paired off and the remainder, stirring feelings of jealousy, and inclining those who hadn't managed to pair off to seek female company elsewhere. Moreover, there was the fear that women may exploit the medical college as a marriage marketplace, so that even if a woman completed her studies, her mind would not really be on the training.

It is within recent memory that a quota system operated for all subjects in US ivy league universities. Similar arguments were behind this. Being pre-eminent colleges meant they had the pick of high-flying applicants. So why miss out on accepting some of the male potential stars by taking a risk on a few women? This is an important point. The normal distribution of talent across the population would produce a larger ratio of men to women in the very top bracket (see chapter five) that the likes of Harvard were looking for, so a quota similar to that for medical schools actually would be consonant with this. Indeed, with the shortage of training places available, it may well be that given the sex difference in normal distribution curves (the heavy preponderance of men at the top end), then a disproportionate ratio of men to women was necessary to avoid compromising on the level of aptitude/ability. On this basis there was no discrimination against women.

Myopic as it is for us to have lost the perspective of the family household as a worthier object for social justice than the individual, it's even stranger that we fail to grasp the overall community interest that was served by a rule-of-thumb discrimination against the really very small sub-group of those few women who applied to medical school. The medical school and the premier universities were acting on behalf of the community, in its best interests in an environment of far tighter resources than we can imagine today. Against that, the disappointment of a few female applicants—if indeed once quotas were introduced there actually was any discrimination—should count for little.

Child custody law was primarily an obligation for men

Child custody is an issue with a large resonance today. With the changing world of the industrial revolution, the common law as it applied to the family became outdated by the late-eighteenth and early-nineteenth centuries, and informal or quasi-legal arrangements replaced it. The law was effectively irrelevant, because only a tiny minority could afford recourse to it, whereas informal means of separation and agreement on custody were cheap, easy, and enforceable. More fundamentally, to make an argument that somehow 'patriarchal' inertia was why the law lagged behind what people desired, supposes that people shared our current mindset regarding the law. They didn't. Legal historians are unanimous that it was only towards the end of the eighteenth century that law moved to the forefront of social consciousness.

There *was* a reason for inertia, and it could be characterised as 'patriarchal'; but most certainly not as feminists would understand the term. The state imposed liability on the father in order to ensure that men never shirked their responsibilities for their children — because the financial burden would then fall on the parish. A statute of 1646 granted guardianship powers to fathers, but although this gave to a father the right to appoint someone as the guardian for his children upon his death — his widow being the obvious candidate — the courts would not allow him to give away guardianship of his children to anyone while he was still alive, their mother included. It was forbidden for a father to contract out of his paternal duties. It was particularly important that the father could not divest his responsibility on to the mother, because being the carer she would be very unlikely to be in a position to provide the necessary financial support as well. The whole point of guardianship was to separate childcare — which hardly required a law to compel mothers to perform — from provision, which necessarily was for the benefit of the child and the mother. Being much more like a burden — an onerous one in some circumstances — provision was very likely to require enforcing in a minority of cases.

The state, if it was oppressing anybody, was oppressing the father; certainly not the mother. The state was supporting the mother on behalf of the community, and it was also supporting all others within the community who would otherwise be called upon to pay higher parish taxes that they could probably ill afford, but which in any case it was unjust to expect them to pay. These others were almost all of the men in the community. Children were, and were seen to be, assets only to their own family, and certainly not to the community, to which they were potentially a burden. In pre-modern and early-modern times — when marginal economic existence was the norm, where competition was local and direct, and where men who were not fully competent were unmarriageable — in these times it would have been unreasonable to expect men to in any way support another man's child, except when there was no conceivable alternative to avoiding a mother and child's complete destitution.

Problems arose indirectly from this when custody was at issue between mother and father, and the all-or-nothing situation loomed where the carer and the provider roles would have to be fused in the person of either the natural carer or the natural provider. Only one outcome was possible. Even if the father wanted to give custody to the mother, he could not do so because necessarily this would be relinquishing his guardianship, which the law would insist he must continue. In any case, a married woman could not bring a legal action against her husband without first obtaining a legal separation in the ecclesiastical court.

Sure enough, the law facilitated vindictive treatment of mothers by fathers exploiting a law intended to protect children, just as today the law pretty much guarantees vindictive treatment of fathers. But there is an important difference. The law at this time tended to reinforce long-term, male–female pair bonds, congruent with community interest, whereas the law today actually works relentlessly against this. However, even at this time, a father could be left in the position of having serious obligations but with no rights even of access to his children, if through cruelty or desertion or some other malfeasance he had forfeited his paternal rights.

Legal experts have convoluted disagreements about whether changes in the law were the driving force that eventually led, by the end of the nineteenth century, to the presumption that the mother and not the father had custody; or whether actually the law had hindered this development. There are mountains of writing about the famous De Manneville case of 1805 (e.g. Wright, 1999), which was the first brought by a woman to challenge custody law. Any and every interpretation has been put on the importance or irrelevance of this case, and the picture is too confused to be teased out here. Any feminist interpretation that the case somehow demonstrates inertia of the legal system in the service of 'patriarchy', in the light of the endless squabbling about what the De Manneville case can tell us, merely shows the lengths to which (supposed) scholars will go to twist things in support of their own position.

The law was in an appalling mess, with still more confusion from case law. By the middle of the eighteenth century, competing laws from the perspective of the different protagonists had asserted themselves. As the rights of fathers were being narrowed, more consideration was given to protection for mothers, by way of looking out for the care of young children, and the welfare and inheritance of children when they were older. Then there was the state poking its nose in as the uber-father. This was just the start of complication, because there were separate court jurisdictions for the different aspects of a separation. Property was straightforwardly in the main legal domain, but it was equity law that applied to custody, whilst the ecclesiastical jurisdiction governed marriage and divorce. To cap it all, there were the coverture (see below) restrictions. Judges must have dreaded these cases.

Generally on the rise was an appreciation that mothers are not just important but vital for children. Common law bequeathed the 'tender years' argument that young children should naturally be in the custody of the mother. However, this was seen to be trumped by the father's role of passing on a skill, educating and generally preparing a child for the outside world. Remember, that until relatively recently, most men did the same work as their father had done. With education in short supply, if it existed at all, a man usually made his way at the start of adult life under his father's wing. So even as the consideration of property ceased to be dominant, and the Infant Custody Act was passed in 1839 to allow blameless mothers to petition for custody of a young child, or for access to older children; the growing consideration of 'the best interests of the child' strengthened the case to award the father custody. What really undermined the Act was the clash of jurisdictions. Judges still looked to the ecclesiastical courts in respect of marriage, going on to consider custody on this basis. The new Act was sidestepped. The effect was to exacerbate the clash between the common law of paternal rights and the growing prevalence of divorce and single-motherhood.

The Infant Custody Act was one of several acts passed to try to free up the legal logjam, but as with most of them, it served to compound the problem. Parliament gave it another go and set up the Divorce and Matrimonial Causes Court in 1858. At first, the judges in the new court granted custody on the basis of a much wider interpretation of what was unacceptable behaviour by husbands, and a marital fault rule was quickly established. But this was scuppered, not by determinations from the ecclesiastical law, but by the equity courts; since they had the power of review. Once again, fathers were denied custody only if they were found to be extremely unfit. What really stymied the whole enterprise, however, was that by using the new concept of marital fault to decide parental rights, the 'best interests of the child' were lost sight of. The idea that women reformers had of treating parenting and marriage as separate legal domains collapsed. Until changes occurred regarding married women's property, a woman's claim to custody of her children would almost always lose, precisely because 'the best interests of the child' directed that it stay with the parent who had legal control over property; who was of course the father. So it was that married women's property acts were introduced and they did seem to drain the legal swamp.

That custody law had changed out of all recognition by the end of the nineteenth century, is indisputable. The scope of aspects of custody that the law addressed had expanded, and the 'best interests of the child' doctrine would have held sway much earlier if it had not been so difficult, because of the law of coverture, to reconcile paternal and maternal rights.

There is no sign here even of inertia, let alone 'patriarchy'. A series of genuine attempts to modernise the law came in quick succession, until finally a practical solution was found and enacted.

If what happened regarding custody in recent centuries does not provide support for a feminist interpretation, then what if we go back a lot further? In Anglo-Saxon law, the rights of mothers were similar to the rights of fathers in the event of separation or widowhood. What is more, a wife could take half the family's property upon separating from her husband, if she also took custody of the children. In common law—which we have passed down to us from Anglo-Saxon times—the mother is her child's guardian, so long as she is not the inheritor of her child's estate (this condition being to make sure that lands would be in the hands of productive workers). And even if the mother did not control the child's estate, the child remained in her custody. There are extant written sources for the unique legal rights of mothers from the thirteenth century, which is the usual extent of survival of documents, whichever topic in history is researched. So we can presume it dates back to time immemorial.

The law was relatively uncomplicated back then. Only in later times did there emerge courts with ill-defined overlapping jurisdiction and competing legal principles; all with their own superseded statutes and evolving case law. This explains the apparent disadvantage of women in the late eighteenth and through much of the nineteenth centuries. Part of the problem, as I have alluded to, was the law of coverture, and I want now to look into this legal peculiarity that women campaigners held in such contempt.

Coverture was an unreasonable imposition on men

Coverture was bound up with the custody issue, being another facet of the view that the family household and not the individual was the unit of society. Husband and wife were treated as one entity, which meant that wives could not control their own property unless specific provisions were made before marriage. This seems pretty Jurassic even to the most non-feminist contemporary outlook, but there are ramifications that again put things in their true light. Perhaps the clearest description of what coverture meant was made in 1765 by Sir William Blackstone, in his *Commentaries on the Laws of England*:

> By marriage, the husband and wife are one person in law: that is, the very being or legal existence of the woman is suspended during the marriage, or at least incorporated and consolidated into that of the husband: under whose wing, protection, and *cover*, she performs everything.

Legally, the husband was responsible for all actions of his wife, and he could be imprisoned on this basis. So, for example, if the wife's expenditure brought the couple into debt, then the husband would be imprisoned, even though he was the breadwinner and had been the one who had built the financial liquidity of the household, and had in no way contributed to its bankruptcy. A wife could knowingly spend money she knew her husband did not have. Indeed, it was a legal obligation to provide a wife essentials on the offer by the wife of her husband's credit, regardless of the consequences. Coverture gave carte blanche to vindictive wives literally to permanently ruin their husbands and condemn them to life imprisonment. In complete contrast, the wife was rendered immune to prosecution, because any criminal activity would be deemed to be under the husband's direction, and he alone was then regarded as the one who had actually *committed* the crime. In time, this was refined to any crime committed in the husband's presence, or any that in his absence the wife was coerced to do — and simply being told to do something was sufficient to be regarded as coercion. Coverture laws remained until well into the twentieth century. Some statutes exempted certain crimes, notably murder and treason. For example, in the USA, the Oklahoma Statutes of 1931 exempted under certain circumstances murder and treason and sixteen other crimes.

Modern interpretations of coverture pathologise what was in fact protection or chivalry. Coverture was the fiercest legal insistence that a man take responsibility for his family, no matter how wronged he may have been, and no matter how capable his wife was of taking full responsibility for her own behaviour. So coverture does not just provide evidence of female disadvantage as against male privilege. It also provides evidence of *male* disadvantage and *fe*male privilege.

A re-examination of legal nostrums of a past age that most people regard as at best quaint, turns out not to show the operation of the feminists' mythical 'patriarchy', but an oppressive paternalism by the state — specifically against men and on behalf of women and children. It has always been the case that children are legally under the ultimate protection of the king — indeed, explicitly so — but it seems that at least by association, women have been brought fully under the king's great cloak. (We know from how biology plays out in human social psychology, that it is in fact the other way round: that women were always fully under the king's great cloak, and by association so were their children.) As in effect the alpha male of the national community, the king had conjugal rights over every woman in the land — some princes, even in modern times, have acted as if they were entitled to this privilege under the modern written law! That leaves men rather on the outside of the tent in this united nuclear family of the whole kingdom. They are the people that women, and by association children, are 'protected' from. In complete contrast, men themselves were not protected in any sense by the Crown, but instead threatened by the king's drawn sword, and typecast as enemies of the state.

Summary

Whatever the contemporary evidence, it's never questioned that, historically-speaking, women were disadvantaged. This is taken as proof that men must have 'power' over women. But the truth is that through history not only were women never disadvantaged but they were privileged. It's always a mistake in looking at the past to impose today's outlook on the behaviour and thinking of people in former times. When you look in terms of what was needed to achieve social justice at the time, then as now it was for the benefit primarily of women.

Up until very recently, people did not think in terms of individual rights, but of mutual obligations within the household in which everyone lived. From this perspective, it would be nonsense to compare the sexes in terms of rights, wrongs, privileges and duties, when the sexes had clearly different but complementary domains that couldn't be compared.

At a time when the wealth available for distribution was so pitifully small there had to be in effect some tough-minded rationing. The necessary division of labour between homemaker and breadwinner made it important that the male breadwinner competed for and received a 'family wage'; whereas any income for the person who was principally the homemaker was in comparison unimportant.

Women, not men, benefited from the 'marriage bar'. This was to ensure the full employment of those women who needed to work. This is why women were the main supporters of the policy – it had nothing to do with ensuring full employment for men. With widespread sex segregation of work, there was little competition between men and women for jobs, as shown by the independence of male and female unemployment.

In times past when training resources for top professions were scarce, it made good sense to take account of the proclivity of women to leave full-time professional life or to compromise it with other goals. This sometimes meant not considering women as applicants at all. But where they were considered, it made sense to place a low upper limit on the proportion of women; not just for the aforesaid reasons, but also to reflect the skew in ability at the top end of performance between the sexes.

Regarding custody law the point was to prevent any man from eschewing his financial obligations towards his children. That women have an inalienable bond with their own children that is not necessarily mirrored in men, is why law was necessary only in respect of enforcing male obligation. As soon as cases emerged of conflict with motherhood, effort was made to change the law, which finally came to fruition after complications were overcome.

Coverture is the legal principle that a man must take responsibility for the actions of his wife, no matter how unreasonable. This has been presented as the creation of a female legal non-persona, but any adverse consequence for women was unusual and minor compared to the serious imposition on men. It can be understood only in terms of the conception of social justice at the time, that the family household, not the individual, was the locus of rights and duties.

Chapter 8

The True Sufferers for Suffrage

Votes not for men

The widening of the national franchise always sold men short

The modern history of the franchise in Britain could be said to have begun with the Great Reform Act of 1832. However women had always had the vote at parish level on exactly the same basis as men, and continued to do so (except in certain places between 1835 and 1869, as I will explain), whilst only a tiny minority of men had the vote at the parliamentary level. Some very late-in-the-day parliamentary acts eventually culminated in a slim majority of adult men being enfranchised. In practice, because of the registration procedure, a majority of men were voteless nationally, right up until the very day universal suffrage arrived. All this against the background that almost exclusively men only were engaged in lifetime full-time work outside the home; the bulk of government spending was on 'defence' and the prosecution of wars—for which, of course, only men had a direct 'interest'—and, in the absence of even a rudimentary welfare state, national government had little other impact on people's lives.

The relevant history with which we have lost touch is the different rationales behind the municipal and parliamentary franchise, which informed the debate about each other throughout the nineteenth century. These are separate histories, subject to separate legislation, but which from very different starting points began under mutual influence to move towards each other; and to cross paths before becoming entwined. To make the arguments clearer, I won't present a simple chronological account, but instead deal with the parliamentary franchise first, without referring to the municipal equivalent. When I go on to local democracy, and so to much further back in time, the true nature of attitudes to men–women with regard to having a say in matters which concern everyone, will become abundantly clear.

* * *

The events leading up to the 1928 act, which finally brought about a universal eligibility to vote nationally, began in prehistory. But sticking with recorded history, events could be said to have begun about 2,500 years ago, in the Greek city state of Athens. Only 40,000 out of a population of two million could vote, and all 40,000 were men, but that number was a mere four per cent of the male population. Yet this was to remain an historical high until mid-nineteenth-century England. English people were still living in complete servitude, formally speaking, 2,000 years later, with no kind of central representation save for disparate elections to a so-called parliament by those serving on county courts. The English Civil War was one of unprecedented bloodiness in which ordinary locally-conscripted men died (one in ten of the adult male population), not least because the conflict was tied up with the call for universal male suffrage.

Nothing significant changed for well over 150 years, so that even by the end of the eighteenth century, only if you were a superior yeoman farmer, if not actually a gentleman, could you be among the paltry two per cent of the population who, through owning land above a certain valuation, had the vote. This included nobody at all in the great industrial cities. Only because of inflation lowering the effective level of the property-valuation threshold, was the four per cent of the male population that was the extent of Athenian democracy, finally overtaken. It stood at five per cent by the time of the first of the nineteenth-century reform acts: the aforementioned Great Reform Act of 1832. So much for almost two-and-a-half millennia of supposed male 'power'. To get beyond a representation of one-in-twenty, the act took Herculean efforts to get through parliament.

For all this, the Act did little to lift the numbers of the population who could vote. Yes, at a stroke it increased the electorate by half as much again, but from such a low base this amounted only to about 200,000 additional voters. And because of the still low numbers, all of these came from the upper reaches of the new middle class. Even this small concession was given only because of the advent of income tax (to pay for the Napoleonic wars). Previously, the state demanded a cut only from the landed gentry, who paid their dues by raising armed forces for the king from their subjects on their estates. Those newly well-off through industry and commerce were in no position to do this. The total electorate now stood at 650,000. That the vast majority of men were not allowed to vote was not even seen as an affront. The attitude at the time was very much that the masses were full of 'bovine stupidity', to quote Walter Bagehot, the nineteenth-century constitutional theorist. This was the time of the Chartists, a radical mass movement that was strong in the industrial cities, with their People's Charter — renewing the demand of two centuries before for universal manhood suffrage. This was supreme boldness; the Chartist movement being perceived as the greatest revolutionary threat facing Britain. It's leaders were imprisoned, gatherings were ruthlessly suppressed, and the mass petitions signed by many hundreds of thousands of ordinary working men were contemptuously rejected.

Few saw any anomaly in demanding a right to vote for men, and not for both men and women. A puny 1,500 people signed a petition in 1866 calling for votes for women, but this proved influential, leading to an amendment to the Second Reform Act of 1867 that actually secured 73 votes – almost a third of the votes cast. The Chartist petition to extend male suffrage, that required several fully-laden cabs to get it to Downing Street, by contrast fell on deaf ears. Yes, in this second extension of the franchise the electorate was almost doubled – through a lowering of the property valuation threshold, and also taking in those paying a high rent – but at well under two million, out of a population of more than ten million adult men, this was still only one in six.

Not that the vote at the time was much use to most of those who could cast it, because until the Ballot Act of 1872, every individual vote was published for all to see in the poll books (Seymour, 1915). This transparency, thought Harriet Taylor, one of the very earliest campaigners for women's suffrage, discouraged selfish voting. (This was typical of the lack of empathy for ordinary people that upper-class Liberal campaigners for female suffrage shared – as I will reveal.) The vote was actually a real nuisance to those who held it, because they risked the wrath of the locally powerful candidate they didn't vote for – or from both candidates if they abstained. Votes were bought, cajoled or beaten out of men by agents of candidates, and a tradesman voter could be threatened from the other end, as it were, with an organised boycott of his business by non-voters. The upshot was that the electorate was almost as completely under the control of the upper classes as it had been before 1832 (Pelling, 1967).

Because of the continuing property criteria, together with residence restrictions, even after the passage of a third act in 1884, it was still the case that the adult men who could vote were in the minority. A further increase in the electorate to a total of something under four-and-a-half million didn't change that. Anyone who was a 'lodger' and paid less than the then lavish sum of five shillings a week in rent, was ineligible. This excluded from voting the large numbers of men who were still living with their parents or other relatives, as well as almost all those in multiple occupancy, of which there were vast numbers in both industrial cities and rural areas.

Both of the reform acts of the late-nineteenth century were brought in primarily for political expediency (Disraeli trying to outdo Gladstone). The party in power extended the franchise so as to get more votes in industrial constituencies especially, and thereby force certain legislation through parliament. In general, however, any expansion in the electorate was regarded as dangerous.

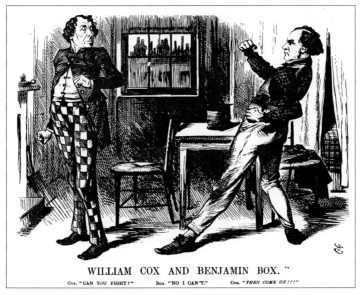

WILLIAM COX AND BENJAMIN BOX.
Cox. "CAN YOU FIGHT?"   Box. "NO I CAN'T."   Cox. "*THEN COME ON!!!*"

The Second Reform Act was introduced primarily for political
expediency — Disraeli trying to out-box Gladstone

By 1910 — the last year of a general election before the first election featuring female suffrage in 1918 — the proportion of men who could vote at long last had exceeded those who could not. But the figures are not all they seem. There were 7.7 million men registered, out of an estimated male population just short of 12 million. That's 65%. However, well over half a million of these were plural votes (many well-off men had a vote in respect of a business as well as residence), so the total of the enfranchised was actually 60%. Even this was deceptive because constituency registration involved literally years of bureaucratic delay, and working men were at the time astonishingly mobile. In the intervening time between registration and the election, typically between a quarter and a third of the urban electorate had moved out of the constituency: usually too far away to come back and vote. This meant that substantially under 50% of the adult male population was in reality entitled to cast a vote in the sense of being both entitled and able to do so.

The situation between 1910 and 1918 was unchanged on the electoral front, but of course the cataclysm on the Western front — the war — inevitably had an impact on the registration arithmetic. The essential truth is that as the year 1918 began, it was still the case that well under 50% of adult men were in possession of a usable national vote.

* * *

After legislation passed in the same year, the 1918 election was the first that in theory all men aged twenty-one and over had the vote, but in practice many men effectively still had no say. This same act gave women the vote, and although women under thirty were still excluded, most men — young men under thirty especially, but also vast numbers of their older colleagues too — were still stuck in France at the close of the war, and had been at war when electoral registration was taking place. Proxy voting forms in great numbers either would not reach the troops or would go astray after being completed. Ditto the registration forms before them. Not that in the thick of fighting and facing likely death would men be of a mind to bother with them. Those who had got back home would have been caught out either by the length of residence qualification or the delay in processing (Pugh, 1978). The result was that, notwithstanding the sudden mass increase in the electorate of women, turnout in the 'khaki election' was actually a full third down on previous elections. Overall, it was not men but women who were the most unencumbered in getting to the ballot box. And it looks like women were heavily inclined to vote, because they were in the great majority of those who had always been at home, and wanted to express their anti-German emotions by voting for a harsh peace settlement. It could well be that more women than men voted. Of course, there were no breakdowns by sex of the 1918 vote, and no opinion polls, so we will never know. What must be strongly suspected is that just as in 1910, the proportion of effectively enfranchised men still struggled to top 50%, whereas even allowing for the disenfranchisement of those women aged twenty-one to thirty, in 1918 most women were. Certainly, more women than men had the vote in the sense of actually being able to use it.

The shift to citizenship

There is a common fallacy that what had brought about an extension of the franchise to include women was their war work. On the assumption that men had the vote in recognition of their work, it's thought that when women similarly became economic contributors they were likewise rewarded. Actually, women's war work was just an excuse for a dignified climb-down for those anti-suffragists in the government whose position had already been untenable before the war (Sharp, 1933). The supposed contribution by women in general to World War One is mostly a myth. War work for women was voluntary, and even by the last year of the war only one in ten adult women had signed up. Less than half of these worked in engineering/munitions, where most chose (as they could do) to do nothing much different to the factory work they had done or might have done before wartime. Production was possible only because of the then new atomised working techniques that allowed complete de-skilling, which itself was possible only with the continuous production that war demanded. The sheer volume of production and the dispensability of the lives of soldiers hid the appallingly low quality of output (shells insufficiently filled fell short on our own troops, and shells with faulty fuses failed to explode or blew up on firing). There was no question of keeping on these women for the entirely different skilled and semi-skilled work that resumed after the war. The much smaller numbers who replaced farm workers accounted for the precipitous fall in agricultural production. All-in-all, women's war work was hardly an advertisement for women as workers.

In any case, there was a more profound basis for exclusive male enfranchisement than economics. Buried by the passage of time, but obvious to everyone at the time, was the grounding of worldly political power in the separate world of the male. The national vote was and was seen to be all about 'imperial' issues — law and order and the like — and therefore clearly the province of men (only men being required to take up arms and only men having an appetite to do so). Helen Kendrick Johnson, writing in 1913 (*A Survey of the Woman Suffrage Movement in the United States and a Discussion of the Claims and Arguments of Its Foremost Advocates*) explains:

> Democratic government is at an end when those who issue decrees are not identical with those who can enforce those decrees....Upon this depended stability, and without stability there is nothing. Stability required a majority of men....Woman's only relation to this defence is that of beneficiary, and therefore her relation to the laws with which that defence is associated must be one of advice and not of control.

This argument could be broadened to an economic one in moving from the issue of providing physical security to taxation. Women voting nationally was considered undemocratic, because very few women paid tax.

Underpinning these arguments was the near universally-held attitude that the world was and should be divided into two spheres of influence: that of children, morality, and the future of the human race (where woman held sway), and that of politics, which was not only much less important, but also much less high-minded (where men held sway). Johnson thought that women were privileged in being able to successfully cross this divide and by influence in effect to exert more power than men could within their own domain: 'The right of petition is not only as open to women as to men, but because of the non-partisan character of their claims and suggestions they find quicker hearing.' Female suffrage Johnson saw as a permanent crossing over to the male sphere of influence, whereby women risked degrading their position in society by a contamination of the relative sanctity of their natural domain with the worldliness of men. These were formidable arguments for a new concept of completely unisexual citizenship to overcome.

* * *

A second common fallacy was that it had taken a world war with millions of deaths to finally make the case for universal male suffrage without qualification; and that by the removal of property ownership or earned income as some minimum threshold of economic standing or contribution, this naturally led to the extension to women. However 'A land fit for heroes' was not the reason. Soldiers after every war are surprised how suddenly their sacrifice is forgotten. This was even more true of World War One than for any other war.

The removal of qualification for male voting indeed was key, but this was not courtesy of the war; rather through a continuation of the political expediency which was at the root of the 1832, 1867 and 1884 acts. It was simply that an ever-greater proportion of the population was necessarily becoming subject to income tax, and this trend had accelerated with the watershed decision of the 1909 Liberal Government to move the taxation agenda towards paying for social welfare. But the real crunch was the cost of the 1914-18 war, which multiplied five-fold the basic rate of tax (from 6% to a whopping 30%). With such a dramatic rise, it was imperative to widen the franchise to avert taxpayers voting out the Government. And widening the franchise would enable the income tax base likewise to be widened, and so reduce the tax rate. There had also been a big expansion of taxes on expenditure, and this disproportionately hit those who were as yet outside the income tax base, though were nevertheless the main house-hold earners: the remainder of the male population. It was prudent to scale down these regressive expenditure taxes in favour of the progressive tax on income.

The upshot is that the vote was not a reward to those who had fought the war, but a recognition that they were now going to have to pay for it finan-cially as well as with their blood. This widening of taxation as the basis of universal male suffrage in turn dissolved any basis for enfranchisement other than simple citizenship, and by default this admitted women. This helps to explain why universal *female* suffrage was not seen by most peo-ple as a separate or even major part of the suffrage issue; but becoming important only inasmuch as it was bound up with the treatment of men.

It was the property/income qualification that not only disqualified many if not most men from voting, but also in effect disqualified women. Given that very few woman headed a household that would have passed the property or income threshold to give the household head a vote, then almost no women would have been eligible to vote even if there had been no distinction in terms of sex in eligibility to vote. Given the focus on the household rather than the individual, the blanket exclusion of women was largely superfluous; discrimination against women being effectively only *in*direct. This betrays the root of what only later came to be seen as unfair-ness; an omission based on the assumption that voting was only of concern to men. In not having the vote, women were not specially excluded, but had common ground with all men who failed to pass property/income qualifications.

Outside the middle/upper classes, most of the few women who ruled their own roosts were widows and would likely fail the ownership or income tests. Any sizeable house would be handed over to offspring, perhaps with the elderly widow given quarters or a cottage nearby. The indirect discrimination against men affected *most* men right into the twentieth century, and this was despite the fact that most of these men were in full-time employment and considered the head of a family. It could even be that a man was a fully productive farmer or industrial worker, with a wife and children, but with his household nested inside his father's, he could not join his father in voting. These were far greater injustices than the system delivered to women.

* * *

The shift of focus to individual citizenship was the principle that allowed for universal suffrage. It had been resisted in favour of retaining some sort of qualification, understandably to ensure the voter's involvement in and knowledge of wider economic and political affairs sufficient to express an informed opinion. (All men were assumed to be informed voters through their inescapable and permanent involvement with work, and through having to support a family or at least to establish themselves as solvent suitors to would-be brides.) Even when the new principle of citizenship was accepted, the qualification notion was not offloaded entirely. Still today, the word 'citizenship' conjures up the sense of an active involvement in community rather than a passive universal entitlement. From this perspective, given that women were much less involved in the economy and politics, keeping some sort of qualification for women was felt to be necessary. An age threshold of thirty ensured that most female voters would, through marriage, the management of the household and attaining maturity, at least to some degree be in touch with the issues of the day.

Excluding women younger than thirty was for another reason that was highly pertinent at the time—to ensure that women would not then have an unfair majority. It was not the natural majority women enjoy through living longer that was of concern, but that there were many fewer men because they had lived very short lives indeed, having been killed in the war. The carnage was uppermost in everyone's minds, and the emotion this aroused is the real reason for the anomaly regarding the female franchise. Ironically, this was the first time that there had been effective direct discrimination against women, and it survived *a mere decade*: from when it was introduced in 1918 to its removal by the legislation for full equal universal suffrage in 1928.

This explanation is supported by the fact that, right from 1918, women were allowed to stand as MPs without regard to the differential age qualification—on the same basis as men, from age twenty-one. This shows that the age anomaly was not 'chauvinism'. The question was seen to be genuinely whether most women were sufficiently embedded in the wider affairs of society to form opinions as the basis for casting a vote. There was not a blanket assumption that all women under thirty were incapable of a constructive engagement with politics. The non-application of the age qualification to standing for election could not be a clearer acknowledgement that some young women were more than able to make a sound judgement about the issues of the day. By definition, a young woman who was able to be selected by her party to be put on a ballot, must be in this category.

If 'chauvinism' had been the real obstacle to full equality in voting rights, then the first thing MPs would have made sure of, was that women could not join them in voting within the House of Commons itself. If women were deemed universally incapable of political understanding – and remember that very few men indeed were considered of sufficient calibre to stand for parliament – then most certainly no woman would have been allowed to become an MP. Again, if 'chauvinism' was the real obstacle, then why, shortly after the 1918 act, were the wives of business voters enfranchised? The decision was taken in parliamentary committee without a division and without so much as a single speech against. If there had been a proposal in any other context to double the business vote, it is inconceivable that Labour politicians would not have vehemently objected. It had been clear for some years that 'chauvinism' was not a part of government legislation when female political power was the issue. Legislation passed in 1902 required every county council to have at least one woman on their education committees, and the 1905 Unemployed Workmen's Act required the same for 'distress committees'.

Of course, the view from today is that the rationale of the time was a prize piece of 'chauvinism', but what nowadays is commonly held to be 'chauvinism' covers chivalry or, as it was then more commonly known, gallantry. Gallantry was (and remains in a less obviously fawning guise) a universal attitude expressed by men which was both intended and received as genuinely respectful and deferential behaviour; a relationship between the sexes where they knew they were essentially different. This is a facet of the usual care and consideration for women, not the excessive or prejudicial loyalty (to the male sex) which is how the dictionary defines 'chauvinism'. In fact, it is excessive and prejudiced loyalty *by women* to their own sex that we know to be a problem, and a substantial one; we know now that men have no such bias (see chapter five). Granting of equal treatment to women to stand for parliament, whilst retaining the age-thirty voting qualification, actually reflected a wider interpretation of what was the basis of being able to vote 'intelligently', in keeping with a looser view of what citizenship was.

Going the extra mile in this way can really only be seen as a privilege for women. The very few idle rich aside, men were universally workers, and either the sole (usually) or at least the main provider for their household. Inasmuch as men were afforded the vote in recognition of their economic activity, this is directly related to issues of taxation and spending. Men were also liable to be compulsorily called up in time of war. At no time and in no sense had men ever been afforded consideration in terms of mere 'citizenship'. On the contrary, the default was no consideration at all unless some well-defined criteria were met; criteria which had until recently deliberately excluded all but a small minority. In complete contrast, women were exempt from all this, so quite different criteria had to be thought up. The age qualification, depending on which way you look at it, was either itself a privilege afforded only to women, or a modest curb on what would otherwise have been a woman-only universal privilege by default. No man could keep the vote if he declined to support his family, or if he declared himself a conscientious objector, and simply cited his birth certificate as proof that he was world-weary enough to go to the ballot box. Any man behaving in these ways would have been imprisoned and thereby automatically deprived of his former right to vote.

That the rationale of withholding the franchise from 21–30-year-old women stood for a mere ten years—before the principle of citizenship entirely regardless of ability to vote 'intelligently' came to hold sway—is further testament to the privilege bestowed on women. It shows that gallantry remained as strong in men's dealings with women as ever. This 'watering down' of the citizenship concept came about precisely in order to allow for the inclusion of women in their twenties, and so to bring in truly universal suffrage. It must be kept in mind, however, that the universality is one-sided, given that any male—but only a male—could be disqualified from voting for failing to meet certain criteria, even though innocent of any criminality.

Kicking in an open door

There is a further set of reasons that lie behind the introduction of the higher age threshold for women, and also for the arrival of (near) universal suffrage, in 1918, as late in coming as it was. The cry of 'votes for women', in great contrast to the brutal suppression of various movements through history which could be characterised as 'votes for ordinary men' (notably the Chartists, little more than half a century before), was a push at an open door. Parliament had been long persuaded of the case, despite the lack of popular demand for female suffrage. The tactic of the suffragettes was counter-productively to try to kick the door in. What is not appreciated today is that it was directly as a result of suffragette militancy that legislation for universal suffrage was not hastened but *delayed*, and introduced not in full but in two stages.

The tactics of the suffragettes were seen at the time as largely counterproductive

THE SHRIEKING SISTER.

The Sensible Woman: *"YOU HELP OUR CAUSE? WHY, YOU'RE IT'S WORST ENEMY!"*

The female suffragist cause was an extremely well-to-do affair generally: not middle- but *upper*-class (Pugh, 2002). The only places in the country where there was any significant involvement by working-class women were some of the Lancashire textile towns. Everywhere else it was characterised by the absence of a working-class or of even a middle-class element, in contrast to other political movements at the time. Very well politically-connected, wealthy, and titled women made up the Women's Social & Political Union. Far from being the case that ordinary women were clamouring for the vote, there was general indifference, as Gladstone, prime minister at the time, remarked.

Militancy confirmed the one fear the general population had about the female franchise — irresponsible behaviour by those who would be newly enfranchised. The twin concerns that the movement needed to address — being unrepresentative and irresponsible — were exactly the concerns that the suffragettes haplessly highlighted and confirmed.

This was of little if any consequence to the suffragettes, because through their connections they well knew they were nonetheless secure in that parliamentary opinion was substantially in favour of women getting the vote, despite MPs knowing that there was little support in the country. They were simply playing at politics, and managed to turn newspapers from offering almost uniform open support to being obliged to attack their

The death of Emily Davison: suicide it was not

methods. The onset of militancy in 1908 spawned The Ladies League for Opposing Women's Suffrage, which by 1914 boasted 42,000 members. They appealed over the heads of the politicians by canvassing female local government electors, whom they found consistently opposed to female suffrage by a factor of four to one, but this had no impact on MPs.

As women, and even more so as well-to-do women, the suffragettes knew full well that they were immune from physical harm, regardless of what they did. The sole fatality in the campaign, Emily Davison, was a well-to-do woman too out of touch with the real world to know that the King's racehorse would not be made to stop simply by jumping out from the rail and standing in front of it. Suicide it was not, it is now known. Suffragettes, unlike Chartists and their ilk, never needed to be brave. They never needed even to fear loss of any reputation. A night or more in the cells was generally seen as a badge of honour, as suffragettes had carte blanche to be shameless.

Unabashed by the fact that men were dying in huge numbers in a war over which half of all men had been denied the expression of any opinion whatsoever; throughout World War I, Sylvia Pankhurst campaigned undaunted, along with The Women's Freedom League. Pankhurst set up a 'League of Rights for Soldiers' and Sailors' Wives and Relatives'. This focus away from those who were the real sufferers, is exemplified in an absurd statement by Isabella Ford, writing in 1915: 'Women have more to lose in the horrible business than some men have; for they often lose more than life itself when their men are killed.'

Two leading suffragette organisations did agree to suspend their window breaking, arson, policemen-hitting and the like, right from the start of WW1, when they realised that their campaign would be seen to be a disgrace. The leader of the whole movement, Emmeline Pankhurst, with her daughter Christabel, toured the country speaking at meetings to recruit young men into the army. Christabel wrote of her mother: 'she called for wartime conscription for men, believing that this was democratic and

Emmeline Pankhurst and Kier Hardie:
The contrasting faces of 'progressive' politics in Edwardian Britain

equitable'. Did she also think it democratic that her supporters handed white feathers to every young man they encountered wearing civilian dress? These would be those reserved for essential heavy industrial work, government employees, those too unfit for service, boys too young to enlist, and convalescents from physical or psychological wounding, as well as those very few men who had indeed taken the sure route to total social ostracism and punishment beatings by declaring themselves conscientious objectors. These last would not include Emmeline's daughter, Sylvia, because being a woman she was free to actively campaign *against* the war effort with impunity. But her mother's white feather brigade contributed to so many children lying about their age in order to enlist, making them even more likely to be killed than the average soldier, on account of the extra vulnerability of their impetuous youth.

It cannot have been unknown to Emmeline, the foremost and most well-known suffragette of all, that even by 1914 and the start of World War One, half of adult men were still not entitled to vote; and that therefore they had no say in the political process that brought about Britain's involvement in the war. For the first part of the war, soldiers were not called up but volunteered, albeit under massive social pressure. Conscription would mean that *all* men below a certain age could be forced into a situation where they could be ordered to take part in attacks in which they faced a very good chance of being killed or seriously wounded, in a war which overall they stood a high chance of not surviving, and an even better chance of being maimed and so unable to live a normal life afterwards. This would apply disproportionately to those men without the vote, because conscription had an upper age limit of forty-five. The subset of younger men aged twenty-one to forty-five was made up of those within the electorate less likely to have established themselves in terms of tenancy, property owner-ship or residence—the very criteria by which many would have failed to be enfranchised. How could Emmeline Pankhurst of all people have had the hypocrisy to actively campaign for conscription at a time when the majority of those who would be conscripted did not have the vote?

* * *

Militancy was not the women suffragists' worst blunder. This was that they saw themselves as quite separate from, and unhelped or even hin-dered by, progressive male enfranchisement. They repeatedly demanded that the next step should be purely in regard to women. The root of their difficulties was a false belief that there was no clamour amongst the work-ing classes for extending the male vote (Pugh, 2002). They could not have been more wrong. (Presumably, they must have falsely extrapolated from the indifference of working-class women for votes for themselves to imag-ine that enfranchisement was generally not an issue for the whole working class.) In fact, the male franchise was a big issue for working men, and their women supported them. This delusion was motivated by something worse than that the women suffragists simply did not care about the extent of adult male suffrage. A common theme in the movement, on both sides of the Atlantic, was that the vote initially should be extended to women through an education qualification. The converse of this was also argued, and quite openly: that *uneducated men should be denied the vote*.

The suffragettes wanted first and foremost an elitist enfranchisement of themselves to join the men of their own upper- and upper-middle classes, and only argued for universal *female* suffrage because it was more politi-cally expedient. Their second preferred option was to give way and allow the vote for the entire 'sisterhood', but only if there was qualified voting for men! The sentiment was here perhaps a little less elitist but decidedly separatist, betraying the common attitude of women of being not anti-male per se, but just against the majority of lower-status men. This is why women prominent in the Labour movement at the time were not per-suaded by the suffragettes and stuck to campaigning for adult suffrage and not for a separate bill for women. The wider perception was that the suffragettes created a needless divide between the sexes, and in the years before politicians were fully persuaded, the tactic of an initial partial extension of franchise for women backfired. It alerted politicians that gal-lantry could be aroused to concede the vote to a section of the female popu-lation, and this would then act as a Trojan horse for a complete capitulation to democratic rule by the masses.

The elitism of the suffragettes' demands is even more apparent when you consider that these privileged women were married to men who often already provided *two* votes for the household in having a business as well as a residence qualification. Upper-class or upper-middle-class women felt aggrieved not so much that their husbands or the husbands of friends (if they were in business or academia) could command two votes to their none, but that the vote had been accorded to other men beneath their social milieu. This is the reason for campaigning for a male educational qualification. Ladies of leisure received an education (falsely) regarded as far superior to the technical education of upper-working-class men, so this was a ticket with which to maintain social differentials.

After 1918 the observation was made by one politician that full male suffrage had taken 600 years to achieve, so why should female suffrage take only ten? But the overriding male deference to women as ever ruled the day. Influential men joined in the women's campaign, and the wider 'chivalrous' principle was allowed to overcome what in any other matter considered by government would have been continuing inertia. Yet this issue concerned the very survival of the elected members of political parties themselves. Any proposed changes to the electoral system make political parties extremely wary. Albeit that the Rubicon had been crossed in 1918; with politics in some turmoil the unpredictable effect of the entire mass of young women suddenly joining the electoral roll must have given politicians of all parties some worry. The underlying reason for the short delay was to see what the great change in the franchise of 1918 would lead to. After being sure that the destabilisation was containable, only then could MPs responsibly proceed further. Ten years, and just a couple of elections, would have been a minimum period to assess this. What makes it still more remarkable is that the assessment could not have been helped, to say the least, by the fact that the very first woman MP, elected in 1918, was for Sinn Féin.

Constance Georgine, Countess Markiewicz, the first woman elected to parliament. Born Constance Georgine Gore-Booth, the daughter of an Arctic explorer, she won the Dublin St. Patrick's constituency for Sinn Féin in 1918, but did not take her seat

Women have always had the vote locally

If so many accounts of the history of the national franchise completely miss the essential truths about women and the vote, is the truth about the local franchise easier to disentangle? And what could it tell us? This history has been largely ignored, so in comparison to the suffragette battles there is little distortion and mythologizing to deconstruct. The point of interest is that whereas any sort of mass national franchise is a recent development, representative local democracy is ancient; so the participation or otherwise of women will reveal an underlying reality.

The history of the national vote, at least according to the Whig narrative, is a transition from autocracy through aristocracy to full democracy, whereas the local vote was always democratic; though it veered towards excluding some of those at the bottom before moving back to full participation. The two histories are separate, but they appear to have influenced each other.

It may come as a big surprise to most people that *from time immemorial, women could and did vote at the local level* — in both parish and manor. Every manor originally had its own civil-cum-criminal court and forum known as the Court Leet, at which everyone over the age of twelve was required to attend. This was a dutiful and in some ways onerous service, and in 1228 a concession to make attendance voluntary was given to nobles, churchmen and to women (Scriven, 1896; Webb & Webb, 1963). Women were here considered as worthily above the common fray — on a level with nobility and the church.

This recognition of female voting rights was not a Norman invention. Women sat on Saxon councils, and it is likely that women were included in decision making in Brittonic and other 'Celtic' communities.

The other decision-making arena common to everyone in medieval times was the church: the open Parish Vestry meetings ('vestry' being the name for a gathering of all parishioners), at which every householder, male or female, could attend and vote (Webb & Webb, 1963). Even holding office had never been conditional on sex, and this was reaffirmed in early-nineteenth-century legislation that explicitly made participation in all aspects of local democracy independent of sex. But then came the Municipal Corporations Act (1835), which is a long document regarding the then new town councils, where the word 'male' occurs just the once. This is in the section detailing the qualification to vote: 'every Male Person of full age (and who) shall have been an Inhabitant Householder'. Afterwards 'male' is dropped in favour of simply 'person'. The bill for this act was debated in a select committee in July 1835. Peter Borthwick,[1] the new MP for Evesham, moved that the word 'male' be deleted, so as to continue to

---

[1] Mr. Borthwick, curiously, was a prominent defender of slavery, but managed to reconcile this with his advocacy for the emancipation of women.

qualify lady householders to vote for town councils; but his amendment was lost in committee. The whole of the House of Commons could subsequently vote only on the bill in its entirety, and — whether unknowing of this ungallant detail, or that the bill was otherwise too important not to be passed — passed it was. There is no record anywhere of why the bill was drafted to include this entirely novel form of sex discrimination. So why was it?

It was hardly in keeping with the political climate of the time. Just three months before, the *Leeds Intelligencer* newspaper ran an article on the problem of Vestry meetings descending into unruly mobs, as the more prominent and level-headed members of local communities stayed away. A statement further away from 'chauvinism' it would be hard to imagine:

> The only method now left to the friends of law and order is to appeal from such packed Vestries to the Parish at large. Nor will the appeal be in vain … Rated females are entitled to vote as well as males. We do not wish for a gynocracy; but we are sufficiently gallant to perceive that too many of the wayward Lords of creation are disposed to make a bad world of it; therefore the sooner the ladies interfere the better.

Interfere, the women could, and in ways that were seen as clearly unreasonable. And this answers the mystery of why sex discrimination arrived in 1835. The problem had arisen four years earlier with the Adoptive Vestries Act, which includes the following:

> In cases where two or more of the inhabitants present shall be jointly rated, each of them shall be entitled to vote according to the proportion and amount which shall be borne by him of the joint charge, and where one only of the persons jointly rated shall attend, he shall be entitled to vote according to and in respect of the whole of the joint charge.

Given that 'he' also refers to 'she' (as the wording of the Act makes explicitly clear), then a wife could be jointly registered as a ratepayer even though she would usually not have any income of her own — indeed, at this time a married woman was deemed legally to have no income of her own. Now, here is the nub: not only could she then vote, but in the likely absence of her husband through work, she could vote twice: once for herself and once 'on behalf of' her husband. In this way, the opinions of the husband — the partaker of the world of moneyed affairs and the earner of the wherewithal to pay the rates in the first place — could not only be joined, but even usurped by those of his wife.

What is more, here in the early nineteenth century, there was no distance between those who received and those who paid for welfare under the parish poor law, and the main recipients of poor law relief — which accounted for most parish expenditure — were women: widows and unmarried or abandoned women with children. So you can imagine how this possibility of proxy voting by women would have gone down.

So the fact that the one word 'male' was put into the 1835 bill was not at all to do with sexual chauvinism in any direct sense.

The restoring of the briefly-lost female franchise

For all that, the change brought about in 1835 was of limited consequence. Through the complexity of local government legislation, the 1835 Act did not apply in most places. In the places where it did, it was short-lived, because the issue of reinstating women voters came up for debate in an 1869 bill. The Earl of Kimberley pointed out that:

> This was not a proposition giving to women the municipal franchise for the first time. Previous to the passing of the Municipal Act in 1835, women did vote at municipal elections, but that Act took away their right to do so. Subsequent local government Acts gave them the franchise in the places in which those Acts were in force; and hence arose the anomaly that, whilst they could vote in the numerous towns in which the local government Acts were in operation, when a town obtained a charter of incorporation they were excluded. Therefore, the Bill merely restored to women a franchise which they formerly enjoyed.

The Earl won the day and the spelling out of equal applicability regardless of sex comes in section nine of the resulting legislation:

> [W]herever words occur which import the masculine gender the same shall be held to include females for all purposes connected with and having reference to the right to vote in the election of councillors, auditors and assessors.

Evidently women playing catch-up with men in suffrage was to do with other factors that vary together with sex, rather than sex discrimination against women per se. The big picture was not only that the great majority of men were disenfranchised along with women but that, much earlier than is supposed, women had the franchise on the same basis as men, and only temporarily lost this because of a link between tax (and therefore earnings) and the vote.

The thinking about municipal enfranchisement crossed over into the parliamentary domain, and vice versa. Originally, the issues of parliament seemed to belong to the world only of exceptionally monied people — necessarily men — whereas parish business seemed largely divorced from considerations of money, let alone war, and was the lot of common folk — women included — even more than of the gentry (who tended to shun the proceedings). Money questions to do with ever-bigger government then meant that just as pressure for widening the franchise for parliamentary elections mounted, the reverse trend was apparent at the parish level. The basis of the parliamentary franchise became assimilated by its parish counterpart. This played out the other way, as the original principles of local representation added further drive to the trend towards universal suffrage for parliament.

* * *

By a proper examination of the parallel but entwined histories of the national and local franchise, the truth about suffrage that emerges could hardly be more different from the standard social history line. It's the same kind of truth we can see across the board for affairs of men–women: that only the men at the top of the tree are/were privileged, and their privilege is/was at the expense of the majority of relatively unsuccessful men, and not at all at the expense of women. For the mass of men there is only contempt by the privileged of both sexes.

Developments in democracy which redressed unfairness to men were begrudged and protracted, but when they finally came they were swiftly followed by, or were even in tandem with, similar changes for women which were in effect still further privileges (that would not have been granted to men if the boot had been on the other foot). In the event of the arising of what was apparently a clear case of different treatment of women – when men and women could be viewed as being on the same playing field – redress for women happened effectively overnight, by comparison to a similar anomaly for disadvantaged men. Taking the history of the vote together with the analysis of marriage, custody, the historical 'pay gap', the marriage bar and the quota-ceiling restriction of entry to professions: it can be shown that there are no commonly-cited issues in history that in fact provide evidence for the notion that women were oppressed in any way.

Summary

Everyone – men and women – historically had their say within their own communities, but at higher levels only a tiny proportion could vote – just two percent of men before the first of the reform acts in 1832. By 1918, less than half of all men effectively had the vote, and most men who fought in the Great War had had no say. This, and the fact that all men shouldered some form of taxation, was the real injustice; not the absence of votes for women.

It was neither women's war work nor a 'land fit for heroes' that secured women the vote, but a new conception of universal citizenship, independent of some sort of qualification. This arose through the necessity of spreading the burden of income tax much more widely amongst men, so as to pay for the war. This took away property and income qualifications to make a universal principle that gave the excuse politicians were looking for to extend voting to women.

With parliament having long been fully persuaded, the political posturing of upper-class women and the militancy of the suffragette campaign was counter-productive. It served actually to delay the introduction of votes for all, and ensured that it was not complete until 1928. The campaigners were not interested in universal suffrage, but in the separate enfranchising of women, who they saw as superior to the mass of uneducated men. This betrayed an undemocratic and elitist motivation – the usual attitudes in human social groups of prejudice against the majority of (lower-status) men.

From ancient times, women have operated alongside men in decision-making in their communities, which is the decision-making level for what most concerned women. This persisted right through the modern period (apart from a thirty-five-year interlude), and only in certain areas; where as a result of a single word change in one parliamentary act, women were briefly denied the franchise, when municipal voting was aligned with that for parliament.

Never the will of parliament, but an oversight after a decision in a select committee, the denial of women's right to vote in their communities was soon decisively overturned. This showed the continuity of the principle of women having the right to have a say in matters that concerned them, which had never been the right of men except for a minority, and usually a very small minority at that.

Chapter 9

Sex at Work

Why women are not in love with work, yet the pay gap is so small

The opportunity for men to compete with each other for status is universally provided by work, for which men receive as reward the proxy for status: money. Status acquisition is the only option for men if they are to have any 'mate value' and obtain sexual partners; either long-term or fleeting. From a biological perspective, women neither need nor have any use at all for status (that is rank as measured in male terms), because they already have 'mate value' inherent in the degree to which they have a combination of youth and beauty. Some people are just more honest about this than others: witness this recent posting on the classifieds website *Craiglist*:

> I'm tired of beating around the bush. I'm a beautiful (spectacularly beautiful) 25-year-old. I'm articulate and classy. I'm not from New York. I'm looking to get married to a guy who makes at least half a million a year. I know how that sounds, but keep in mind that a million a year is middle-class in New York, so I don't think I'm overreaching at all.

This led to an equally candid response from a (male) merchant banker:

> In economic terms, you are a depreciating asset and I am an earning asset. Your looks will fade and my money will likely continue into perpetuity. You're 25 now and will likely stay pretty hot for the next 5 years, but less so each year. Then the fade begins in earnest. By 35, stick a fork in you!

Men never choose women on the basis of status; such male criteria being, biologically speaking, a meaningless way to view women. Work is consequently very much on the male side of life's equation, and it must be expected that men will tend to want much more of it than do women — both for the monetary reward and to 'climb the greasy pole', for which they will be prepared to put in more effort regarding the task, and to enter into more competition. Inevitably then, for this reason (even before we consider various others) men will always, on average, outdo women — in top jobs especially — but also across the board, in terms of pay and promotion. This is reflected in what is found when looking in the most general terms at the difference between men and women (see chapter five). In measuring almost any ability or performance, men on average outdo women, and even a small average betterment translates into overwhelming male preponderance at the top end because of the different nature of distribution according to sex. Male performance generally is spread wider, with both over- and under-performance compared to that of women, which tends to bunch in the mid-range (see chapter five).

Women in going backwards can't be 'catching up'

Even with perfect equality of opportunity, it should be expected that for a top job like director of a leading company, men will easily be beating women into the boardroom. And so they are. Not only is the proportion of women directors of the top hundred UK companies just one in ten, but almost all of them are non-executive. Even across the top 250 UK companies, at the time of writing (2007), there were less than a couple of dozen women who have any executive responsibility. Yet government ministers, quangocrats and activists continue to claim that it's merely a question of time before women catch up with men at the top. This social inertia notion might have more credence if the number of women in positions that are a springboard to the directorial board was increasing. They're not. They're *declining*.

Of the senior management posts in the 350 largest UK companies, only 22% were held by women in 2007, compared to 40% in 2002. That's an enormous drop in just five years. The exodus is still greater if you look at the less high-powered 'head of function' roles (that is, positions where there is anyone reporting to you) in the 250 largest UK companies, where women declined from one in five in 2002 to just over one in ten in 2007. Senior and 'head of function' managers are the pools of women from which future board members could be drawn, so we can expect corresponding falls in the numbers of women on the board, even though it's from a very low base. This is already happening. Of the top 100 UK companies, there were just twelve executive directors in 2006, which is almost a halving of the number from the previous year. It's been happening for some time: the same story of decline in women on the board and executive directors had been apparent at the onset of the new millennium.

The news had appeared to be advancement, when in the decade up to the millennium the proportion of all companies boasting a woman on their board had climbed from just two percent to ten percent. This is illusory, however. Many of these are minuscule businesses, directed by the owners themselves. Most business growth has been of such concerns, and a significant proportion of this has been by women. There are now a million self-employed women in Britain. In business, women tend to be present as decision-makers in inverse proportion to the degree of hierarchy. In big companies, not to have a token woman board member is bad PR, and there is no commercial risk if an appointee is non-executive; and this accounts for most of the relatively small numbers of women there are at this level. Likewise in management, the rise of women is not in private-sector line management but in public-sector staff roles, as would be expected with the recent growth in the public sector. There is no likelihood of reversing the decline of women in the commercial hierarchy, looking at the figures for those enrolling on business courses. The London Business School's female intake is only one in five of the total, and this is mirrored in business schools nationwide. There is subsequent heavy attrition in numbers of females, not just owing to their family commitments, but also, compared to men, through their having less focus and more other interests that conflict with both the desire and the effort necessary to climb the hierarchy. And this does not take into account the high proportion of men who will get there through other, less direct or riskier routes, who never went to business school. Business is the field of the entrepreneur, after all, who is born with the attitude and the drive. He's not a product of a college course. Just ask Sir Richard Branson or Sir Alan Sugar.

* * *

All this is astonishing in the face of the constant media exhortations and government pressure to get more women into senior positions. It takes time to climb the corporate ladder, but the aspirations of women at least to get into the lower echelons of senior management should have been fully realised many years ago now. Social inertia explanations have been replaced with a resurrection of the old rhetoric about discrimination; though now supposed to be in ever subtler form. There is refusal to face up to the simple fact that women do not cut this particularly competitive kind of mustard in the way that men do.

Instead of going into business, women have concentrated further in areas where they have always been established: the public sector in general, but particularly in education and health. Anywhere where real competition, risk and innovation are less important. Even then, near the top of an organisation in a 'female' employment niche/sector, the sheer hassle puts women off. (Actually 'female' sex-typical work has shrunk no less than the male equivalent: the growth is in sex-neutral work.) Managing a company at the top is all about dealing with irreconcilables in a moneyed world. Conflict, in other words. This is not what women are looking for at work, as I will explain.

Women are not orientated towards work

How women behave with respect to seeking top jobs is a reflection of women's attitude generally to the world of work. In whatever field, that the pattern of work amongst women has changed hardly, if at all, was first highlighted in 1996 in the first of a series of books by the world's leading expert on women in work, LSE sociologist Catherine Hakim. Over a thirty-year period, British women certainly did take up work, but all of the extra working was part-time, with no increase whatsoever in full-time permanent work:

> All the increase in employment in Britain since 1950, from 22 million jobs in 1951 to 26 million jobs in 1997, consisted of growth in female part-time jobs. By the early 1980s, two million full-time jobs were lost in the male workforce, most of them in manufacturing. Another one million jobs were lost in the female workforce, but then regained in the early 1990s. The only increase in female employment since the 1950s, and indeed since 1851 or before, is the massive expansion of part-time jobs, from 0.8 million in 1951 to 5.5 million by 1997....The headcount increase in female employment conceals an almost unchanging contribution of total hours worked by women, which remained below 33% up to 1980 (Hakim, 2004).

Remarkably, the proportion of women in full-time permanent work in Britain is the same now not just compared to what it was a few decades ago, but compared to what it was *150 years ago*. I checked with Hakim that the conclusion remained, and she replied (citing Hakim, 2003):

> That conclusion is not altered: there is no substantial difference in full-time permanent female employment. In fact, researchers in several other European countries report the same finding, if they compare figures over a long period. And additionally, current evidence for Britain suggests that women's continuity of employment is declining rather than rising, so full-time and continuous employment actually covers only about 10–15% of women in Britain—and many other European countries where appropriate data exists.
>
> The importance of this finding is difficult to overstate. It means that all the expectations of social and economic change, of greater equality between men and women in the workforce, and in the home, have rested, in practice, on the creation of a large part-time workforce. This is clearly nonsense. Even if part-time workers were identical to women working full-time in terms of qualifications, occupations and work experience, differing only in their shorter working hours, they would be poorly placed to provide the vanguard of change in the labour force, and the catalyst for wider social and political change.

Recent Labour Force Survey figures (2003) show that there are not far off twice as many male full-time workers as there are female, but there were only a quarter to a third as many male part-timers as there were women. So the labour market is enormously skewed according to sex in preference for full-time over part-time work or vice-versa, for all the media talk about work now being a woman's world after structural changes favouring the service economy. Surely there must have been a substantial change in the most recent years to coincide with women having children later and later in life, and the much lower starting base for women compared to men? Well, between 1995 and 2003 the number of women in full-time work went up by about 200,000, but the increase in part-timers was almost exactly one million—five times as many. The result was that the percentage of the female workforce in part-time as opposed to full-time employment was not just maintained but actually rose from 44% to 48%.

What's going on? It appears from the latest research that just as with women in top jobs or jobs not obviously appealing to women, there are signs of a counter-trend leading to a decline in numbers of women in any kind of full-time employment; women preferring instead to work part-time. The Institute for Social and Economic Research published the most extensive study on this issue anyone had so far attempted which showed that:

> Over 40% of women employed full-time prefer to work fewer hours at the prevailing wage, while only 4% prefer to work more hours. However, almost three-quarters of women who work part-time are unconstrained in their work hours, 10% prefer to work fewer hours and 19% prefer to work more hours....In 1991, 28% of women in employment wanted to work fewer hours at the prevailing wage, while 10% wanted to work more hours. By 1998, 34% wanted to work fewer hours, while only 7% wanted to work more hours (Böheim & Taylor, 2001).

Men showed the reverse and even more strikingly in all categories. The authors discuss at length possible constraints on choice of working hours, and show that while there are some, they are not serious obstacles. The choices made by the women about what they would prefer as ideal are real preferences, so over time they are likely to translate into actual working patterns. Notice that the ten percent increase over the decade of women dissatisfied with full-time working roughly corresponds to the increase of women in full-time work from 1995. It appears that most of the extra new recruits to full-time work either never really wanted to be there, or having tasted it realised that the grass, instead of being greener, was parched. Perhaps too, disillusion had started to set in amongst more longstanding women workers who had tired of the novelty of juggling home and work.

It might well be that the dissatisfaction is far more even than the ISER research shows, and that this could be shown if women are allowed to be more candid. In June 2001, *Bupa/Top Santé* published a survey of 5,000 full-time working women in the UK and found that only *nine percent* said they would still work full-time if they had a realistic choice. This compares with a *majority* of men, because men have no concept of an alternative to life-long full-time work which does not mean criminality or poverty, and—more to the point—loss of esteem. The minority of men who would give up work would do so only for a guaranteed independent income. Women, on the other hand, have every prospect of being 'kept' by simply staying at home and relying on their husbands to continue working full-time. Until very recently, this was actually the norm even in the poorest of working-class districts.

It seems then that more women are set to move away from full-time and into part-time work, and this already seems to be happening. The shakeout of stay-at-home women from the era in which they were not expected to go out to work had run its course some time ago, so the effect of a shift to part-time work will therefore mean a reduction in women full-timers. This is likely to be boosted further, and quite considerably so, by the reaction already apparent against what is being seen as a burdensome expectation the other way: nowadays women are generally cajoled into work, and this is becoming a focus of resistance. Well publicised middle-class female 'role model' figures have become vocal on this question. Job sharing is moving up-market, and many of those women who do achieve better jobs and pay but do not go this far, are likely to readjust their work–life balance to reduce working hours. This will have the effect, of course, of slowing or halting their rise into the topmost positions.

* * *

Women have woken up to not just the stress and thorough lack of empowerment that work actually provides, but what is for women the pointlessness of it. Their message will be more and more warmly received, though working-class women have always known the harsh reality of work. The push towards women treating work in a similar way to how men do, though clearly still persisting amongst a small minority of women, will seem in retrospect a short-lived bubble, with women who do remain in full-time work doing so only through a perceived necessity. This not least because house prices have risen owing to the rise of the dual- earning couple, so women are to an important extent now locked into work. (Another consequence of the dual-earning expectation is the depressive effect on real wages: 2006 being the only year in the last two decades when there was a zero increase in disposable income. In the US, inflation-adjusted hourly and weekly wages in 2006 were below where they were at the start of the recovery in November 2001.) Hakim cites further research showing that secondary earners forced to work full-time are the most dissatisfied of all workers. So again, the social inertia theory to try and explain disparity between the sexes is a hopeless fit to figures which show precisely the opposite of what it predicted. This is all the more remarkable because it comes in spite of the relative collapse of the female archetype of homemaker and mother, which has had a profound impact on women, and as a psychological 'projection', is the source of the bizarre notion that the male is redundant. The redundant sex is actually the female.

Underlying all this is what Catherine Hakim has identified as a persistent set of alternative lifestyle preferences that women make. Only a minority of women (between ten and fifteen percent) are 'work-centred' and so work continuously in permanent full-time jobs, whilst a rather larger proportion (a fifth) are 'home-centred', giving priority to children and home-making, and don't want to work at all. That leaves the bulk of women making up the balance in the 'adaptive' group, who fit employment around family responsibilities, either working part-time or moving in and out of full-time jobs. The women of the 'work-centred' sub-group are the least representative of their sex, because the attitudes of women in the 'adaptive' group are very similar to those of the 'home-centred'. They see work as not primarily about bread-winning or having a career, or of developing an ability or skill; but more as a social activity providing supplementary income. They also have the same attitude as 'home-makers' regarding the sexual division of couples into a wage-earning male and a home-making female. Only about a *quarter* of women who hold full-time jobs view their working life as a career.

Hakim herself sees the distinctions between women's preferences as a normal distribution curve, with the more extreme minority choices at either end and the bulk of women in the middle. But at the same time, she sees the three categories as enduring and qualitatively different. However, she ignores an underlying homogeneity, as revealed by the remarkably similar attitudes of women across the first and second most populous categories. This similarity is because women do not compete with each other in the way that men do — for status. The difference that makes the 'work-centred' women stand out is that they have elected to progress up a career ladder. For some this will be through intra-sexual competition (with other women), or because the job had become an end in itself; but these motivations are usually far weaker than they are in men. Ultimately women's 'climbing the greasy pole' is not for the reasons that men have to, but — as evolutionary psychology would suggest — so that they place themselves in the milieu of higher-status men. They may have careers but their working is anything other than an end in itself, in common with most women who work. Some women carry on, forever trying to climb; forgetting to jump off as their working life becomes an unintended end in itself. These women *appear* to be very like men, but they are not.

In trying to apply her 'Preference Theory' to men, Hakim finds that the overwhelming majority are careerist, with a very few 'home-makers', and the remainder she sees as 'adaptive', similar to the predominant group in women. But this would be to assume that, like women, men are compromising between working and home-making. It's clear to me that men are not doing this. They are dividing time between work and alternative means of acquiring and maintaining status — sports, hobbies, pressure-group politics, some blind-alley obsession, developing something that may turn into work, serving in an official body of some sort; a vast array of activities that are competitive in some way. If a man's work is low-status, dead-end or in some way unsatisfying, then he can spread his options of how to make his way in life. One option he is not interested in is to become a home-maker. A 'home-protector', yes; and to some extent the builder of the nest the woman then tends. If he has no option, of course, a man will become a home-maker as a single parent; or as the one who stays home simply because he earns much less that his wife, who otherwise would have to. These are forced choices though, and in this scenario divorce rates multiply several fold as women seem to see their husbands as having lost the status which was the basis on which they married them, and men register within themselves such a diminution; so both parties become dissatisfied with their situation. Hakim's three alternative preferences of work that she sees as applying to both sexes is her interpretation, but a better one is that they are unique to women. They don't apply to men. Hakim assumes some form of social construction model which does not admit of a natural sex difference, and so she doesn't look for underlying evolutionary explanations. She sees her findings as necessarily having to fit a unisexual model.

* * *

Long-term data show that women's preferences (rather than circumstantial constraints) are increasingly important in their decisions about work, especially for younger women (Blossfeld, 1987). Furthermore, this is so regardless of their level of education, social class, and whether or not they have children. Contrary to what most would imagine, research demonstrates that women are not constrained from working by childcare and home-making. This further underlines the homogeneity of the three preference groups, and points up that there is a fundamental divide between men and women in a systematic and uniform difference in attitude to work or, more precisely, to status-seeking. The upshot is that no steady increase of women in work can be expected. The opposite is likely, as in France where the 'home-centred' group has swollen to a third of all women.

For a look in detail at the preferences of women in a professional group in Britain, Hakim chose pharmacists. The women had the same qualifications as their male colleagues, but markedly different work patterns. Male pharmacists see their work as a platform to launch into self-employment or management, whereas women see it as a haven for flexible, mother-friendly, part-time employment with no responsibilities to interfere with those of the family. And there seems to be another, time-honoured, aspect to this female 'pseudo-career' path revealed by Hakim's findings. Going into jobs requiring high levels of education is as much making use of qualifications to 'trade up' in the marriage market as it is in the market for jobs. The statistics in many countries show that the husband is now much more likely to be the better-educated spouse. It's not just that women are using education to ensure meeting Mr Right, but that Mr Right is, as ever he was, a man not so much able to offer more resources than a woman can muster — after all, she is now often anything but poor herself — but a man high in status.

* * *

The commercial office world, far from becoming 'feminised' has actually got more cut-throat than ever before. Yes, there are fewer heavy shop-floor industrial jobs to soak up unskilled male labour, so the workplace overall has in this sense become less of a man's world than it was. Equally, though, 'feminine' jobs have disappeared or have become 'gender neutral', and this is an ongoing trend. Nobody anywhere is saying that work has got softer: everyone agrees it's more than ever dog-eat-dog. Women can compete alongside men, but this suits only a minority of women, and not a large one at that; and even then, they won't be motivated at root in the way that typically men are. (This is not to say that some women are not indeed highly motivated. Some women have male 'brain patterning' and so may be 'focused' in a male manner; and/or they may be particularly strongly driven to seek high status males.).

There is no reason why those women who feel cut out for it should not opt for a work life as a 'pseudo-male', as it were; as increasingly they have been encouraged to do. It's just that the majority of those women who want to work full-time have ample scope to choose a different, less overtly competitive sector or niche. Something that has a more social front end; more to do with care; perhaps more creative, rather than, say, ruthlessly deciding between irreconcilable options in the boardroom. This is one reason why employment sectors and niches have always tended to polarise the sexes, and why we should expect not less but more of this. That most women still continue to shun the male work model confounds social-trends predictions and undermines the tediously regular claims of discrimination by the late and unlamented Equal Opportunities Commission. Conversely, the convoluted and flimsy excuses used to explain women's lack of progress is evidence itself of a root deeper than social norms — evidence which gets stronger with every year that passes. And all this is despite the collapse in female roles — housewife, mother, even exclusive sex-provider — which has left women feeling they have less scope, and so further encouraging them to fill male roles.

The sexual division of labour

The distinction between male breadwinner and female home-maker roles that underlies the different attitude of the sexes to work, is so great that it's often claimed that housework is somehow imposed on women as part of men's supposed 'oppression' of them. Men's burden as 'wage slaves' is said to be more than offset by women doing all the housework, which curtails the scope women have to participate in the jobs market, making their choices, such as part-time rather than full-time working, forced.

This is all myth. The cry of 'women work more' has by repetition assumed truth. Hakim is absolutely conclusive:

> Adding together market work, domestic and childcare work, the evidence for the 1970s onwards is that wives and women generally do fewer total work hours than husbands and men generally, and that women's dual burden of paid work and family work is diminishing.

The gap was five hours per week in the USA in 1991, though very recent studies—as Hakim has pointed out to me—show the total work hours of the sexes to be the same.

A misleading picture of overworked women has built up partly through a focus on mothers with young children, as if this period is typical of their whole life. It's typical of only a few years. Children need far less care as they get older, and then leave home. More misleading still is to include as work women's natural nurturing behaviour towards their children, as if it's an onerous task on a par with working for an employer. Economists would see it not as productive work but as consumption, because it loses its value to the mother if someone else was substituted to carry it out. Much housework would also not be work, given a reluctance to delegate even to the husband. And it can't be claimed that women who stay at home or work part-time are doing unpaid work. They are paid directly for doing housework and childcare by their full-time working partners.

That women who combine work proper and housework are not having the hard time juggling demands on their time that it is made out, is provided by analyses of what women get up to when they are full-time home-makers. Inefficiency is hardly the word, according to Hakim. If you include activities that look like housework but are done for pleasure, then half the hours are wasted and far from being work really represent consumption:

> Studies of full-time home-makers reveal a remarkable lack of concern with efficiency; on the contrary, tasks are constantly expanded into huge amounts of unnecessary make-work...endlessly repeating the same unskilled tasks. Full-time home-makers cleaned and shopped daily instead of weekly, washed and ironed sheets twice a week instead of once a month....Variations in hours spent on domestic work are not explained by the number of children being cared for, access to labour-saving equipment and other amenities, or the purchase of more services in the market. One explanation for the reluctance of husbands to help with domestic work is the suspicion that there might be no need for it (Silverman & Eals, 1994).

Men by contrast are reluctant to divert effort into looking for dirt they fail to see—research confirms that men are poorer than women at spotting objects in an array, and this explains why men literally tend not to see dirt. Why should a man do housework to a partner's higher standards than his own, when this is his partner's domain, and is something she does well and (as studies reveal) is not so easily bored by — and may even enjoy?

* * *

The family is a beautiful example of a mutually-beneficial division of labour, with the sexes respectively doing not just what they do best, but what they like doing best. Just suppose that the extreme feminist line of a universal 'superwoman', always better than men, was not nonsense but true. Let us imagine that women are not just the best at rearing children but also model workers. Surely this would then mean that women should do both, with men filling in around them with complementary, albeit inferior, contributions on both fronts? Well no, this is not how things would pan out. The most fundamental insight of economics — the law of comparative advantage — tells us why. Instead of making all kinds of items you need, it's far easier to make just those things that you can make easily and quickly, and trade with those who also can make what you make, but less easily and less quickly. This is what human beings have always done, long before any law and customs to do with trade were devised. Trade with a division of labour between a man and a woman makes sense regardless of their relative merits in whatever sphere.

Even if women were better at everything than men, nobody seriously doubts that men are better in the work sphere than they are homemakers. Few people doubt that women make better carers of young children than do men. Men would (nearly) always be the primary breadwinners simply because they are *less bad* at this than they are at bringing up baby. Women would (nearly) always be the primary carers because they are clearly evolved for this function whereas men clearly are not. These differences reinforce each other in a positive feedback loop and lead to polarisation. Given that all men and women are either in a sexual relationship or looking for one, and equipped psychologically to anticipate the consequences, then the family scenario is the default social expectation guiding economic behaviour. Factor in the related intra-sexual competitive drive of men, which has only a weak parallel in women, and it's obvious to anybody that the feminist ideal of a world of work devoid of any parameters related to sex, is perpetually unrealisable.

Why there is a pay gap, and why it's so small

With the failure to understand the sex differences in attitude to work, the pay gap supposedly results from sex discrimination. And just as with the failure of women to get anywhere near parity with men in getting into top jobs, the stubbornness of the pay gap to close is put down to social inertia or ever more subtle forms of sex discrimination. I'm not dealing here with the historical pay gap that certainly did exist (which I dealt with in chapter seven), but which was actually not in any way against women's interests in the context of a view of social justice that focused on the family household. Here I will confine myself to the contemporary pay gap—with women on average earning four-fifths of what men earn.

That the pay gap has nothing at all to do with discrimination was confirmed in the 2006 report by the Women and Work Commission, which instead blamed the culture in schools and the workplace (but which was an indirect way of saying that actually it's down to women's choices). It remains anathema to say this, because it reveals that women have not and will not change—that is, they will not change the basis of their preferences, though they will react contingently. Not only is the pay gap not due to discrimination, but that it's as low as it is indicates sex discrimination *against* *men*. (I will come on to the proof of this discrimination at the end of this chapter.)

The pay gap is easily explained by men tending to have harder jobs, putting in longer hours, taking more responsibility, etc; which in turn is easily explained by multiplying together the impact of the sex difference in how performance generally is distributed, and the radically polarised attitude to work of the sexes. Then there is the drawback women have in moving up any employment scale in having and raising children. Breaks in employment or reducing full-time work to part-time, inevitably hold women back, and there is nothing corresponding in men's life that systematically produces anything similar.

There are still other reasons behind the disparity in average income between the sexes, to do with the predilection of women for work that is more in keeping with their natural tendency towards social networking, as opposed to the natural male inclination towards goal-directed competition. Jobs that are at the social front end, such as receptionists; and caring roles, such as nurses; are overwhelmingly female staffed. Most of the sex-typical female kinds of employment—even when full-time—tend to be low paying, for simple supply/demand reasons: they are pleasant and socially rewarding positions that are easy for employers to fill. It's certainly true that female sex-typical work *sectors* are very much reduced as a proportion of the economy than they once were—going 'into service' was by far the most usual female job prior to the First World War—but female sex-typical work *niches* within the full range of work sectors are abundant, and 'gender neutral' jobs in administration that are at least conducive to women have grown substantially. With thoroughgoing equal-opportunity initiatives, most of the population is considered eligible for recruitment, so pay levels can be pitiful, which puts men off. Women have made up most of these new recruits, so again average female pay across the whole economy will be further reduced.

* * *

The 'pay gap' is a misnomer when you consider that it's less important than the 'family gap': the difference in earnings between partnered mothers and single childless women (Harkness & Waldfogel, 1999; Bayard et al., 2003). A woman without children who is also not partnered, on average has roughly the same earnings — actually slightly more — as the average man (Hecker, 1998). Even more telling are the pay differentials between hetero- and homo-sexual couples (Berg & Lien, 2002; Carpenter, 2005). Lesbians enjoy an earnings premium of 20% compared to heterosexual women. The difference between lesbians and all other women may best capture the impact of being female: compared not to men but to a null baseline. Whereas being a woman with a family normally is a brake on earning, for men with a family it may be a spur. Married men earn on average 25% more than do single men (and also, interestingly, compared to gay men).

Is this because women choose better earners as marriage partners? Or is it that men, once they have a family (children and/or a spouse) are then motivated to earn more money? (Cohen & Yitchak, 1991.) Correspondingly, do women who don't have primary responsibility for earning then take their foot off the pedal and/or displace their own expectation for earning on to men? It's not that a wife frees a man from domesticity so that he can concentrate more on earning, because single men have little domesticity to offload, and may well take on more in a female-run household where standards are much higher. The other explanations are probably all part of the picture. The point is that all of the differences are between individuals of the same sex in different situations. The 'pay gap' resolves into a within-sex, not a between-sex difference. The 'marriage gap' amongst men reflects a difference in motivation between sub-groups of men, but it says nothing about the overall difference in motivation between men in general and women in general.

There are a host of reasons, many inter-related, that might incline us to the view that the actual figure of circa 20% seems far smaller than it should be. The standard PC viewpoint may well posit the problem in reverse: instead of women being discriminated against, either men are being discriminated against or women are being given preferential treatment. Or both. The lamentable understanding of what lies behind the pay gap is evident in the slew of books in the late 1990s demanding its end. Authors such as Suzanne Franks (a truly risible analysis titled *Having None of It*) marshalled the supposed evidence for sex discrimination in ever more ill-thought-out fervency.

* * *

The intransigence of the pay gap to fall progressively to zero is one thing, but in many developed world countries the pay gap is actually *widening*. And it's widening in the very places where there is most effort to close it. In Sweden, the pay gap hit a floor of 18% in 1981, *more than 20 years ago*. By 2000 it had risen (on comparable, adjusted figures) to 21% (Spant & Gonas, 2002). Sweden is ahead of any other country in measures of trying to combat the pay gap, so Sweden should be furthest down the road to getting the gap down to zero. The pay gap has defied feminist theory in not falling to zero, but instead bottoming out nowhere near zero and then going into reverse.

The Swedish experience is caused by the very family-friendly policies designed to get women into work. Because women have a fundamentally different and often antipathetic attitude to work, then the higher the proportion of women who feel compelled or deceived into working, the ever greater proportion of these will be women who really don't want to. Instead of embracing work, they go into poorly-trained, sex-segregated jobs that demand little or no commitment or compromise and which pay correspondingly poorly. This drags down the average female wage.

In countries where women are more or less universally compelled to work, so that even the core 'home-makers' are begrudgingly at work; then the pay gap can be very much larger — up to 50%. This was the case paradoxically in the very country where sex equality was most explicitly articulated — prior to 1989 in the Soviet-block state of East Germany.

Will there be a pronounced retrenchment of the pay gap everywhere? It's hard to see why there won't be. And there is another factor that is surely set to come into play, in addition to the attitudes of most women to work. Given the DH-inspired propensity of men to compete with each other for status, and with income being the most straightforward proxy for status, then albeit that their aim is success in competition with other *men*, men gauge their relative status in part at least by their income above a general baseline, and women's wages are very much part of this. So although men are in no way competing against women, women's wages insofar as they register and are generally assessed, represent in men's minds the sort of money you would earn *if you weren't trying*, as it were. Men correctly surmise that if they can manage to earn only what lowly-paid women typically earn, then few women will be interested in them as potential sexual partners. A 1996 ICM research poll showed that the majority of men will not take on what they regard as women's work. Research has also shown that men have cognisance of a reference income with respect to total benefit levels: men (but not women) think in terms of the 'reservation wage', which is that wage level which is sufficiently above benefit levels to make work even begin to seem worthwhile. The general baseline of earned income has risen in the wake of measures equalising pay between the sexes, and also more particularly through in-work benefits/tax credits that are skewed to help women. Inevitably therefore, men on average will take action to boost their incomes so that they are restored to something like previous differentials. Apart from ways of doing this that exploit loopholes that can be closed, an increased sex difference in pay cannot be clawed back by measures of sex equality, for the simple reason that such measures have already been introduced and their impact is a one-off 'gain'. There is nowhere else for feminists to go except to overtly discriminate against men.

The value we put on jobs, and their sex segregation

The argument that the pay gap is discrimination is tied up with a widely-accepted notion that women's jobs are less valued than men's jobs, simply because women do them. This is not just a reversal of cause and effect, but assumes that the prestige of any job is arbitrary. Job prestige is not arbitrary but bound up with remuneration, which is a strong reflection of profitability, supply and demand, etc. Status is attached to a job because the qualities required to gain the position are in short supply. Status in the world of work, where employers have to stump up hard cash, is never arbitrary.

In the mid-nineteenth century office work was a high-status male preserve . At the cutting edge of the labour market, it required a level of education obtainable only by a very few. A combination of book-keeping skills, writing and record keeping, and a sound knowledge of most aspects of the business were prerequisites. The scarcity of these skills attracted a premium in pay that was the necessary 'family wage' for a man. As education levelled upwards, and as women were now themselves being educated above primary level, then it became far easier to fill posts. Consequently, salaries fell. Advances in technology allowed for de-skilling and the separation of tasks from each other and from managerial functions resulting in the office coming to resemble the factory. This was just the sort of work educated and upper-working-class or middle-class women were seeking. Factory work was often unsuitable for women, because it sacrificed femininity and (usually) hygiene. The affordability of this workforce ensured mass availability of jobs in large organisations. As ever in search of (and being pushed into) a breadwinner's pay, men were obliged to move on to more challenging pastures either outside of this area of work altogether or by moving up into management. So it was that women predominated in clerical work by default, and it became routine and female.

At the other end of the spectrum of jobs that men but not women do (or used to do), jobs are anything but more valued. These jobs are *less* valued and may be paid well only by virtue of how dirty, heavy and dangerous they are. The supply of labour to do such work is restricted by the willing-ness of people to do it, and by fitness requirements; but also through unionisation to turn a weak bargaining position into a strong one. Male coalitional behaviour is particularly useful here. A major constraint on labour supply that helps to keep wages buoyant in these jobs is that natu-ral care and protection of women has nearly always precluded them from this type of employment. At most times in history, and still today, we oblige men to do all the work that might in any way compromise a woman's ability to safely bear children, her beauty or her dignity. To expect women to do such work would reflect badly on the men around them: they would be seen not least by other women as having fallen down on their universal 'care and protection' role, and this would translate into loss of status. A notable exception here is the 'cleaning lady', but it's excep-tional because it's just an extension of domestic cleaning duties that are part of a woman's sense of being a home-maker. When any cleaning work moves far beyond any parallel with the housewife role, then it becomes all-male.

There have been times in the past when economic necessity has meant that all household members including children, let alone women, had to join men in dirty and dangerous workplaces; notably the coal mine. How-ever, women did the less onerous, lighter jobs away from the face, that were consequently lower paid; but which in any case came to an end after the public uproar when they came to wider attention. Reports in the early-nineteenth century of coal-blackened and bare-breasted women working underground prompted a royal commission and then an act to ban it. (The jobs were sex-categorised, but it wasn't possible for the sexes to physically segregate in a coal mine, and this is what caused the uproar.)

Women could be found in several hazardous industries. They might contract the respiratory disease *byssinosis* (Brown Lung), working in the carding rooms or loom sheds of cotton factories; but they were kept out of areas where cotton-dust levels were really high, which were all-male envi-ronments. Likewise regarding asbestos. These were factory environments, where sex-segregation was possible, not just to keep women away from most danger, but so that each sex could associate separately. The same was true at Bryant & May's London match factory in the late-nineteenth cen-tury, where exposure to yellow phosphorus fumes in the stages of manu-facture (mixing and dipping) led to the fatal poisoning of many of the completely male workforce. Women were not allowed anywhere near this, and merely boxed the finished product, in what was a correspondingly all-female environment. Although ventilation was an issue, it was mainly if instructions regarding hygiene were not followed that there was any major risk of contracting the condition known as 'phossy jaw' (necrosis of the jaw bone) which, if left untreated, might be indirectly fatal, but usually caused partial facial discolouration and a foul-smelling pus, that led at

The 1888 Match Girls Strike was the most famous in history, even though the incidence of phosphorous poisoning among male workers was far worse

worst to disfigurement. Nobody called for action on behalf of the men, but in 1888 the women were spurred to the most famous strike in history by the prospect of massive public and media support organised for them by the leading social reformer Annie Besant. Evidently, women's physical beauty was of far greater public concern than the death of men (a view that seems to remain, given the long struggle by the mass of miners for compensation for terminal respiratory conditions). Again, the underlying story is of sex segregation. It was the existence of female single-sex zones within the workplace to partition women *away* from danger, that ironically led to spurious stories about working women being comparatively hard done by.

Women are perfectly capable of doing many dirty and/or dangerous jobs, as they have to do in wartime (though even then, the men do the heaviest 'reserved' work). There are always a few women car mechanics, plumbers, etc; as we'd expect by virtue of the small percentage of women with 'brain patterning' along male lines. It may be that there are no remotely typical women in these jobs at all. It's still the case that all of the very worst jobs—in terms of work environment, physical demands, promotion/redundancy prospects, stress, likelihood of injury or death and extra hours of work regarded as the norm to make up reasonable pay—are *man*ned 95-100%. Women do not look for jobs that pay a bonus for being 'dirty' or 'dangerous' because for them it would be essentially pointless, as a biologically-based analysis reveals. But it's the fact that they are jobs that tend to be held by men that seals it. It's self-segregation of the sexes that underlies why many light-assembly factories have for generations employed either nearly all women or nearly all men, for reasons nobody can remember (rather, it was for reasons we are but dimly aware of).

* * *

Most women are in the lower echelons of the economy in a separate all-female labour market. This is so pronounced that this horizontal job segregation has no impact on the pay gap, which is produced by vertical segregation (differences in the position in the organisational hierarchy). This is reflected in the fact that male and female unemployment rates are almost independent of each other. As Hakim concludes, competition between male and female workers does not happen. Equal pay laws have nil effect on female unemployment, despite economic theory predicting that as women's wages rise relative to men's, then women would tend to become progressively less employable. This didn't happen, because women's jobs were mostly segregated — largely self-segregated — from men's.

The sexes together and confused in the workplace: teamwork, harassment and hazing

In the light of the voluntary segregation by sex in workplaces: is a mixed-sex work environment just a recipe for conflict, or do many or most people find that the sexes are complementary in this situation? When the sexes are forced to be together, does one sex stick together at the expense of the other? How does performance and commitment alter according to whether the workplace is all male, all female, or a mix?

We know to expect differences, because women are found to favour other women far more than they do men, and women can have membership of the female 'in-group', no matter how unconnected. This is in contrast to the kind of 'in-group' formation by men that particularly suits the workplace as a natural locus for male coalition building. This complements the research which suggests that whereas women tend to be more relationally inter-dependent, men tend to be so more collectively.

Answering her own question in a 2001 review article entitled *Are Men or Women More Committed to Organizations?*, Kim Malloy finds that the problem of commitment comes from mixing the sexes. Men in particular don't want to commit to the workplace when they are significantly in the minority, and tend to leave. Efforts to integrate the sexes actually worsens this problem. This is not because of the presence of women, but the lack of other men to compete against.

Men compete with other men, and instead of competing against women, show deference to them. After all, women are what men compete *for*.

The Sugar Daddy

Viewers of the fascinating BBC television series *The Apprentice*, in which the businessman Sir Alan Sugar obliged teams of women and men to compete against each other (with the weakest performer facing dismissal) might well argue with the nostrum that only men are status-seeking. If anything the male team members were relaxed and co-operative and the women confrontational and status-obsessed. (And, although the producers of reality TV programmes deliberately select non-typical contestants, viewers will confirm that this was more genuine than the average reality TV freak show.)

How can this be? Men, being naturally task-oriented, are happy for their performance (and resulting position in their DH) to be determined by results. Just as in a game of cricket either you win or you lose, and most men—not just those who have gone to public school—are resigned to accepting the outcome with good grace (witness their relative lack of histrionics on receipt of Sir Alan's catchphrase, 'You're fired').There's always another game.

Women, however—even high-flyers like *The Apprentice* contestants— when pitched into a task-oriented environment may fail to perceive that the *outcome* is all that matters (rather than the impact of the task on their social network) and so become obsessed by their perceived position—in other words they tend to psychologise something that men see in purely instrumental terms. This explains the paradox that women might superficially appear to be the most status-obsessed sex in the workplace despite men being much more strongly motivated in this regard. Men are not obsessed with status so much as achievement—status naturally following on from success.

Women do not compete with each other on anything like the scale that men do, and suffer no social stigma in competing against men if they so choose. They can swap with impunity between competitive and sexual modes in their dealings with men, whereas men are severely constrained in reciprocating. Entrench this institutionally and politically, and no wonder men will be disillusioned in a workplace where female employees greatly outnumber them. They are at sea in the relative absence of others who are psychologically salient to them as competitors.

The silly notion that men perceive women at work as some kind of threat, is just feminism-inspired wishful thinking. Men perceive nothing of the kind, even though in a particular important sense they would be quite correct if they did. Women network in a different way to men. They are much more co-operative in a personal sense, whereas men are co-operative as regards the task and can get on with people they don't like. This means that the perception by women of actual achievements of fellow workers tends to be subsumed under personal considerations, and 'relational aggression' may result in social ostracism. Again, this is the reverse of the popular fallacy of an all-male club. Men co-operate as an alliance to serve competition, and this can easily be focused on a task, which is why men function well in organisations. Women co-operate so as to form a gossip circle. First, to 'find out' men—the minority of winners and majority of losers in their eyes; and second, to assort to some degree amongst themselves. Achieving things outside these social concerns—not least the tasks to be done in the workplace—is something female co-operation can be co-opted for, but is some distance from the reason for its existence.

The reality is the opposite of 'male chauvinism'. Women, not men, club together in this way (male coalitional behaviour being a different phenomenon). And women, not men, treat members of the opposite sex unfavourably. After all, women sift through men and very reservedly choose a man as either a long-term sexual partner, or—if he is rather more extraordinary—as a one-instance sexual liaison. Men are radically different, being open to virtually anything with any and almost every woman if sex is a prospect, however far removed or unlikely. In ordinary social life, this translates into women taking good care to keep at a distance from many or most men, and they do this both individually and collectively.

* * *

At work, the most extreme potential flashpoint, obviously, is when sex becomes salient as actual sexuality. Women inevitably have to brush off advances, which normally they not only take in their stride, but as compliments that help them to choose between men. Problems come when a woman lacks resourcefulness, and/or is politically encouraged to pretend likewise, to deal with this normal part of life. Now that we have the bizarre

nurturing of woman as social moron in the legal wormhole of a harassment charge, the small number of genuine cases of sexual harassment are
lost under an avalanche of the trivial or bogus, that would be of no issue
were it not for a precautionary principle deeming them worthy of investigation—to avoid being sued, and to satisfy over-zealous corporate or
statutory 'equal opportunities and diversity' policies.

By enacting legislation focused on the often false perception of the supposed victim (Sorenson & Amick, 2005) rather than the intention of the
putative assailant, the law is being used to misrepresent and criminalise
normal interaction. So what is going on when flirting becomes harassment? Generally, a man who appears a skilful flirt is actually simply a man
sufficiently high in status to attract the woman he is flirting with, and for
that reason can keep her interest, and even get a date. At worst, he'll get a
reputation as a 'bit of a card'. A man who instead appears simply to be
unwelcome in his attentiveness is usually just a man insufficiently high in
status. This will trigger in the woman her 'cheater-detection' mechanisms,
that will cause her to perceive the man in various unwarranted negative
ways, and he'll fall foul of the gossip network. Even if his attention is just
genuinely friendly playfulness with little real sexual intent; for a slight
lack of judgement of respective 'mate value', the man runs the very real
risk of a criminal charge.

However, matters seem to be more complicated than this in the workplace. We would expect that here women interact both through their personal network—their normal mode of interaction—and through the work
hierarchy, in which they are in effect acting as surrogate males—part of the
(male) dominance hierarchy. A woman places herself, or has been placed,
in a situation that she can use to her advantage, but which is also a potentially compromised position, whereby a man can take advantage of her
position in the work hierarchy rather than to engage with her through her
personal network. If a woman perceives a man's approach to her as being
not through her personal network but as being within the status hierarchy,
then she may interpret this as harassment. This is a measure of how out of
kilter a social network organisation is when placed within a hierarchy.

This analysis reflects just what researchers have found. Women don't
feel harassed when 'hit on' by high-status compared to low-status men
when they are outside work. We can interpret this as being because there is
no confusion in a woman's mind between personal network and hierarchy. At work they actually feel *more* harassed when 'hit on' by a high-
status work colleague than by a lowlier-one (Bourgeois & Perkins, 2003).
And this would seem to be because here they are confused between their
natural and surrogate roles (in the workplace DH).

A man cannot second-guess the distinction women intuitively make. It's
bad enough that a man is saddled with the cost of misjudging the relative
'mate value' whenever he makes a sexual approach. But here, even if he

makes a non-sexual approach, he may still be accused of harassment. Furthermore, because a dominance display is part-and-parcel of a sexual approach (the evolutionary process having co-opted dominance signalling for courtship), then the normal behaviour of a work superior could be easily misconstrued as harassment. This is transparently an unfair position for men to find themselves in.

* * *

Another and far more common source of confusion for the sexes interacting in the workplace is when the usual ways that people get along with others of their own sex crosses the sex boundary. The universal way that human males carry on is by 'winding each other up' — men always do this to find out if a new recruit is trustworthy, how clued-up and socially skilled he is, and if he is interested enough in being there. A series of tests are used to make sure someone is worthy of being admitted to the 'in-group'.

In a male single-sex environment, new recruits in many establishments get 'initiated' or hazed (to use the American expression), especially when bad teamwork would be life threatening — notably in mining and the armed forces. Notwithstanding the occasional excess, it's a very pro-social phenomenon, and most men in most situations where it occurs have little trouble enduring what is an acceptance ritual into a new coalition. Traditional craft apprenticeship, street gang and college fraternity initiation rites can also be understood in this way.

Winding each other up is a highly constructive form of harassment, as Warren Farrell analysed (Farrell, 1994). It de-individualises men to prepare them to sacrifice themselves for the survival of the group (especially the survival of the women in the group), or even for no better reason than that they just became an unproductive burden. This is quintessentially male and quite alien to women. Not just team- orientated, men are also task-centred more than they are relationship builders; and hazing is about whether you are up to scratch rather than how you click with other people. But it's a joining ceremony, and about inclusion, not exclusion — on certain terms, and likely not a favourable place in the informal hierarchy; but inclusion nonetheless.

There is no equivalent in female single-sex workplaces, though it may appear that there is a more subdued version. Women do not have to offer themselves as sacrifice for anybody (except perhaps their own children), and don't form teams of those at hand, and nor do they tend to be orientated to the task. So here recruitment is simply into a gossip network of individuals that extends well beyond the group of women on site. This is so open that initiation would hardly be needed.

Neither of these scenarios fit the bill when the opposite sex is also recruited, because neither team-building nor personal networking can be applied, and the whole workplace culture can be damaged. Women know that in places where men predominate they might get wound up by the men—suspicious that women are getting a better, cushier deal from management at their expense. Such disparagement would not be unfounded: the women cannot be tested out as they would be if they were men, and (as men know all too well) women can hop between a work role and natural sexual mode according to what is advantageous for them. Men get a considerably harder time than this if they go for work labelled 'woman's', as some men have done following on the closure of heavy industry.

What might happen to a woman in an otherwise male work environment? There would be engagement with her, not least because a woman is invariably of interest to men. Men always bring women in to their 'in-group'. This gets round the problem of trying to get along with someone who, being a woman, cannot be assimilated normally by male team building. In that the male style of team building would be more likely to be inclusive than the female personal network, she may somehow be co-opted, with the woman treated in some respects as an 'honorary male'. But perhaps the men would be in two minds whether to view her in this way or to display to her. A mixture or an alternation of mild hazing and mild flirting could be a dangerous cocktail for the male team members though. Men would realise this, and be accordingly stand-offish.

A woman on the receiving end of this might read sexuality into what is mild hazing alongside flirting or simple friendliness, and then—given how easy it is to do, and the encouragements on offer—may initiate a harassment charge purely on the basis of her own misperceptions, regardless of the innocent intent of the man she accuses. This destroys teamwork and may even result in a team builder losing his job, whilst the socially incompetent woman retains hers. It would not take much of this before eventually the whole organisation would be unable to communicate internally about anything.

The stakes have been raised by legal precedents and, since 1997, an EU directive which makes employers liable if for any reason they fail to protect an employee. The onus of proof is entirely on the employer, who then has no choice but to side with the complainant, leaving the falsely accused isolated. Once again, codified in law is a subjective flexibility for a woman rather than an objective rule by which people can know where they stand. The absurdity is complete with the general adoption into codes of practice by organisations and firms of the notion of harassment as anything considered as such by either the recipient or any witness. Yet more disturbing still is the incorporation of this 'principle' into law.

Meryl Streep and Anne Hathaway in The Devil Wears Prada *(2006)*

Women tend to revile women bosses

It might be expected that, with the separate social organisation of the sexes, having a boss of the opposite sex might be problematic, and that with women sticking together the most benign arrangement is women working for a woman boss. Paradoxical though it seems, nothing could be further from the truth. Organisations function best where bosses are male—whether their underlings are male or female—and worst when bosses are female. They function worst of all when a woman manages women.

Research reveals that women overwhelmingly prefer not to work under another female. This is a profoundly negative feeling about women as line managers and not a positive feeling about men in the role. A useless male boss is preferred to a competent female one. It's not just an issue of women not liking working for women superiors, but that they don't want to co-operate with or even acknowledge them (Molm, 1986). Some female secretaries actually walk out of recruitment when they find that their prospective boss is a woman. (The squabbling on *The Apprentice* came to a head when Miranda Rose got the boot for disloyalty after being appointed P.A. by the power-hungry Adele Lock. The job appeared to have no purpose other than to improve Ms. Lock's level of self-esteem and had disastrous consequences for the female social network as well as for the 'enterprise'.) A survey for the Royal Mail in 2000 reported that only seven percent of women preferred a female superior. In a 1991 survey, of women who had worked through the Alfred Marks agency under both men and women, less than a fifth said they would want a woman line manager in future, and two-thirds said they would never work under a woman again and wanted their boss to be male. Almost the same proportion (three in five) expressed just the same to researchers for *Harper's Bazaar* magazine in 2007 — and these were professional women in top jobs.

Women's unwillingness to work for a woman line manager is greater compared to *men's* (Mavin, Sandra & Lockwood, 2004; Mavin, Sharon & Bryans, 2003). Women can positively welcome work beyond their job description when it's for a male boss. However hidden, it appears that a sexual frisson — which can be very widely manifested, in many not overtly sexual ways — makes a dull job sparkle. Inter-sexual social reality is what is most salient.

Women complain that female bosses have favourites and are inconsistent because they deal in personal relationships instead of focusing on the job, whereas women feel they get fair treatment from male bosses. The predominantly personal dimension of women's managerial style leads to sniping or awkwardness; or a sense of superiority and trying to prove a point when giving out work.

Something powerful is at play here. Women have an acute awareness of the separate worlds of the sexes. Underlying the negative feelings women have for same-sex bosses, is that they are aware of the instrumental motivation of women to try to travel up organisational structures, of being more in the company of higher-status men. From the perspective of evolutionary psychology, women don't acquire status, except in the sense of acquiring it indirectly from their long-term mates; so women placing themselves over other women according to the criteria of a male competitive status hierarchy may be seen by their female underlings as incongruous — cheating even. Women's natural predisposition to networking exacerbates this. A female boss is not centred on the workplace as a coalition as are men; instead being more concerned with what she perceives as her 'in-group' of women, most of whom are likely outside the organisation, with whom the women under her may well have no connection.

The women bosses with their favoured women underlings stick together, and the selective bias women have for other women will come out in interviews for promotion. There is an irony that women, as the people women least want to see manage them, will tend to end up with positions of responsibility, thus driving further workplace discord amongst women, and further discrimination against men.

Women's preference for their own sex: serious sex discrimination against men

The fourfold female preference for their own sex, and the 'in-group'/ 'out-group' differences between men and women (see chapter four) means that employers entrusting recruitment to women are likely to get not the best man for the job but more likely a mediocre woman. It also means potential problems of female performance in the job, irrespective of ability. The upshot for men is serious sex discrimination against them.

In recruitment, whereas women candidates will tend on average not to suffer discrimination—even if the interview panel is all-male—men candidates will probably suffer worst outcomes the greater is the proportion of female interviewers. If the panel is all-women, then not only is this effect at its maximum, but there is no male perspective to counteract it. Women interviewers will prefer women (even aside from any feminist political attitudes, or any acceptance of notions of supposed oppression of women, or pressure through equal-opportunities policies). There would seem to be two complementary reasons for this. First, the interviewer tends to feel a potential personal connection with any and every female applicant, even though she may be a complete stranger—there need be no shared 'in-group' for this to occur, as would be the case for men. Second, prejudicial preference will go relatively unchecked (compared to how men would feel) given that women have a very different sense of 'in-group', and so will be less concerned about the impact of making a decision that may not be in the best interests of the work group.

I encountered this when I first applied for a lowly job at the Home Office. The all-woman interview panel rejected me, ostensibly—and, to say the least, ironically, given future events—for lack of 'communication skills'. It turned out to be a case of a mismatch between male and female communication *styles*, with my use 'in inverted commas' of two colloquialisms one interviewer labelled 'swear words'. (Ten months later I had another interview for a job in another part of the Home Office, but this time I faced a lone female, and not from HR but an ordinary worker. Evidently I ticked too many boxes for them to fail me a second time.)

Regarding internal interviews for promotion, the problem is still worse, because by now the female interviewee may well be within the female interviewer's personal network.

Performance in the job by female workers will tend to be problematic because of the relative failure to identify with the 'in-group' of fellow workers, and to focus instead on personal connectedness rather than the task at hand. This will reduce efficiency in the workplace directly, but there is also a further impact in that those members of the work group that the top clique of female workers do not feel personally related to, will feel rejected. As a result, they will either become de-motivated, or work more for themselves and competitively against the group. This is the opposite of how male workers would tend to behave. Men experience a mutually reinforcing sense of belonging to a group, and competitiveness on behalf of the group (as well as individual effort within it to try to rise to the top).

The current notion though, is that women make better employees than men. Men are thought to be 'bolshy' and women compliant. Yet the more rule-based existence of men—apparent right from the days of school play-

ground team sports—makes them likely to be more predictable and reasonable than women. Countless television advertisements (exemplified by
the excruciating BT 'work smarter' series, but long ubiquitous), proclaim a
contest of male 'dimwits' versus female 'smarties'. In fact, the average
intelligence difference of five IQ points is in men's favour, which is amplified by the male sex-typical distribution (see chapter five). The problem is
female mediocrity, which appears virtuous and high-achieving, especially
by contrast to how men are seen, because of the prejudices born of the
social psychology of 'cheater detection'.

Some think that men are too status-orientated, without seeing that there
is a problem with women employees of being too person-centred. Both
male and female sex-typical behaviours could be regarded either as distractions from or contributions to the work culture, but employers certainly do prefer women (as a 1996 Rowntree report showed). Yet it is men
who have the additional clear attributes of being both task-centred and of
forming teams within the workplace, rather than personal networks that
may well be more connected with life outside—though sometimes female
work teams are as effective as male ones. Currently, there is a misperception that inter-personal facility necessarily makes for constructive co-operation, and that relational aggression makes for fruitful competition.

* * *

Conclusive evidence of widescale discrimination against men at the job
application stage was uncovered in 2006 by Peter Riach and Judith Rich
(*An Experimental Investigation of Sexual Discrimination in Hiring in the English Labour Market*). They had sent pairs of résumés to employers: one from
a mythical applicant called 'Phillip' and another from a no less fictitious
'Emma', differing from each other only in the most minor details, but sufficient to ensure they would not be detected as being identical. The experience, qualifications, age, marital status, socio-economic background—
every relevant detail—were as near to identical as could make no difference. They awaited the offer of an interview (or a request for a telephone
discussion) or a rejection note (or silence).

Nobody was prepared for the result. Not even the direction of it, let
alone the size. It was not women but men who got the fewer offers, and by
not a small margin but by a massive factor of *four*. Uncannily, this is precisely the same factor by which women prefer other women to men, as discovered in research into the female social psychology of 'in-group'. Have
workplaces completely capitulated to basing their hiring entirely on
female prejudice? (HR is a predominately female profession.)

If the fourfold disparity was not startling enough, compounding the
surprise were the job sectors where this applied. The persisting problem of
serious discrimination against men trying to get secretarial jobs was found

thirty years ago in the USA (Levinson, 1975), and it was at almost exactly the same level as it is today—applications being twice as likely to be rejected. It was and is much harder for men to get accepted into 'female jobs' than for women to get in to 'male jobs', even though in content they are 'gender neutral'. There are two reasons for this. 'Female' jobs are more to do with sex-typical aspects than are their 'male' counterparts; and men are perceived as odd to be going for a lower-status 'female' job, whereas women are not in any way looked down on or viewed as deviant in applying for a 'male' job. This is because only men are judged in terms of status. This world of female sex-typical work carries on as if in a previous age. Jobs are advertised in magazines like *Girl About Town* using key words like 'bubbly' and 'vivacious', and obtained through agencies such as *Office Angels*. Employers relate that agencies ring up and ask: 'I've got a gentleman for you; will that be all right?'.

It's common knowledge that sexism towards men remains rife in female sex-typical jobs like the secretary, but nobody would have thought that this extended to professional work, but this was the focus of Riach and Rich's research. The shock is that there is now even more discrimination against men in male sex-typical jobs: and in the higher-status professional jobs, at that. This is notably in accountancy, and also in what is possibly the most obviously male sex-typical work sector of all—information technology—and in the very niche within this which is most so: the job of computer programmer/analyst. This may well have something to do with the fact that the numbers of women in IT, that were never high, are now declining.

The study's authors point out that their findings are consistent with all previous research that shows that the vast bulk of discrimination occurs at the invitation to interview stage. This preferential choice of women for interview is clearly 'affirmative action', which is illegal, and could see many occupations becoming 'female-dominated'.

Employers must now not merely ignore the problems they are likely to experience with women employees—maternity, greater sickness absence, and a less committed attitude to work, the workplace and to colleagues that recent research shows—but perversely preferring women in spite of them. It's not that employers have *objectively* recognised women to be better than men. In the absence of objectivity there is only prejudice.

There may also be damage limitation. Those who run small- to medium-sized businesses complain that they are not in a position to decline female applicants, because they simply cannot afford the cost of employment tribunal cases for sex discrimination. It's easy for a woman to bring a case of little if any substance, with an easily-made prima facie argument at no cost to themselves, but at crippling cost to employers regardless of the outcome. It could be that in larger organisations, this consideration, allied to a desire to engage in 'positive action', significantly exacerbates the prejudice towards men to account for the scale of sex discrimination against them.

* * *

Men are starting to do something about discrimination against them — reluctantly, as usual — and now make up *more than half* of the complaints about discrimination. There have been high-profile and blatant cases that raise public awareness — such as at BT and the US cosmetics firm which refused to promote or even to employ men. But through the usual prejudices, these have been quickly forgotten.

The laws on sex discrimination may have started to break down some anti-male barriers, but there is abuse of sex-discrimination law itself, whereby women can actually avoid being treated equally to men, and instead be given special favour. This was exemplified by an Employment Tribunal case in 1990 when a civil servant, Mrs Meade-Hill, sought to be exempted from the 'mobility rule' whereby anyone on her job grade may be required to relocate. Her argument was that as a secondary earner to her husband, she would have to get his agreement, which was unfair compared to a man in a similar situation. As the salaries of wives are typically much less than their husbands', then it was considered that her situation fell under 'indirect' sex discrimination. She won. This was despite her job paying a primary earner's salary — as shown by half the staff being male — and despite the 'mobility' rule being apparently no problem for women staff — as shown by the other half of the staff being female.

The point is that the 'mobility rule' is no less resented by men, who could with equal or even more force argue that their wives as mothers were firmly rooted and also the key decision-makers in the household, making it impossible to move.

What this case shows is that sex discrimination law favours women in both ways. *Direct* sex-discrimination law precludes a woman being treated in her job as a secondary earner and being disadvantaged as such, but *indirect* sex-discrimination law precludes a woman being treated in her job the same as everyone else — as a primary earner — if this somehow disadvantages her. A man would always be considered a primary earner, whether or not this disadvantaged him. If a man was a secondary earner in his individual circumstances, then this couldn't be used under indirect sex discrimination law, because this is not a typical situation for a man. And even where for men their typical situation does disadvantage them, the law still doesn't work for them. This is clear sex discrimination in the sex-discrimination law itself.

I came up against this when the company I worked for stopped paying sick pay until after the first three weeks of any sickness. This was more bearable for the majority of the staff, who were women part-timers with a full-time primary earner to support them. As one of the minority full-time male staff, I pointed out that I had no such fallback, and that it was sex-typical for a man to be the sole or main provider for his household, as I was. It was clear indirect sex discrimination, but the employer disagreed, as did my local law centre, and an angry female ACAS advisor. (My employer settled ahead of an Employment Tribunal, so I was denied the chance of testing the law.)

The law is therefore being applied to make for equal treatment except where this is disadvantageous to women, when it is then applied to make for *un*equal treatment. That sex-discrimination law actually *produces* sex discrimination is an amazing state of affairs, but this is even the case when it comes to the Equal Pay Act itself, and here it is even more systematic.

It was thought that the Equal Pay Act (1970) would end pay discrimination, but rate-for-the-job parity long ago ceased to be an issue; cases being vanishingly rare. Sex discrimination in pay has long been the deliberate confusion between rate-for-the-job parity and a between-sex equalisation of average wages. So an amendment to the Equal Pay Act in 1984 artificially extended the concept by the 'equal value' ruse to the rate for the *similar* job. This has been an open door for bizarre comparisons between what actually were highly *dis*similar jobs, such as in the famous Enderby case. Here, the bogus, but eventually successful, claim was made that the job of speech therapist was comparable to the jobs of pharmacist and clinical psychologist. Yet the reason speech therapy is a female profession is that essentially it's personal care and teaching with a very narrow technical component, and consequently easily attracts recruits without needing to offer high pay.

The notion of 'equal value' is seen to be bogus when you look at all kinds of jobs whose comparability seems sensible at first glance. But they are usually close to meaningless, especially if they are across employment sectors. It's highly misleading to directly compare line managers when, for example, one is a site manager of an oil drilling platform (almost certainly male) and the other a housing benefit department supervisor (often female). The pay disparity would be obvious and well justified. The culture of a public service body could hardly be in starker contrast to a lean and competitive company. Just as misleading would be to directly compare sales personnel to include both the lowly invoice clerk (usually female) and the high-pressure sales 'closer' (usually male). The stress profiles are incomparable, as reflected in the closer's pay as bonuses for results instead of salary. He is paid generously by results because relatively few people are either willing or able to do this kind of job.

'Equal value' is open sex discrimination against men, used to destroy the pay premium for 'dirty' or 'heavy' jobs that is the entire reason that men take them. Councils have been under pressure to equalise the wages of staff such as part-time school 'dinner ladies' with those of full-time 'dustmen'. Catering staff, care workers and the like, across the land, had been inspired by the victory of a Liverpool cook in undermining the legitimate pay differential with outdoor workmen. It's clearly nonsense to equate such radically different jobs. Nobody other than the politically-motivated would seriously argue that a 'dustman' should not be paid very significantly more than a 'dinner lady'. Of course, if pay differentials are artificially removed, then reality will have to be engaged with, to get round the inappropriate application of the law, by special bonus payments to stop workers quitting. A job that pays the same as the lowly-paid jobs that some women do, is actually worse than useless for prime working-age men, who are universally expected — and have expectations of themselves — to be the main breadwinner.

The most serious sex discrimination of all is that institutionalised in the use of targets to try to artificially equalise male and female employment at all levels of organisations. The Home Office has what it terms an 'aspiration' to equalise the rates of employment of the sexes at all higher grades. The official stated policy is that 45% of employees at grade six and above should be women. It's termed an 'aspiration' in an attempt to circumvent the law, but it's indistinguishable from a target. Note that instead of 50% it is just short of this. Again, this is a ruse to try to get round the legislation. The problem is that given that the sexes have very different sex-typical normal distribution curves re performance (see chapter five), then even apart from other considerations (such as those that explain the pay gap), it would be expected that the proportion of males in an organisation increases dramatically as you move up the levels in an organisation. To achieve what the Home Office desires cannot be done without wholesale direct sex discrimination against men in respect of promotion. Sooner or later someone is going to test the law. Class action anyone?

Summary

Work is the main arena where men compete with each other for status, which men have to do if they are to have any 'mate value'. This does not apply to women, whose 'mate value' is inherent. Inevitably then, men will always tend to outdo women at work.

The difference in motivation between the sexes is most telling when it comes to top jobs, and we would expect this from the contrast in the sex-typical distribution (see chapter five). Sure enough, not only are women not getting into the boardroom, but even as senior managers their numbers are collapsing. This belies the idea that men and women are essentially the same and that their behaviour will converge over time.

A fraction only of women view work in the way that men do. The small proportion of women in continuous full-time employment is no greater today than it was 150 years ago. Instead women mix work and home-making. They overwhelmingly prefer to work part-time if at all, and this is a free choice. This makes sense in terms of the economic law of comparative advantage. If any sex overall does more work, it's not women but men; and that's even without taking into account that most of what women do in the household does not fit agreed definitions of work.

The pay gap is far less than it should be given male–female differences in motivation and distraction by other duties. The gap disappears if you compare like with like: that is, single childless people. It becomes ever more apparent where more and more women are being cajoled to enter the labour market, given that these tend to be women who would rather be home-makers. This is why the pay gap is actually widening in countries where policies to reduce it are strongest.

Women's jobs are not regarded as low-value because women fill them, but because the jobs women do are more easily filled. Women eschew work that compromises female dignity or does not fit female predilections. Furthermore, women naturally assort with same-sex co-workers, so the sexes work not so much in a hierarchical divide as in parallel.

There are major implications of the radically different social psychologies of the sexes in terms of the 'in-group'. Men make more natural team workers and can better assimilate new workers, whereas women's personal networks can get in the way of this. The use of both work and sexual modes by women is bound to lead to crossed wires and unfairness to men in harassment claims.

The work hierarchy is antithetical to the female personal network, so women tend to view those women who climb the hierarchy as 'breaking the rules' and resent them accordingly. So there are intra- as well as inter- sex problems that come from women in the workplace.

That women tend to prefer their own sex to men by a factor of four, whereas men have no preference for their own sex, cannot but impact seriously on the workplace, notably in recruitment and promotion. Men are not welcome in female sex-typical jobs, whereas women don't suffer the reverse.

Sex discrimination law produces preferential treatment of women and sex discrimination against men; notably by equal-pay law regarding jobs supposedly of 'equal value'. It also allows for either special treatment for women or treatment identical to men, whichever is advantageous to women in the particular case. Employers now unfairly favour women four times as much as men for professional jobs – even those where men have always tended to excel more than women.

Chapter 10

Home Lies

Violence between partners is *not* mostly by men

O f the various ways that men are supposed to have 'power' over women, perhaps most people would say that domestic or intimate partner violence is the clearest. A key phenomenon of the late twentieth/ early twenty-first century is the complete blindness to the truth that domestic violence (henceforth DV), or 'intimate partner violence' is not a male-on-female issue, but is *non*-'gendered'. That is, it's perpetrated by both sexes. In fact, it's predominantly a *female*-on-male phenomenon. If it is 'gendered', then it's not a male crime but a female one.

This general conclusion is one of the most emphatic in all social science. Comprehensive overviews are provided by the leading UK experts, Dr Malcolm George (George, 2003) and Professor John Archer (Archer, 2000), as well as many of the leading US researchers, such as Murray Straus (Straus, 1999). Most damning of all for the feminist advocacy position is that published in 2005 by Donald Dutton and Tonia Nicholls (*The Gender Paradigm in Domestic Violence Research and Theory*). But my role here is not to produce a deluge of citations. It's to cut through to the main points, and examine why 'advocacy' retorts are empty.

Quite apart from a simple comparison of the incidence or prevalence of DV according to sex, there is another way of looking at DV that is illuminating. This is to look at the violence of each sex against the other as a proportion of all of the violence that each sex engages in. A very small fraction of violent acts by men are against women, whereas women are violent towards men at twice the rate that they are to their fellow women. (Though when women are on their own, in prison, in almost ubiquitous homosexual relationship, then they tend to be considerably more violent even than their male counterparts.) In this sense, DV is indeed 'gendered'. It's the most common mode of violence by women, but the least common by men.

The collapse of the idea of 'gendered' violence

The root of the popular misapprehension that DV is a women's issue is very simple. If you only look at those in (women's) refuges or in criminal proceedings; or if you only ask women, or both men and women but only about DV as a *crime:* then unsurprisingly you will find that there are few male victims compared to female. It can appear to be 'gender neutral' to ask men whether they have themselves been on the receiving end of the crime of DV, but they will often or usually answer 'no', even if they have been persistently and seriously assaulted by their women partners. This is because men don't usually regard physical assault against them by their partner as criminal, no matter how serious.

To get the real picture of what is going on violence-wise between the sexes in *both* directions, all you have to do is to remove the 'demand characteristic' that responses are about crime per se, and instead to make a graded list of kinds of aggressive actions, and hand them out to people of both sexes, reassuring them that it is an anonymous social survey about violence in the home. Then men will reply far more honestly, and the real extent of women's DV is revealed. This is then corroborated by asking questions using the same graded list not just about sustaining DV but also perpetration, and again by both sexes. To provide still further confidence in the findings, both men and women partners in the same couples are studied. Such a graded list has been devised, and then refined to put the specific violent acts in context to get a better handle on their actual seriousness. This is the Conflict Tactics Scale (CTS). For upwards of twenty-five years, studies using this have bulked into a body of data where female-on-male DV can be compared with male-on-female.

Professor Martin Fiebert has compiled a regularly-updated reference list with abstracts of *all* studies — not a cherry-picked subset — where male- and female-perpetrated DV are compared (Fiebert, 2007). Of the now over 200 studies and overviews, *not a single one* shows significantly more aggression in the male-to-female direction. Some of the studies show a roughly equal perpetration, but most show either a significant or a considerable preponderance of aggression female-on-male.

They provide a comprehensive picture of the variety of DV. The great majority of it is low-level and tit-for-tat, that most people would hesitate to describe as violence. Even if they did, they would regard it as trivial. Most of this is female-on-male. At the other extreme, where there is no doubt that serious and/or serial violence is being used against the other partner, again women predominate as perpetrators. Where women most outdo men in perpetration is actually for the *more serious* as well as the least serious violence.

Seeing as only a very small proportion of couples experience severe DV, and as DV is not 'gendered', then DV is not the social problem that feminist advocates would have us believe. It's not even remotely on the scale or direction required by a theory based on supposed 'patriarchy'. And male- on-female DV has fallen dramatically in recent years.

Even crime surveys are now destroying the notion that DV is over-whelmingly a problem for the one, female, sex. Famously, in 1996, the Home Office's own supplement to that year's British Crime Survey (BCS) returned exactly the same proportion (4.2%) of both men and women reporting being the victim of DV at some point over the previous year. Vic-timisation was 50/50. This roughly accords with the figures in the supple-ments to the BCS since 2001: male DV victims as a proportion of all victims have varied around 40% — which in turn is in accord with similar data in developed countries around the world. Even the cruder measures in the BCS come out at an average of 24%. The point is that at a quarter or a half; either way, male victims are a substantial proportion. In the face of the rea-sons unique to men for under-reporting then, for all the Home Office knows, these figures could hide a large number of male victims, perhaps twice the female total, as some of the proper social science research indi-cates. Still at least the Home Office does now publicise the least inaccurate of the crime-based measures. The standard line now is that men are 40% of DV victims, though the Home Office puts it in terms of 'lifetime' risk: one in four of women, and one in six of men.

The use of 'lifetime' measures serves to inflate and so misrepresent the scale of the issue, of course. And this is augmented by changing the label from DV to 'domestic abuse'. 'Abuse' is of course a meaningless notion in the hands of those who consider that axiomatically all that men do to women is abuse. It's very easy to elide distinctions between serious and trivial DV, and to relentlessly define down what DV can run to; then to present it as the burning issue of the times. The redefinition to 'domestic abuse' backfires badly though, as I will explain.

In the face of undeniable findings available for the last decade or two, there has been relentless misrepresentation by a research–activist commu-nity (distinct from the social science research establishment proper), serving political rather than scientific goals. Objective social science research is ignored, activists insisting instead on using only data that came from crime surveys, or from those presented to respondents as *female* vic-timisation surveys, and/or with demand characteristics and filters to minimise or eliminate males reporting on their own victimisation. If all else failed, studies were either published with all data on male victims omitted, or the entire study was suppressed (examples are well docu-mented and an overview is provided by Christina Hoff Summers in her book, *Who Stole Feminism*). The bogus conclusions from the activist-inspired studies allowed extreme feminists within both academia and the media to bring about a climate of opinion which encouraged politicians to formulate policies that targeted the female vote.

* * *

There have been a number of increasingly desperate defences, but each has collapsed. First was the attempt to distract from the aggression uncovered in women through focusing on physical injuries sustained. It's usually but mistakenly accepted that twice as many women are injured as men, but even if this disparity were true, a considerably greater disparity than a twofold difference would be expected – given the weaker and more fragile female body. You have to consider not just the sex dichotomy in strength, but also that of resilience of the body frame. A good comparison here is with the very large sex difference in the injury rate between men and women in military training. Women have been pulled out altogether from many training regimes, or requirements have been drastically scaled down, because of the unsustainably high attrition rates through injury – very many times higher than for men. Military training, however, does not have the 'double whammy' of both fragility and relative weakness: the disparity in injury rates is through the sexes pitting themselves against the same inanimate assault course, whereas in DV they are pitted against each other. Here one would expect that the much higher upper-body strength of men would make a dramatic difference. Multiplying these two factors together should push the sex difference 'off the scale'. Evidently the disparity in injury does not go 'off the scale' or anywhere near, so it appears that the general male inhibition from hitting women (see below) prevents the upper-body strength differential coming into play.

A mere two-fold disparity in the rate of injury – rather than a multiple of, say, ten times or more – could be explained only by a predominance of violence *from* women to men. But even a mere two-fold difference is not what the data is now showing (see overviews by Dr Malcolm George). There are many studies showing men suffering more injury than women at all levels of seriousness, but especially regarding severe injury. Particularly galling for the American National Violence Against Women Prevention Research Center, an analysis of their own data (Felson & Cares, 2005) showed that while men more frequently than women caused minor injuries in those they aggressed against, this was not the case regarding severe injuries. It was men who suffered in this far more worrying way. Yet this is from results obtained from a survey actually presented to respondents as one about female victimisation.

The previous masking of this reality is not least because of the relative failure of men to present themselves for medical treatment; or, when they do, not to reveal that it is the result of DV. Men are not asked if this is what gave rise to the injury – women are routinely asked as a matter of 'preventative healthcare'. When men do report DV, they tend not to report injury, even in confidence in a one-to-one interview with a researcher (as opposed to filling in a self-completion survey). In any face-to-face situation, such as

A licence to kill

A uniquely female ploy to rebuff a murder charge is the plea of 'delayed self-defence'. This is the invented notion that whereas men cool down over time, women instead boil over. Underpinning this is the equally bogus concept that what makes females peculiarly fume over a longer timeframe is 'cumulative provocation'. Of course, this allows women to premeditate murder at a juncture when the spouse has dropped his guard and can't use his strength to restrain her. The legal system now actively justifies and thereby encourages this. A string of women convicted of murder for killing their husbands whilst they slept and/or poisoning them all had their sentences reduced to manslaughter through 'diminished responsibility'.

The most famous of these women, Sara Thornton, drugged her husband Malcolm to sleep before knifing him to death. Convicted of murder, when re-tried on the basis of the new defence, she claimed that it was not her husband but herself who was the victim, with a supposed history of 'battery'. Yet no evidence was presented in court to substantiate this and Malcolm's relatives were certain that he was in no way violent. His first wife said Sara's release was 'a licence for any woman to kill her husband and say whatever she wants to say about him after he's dead.' Even Sara's own father and step-mother were against her.

It was clear that not only was there delay between any provocation and the murder, but also premeditation. Four days before the murder, Sara told a colleague that she was going to kill Malcolm, and she had fed him a meal laced with tranquilisers. Just 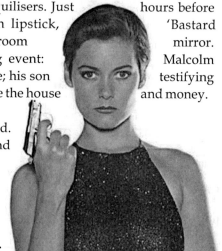 hours before the crime she had scrawled in lipstick, 'Bastard Thornton, I hate you' on the bedroom mirror. There was a clear precipitating event: Malcolm had told her he wanted a divorce; his son testifying that she feared that she might lose the house and money.

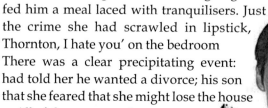

All of the women whose cases were re-examined were acquitted. Carol Peters drugged her husband and then stabbed him 39 times; Pamela Sainsbury strangled her husband with a rope while he was sleeping; Zoora Shah administered a fatal dose of arsenic; Josephine Smith shot her sleeping husband in the head; and Kiranjit Ahluwalia burned her husband alive in his bed.

dealing with police, CAFCASS (regarding family court proceedings) or other public bodies, then both DV and injuries tend very much to be played down, for pretty obvious reasons. That rates of injury are in fact similar or the reverse of that often claimed, confirms that the aggression must be predominantly female-to-male.

With no concrete evidential base for the extreme feminist DV edifice remaining, the next staged retreat was to declare all of the research beside the point, on the grounds that the violence by women is retaliatory self-defence. The data comprehensively rules this out. Not only are women responsible for most DV, but they also account for most of the initiation. Roughly speaking, there seems to be an equivalence, with about half of DV so mutual that it is hard to tease out the initiator from the retaliator; and of which a very small proportion is severe violence and fully mutual. The other half is split between male and female strikers of the first blow. Within this overall picture, however, is hidden a threefold excess of women among those who unilaterally aggress against either completely non-violent or only minimally aggressive partners. And this is evident whichever way round the reporting is done: from the victim or from the aggressor (Stets & Straus, 1992). When you consider *serious* violence with minimal or nil violence in return, then the sex difference rises to between three and six times as many women perpetrators (Stets & Straus, 1990).

Closely examining families where wives are known to be violent, in 2004 Sotirios Sarantakos interviewed all of the children, friends and relatives he could find; and found that even the wives' mothers disputed any claim that their daughters' violence was anything to do with self-defence. Research clearly shows self-defence to be a minor motive for female violence, and that conversely it is men who are having to use self-defence, by attempting to restrain women attackers (which is itself misconstrued as DV).

Viewing female DV as self-defence is tied up with a raw anti-male prejudice that men are the real agents of anything that is negative, whereas women's violence is supposedly flash-in-the-pan and a reaction to something intolerable that has been bottled up. (Presumably, extreme feminists mean that somehow it has been put there by a man.) On this model, female DV is characterised as 'expressive' whilst that of men is 'instrumental' — somehow channelling 'patriarchy' in order to exercise control. This un-scientific assertion lasted only until the research community got around to analysing the contexts of when DV occurs according to sex. The instru-mentality of most male violence towards women is nothing more than restraint, which is merely the minimal use of a strength advantage to react to an emergency. It has nothing to do with the instrumentality extreme feminists suppose. Not only is 'expressive' violence at least as much in evidence from men as it is from women, but women actually use violence *more* instrumentally than do men. Even a vague understanding of the nature of female violence would tell you this. Women actually prefer to use 'indirect' or 'relational' aggression, at which they are expert; this being a much more strategic, risk-free approach to behaving maliciously (as befits the sex that is the more prized, being the 'limiting factor' in reproduction). With DV redefined to include 'psychological abuse', the instrumentality of women's DV becomes starkly apparent.

Fear

The next extreme feminist defence is to deny not just all of the evidence, but even the possibility of evidence. This is the phenomenological appeal to subjective experience—that there is something special about being a female victim not shared by men. Women feel specially threatened and frightened, we are told, making DV a qualitatively different experience for them.

But fear is not merely subjective, it is squarely based on an objective calculation of risk that we've evolved to cope with. And it can be measured. Fear tends to be on full and exaggerated show in women because of its benefit as a ploy to attract male care and protection (unlike in men, where displaying fear clashes with the imperative not to show weakness). Sure enough, women are unreasonably scared about the actual risk (adjusted for respective probability) of being killed by a partner. That they are naturally twice as fearful compared to men is no reason to justify the special pleading to view DV against women as distinct.

Amongst the multiple misunderstandings here is that only men can intimidate by malicious control, and that physical injury is the only serious harm that can be threatened and feared in a domestic situation.

Just focusing on physical violence: what is particularly disturbing for the serial victim (of either sex) is never knowing when the mood of a partner is going to suddenly turn to precipitate violence. But for most women, the fear from a partner is always tempered by the realisation everyone shares that all normal men have a deeply-ingrained inhibition from striking women, so that even if a woman is in a DV situation, she knows she would be very unlucky to be seriously injured. This does not apply if the perpetrator is a sociopath, but such aberrant individuals are very thin on the ground, and in any case the only women prepared to partner them usually are complicit in being 'violence-prone'. Erin Pizzey, the founder of the women's refuge movement, revealed—to the fury of the feminist movement—that many of the women who took refuge had a personality such that they sought abusive relationships, and most were as or more violent than their partners..

By contrast, for men there is a double problem arising from the inhibition from hitting women all normal men have. They are at risk of sustaining serious injury if they only have recourse to attempts to restrain; and

Erin Pizzey, founder of the women's refuge movement was denounced by feminists for revealing that many of the people she helped were psychologically 'prone to violence'

women are indeed capable of inflicting serious injury because they have no corresponding inhibition against hitting men. Even just attempting restraint causes problems for a man. It's liable to provoke an escalation of violence by the woman, and if holding her wrists or neck causes minor injury, then this can easily be sufficient for the woman to get him arrested as not the victim but the perpetrator of DV. This is very likely, because women use 'relational' or 'indirect' aggression as their preferred mode, and most police forces have still not officially wised up to this travesty, notwithstanding that DV recently has been redefined to include all kinds of abuse and supposed abuse. Not having a corresponding inhibition, women not only readily use more severe violence, but they take a no-holds-barred attitude. The great majority of weapon use in DV is by women: notably the use of knives, but also any object that comes to hand. Head injuries caused by heavy thrown objects is common only amongst male DV victims. Women take advantage of the fact that for most of the time a partner cannot be on guard, and commonly attack men when they are sleeping or otherwise off-guard, whereas men never do this.

In trying to understand the fear of DV, what is missed is that it's not about the risk of being physically injured, but the risk of losing what the victim in staying in the domestic situation is trying to hang on to. For men, an especial and very real fear — one that is supported by abuse statistics —

is that women who practice DV are also physically abusing their own children. A male victim knows that it's easy for him to be thrown out of his own home, which then leaves his children entirely at the mercy of the woman perpetrator. In the absence of him to function as the main punch-bag, the children may become objects of her violence by displacement. Because men feel very strongly that they are the protectors of their family, then any aspect of the home situation that is out of control or is at risk of being lost is both a great worry and destructive of their personal sense of worth. For any man, the relationship with the woman of his life is in itself central to this. Men are unlike women in usually having no emotional support network outside their own family. With the prospect of losing his partner, contact with his children, the roof over his head, all savings and most of his income; a man has much more at stake in the family household than a woman has. All she stands to lose is her partner.

Women do not have this constellation of factors to compound their anxiety, or not to the same degree. In particular there is no real corresponding fear of violence to their children. As data readily shows, most physical abuse of children is by either the mother or a step-parent. Natural fathers are by very many times the least likely to physically abuse their own children—especially if they are married to the mother. (For the very reason that the data readily shows this, figures for physical abuse tend no longer to be broken down. The NSPCC notably and unforgivably continues with this, despite it being repeatedly pointed out to them. The very large differential between natural- and step-parents in this regard is very well researched because it relates to a fundamental evolutionary principal that those who are genetically related have a mutual consideration on a much higher plain than that between non-kin—I discuss the date in chapter 14.) With violence the substantial thing that women have to fear in DV, they know that they will attract support wherever they seek it, and that this is in itself a highly potent weapon against the man who is, or who is threatening to, victimise them. She can even kill him and claim a 'delayed time' self-defence that is evidently only available to women (see panel on page 164, above). No such support—indeed quite the opposite: age-old ridicule or an assumption that his injuries are through self-defence by the woman and that he is therefore the real abuser—is what a man can expect. This traps him in silence. He is already disadvantaged by the very locus of his nightmare being formerly his sole or main source of emotional support.

The fear that a man has in a DV scenario is the possible destruction of everything he values in his life outside work (which a man often if not usually views as a major cost—endurable only for the sake of his family), the collapse in his sense of self-worth, and serious injury: in respect of all of which he has little if any prospect of avoidance, support or redress. The fear that a woman has in a DV scenario is usually superficial injuries.

Plays such as Who's Afraid of Virginia Woolf *and* Abigail's Party
demonstrate that domestic abuse doesn't have to entail physical violence

A full picture of the horror of these situations for men can be found in a 2001 summary of unstructured interviews with men from a variety of backgrounds by Ann Lewis and Sotirios Sarantakos. What comes across is the sheer range, inventiveness, multiplicity, manipulativeness and ruthlessness of the women's abuse. Extreme controlling and intimidating behaviour was to the fore, including direct challenges to the man's sense of care and protection of, and responsibility and fear for, his children, by threatening to and actually harming them. In particular there were false allegations of DV to authorities. Uniformly the men felt pain, loss, an enormous feeling of betrayal, chronic collapse of self-esteem; and ... *fear*. Fear that was chronic to the point of manifesting as psychosomatic symptoms. Apart from despair, powerlessness and confusion, persisting through all this was a feeling that the situation was their own fault. Suicidal thoughts were common. All of this was on top of serious physical injuries. However you may characterise the collective experiences of these male victims of DV, it's not less serious than any amount of distinctively female 'fear' that women victims may feel. The special pleading on behalf of women of fear is yet another handful of sand in the face of the truth.

* * *

With the collapse of the extreme feminist position regarding DV, the advocacy lobby can only try to save face by recycling previously discredited positions under a new guise. One way is to change the goal-posts by redefining DV as 'domestic abuse'. But as an examination of the question of fear illustrates, and as we would expect from the female predilection for 'relational aggression', this puts the boot very much on the other foot. The preponderance of female perpetration by this new measure is likely several times more than it is by men. DV has indeed now become 'gendered', but in the opposite direction.

The other option for the advocacy lobby to try to save face is to give in and agree that the research community is right, but that so too are they. This is the position of Michael P. Johnson, who first proposed his now much discussed DV typologies in 1995. Johnson distinguishes between on the one hand mutual 'situational couple violence', and on the other unilateral 'intimate terrorism' and the possible reaction to it of 'violent resistance' (which somehow may not be restricted to self-defence), or (more rarely) 'mutual violent control' (Johnson, 2005, 2006). The analysis is just the usual notion of 'patriarchy' but in still more pejorative terms, though with the addition of a 'non-patriarchal' form. The idea is that 'gendering' applies only to 'intimate terrorism' and (in reverse) to the possible response to it; but again, it's only rehashing positions that have been found wanting. Johnson sees the factor underlying the distinction between his DV types as 'control', but this is just to reassert the contention that men instrumentally generate a special fear. So, of course, as soon as the research community look into this typology, no 'gendering' is found (Graham-Kevan, 2007; Graham-Kevan & Archer, 2005). Graham-Kevan concludes in one of her two 2007 papers: 'From the literature reviewed here, it is clear that controlling behavior and physical aggression co-occur and that the use of controlling behavior is not a male or a heterosexual preserve.'

Why does DV happen? 'Mate guarding'

'Control' is actually a useful concept in the aetiology of DV, but of no help to the advocacy lobby to get it off the hook. As with any violence, DV has a complex set of causes, and it comes in various forms. There are the dysfunctional mutual batterers who seem to need each other's violence, that Erin Pizzey discovered (and Johnson, apparently, also discovered). These are outliers who have an abnormal relationship dynamic all their own. Then there are those with psychological borderline states and personality disorders that predispose to more unilateral explosive violence. Surprisingly, these are mainly women—a threefold preponderance, and these conditions are linked to female sex hormones (Evardone et al, 2007).

The most famous case of a female personality-disordered DV perpetrator is that of Sara Thornton (see panel on page 164, above). In 1995 Thornton was released from prison after her retrial reduced the conviction to manslaughter on the grounds of diminished responsibility. She had murdered her defenceless husband and then murdered his reputation, and the personality disorder that underpinned her violent behaviour was actually cited as an excuse for her premeditating murder, rather than being used as evidence of her predilection for DV and hence culpability. Needless to say, there are no cases of a similar scenario with the sexes reversed. A personality disorder is no defence for a male.

Mild derangement may explain a minority of serious aggressors, but it begs the question of just why women should be prone to being violent here, when in other scenarios they are not. In any case, these rare kinds of DV don't tell us what is going on more generally, especially with the far less serious and mostly quite minor violence that is the great bulk of DV.

This brings us back to 'control', which potentially can become pathological to the point of making life hell for the other partner, such that he/she is in constant fear of what might come next. Normally, however, 'control' is benign; and more than that, it's a healthy sign in a marriage, and it's mostly by women. That it's by women might be expected given that the domestic domain is very much a woman's sphere of influence in the separate worlds of the sexes. It's her 'power' base. This is common 'folk' wisdom, that we regularly confirm from our own social knowledge of how men and women relate in couples. Very recent research (Vogel & Murphy et al., 2007) showed that women take responsibility and power in marriage. Murphy summed up: 'Women are responsible for overseeing the relationship—making sure the relationship runs, that everything gets done, and that everybody's happy.' Vogel's take on it is that men go along with what women say—agreeing or giving in.

Men are here being deferent, which as I've explained previously, is not submission behaviour, but non-engagement (in dominance terms). Vogel, Murphy et al., talk of wives being more 'domineering and dominant' than their husbands, but this is not interpretation based on observation so much as bogus convention. There are none of the hallmarks of dominance in what I refer to as 'control'.

The 'control' here is what biologists and ethologists call 'mate guarding': behaviour to stop a long-term (pair-bonded) partner from straying. Men, like the males of most species, employ tactics to try to head off the possibility of raising offspring who aren't their own. Effort is directed mainly at male rivals—would-be adulterers—but also at the partner to try to prevent her from briefly going off with another man and having sex. This male mate guarding can be seen clearly in all societies, not least the more 'primitive'. For the usual reasons of bias stemming from the male being the agentic sex, it's been assumed that mate guarding is a peculiarly male behaviour. The corresponding mate guarding by women has only now been picked up by researchers — notably by John Archer and his team, who see it as being quite different from the male version (Archer et al., 2001; personal communication, 2005).

Female mate guarding is not a recently evolved phenomenon. There is a high level of unilateral female-on-male aggression in some primates, notably the Mongoose lemur, which has been found to concern mate monopolisation by females (e.g. Anzenberger, 1992, 1993). Females in most primate species have the problem that males are always much more inclined than they are to try to obtain sex outside of a pair bond — women most certainly not excepted. In humans, mate guarding is inherently a bigger problem for women. However, it's not, as with men, designed primarily to prevent a partner's brief sneaky bout of extra-pair sex. There would be less point to this for women because it doesn't threaten the long-term pair bond from the woman's point of view. Women always know that their children are their own! Instead, women are trying to ensure the continued strength of the pair bond.

This, as opposed to 'patriarchy', is why wives so often stick by their unfaithful husbands, whereas men more usually desert wives at the first instance of their adultery. And it's why extreme jealousy is aroused very differently according to sex — a now heavily-researched finding. Female jealousy is typically aroused by emotional rather than sexual infidelity.

In long-term partnerships, men are valued by women for a combination of their male status and their reliability as providers, so female mate guarding is similarly for the long haul. Any sign that the man is losing interest and becoming blasé about the relationship is a sign that he might not just be seeking occasional sexual variety (which she may well tolerate as a safety valve, and even as confirmation of his continued desirability), but seeking a replacement long-term partner. This is a real fear for women, because as they get older they become less and less attractive. The prospect of desertion is even more threatening to a woman than a partner's extra-pair sex is to men.

Female mate guarding is akin to the hoops women make their partners jump through in choosing them in the first place. A woman continually checks that her partner is up to scratch as likely to be in the relationship for the long haul. There is no equivalent for men, who lose much less if the relationship dissolves. Given that a man's main concern is that the children are indeed his, after conception has become apparent a man's concerns disappear. A woman cannot conceive anyone else's child whilst she's gestating, nor after birth for the whole period she's lactating, which is several years in traditional societies. Male mate guarding therefore can be on hold for years at a stretch. In any case, once his wife has children, a man knows she depends on him more, and that she is progressively losing her attractiveness to other men, both through having children and through increasing age. Female mate guarding, by contrast, not only can never be on hold, but the need for it progressively increases. The absurdly jealous female spouse is not just looking for the concrete evidence of sexual intercourse—an event the occurrence of which is open to clear proof and disproof. She's looking for any attitude—absence of ardour, or any interest in any other women—that might suggest transfer of emotional fidelity. There is no limit to the demand a woman can place on her partner to demonstrate that he's still committed. After all, an emotional attachment can grow from nothing, and grows most assuredly from the very kind of sexual situation that women know only too well that all men are not just vulnerable to, but are likely to succumb to with enthusiasm, if indeed they don't actively seek out possibilities themselves. Women know that other women are likely to use sex as bait to try to develop a committed relationship. The normal attitude of a woman is more likely to be one of permanent suspicion. This means that, unlike for a man, mate guarding by a woman tends not to damp down but to ratchet up. It would seem that the potential for pathological attempts to 'control' the partner is greater for a woman than it is for a man. This is where the stereotype of the 'nagging wife' stems from. Like most 'stereotypes', it is in fact an accurate observation—though it's a comical portrayal of such women, that plays down the pathology of it and the potential for violence.

The unnatural state of modern society exacerbates the problem. Much of what would normally (in traditional societies) be public is instead private; and the 'public' would formerly have been largely your own relatives, looking out for your interests. Living as we do so anonymously, our behaviour cannot be informally 'policed' in the way that it would have been in the past. This makes mate guarding much more difficult, or impossible. We are off the scale of the normal range of contingencies that mateguarding behaviours respond to. This includes the sheer vastness of what today we perceive to be the social environment. There is an ever-expanding pool of those we perceive to be potential rivals, irrespective of the chances of any becoming actual rivals. For a woman, it's the unlimited exposure of their mate to highly attractive young women. No matter that most of these women are on TV and in magazines, or that the closest that the great majority of potential rivals get to impinging on her life is that by chance they pass close by in a car. That they could not possibly threaten the stability of the woman's own pair bond does not diminish her natural response of jealousy.

All this serves to allow pathological mate guarding to blossom. There is a possible underlying biological exacerbation: that mate guarding is an extension of sexual selection. The criteria by which women choose men develops along various lines, one of which may well be tolerating female provocation. Such a test would serve not merely to test male vigour, but it would confer the advantage to women of better guaranteeing that a man would be reliable over the longer term. The process could move on a stage further and pre-emptively provoke men, possibly with behaviour beyond anything men would normally be expected to have to face. DV by women may in part be a test of male quality, perhaps a test that has long been in the female repertoire but that emerges in conditions of social breakdown.

If women are the ones who have control of the domestic domain, rooted in mate guarding—which is more likely to become pathological in women—why does it then lead to violence? For the simple afore-mentioned reason that women, unlike men, have no inhibition to being violent to the opposite sex, and little reason to fear retaliation if they are. This is firmly rooted in the basic fact that separates the sexes: that the female is the 'limiting factor' in reproduction. Males necessarily must have in-built blocks to aggressing against females, for which there will be no counterpart in females. Normal men 'hold back' from hitting women, and would be held in disgrace if they break this taboo. Far from there being a taboo against women hitting men, this is itself a disgrace for the man. Up until the very recent past, a cuckolded and/or beaten husband could expect to suffer ritual mocking by members of his community, in the shaming customs known as the 'skimmington ride' or 'riding the stang' (George, 1994, 2002). Locals would gather outside a cuckold's house to make 'rough music' (a cacophony using household utensils) either with the man or couple in effigy, or they may drag out the man, or the man and his wife, to place him/them on animal back (with the husband facing the rear), to then make a procession through the locality, to general raucous amusement. These appear to be female-instigated customs that were in origin fertility rites, but adapted to register and advertise a man's lowered 'mate value'.

A man is in a 'catch 22' scenario at every turn, in that there are severe constraints on what he can do either to prevent his wife from sexually

Since time immemorial, the cuckold has been a figure of contempt
(William Hogarth, Hudibras Encounters the Skimmington)

straying, or to hold his wife responsible should she do so, to try to prevent any repetition. However angry he may be with his adulteress wife, he will appreciate that any aggression will in some respects turn his wife against him at the very time when she has already shown that she is reckless as to the continuation of the marriage. He needs to draw her closer and convince her he still has the qualities that had attracted her to him. She has herself, by virtue of her adultery, already dented his status, but he won't want to seem still lesser in people's eyes by injuring her; which would also jeopardise her faith in him as being reliable. Ambivalent though he may feel towards his wife, he is obliged to take her on trust. A man's anger in any case will be directed primarily against potential or actual rivals, and only secondarily against his wife. Retaliation against the rival may well assuage much of the aggrieved husband's anger. The rival may end up by displacement also the recipient of the husband's anger towards his wife, because violence against him is admissible, whereas against his wife it isn't. This applies notably in the most 'primitive' and violent societies, such as the Yanomamo. Men are highly likely to be killed by other men over various sexual indiscretions, and a male adulterer will face the husband, his relatives, and the husband's wife's relatives. An adulteress wife, on the other hand, at worst will suffer severed ears or an arrow in a limb. Everything is, as they say, relative! (The very different experience of Muslim and Hebraic cultures — where social practices are derived primarily from canonical texts rather than the codification of biological imperatives — is the exception that proves the rule. Indeed a plausible argument could be made that the 'patriarchal' moral and legal codes deriving from the 'religions of the book' are an attempt to redress the imbalance revealed by the practices of 'natural' societies.)

In short, DV is mainly female-on-male because men 'hold back' through not wanting to be violent towards their partners and being in any case heavily restricted from being so; whereas women 'let rip', because they both want to, and can.

Extreme politicisation

The politicisation of DV is now comprehensively discredited, yet when she was Solicitor General, Harriet Harman (Harm-man?) pressed ahead with a change in the law allowing restraining orders to be placed on men despite being *acquitted* of any charge of DV. We know that Harman means that it's to be applied only to men, because this is how she described it:

> A tough new law which will protect women and offer violent men a choice — stop the violence or you will face prison.

Any man breaching a restraining order will go to prison despite never facing a criminal charge. A restraining order is merely part of the civil law, so any hearing about its breach will itself be subject to the (lesser) civil standard of proof, 'on the balance of probabilities'. So at every stage, applying the criminal law is evaded, and the invitation is clearly made to women to level false accusations in the knowledge that the absence of evidence will be no obstacle to conviction. As in rape, the 'woman's word' is regarded as trumping the word of a man in order, supposedly, to arrive at the truth. And a man's word against a female perpetrator is hardly ever to be heard, because just five percent of cases in special DV courts are of women.

Harman is convinced that DV is a male crime, and enshrines this in a section of the document on DV she oversaw produced by the CPS, where it is spelt out that: 'the overwhelming majority of victims are female and abusers male'. She could not have been clearer than in a speech she made in 2002, that Erin Pizzey described as 'an outburst of hatred against men'. According to Harman:

> Domestic violence is a crime which is a throwback to when men expected to be the boss and were entitled to control their wives and entitled to assault them.

This demonstrates a conception of DV that is wrong-headed in every aspect. When I pressed him about why women should be given all of the attention and resources on the DV issue, Harman's then boss, the Attorney General, came up with two reasons. First, that women are more likely to get injured. Second, that victimisation is greater during pregnancy. The former has been rumbled as a red herring by the research community, as I have explained. The latter is new, but a herring nevertheless.

Far from there being increased DV male-to-female during pregnancy, DV decreases. This is what was found by the US Center for Disease Control and Prevention (CDC), which is the one reliable source of any information about DV and pregnancy—there being no reputable studies; that is, research not using self-selecting samples (US GAO for CDC, 2002). In any case, there is a reason for a false perception here. Younger women are considerably more likely to attack their partners than are older women, and than are younger men. This is particularly so for women from the former working classes, who are the most fertile, most numerous, and who get pregnant at very much younger ages than the average. Without controlling for this, a spurious figure of elevated DV during and after pregnancy is to be expected. Furthermore, it needs to be shown whether or not men are simply blocking or restraining attacks by these younger women—who are still more likely to be perpetrating violence through emotional upset during gestation or post-natal depression. Definitions of DV used by the government wrongly include all restraining/defensive behaviour that men may typically use. Given the findings that men are routinely arrested and in various ways appallingly treated when they are themselves the victims of unilateral violence, then any research is deficient that does not look carefully at the actual nature, severity and mutuality of abuse. It's very apparent that overwhelmingly men are even more than usually caring and protective of their pregnant partners. In the situation where a woman has effectively entrapped her partner by deceit, then this normal care and protection by the man might well not be provided; but in this scenario, according to new definitions of DV to encompass 'abuse', the woman is herself a perpetrator by her emotional behaviour and financial exploitation. This is, after all, classic 'indirect aggression'. To add all forms of 'indirect aggression' by women against men to current figures would turn women from being merely the predominant perpetrating sex to being overwhelmingly so.

The complete refusal to accept that women are the major abusers in most instances is a huge problem in the family courts, staffed as they are by highly-politicised CAFCASS officers (who have a unionised and institutionalised anti-male sexist doctrine of always believing the 'parent with care' and actively challenging the notion that men have any part to play in the family—see chapter fourteen, below). The most obvious locus of harm is the police, where archaic and female-protective attitudes conspire with the successful take-over of 'consultation' by women's activists. Added to the pressure to reduce violent crime statistics through focus on the 'soft' end—to meet Home Office targets—this destroys the integrity of the police to the point of facilitating the prosecution of victims. Large organisations such as Women's Aid and the whole activist–research community stand to lose funding once the truth becomes widely known. All these stakeholders are becoming aware that the extreme feminism at the heart of what is starting to resemble 'PC fascism' will start to be undermined.

The bias against male DV victims has been revealed in North American and Australian research, in surveys in this country for the Channel 4 *Dispatches* programme, in a 1999 Home Office Research Study and in a report based on a survey of male DV victims (George & Yarwood, 2004). Considering the seriousness of the abuse compared to the response, the statistics are alarming. Try inverting the sex of the abuser/victim when you consider this: three-quarters were assaulted once a month or more frequently; over two-thirds had been assaulted more than ten times; half were threatened with a weapon, and a similar proportion were severely bruised; a third were kicked in the genitals; one in five were burnt or scalded.

The police response? A quarter of the respondents said that they themselves had been arrested despite being the victim, half were threatened with arrest despite being the victim, and most of the remainder reported that the police had totally ignored what they had to say. In just three percent of the cases was the violent female partner arrested. Most tellingly of all, female assailants called the police nearly as often as did the male victims. Of the few female assailants arrested and subsequently charged—despite the serious injuries some of the male victims had suffered—not one was convicted.

Summary

The most obvious expression of men's 'power' over women is domestic violence, but this cannot be. The phenomenon is not 'one-way' but 'non-gendered': both sexes are perpetrators. What's more women, not men, predominate – substantially at the rare serious levels and in younger age groups. The feminist advocacy lobby has retreated behind staged special pleadings that the findings are irrelevant, but all have collapsed, including the bogus idea that for women DV is self-defence.

The residual notion of why DV is a different experience for women is fear, but men have not dissimilar responses which the much more ruthless DV by women justifies. Men have much more to fear than violence—the destruction of all family life—and the violence is likely to be completely uninhibited (use of a weapon, when the man is asleep, etc).

The root of DV is 'controlling' behaviour, which both sexes do, but more usually women. This is based on 'mate guarding', which women practice in a different way to men, and which tends more to be pushed to extremes. This, together with the instinctive holding back that men display but which is conspicuously absent in women, may explain why DV is predominantly female-on-male.

Ignoring all evidence, the government allowed the hatred of men to guide law-making. Extreme bias against male victims is now proven. The refusal to in any way accept the evidence leads to women quite literally getting away with murder.

Chapter 11

Rape: Fact, Fantasy and Fabrication

The crime that's 'worse' than murder

Being the ultimate crime of sex difference where, of necessity, only men are perpetrators and only women are victims, rape is a quintessential example of male 'oppression'. This is undermined by the revelations of the scale of 'male rape', but nevertheless rape is an irresistible platform for unbridled hatred towards men. Both public institutions and the media parrot Orwellian and Kafkaesque wrong-headedness about rape. The general public assumes that the law on rape is dispassionate, but it's now completely compromised. The vitriol expressed for the men accused — whether subsequently found guilty or innocent — is on a par with that reserved for murderers (and sometimes worse).

There are several questions key to unravelling the phenomenon of rape to see if the idea that it is male 'oppression' stands up. Is rape on a sufficiently large a scale? Does the experience of rape invariably give rise to serious psychological consequences? Is rape essentially not a sexual but a violent crime? The answers to all these questions is a resounding 'no'. Why is rape considered to be such a heinous crime as to be on a par with murder when — nasty though it can be — self-evidently it isn't? This is the interesting question, the answer to which has deep evolutionary roots.

An epidemic of 'false rape'

Rape is not a ubiquitous phenomenon, as is evident to all of us through our personal and social networks. We may know or know of *a* woman who has been raped, or even of more than one, but out of all of our women friends and acquaintances, for almost all of us, it's but a tiny proportion. This is notwithstanding the defining down of rape to include sex where consent is not fully explicit: the usual scenario in so-called 'acquaintance' or 'date rape'.

To point out that classic 'stranger rape' is not the only or even the main form that rape takes is important. Certainly some dates turn into clear instances of rape, and may be as bad an experience for a victim as a 'stranger' rape (though we don't know: the research is too limited); but distinguishing 'date rape' as a separate category is more to do with a refusal to accept the dynamic of normal sexual encounter, where usually the woman acts coyly until she is sure the man who is interested in her is interested in a lot more than just sex. The man gets 'come on, but' or 'come on' followed by 'no, not yet' messages (Muehnenhard & Hollabaugh, 1988). In a way, women in part precipitate their own potential victimisation, but men are quite capable of reading the signals. Of those men who cannot or will not do so, there is a subset of men who might then go on to rape, but only a tiny one (judging by the rape statistics). If we all followed a strict code that consent was nothing short of an emphatic repeated 'yes', then people would have to more or less give up trying to have sex.

It's now widely acknowledged that 'date rape' law has given a licence to retrospectively revoke consent for what had turned out to be 'bad sex', as Katie Roiphe famously argued over a decade ago in her heavily debated book, *The Morning After* (Roiphe, 1994). That redefining (dumbing down) rape was a very dangerous move is shown by the enormous scale of fabricated rape allegations, which it further feeds.

That there even exist bogus rape allegations (often called 'false rape'), let alone that the incidence is extraordinarily high, is but one of the taboos surrounding rape. This is still so, despite the huge number of cases and the many cases that have made national front-page news in the last few years because of the celebrity of those unjustly accused. There was Craig Charles, John Leslie, Mick Hucknall, Paul Weller, and a string of footballers, but most notable was the known serial fantasist, Nadine Milroy-Sloane's invention of rape by Neil and Christine Hamilton. This was subsequently trumped for sophisticated wickedness by Alison Welfare's attempt to frame her boyfriend, that entailed gagging and tying herself up. Most ironic was the gang-rape fiction by Desirée Nall, a Florida campus president of the US National Organisation of Women. If a campaigner can fabricate rape merely for political illustration (adding spice to her college's Sexual Assault Awareness Week), then we can imagine how much more likely is a woman to seize the opportunity of claiming 'false rape' to bury a personal problem.

There may be the flimsiest of instrumental reasons for lodging a fabricated complaint; not least trivial financial gain. For example Susan Warburton accused a hotel worker of overpowering her whilst asleep when she was on holiday in Cyprus. She did it in the mistaken belief she could claim some sort of compensation on her insurance. A fortnight earlier, the same court convicted Annette Mangan, who was trying to get her own back on two men (she claims) who took photos of her having sex. (Mangan got only four months and Warburton was merely fined.)

When Naomi cried Wolf, Katie said baaah

A decade ago Katie Roiphe, then a 25-year-old Princeton graduate, proclaimed the epidemic of 'date-rape' a hoax; most instances being nothing more than 'bad sexual experiences'. (This led to several sacks of hate mail, campus petitions, threats or expressions of hope that she'd be killed or raped.) Writing in *The Morning After: Sex, Fear and Feminism On Campus*:

> We have to learn to separate bad sexual experiences from rape. We have to be able to say there are experiences when you feel bad or regret something, or something happened which you feel miserable about, but that's not rape. [Rape is] the use of physical force, the serious threat of physical force, or sex with somebody who is incapacitated, such as a passed-out drunk. What I object to is an expanding definition of rape to include things like verbal coercion by the man. I also object to the notion that if a woman is drunk that is enough to constitute rape. I am not saying that some men don't go out, give women ten vodkas and then rape them. But does it happen with the frequency we are being led to believe? I really don't believe it does.

Roiphe compares the rape pamphlets given out on US campuses with the Victorian circulars admonishing the women of that era about virtue. She believes that what the 'rape-crisis' feminists are saying, implicitly, is that women can't take control of their own sexuality. In a London debate with 'anti-cutie beauty' Naomi Wolf (author of *The Beauty Myth*), Roiphe insisted that, drunk or sober, 'when you are conscious you are responsible for your actions'. Then she dropped a cluster bomb: 'I do not believe all men are potential rapists'. Wolf challenged with a study revealing that one in nine men said that they would commit rape if they thought they could get away with it. 'I just don't believe that', Roiphe retorted, 'I don't believe that about men'.

(Perhaps both sides miss the point here. There is a chasm of infinite size between an action and the mere idea of doing it. It is the very nature of such fantasies, especially when they are more serious and personal, that they serve to relieve whatever produces them. The man who has had to suppress his rage or lust is almost invariably a better man than one who has never had to seriously deal with such emotions, and is a man who is more able to show compassion to others.)

'I was reacting to a political climate that really was not allowing for free conversation', said Roiphe. She then takes her logic right into the courtroom and agrees that the anonymity of rape victims needs to be reconsidered:

> We don't protect other types of victims, why should we protect rape victims? The real reason is because rape is considered so shameful. Rape should not be considered shameful to the victim. It should be considered shameful for the rapist.

A series of incidents in Britain in 2005 were less inventive than implausible, and though they had all the hallmarks of fabrication from the outset, were nevertheless vigorously and protractedly investigated by police forces—less through gullibility than politically hounded into action. In March of that year, in Basildon, there was a classic case of wild invention by a young girl, under ten years old, supposedly raped at night in her bed in the same room as other children were sleeping. There were six in the house at the time, with the parents in the next room. The attacker she described as a black man with dirty teeth except one very bright one. He had supposedly somehow got in without making any sign of entry. This case shouted 'fabrication' from the very outset, but it was prominent in the news for months before police eventually admitted it was a fiction. Several months later, a not dissimilar incident in Yorkshire was made much fuss of by both police and local media, heedless of the possibility of fabrication. Then a story emerged of a gang of serial rapists in Northampton. Three 'stranger' rapes and two abductions led to a massive police hunt and the town's female population feeling under siege, encouraged by a police poster campaign. The story of a gang committing 'stranger' rape and, conveniently, identifiably from overseas (so that when they weren't traced they would be assumed to have gone back home): shouldn't that have rung alarm bells? Months later, police announced that the whole thing was a hoax and two women were to be charged (though why only two and not the five who had made formal accusations was never explained). Copycat 'false rape' had arrived in Britain; or rather, had become more visible.

'False rape' culprits are usually not prosecuted, and frequently not even cautioned, and consequently remain protected by legal anonymity. If jailed, the sentencing is feather-light—usually just three months or at the most six. This is even when a man has been falsely named and lives in fear of being seriously injured in reprisals. For examples amongst many, and just staying in West Yorkshire in the last couple of years, Tracey Rowe named a man she'd never had contact with as her 'stranger' rapist, to cover having sex with someone else. As a result, he was fired from his job and attacked, whilst his wife lost her own job, and the stress led to her leaving her college course. Even after being been told of an arrest, Rowe did not admit the truth for a further three weeks. Similarly motivated to Rowe, Emma Louise Goodwin's refusal to recant kept a man in jail. A still unnamed Bradford woman got a man arrested, but her sanction was not even a few months jail; just a fixed penalty ticket for wasting police time.

With many instances of 'false rape', there is at least one male victim who not only may spend weeks or months in prison, but he then goes through months or years of hell, including losing partner/wife/children/job/friends/home/life, and ongoing community hostility against which he has no defence, such is the impossibility of convincing a gossip network and proving a negative. This makes fabricated rape the most heinous form of 'indirect aggression'. Indeed, many people have called for sentences equivalent to what the accused man would have received had he been convicted; not least as a long-overdue deterrent measure to start to reduce the prevalence of this crime.

The men put through the mill in these cases where 'false rape' was detected were the lucky ones. It's not only the gullibility of the police in bowing to the PC lobby that leads to so many women not being found out, or found out quite a long way down the road. The government facilitates this in having made evidence about a woman's past sexual history inadmissible. The government even tried to make this inadmissible when the accused was himself that sexual history! Jack Straw, when Home Secretary, challenged a Court of Appeal ruling against this very nonsense, and lost only when the Law Lords concluded that it would 'disembody' the case.

On top of this there is evidence of serious mishandling of investigations. Even of the relatively straightforward 'stranger' rape cases, in the USA one in three are found by retrospective DNA testing to be miscarriages of justice. Evidence that would exonerate falsely-accused men is not obtained because the police have so low a bar to get a case past the CPS, that they don't need to allocate resources to proper investigation. Having spent nearly three years in jail as part of a seven-year sentence, David Luxford was cleared in late 2003, but only after his wife hired a private detective who proved that her husband could not possibly have committed the rapes he had been accused of. The conviction was on the basis of no medical evidence or corroboration: 'It was her word against mine', Luxford protested. 'All I could say was "I didn't do it".' As usual, the defendant was in the impossible position of being asked to prove a negative.

Even in some cases where the most crucial evidence has been obtained, it might not be taken into account. In 2004, Leslie Warren, having served two years, had his conviction for raping his ex-girlfriend quashed when it was discovered that a detective had failed to pass on information about false allegations the woman had made against other men. She later admitted she had lied.

The failure to check for a history of false allegation by an accuser is a routine omission in rape cases, and led to a senior judge demanding a register of such women. Famously, Roy Burnett spent fourteen years in jail before he was finally released in 2000, after his false accuser made a similar and obviously bogus allegation in 1998. His conviction was based solely on being picked out in an identity parade by a woman whose boyfriend and a close friend eventually came forward to reveal she had actually claimed she'd never been raped fifteen years earlier. Inexplicably, this woman, like so many other fabricators, still retains her anonymity.

Was Cora (Jessica Lange) being raped by Frank (Jack Nicholson) or having consensual sex with him? From The Postman Always Rings Twice *(1981)*

'False rape': the figures and the reasons

Reliable statistics from the British police and the FBI (which has examined in depth the motivation of women to make such inventions) leave no doubt that a large proportion of rape allegations are indeed entirely false. The Home Office study on rape in 1999 reveals figures that are, to say the very least, alarming (and were replicated in a subsequent 2005 study). The majority of rape complaints were categorised by police forces as either 'no crime' or 'no further action'. 'No crime' means just that: no crime took place. In 1985, the figure for this was a staggering 45%, but then the Home Office stepped in with a directive instructing forces to rig the figures by recording 'no crime' only when 'the complainant retracts completely and admits to fabrication'. In one move, police were gagged from revealing most of the extent of fabrication. Only the women accusers themselves were from this point allowed to define their own allegation as false—a unique privilege in law-enforcement, inverting due process.

Nevertheless, the figure remained very high. A decade later, the censored 'no crime' figure was still a full quarter of all allegations. Part of the reason it remained so high was that police were in part ignoring the Home Office directive by breaking down the 'no crime' figure into three sub-categories. Almost half, still, were because of an admission of malicious allegation; over a third because the allegation was withdrawn; and five percent because of lack of evidence. The telling thing is that the police recorded all under the 'no crime' umbrella, clearly demonstrating that in all of these cases officers were firmly convinced that the complaints were bogus. This was confirmed through interviewing detectives the following year: according to law academic Jennifer Temkin (1997), they believed that a quarter of complaints were false; an exact tally. It's not a question merely of belief, however, because the sub-categories within the 'no-crime' bracket are themselves subsets of categories that were distributed between

Cartesian meditations

It is ironic that the recent focus on a woman's exercise of her 'free choice' in sexual matters has happened just at the time that neuoro-scientists and psychologists are rejecting the very notion of un-constrained free will (Wegner, 2003). The 'freely-choosing' self cham-pioned by the feminists is predicated on Descartes' conception of the disembodied mental subject acting independently of body and envi-ronment, thus the notion of 'consent' is viewed as absolute.

But this view has to be misguided, as volitional consent at the time of sexual intercourse is clearly a product of a complex combination of cognitive, emotional, hormonal, pharmaceutical and environmental factors (including alcohol consumption). On the absolutist criterion, at what precise frame in *The Postman Always Rings Twice* did the coupling in the famous kitchen-table scene make the transition from rape to consensual sex (or, more controversially, in Peckinpah's *Straw Dogs*)? The question is just as undecideable as the issue of at exactly what point a foetus becomes a human infant (an issue on which pro-choice feminists take a rather different philosophical position).

This absolutist view of free choice is also extended to the supposed assailant — men being required to stoically ignore any degree of provo-cation, encouragement or enticement. The traditional, prudential wis-dom that a girl out on a Saturday night wearing next to nothing and with half a bottle of vodka inside her was 'asking for it' falls foul of the Cartesian ethics beloved of the feminists.

Psychologists are also equally disinclined to accord privileged sta-tus to memory or a subject's perception of an incident. After the demise of the computational analogy in psychology, memory is now largely seen as a process of construction, which may explain the fre-quent delays in reporting alleged rapes. Psychologists have found that new (and false) memories can easily be constructed by a simple pro-cess of mis-remembering or suggestion, a con-dition known as false-memory syndrome — the basis of many cases of supposed child-abuse (Loftus and Ketcham, 1994). The retro-spective redefinition of rape as consensual sex once a relationship has been re-established shows just how malleable and constructed perception, memory and volition is, and the consequent folly of making the criminal law dependent on this alone.

Feminist metaphysics — stuck in a Cartesian time-warp

'no crime' and 'no further action'. This still leaves scope for a much higher overall proportion that may well be 'false rape' but of which the police were not sure. The 'no further action' umbrella accounted for another third of all complaints; and nearly half of these were because of insufficient evidence, and between five and ten percent due to the complainant's refusal to co-operate in the investigation of their own complaint. The remainder were still down to malicious allegation (and which should have been 'no crimed'). In all, two-thirds of complaints leading to 'no further action' were withdrawn by the accuser and, together with the further five or ten percent who refused to co-operate (effectively a withdrawal of the complaint), that represents a further one in five of all rape allegations.

It must be true that complaints are sometimes retracted for reasons unconnected with their veracity. The obvious scenario here is the rapprochement between lovers. But this itself begs the question of whether or not any crime took place, if in retrospect the supposed victim now has a restored relationship with the supposed perpetrator. (If women can retrospectively redefine a sexual encounter as rape then equally they can redefine what they considered rape as actually a consensual sexual encounter.) Doesn't this suggest that the original complaint may have been a device used by the complainant to lever the relationship? It may be that a proportion are retracted under some kind of duress, but the power balance in the wake of an initial allegation is strongly weighted in favour of the woman accuser.

It must be true that a high proportion of the attrition in alleged rape cases is because the complainant does not wish the truth to be tested, for the simple reason that there was no truth to the allegation. That is certainly the case with the withdrawals under the 'no crime' category, but the withdrawals under the 'no further action' category must contain a proportion of fabrications. It's simply that the police don't have the evidence to show this. With the death of prudery (or what used to be referred to as modesty), the support for rape complainants, and the undermining of the rights of rape suspects, this suspicion can only grow stronger. It's an unusual step to withdraw an accusation of a serious offence, and rape is the one accusation other than domestic violence that the judicial process attempts to ensure gathers momentum. Nobody can reasonably cite a lack of faith in the system not to take a bona fide case to trial. In any case, if there was any dissuasion by police, then the last reaction is to withdraw a complaint and so officially deny it ever took place.

It would be a conservative estimate that of the quarter of all rape allegations that are withdrawn by the complainant herself under the 'no further action' category, half are actually instances of 'false rape'. This would add ten percent to the overall percentage of 'false rape' out of the total of all rape allegations. This gives us a rough low estimate for the rate of 'false rape' of over a third of all complaints to police: an astonishing statistic and

The 1985 Police Foundation report that found that police rape investigators privately thought that between 50% and 70% of rape complaints were bogus was authored by a young copper named Ian Blair.

a major civil rights scandal that requires diametrically the opposite approach to that of the Home Office for the past two decades or more.

Confirming that police generally are unwilling for 'politically correct' reasons to use the 'no-crime' category where if it was any other type of crime this is what would be recorded; an actual comment from police is cited in the Home Office report:

> If rape was treated as any other crime, you would probably no-crime a lot more. But because rape is treated as something special, and indeed it is a serious crime, it is much more difficult to no-crime it.

What then do police officers with experience of rape cases actually believe to be the proportion of bogus complaints? — not what they write in official reports, but what they say in anonymous interview in studies by unbiased researchers? Of research collating interviews around the world: in the UK it came in at between 50% and 70% (Blair, 1985); in New Zealand 60% (Anstiss, 1995) — though 80% is the figure bandied about in police training workshops; in the USA 60% (Feldman-Summers and Palmer, 1980); and in Eire up to 90%. This last tallies with an anonymous statement by an officer who had just retired from the Irish force:

> Female officers investigate a majority of our rape complaints, and none of the female detectives or uniform officers I know would estimate higher than approximately 20% of rape complaints are genuine (Farrar, 2005).

For reasons of wanting to keep hold of their jobs, this is not what the Home Office hears from British policewomen. The Home Office periodically berates police specifically on the question of what officers believe to be the rates of 'false rape', on the assumption that this is a measure of sexism. Recall that before the figures were rigged, British police 'no crimed' just less than half of all rape complaints. Privately, as I've just mentioned, they reckoned with their hands untied it would be between half and three-quarters. It's therefore highly likely that the majority or the great majority of what is supposedly rape is in fact fabrication.

False reporting of crime in general is around two percent, so 'false rape', at multiples of an order of magnitude more serious than for other crimes, is a uniquely serious problem. It's impossible not to infer special motivation for rape fabrication which does not apply to other crimes, putting the onus on the legal system to build in extra safeguards to protect accused men. Instead we have the very reverse.

* * *

The motivation behind 'false rape' has been looked into by Professor Keith Soothill (Soothill, 2004; Soothill & Piggott, 1999), who sums up:

> Women tend to make false allegations to get themselves out of trouble rather than to get men into trouble. They lie when they feel constrained, when they're in a tight spot. The whole thing gets out of hand and there just isn't the opportunity for the woman to bail out. The process begins to take over.

A clear window on this is provided by the recent protracted 'drug rape' scare that was found to be a complete hoax. The Forensic Science Service investigated over a thousand supposed cases of women who had made complaints to police of having their drinks spiked by men to facilitate rape. Each had blood samples taken in hospital, and *not a single sample* proved positive (Scott-Ham & Burton, 2003). A third of the women were not intoxicated with anything, a third had taken standard illegal drugs, and a third had alcohol poisoning. This astonishing finding was replicated subsequently in another study (Hughes et al., 2007). A complaint of 'drug rape' turns out to be simply cover for embarrassing behaviour.

Although many rape allegations are clearly malicious, the sheer scale of the problem and that it is so hidden, means that much must be irresponsible and self-delusional rather than malicious. The range of situations for which women are attempting to cover that Soothill teases out, are similar to those cited by the FBI in their comprehensive research into the motivation behind false allegation and the way that police deal with rape complaints. Leading expert Dr Charles McDowell (McDowell, 1985), produced The FBI Behavioural Science Unit's *Manual on Recognizing False Allegations* after finding that out of well over a thousand police investigated rape claims, a full quarter were verified as false allegations, either by full admission or incontrovertible physical evidence. Exactly the proportion the police in Britain find.

Just why women make false allegations was of particular interest to McDowell because, as he points out, 'false rape' is usually not recognised by investigators for what it actually is, and being so explosive the subject is almost totally neglected. All experienced investigators have been misled by rape complainants, and apart from the injustice to those falsely accused, a failure to recognise 'false rape' is a failure to spot a complainant's actual problems, which may be worthy of attention in themselves.

McDowell cites defence mechanisms used to avoid responsibility for shameful conduct or to recover self-esteem, such as choosing to 'forget' aspects of what happened (notably a woman's own willing involvement in a sexual episode), eschewing responsibility (ultimately placing it upon the police), projecting blame on to somebody else, or simply drifting into fantasy. Motivation is to dispel the impression of being 'too easy' in having sex with a relative stranger; to get back at someone; needing an excuse to cover an imagined risk of STI infection; hiding evidence of an affair; to test a partner's love; to gain concern and sympathy; and sidelining multiple but quite ordinary problems.

In a nutshell, 'false rape' is 'self-handicapping' behaviour, where the individual appears to put herself at a disadvantage or risk, but actually is seeking a protected status to in turn hide manipulation of some scenario which otherwise would be beyond her control. Either consciously or unconsciously, 'false rape' is clearly a variant of the quintessentially female behaviour of 'indirect aggression', and related to the female predilection for parasuicide (a cry for help or attention-seeking, masquerading as attempted suicide). McDowell found that in some cases, the complainant goes to extraordinary lengths to support embellishments of assault, intimidation and even extortion, with ruses such as threats written in blood and poison letters.

Though careful not to pathologise too much, he makes a comparison with those conditions classed as 'medically achieved coping mechanisms': malingering, hysterical conversion reactions and self-mutilation; especially those who claim to have illnesses. These patients have been very well investigated in medicine. They stubbornly refuse to confess to the hoax, and are enraged at any suggestion that their illnesses are anything but genuine.

There are tell-tale signs which individually may mean little but, taken together as a suite — an 'offender profile', if you like — may betray the 'false rape' complainant. First, there is the anonymity of the supposed rapist. Either a total stranger or at best a slight acquaintance makes a good imaginary assailant in that it tends to put the possibility of the complainant's contributory negligence out of the frame. It also makes it impossible for the police even to 'fit up' a suspect, so prolonging the case, shifting responsibility firmly on to police for their lack of progress, and absolving the claimant of the risk of having to deal with an actual person labelled as the offender. Next comes the unusually high level of reported violence — minimal or non-existent in the great majority of actual rapes. Despite the violence, however, assailants seem unusually well behaved in terms of sexual repertoire, rarely engaging in anal sex or forcing fellatio. The incident overall tends to be described either vaguely, with excuses of having eyes closed or of passing out, or in too much detail but with no emotion. Self-inflicted injuries are common, but they're not the sorts of injuries sustained in the small minority of actual rape cases where non-trivial violence is used. Sensitive areas are not involved, and the injuries are from scratching or a sharp instrument within arm's reach, often inconsistent with an attack, and made to appear worse than they are, but to which the 'victim' displays a strange indifference. Even the way that a complaint first surfaces can offer clues: a significant delay and then, instead of going to the police, friends are informed, or a hospital is the first port of call because of a (supposed) fear of pregnancy or STI.

Considerations of personality and lifestyle may also be indicators. The supposed victim may have a previous record of being raped or assaulted and under similar circumstances, and becomes outraged if challenged to corroborate her story. An extensive record of dramatic injuries or illnesses, a history of mental or emotional problems (especially self-harm and behaviour displaying borderline or hysterical aspects), and current difficulties in a personal relationship: all may raise suspicion. Not to be dismissed as another possibility would be an imitation of a recently-publicised similar crime. Then come the usual inconsistencies in evidence, such as the 'victim' being unable to recall where the crime took place (and thereby conveniently keeping forensic routes to her discovery at bay). Damage to clothing may also be inconsistent with injuries received, and serological evidence may be entirely absent—as obviously it would be if there was a significant delay in reporting the invented assault; such a delay often being instrumental in this regard.

The way the FBI deals with rape complainants is canny. Out go any confrontational tactics in favour of a scrupulously non-judgemental attitude; the investigator leaving questions to do with the possibility of a false report to his supervisor. Rapport obviates the complainant's need to defend herself, allowing her to see the inconsistencies in what she's herself provided. Concoction is sympathised with, as understandable and quite common. She's reassured that her distress is recognised and unlikely to be made public to add to her problems; but at the same time the complainant is pressed to face up to what she's done.

Reactions even to this gentle approach vary from an emotional confession and relief, to outraged and ever further-entrenched denial. Very far from foolproof, the approach undermines the proper punishment the absence of which causes much of the fabrication in the first place. Still, it's the best anyone's come up with to stop a lot of the injustice to falsely accused men, and we need it here in Britain.

The myth of 'rape trauma': there is no standard
or serious adverse reaction to rape

To question the supposed 'trauma' experienced by women in key areas of female experience is quite a taboo. It's commonly stated that abortion is always experienced as a trauma, yet the research is conclusive that 'post-abortion trauma' is a complete chimera. Indeed, the reaction of almost all women who have abortions is one of relief. There is a much more complete taboo to ask the same question about rape. We surely can assume that for most 'stranger' rapes at least, the experience is an awful one. We would expect it to be, because of the usurping of mate choice and the pregnancy it might well lead to; but a terrible experience does not mean necessarily any damage that is in any way lasting.

The last time someone had a comprehensive look was over twenty years ago. Gillian Mezey of the Maudsley Hospital, London, trawled through all of the studies (Mezey, 1985). Her conclusion? Even if depression does occur following rape, it lasts on average only two to four months, *even including* for those who undergo a 'compounded reaction' because of prior psychological or serious medical problems. This is the problem of pre-existing conditions, or predispositions to which rape could merely act as trigger, that is very evident from the FBI's research. Mezey explains why most of the studies are useless:

> Unfortunately, of the studies that look at psychological sequelae of rape, very few make any attempt to describe the 'pre-attack' characteristics of the woman, which make it difficult to draw conclusions as to the significance of any documented post-traumatic change....There are five major problems. First, many studies are actually concerned with victims of sexual assaults other than rape...Secondly, some studies include subjects of all ages including children which may bias results. Thirdly, few studies rely on the legal definition of rape...Fourthly, although some studies include victims who claimed to have been raped by a lover, others just look at 'stranger' rapes. Finally, subjects may be drawn from different sources of referral which may influence results.

The problems multiply:

> Lack of control studies: many studies lack comparison groups of non-victimised women. No study has compared the rape victim directly with victims of other violent crimes. Few studies use systematic follow-up techniques with the victims and no study follows the victims up for more than 18 months.

The idea of 'rape trauma syndrome' is discredited for the incontrovertible reason that rape cannot be diagnosed from the supposed trauma symptoms. This is why even the US psychiatric establishment is not convinced: 'rape trauma' is not recognised in the DSM psychiatric classification system. Yet in America, any response to rape is held to be consistent with trauma, so 'experts' are called to testify in court regardless of how mild or severe was the reaction of the alleged rape victim. This is an entirely circular logic based on the assumption that all allegations are true.

Indeed, the entire concept of psychological 'trauma' and especially of 'post traumatic stress disorder' is increasingly dubious and, on thorough analysis, an entirely bogus concept (Leys, 2000).

If serious lasting harm from rape is evident anywhere, it should be in war-torn areas where there have been mass rapes. Investigators of just this phenomenon in Bosnia reported that the absence of severe trauma was the norm. All of the investigators were women, so a charge of lack of empathy because of the sex of the investigator can't have been a factor. Perhaps everything else that had happened to these poor women — their men-folk killed, homes destroyed, sons returning from the front maimed and mentally unhinged, and forced relocation as refugees — had numbed them to the point that little could damage them further. Either way, these reports must be considered striking, providing further evidence that a supposed ubiquitous psychological harm resulting from rape is a fiction.

There is nothing of the behaviour of the putative victim in the aftermath of rape that reliably indicates that a rape actually took place, yet the Home Office recently proposed allowing rape prosecutors to present evidence that the putative victim was displaying psychological symptoms of having been raped. This follows such 'behavioural evidence' being used in the USA to artificially force up the conviction rate.

Male rape

Rape as a unique claim for female victimhood is compromised by the existence of rape of males, albeit that males can't suffer the sense of violation that women have in the usurping of sexual choice and the possibility of pregnancy; and men are still the perpetrators. But could male rape bolster the notion that rape is not to gratify sexual impulses but to express 'power'?

Male rape is very under-reported and consequently the scale of it in wider society is unknown, but it is known to be rife in prisons, where some handle on its nature can be obtained (Dumond, 1992; King & Mezey, 1989). What occurs in US prisons dwarfs all rape on the outside. Academic studies of state and federal prisons in the previous decade reported that fifteen percent of all male inmates are raped — and that is not including prisoners who pair off with stronger inmates, exchanging sex for protection 'voluntarily'. That would add up to at least 200,000 prison inmates across the USA, which is about *three or four times* the total number of rapes of women anywhere in the USA, even adding in best estimates for under-reporting. Even this now appears to be an under-estimate. A more recent Human Rights Watch report estimated that anywhere from 250,000 to 600,000 prisoners are raped every year in American prisons. With the recent growth in the prison population, at any one time there are well in excess of two million men in US prisons, but the annual throughput is several times that figure. This is what lies behind the staggering scale of the problem, given the predilection of men for novel sexual partners and the fiercely hierarchical and brutal social system of the inmates, where bullying is normal. Clearly, in terms of scale, male rape dwarfs the problem of rape of women. There must be an equivalent problem in Britain but the prison service simply refuses to acknowledge it and doesn't keep any data; not even in connection with the many cases of prison suicide which are likely to be rape related — repeat victimisation being a profound indication of rock-bottom status in the male hierarchy. (The only concern is with the much fewer female suicides, most of which are likely to be self-harming incidents gone wrong.)

Far from being unacceptable to the US public, brutal rape as routine prison experience is regarded as part of the punishment to be expected, and somehow actually deserved. Part of crime deterrence, it's become an open cliché and a joke throughout American society, despite the very high incidence in US prisons of HIV and intravenous drug use meaning that the tissue tears usual in forced anal rape make US incarceration a likely death sentence.

Any inmate can expect to be raped within their first or second day of incarceration, and rapes are often brutal, frequently resulting in severe mutilation and prolonged hospitalisation. Most prison male rape is necessarily brutal because in going against the sexual orientation of the great majority of men, it's unimaginably disgusting to them, and in any case involuntary anal sex is difficult to achieve. Men have strength that they are willing to use, and with no inhibition of violence male-to-male. Subjugation of any kind — let alone subjugation as complete as is male rape — will be resisted because of the severe reduction in status that it causes and indicates.

That male rape is such a feature of prison life is because of the combination of the complete unavailability of women, the fiercely hierarchical and ultra-male social system that asserts itself, the inability of inmates to control impulse or to secure greater rewards by delayed gratification, and their existence much more in physical action than in thought. These factors are not a little to do with how men get themselves into prison in the first place. In the absence of females, male bodies that in some ways approximate to those of females, become objects of attraction. When you consider also that homosexuals are greatly over-represented in all prison populations (and with both victims and perpetrators of male rape, data shows that fully half are *not* heterosexual), then male rape is very much what it appears: essentially sexual rather than violent behaviour.

Notwithstanding the prison situation of abnormally intense dominance/submission behaviour, violence in male rape is instrumental. It's necessary to effect the rape, not inflicted for its own sake. Male rape is clearly to satiate sexual desire. To think that rape here is in the service of establishing dominance is to have it backwards. It's the establishment of dominance that then facilitates rape. If this is the case even in male rape, then between the sexes — where there is no dominance interaction — rape must also be as it seems: essentially sexual behaviour.

Rape is about sex, not violence

To further the line that sex is an expression of 'power' in the service of male 'oppression' of women, current taboos in the discussion of rape extend beyond the supposed effect on the victim, to the motivation of the perpetrator. Just as any suggestion is disallowed that there could be an outcome other than protracted trauma for the victim, so too is disallowed any motivation of the perpetrator other than the violent imposition of 'power'. That men rape to gratify frustrated sexual desire (self-evident though it is), you are not supposed to say.

Feminist advocates rationalise this by pretending that even if the claim is in itself untrue, it's necessary so as to shut down the defence of perpetrators that a rape victim was complicit in some way. This is just what Gillian Mezey does in the introduction to her overview of the psychological impact of rape. She calls rape a 'pseudo-sexual' act:

> By focusing on the sexual aspect rather than the violent nature of the assault, the rationalisation can be made that both victim and offender are seeking mutual gratification and that the victim must in some way have welcomed or even provoked the attack.

The idea that rape is the expression of 'power' has it backwards. Inasmuch as it makes any sense at all to talk of 'power' here, rape is an expression of how power*less* is the perpetrator. Rape is obtaining sex outside the social order instead of accessing it in the normal way via status obtained within the DH. It's the most direct subversion of the DH, and the behaviour that is most strongly 'policed'. A man knows that forcing sex on a woman within his social group will at the very least result in his total ostracism, let alone loss of all status. Such a drastic tactical move is one only the powerless would consider.

This is why rape is several times more common in poor US neighbourhoods than in prosperous ones. That's despite the expansion in the definition of rape by and for the middle-class to include date rape and rape within marriage, which heavily inflates the figures in well-off areas. In poor communities there is by contrast under-reporting. If you were to include the poor in the re-defined rape statistics, then the far greater proportion of rape perpetrated by low-status men would appear far greater still.

The 'not about sex' line is completely contradicted by the bare minimum if any force used, and by the high sexual attractiveness and fertility of victims — their ages scatter around the age of greatest fertility. The FBI manual states that in only thirteen percent of rapes does violence play any significant part, and that typically little if any is used. If violent subjugation rather than sexual gratification was the motive, then violence attending rape would likely be out of all proportion to that needed merely to subdue the victim in order to carry out the sexual act. Likewise, if sex was not the motive, then attractiveness and fertility would not be an issue, and women across the whole age spectrum would be victimised. They aren't. Rape victims are almost exclusively women of reproductive age, and overwhelmingly at the young end.

This is shown in detail in the 1999 Home Office study on rape. A profoundly strong correlation between the age of rape victims and fertility is further skewed — apparently to take into account years of future fertility, and the likelihood of virginity or of not being pregnant, which are factors in how males choose females. Well over half of victims were aged sixteen to thirty-five (of which twice as many were below twenty-five as were above it), another quarter were under sixteen, and only five percent were over forty-five.

The substantial proportion in the small age band below sixteen is explained by the low age of menarche. A girl of sixteen typically has already had five years of her reproductive life. She hasn't yet peaked in fertility, but it's high, and being so freshly out of puberty, she's likely to be a virgin or at least less likely to be already pregnant or to have a long-term partner whose semen would be present to compete with that of the rapist. This means that boys/men have evolved to find these girls especially attractive for the reason that sex has a disproportionate chance of resulting in pregnancy. That girls of this age have their entire reproductive life ahead of them is also an attraction. This is because sexual interactions are potential long-term relationships, and establishing a pair bond as soon after puberty as possible means that the male has the female potentially for her full reproductive life. Even if the bond doesn't last this long, the years a man has her are those that span when she is most fertile. (It's just for this combination of reasons to do with attractiveness that catwalk models start their careers at the age of just thirteen or fourteen.) Young post-pubertal girls are also more likely to be un-chaperoned by a male compared to a girl in her late teens or twenties, and her inexperience my well mean she's less likely to resist or to know how to. This makes her more vulnerable and more targeted for both 'stranger' and 'acquaintance' rape.

The number of over forty-fives is small enough probably to exclude all post-menopausal women, and what victimisation there is can be accounted for by the youthful appearance of a significant minority of middle-aged women in contemporary societies, with their low workload and good health. That the over forty-fives were the most likely to report a 'stranger' rape, suggests further explanations. There are constraints of opportunity in that young attractive women are very likely to be 'mate guarded' by a

Why is rexy so sexy?

Kate Moss has been known to compliment her size-zero friends for looking so [ano]-rexy, and the modelling trade is blamed for the epidemic of eating disorders. But why is it that men find thinness so attractive? Women take no pleasure in submitting to a permanent starvation diet, and blaming models and the media just begs the question.

A clue can be found in the rape statistics — 25% of victims are under the age of sixteen. The male preference for youth (along with the universal ideal of virginity) seems to be because the younger the girl the less the chance that she will already be pair-bonded or even pregnant. (It makes no sense, from a biological perspective, for a man to have sex with a pregnant woman, or to provide an heir for another man — hence the disobedience of Onan). Similarly, *the thinner the figure the less opportunity to conceal pregnancy.* The current fad for exposed midriffs — even in winter — is not so much a fashion statement, more a case of saying 'look at my flat, toned stomach, I'm not pregnant.' (Needless to say feminist authors see things differently: 'the bare-midriff fashion functions as a post-feminist declaration of an "acceptable" commodification' (Hall, 2006). Hmm...

This biological preference for thinness is then *amplified* by ferocious female intra-sex competition, hard-wired into the genotype. An additional amplifier is provided by a universal psychological mechanism called the peak shift effect (Ramachandran and Hirstein, 1999). If a rat is rewarded for discriminating a rectangle from a square, it will respond even more vigorously to a rectangle of exaggerated proportions. Human agents respond in a similar way, so thinness can run amok. The male preference for thinness (BMI) is more important, by a factor of twelve, than waist-to-hips ratio (WHR) and is also true for non-Western cultures such as Malaysia (Swami and Tovée, 2007).

This is not to deny the importance of youth and fertility, but it's plausible that the male preference for thinness developed via a different mechanism. The low mean life expectancy and lean diet in the environment of evolutionary adaptation (EEA) would have meant that *most* women would have been fertile and slim for all their lives. Granted the advantage of pair-bonding as soon as possible after menarche, there are more certain signs of extreme youth than thinness — height, voice pitch, skin texture etc. The avoidance of females who were already pregnant, however, would require a distinctive cue.

The theory could be easily tested with a cross-cultural study of erotic art (Rubens' figures are amply fleshed, but they're not fat, and ancient (pregnant) fertility statues are more akin to a Harvest Festival than the stone-age equivalent of *Playboy*.) And if you think that thinness is a recent fad, then just take a look at an Elizabethan or Victorian corset. Women will undergo considerable suffering to display thinness.

Given that the pressure on girls to be thin has its origins in biological preferences there is no point blaming models and the media. But culture has it's own protection against cruel nature — traditional dress codes. If girls were to rediscover modesty then the problem would decline. This is why Western women converting to Islam often say they find it an intensely *liberating* experience (the irony being that the original name for feminism was the 'women's liberation movement').

This kind of secondary-level evolutionary psychology (EP) hypothesis explains how women react to a male biological imperative. This is still EP, but mediated through culture. Culture may only be an amplifier rather than a primary cause, but in the human species secondary phenomena often take priority. This sort of theory is best described as non-reductive EP — you can't reduce every emotion and behavioural tendency to survival fitness as you don't need a teleological explanation for *reactive* emotions/behaviour. They're simply reactions, nothing more, and often strongly dysfunctional (excess dieting can trigger anorexia in subjects with the genetic predisposition (Guisinger, 2003).)

Sex during pregnancy

The motivation behind the display of thinness is *unconscious*. So overweight women are just as likely to display their bare midriffs, without realising they are effectively saying 'hands off, I'm pregnant'. Male discomfort with sexual relations with a woman carrying another man's child helps to explain why lesbians are often fatter than heterosexual females (what better way to avoid the unwanted attentions of men?) However there is considerable pressure on male homosexuals to exercise, due to the innate male preference for slim partners (Grogan *et al.*, 2006).

The screenplay for the film *Waitress* — in which a married pregnant woman has an illicit affair with her doctor throughout the term of her pregnancy — could only have been written by a woman (the late Adrienne Shelly); to male audiences the film is a 108-minute cringe.

man, or to be with other young women, and unlikely to venture out on their own in quiet spots or late at night. Older women therefore are more likely to be available as targets, and in the dark with the hiatus of a rapist pouncing on his victim, middle-aged women may well be chosen under the misapprehension that they are younger.

The very small numbers of real outliers in age at both ends of the spectrum will be down to paraphilias — unusual sexual attractions: for either old people or pre-pubescent children (of which the latter is mostly incest).

The same Home Office study on rape is just as revealing about the marked lack of violence. Some degree of violence was recorded in over half of 'crimed' cases, but in well under half of the total sample of nearly 500 cases processed by police.

> Mostly this amounted to rough treatment such as pushing, but sometimes involved beating, punching and kicking....Three-quarters of stranger attacks involved violence. In eleven of these incidents the attacker threatened the complainant with a weapon, usually a knife, and in four other cases he threatened to kill her. Of the 211 women for whom some level of violence was recorded, four suffered fractured or broken bones or cuts requiring stitches. Nearly 100 received physical injury, including mild bruising, scratches or bite marks; 34 suffered vaginal or anal cuts or hymenal tears; 31 suffered more severe bruising, including black eyes and lacerations.

This is a relatively low overall level of violence, even in respect of the subset of 'stranger rape' — that necessarily requires a victim to be subdued and coerced for an act during which the assailant renders himself vulnerable. You would expect extremely serious threats and likely injury, if not to incapacitate then to reinforce threats; yet there was very little of this. A handful only of threats to kill and hospital cases, and less than a quarter where any threat was made with a weapon. Only one out of five victims was injured in any way at all and, other than the handful of hospital cases, only one in twenty sustained so much as serious bruising, and many more than half endured not even the most minimal violence. Most of those injured had cuts or tears to genitals — the damage that may occur through the sexual act itself. The picture of the typical absence of violence is even stronger when you consider that what injuries are recorded are likely to 'overlap', as it were: to be suffered by the same few individuals.

The four more seriously injured in the survey almost certainly would be victims of rare aberrant individuals: either sociopaths or 'obsessive-compulsive' rapists. Sociopaths have a pathological disregard for the feelings of others and no inhibitions about using violence in pursuit of what they want, and rape is not special in this regard. 'Obsessive-compulsive' rapists have wrongly learned that aggression is necessary to obtain sex, but they don't use violence gratuitously. An interview with such a rapist is revealing: 'Some are mouthy when I catch them, but I rough them up and then they are mostly scared. They try screaming and fighting. A few punches and kicks and they become gentle as lambs' (Lowenstein, 2000a).

The use of violence here is to render the victim quiescent and no more. Just as do psychopaths, these individuals do not see sex as inherently violent, and are using violence *instrumentally* to effect a rape.

The picture overall is very much one of the use of violence barely sufficient to initiate and complete sexual intercourse, and nothing more. Not only is there no gratuitous force, but there is no violence to facilitate escape by somehow immobilising the victim from either pursuing or raising an alarm — which is surprising given the punishment if caught. Even if there were, this would be instrumental to successfully completing the sex act rather than being in any way gratuitous.

Clearly, the case for rape being seen as in any way a crime with violence as a central component, let alone that it could be primarily a violent crime, is completely undermined by this evidence. It's also undermined if you look at how victims react to rape. It's the rape victim of reproductive age who is much more likely to suffer distress. Old women and pre-pubescent girls tend very much not to. This is for the obvious reason that women of reproductive age are liable to become pregnant. This shows that it's only or mainly the usurping of choice over reproduction that peculiarly upsets victims. To women, rape essentially is a crime concerning sex.

Why rape is seen as equivalent to murder

Rape as a crime in either civil society or war is regarded as being of the ultimate severity on a par with murder or even more serious. Compared to murder, rape is harder for a perpetrator to live down. It was the rapes in Bosnia and Kosovo that the civil wars in those countries are often remembered for, even though men by the stadium-full were shot, bludgeoned or knifed and buried in mass graves; first in 1995, and (because nobody made much fuss about it) again in 1999. How can this be? There is an incomparably greater impact on a victim to be murdered than to be raped, and likewise there is a much more serious impact on the community of all potential future victims that necessitates deterrence.

We know that rape generally has no serious long-term impact on victims, yet the justice system hands out punishment far in excess of that for crimes that have a demonstrably serious impact on victims. And this is despite a re-offending rate for rape of just four percent (and almost all of this will be by thoroughgoing serial rapists), so the need for deterrence is not the reason. A criminal who inflicts life-destroying mutilation can easily receive a lesser sentence than a rapist, yet if we were to crudely ask women if they would rather have parts of their bodies severed than be raped, the reply would not be 'which parts are you talking about?' They might express consternation at being presented with such a choice, but they would chose rape as certainly the lesser of two evils.

The punishment of attempted murder is in some respects actually less than that for rape. Even before more stringent sentences for rape were introduced, breakdowns of Home Office figures reveal that a much greater proportion of convicted attempted murderers stayed out of jail than did rapists, and of those who did go to jail, sentencing was comparable. With recent longer sentencing guidelines for rape, rape is now in all respects more heavily punished than attempted murder. For victims of GBH, justice—in comparison to rape victims—is truly laughable. 1993 Home Office figures are that almost half of those convicted of GBH never saw the inside of a cell, and not one got a sentence more than the recommended minimum for rape; the average stretch being a mere fifteen months.

The only possible explanation for all this is an evolutionary one. The victims of murder overwhelmingly are men, and men of lower status. Their deaths may or may not be directly through 'policing' of the male hierarchy, but either way are of little consequence to the reproducing group, because as low-ranked males they are more or less reproductively superfluous. By contrast, with the female being the 'limiting factor' in reproduction, no female is superfluous to the reproducing group. Not only murder, but any injury, or anything that compromises female fecundity is a problem. This is especially so if the compromise *directly* concerns reproduction. Rape is the by-passing of the allocation of sexual access through the male DH. It's the tactical subversion of the way that men allocate amongst themselves sexual access, and of how correspondingly women choose men according to men's status. Rape therefore compromises the mechanism whereby the whole reproducing group skews reproduction towards the fittest individuals. The draconian punishment for rape is an extension of the 'policing' of the male hierarchy.

This cannot be right in a (supposedly) equitable society, especially when you consider that technology has now dealt with the potential consequences of rape. No woman suffers the prospect of having a baby she doesn't want. Even if a woman was not taking hormonal contraceptives, there is the 'morning after' pill; and failing that, simple, safe and reliable early abortion (and, as I previously mentioned, there is now comprehensive evidence that the supposed 'post-abortion syndrome' is a complete myth, with the great majority of women simply experiencing relief). There is still the psychological impact on the victim that will have evolved and which will not change just because the former consequences of rape have been circumvented. But we know there are usually no serious psychological consequences of rape, and, as I will explain, there is a reason for this—the rape scenario is more complicated than it appears. In the following section I discuss rape in an evolutionary context. A consideration of the unconscious motivations of both male perpetrators and female victims, developed in our distant past, will cast a very different light on the problem of rape in modern societies. The contrast between conscious choices and unconscious cognitive mechanisms (for which evolutionary psychology is renowned) is troubling to modern sensibilities, given the privileging of the former and the rejection of the latter after the demise of the Freudian project. Psychoanalysis was in no way science, but EP is, and may well be the only way of explaining some of the strange behaviour surrounding the modern phenomenon of rape. As I explained in the foreword, EP theories are testable, just as are other scientific hypotheses and theories. The hypothesis of female response to rape here outlined is a counter-intuitive proposal—to say the least—that an adaptation to increase fitness causes the several hitherto unexplained phenomena associated with rape. (The adaptation is not the behaviour itself but the neural structure that underlies it; but detailing this neural structure is not required for the theory to have substance.) It is possible to come up with alternative explanations to account for the various aforesaid phenomena, that don't involve an adaptation to directly increase fitness. They will have an uphill task because the hypothesis here has the distinct virtue of being parsimonious—it explains all of the phenomena simply and collectively, rather than just one or other phenomenon separately.

Rape is ostensibly forced sex but may be unconsciously desired

The only way to understand the complex phenomena surrounding rape from the woman's point of view—'false rape', 'rape fantasy', and the inert reaction of women when being raped—is from an evolutionary perspective. There is not much to say about the motivation of the rapist apart from that the social psychology of 'in-group'/'out-group' operates to an extreme in wartime and related situations, and is clearly germinal to rape when it's perpetrated by normal men. In other contexts, rape is a social aberration. Either the rapist is afflicted with some kind of psychopathology, or there is something pathological about the general social organisation within the society, where the sense of 'in-group' is breaking down. There is, in contrast, much that we can infer from the behaviour of women who are raped, of what seems to be going on psychologically (non-consciously, that is). What I outline here is a view of rape using what we know or strongly suspect was common to the social environments throughout hominid history.

In the ancestral environment, as in extant hunter-gatherer societies even today, people are thought to have lived in small communities between which were mutual enmities, with coalitions of males sometimes making raiding forays into each other's territory. Males strayed alone near the edge of their home ranges at their mortal peril, and women risked kidnap to become the wife of her abductor in his home village. This is now thought to be the origin of warfare. We know from the Yanomamo that the object of their raiding is to seize women (Chagnon, 1979), and as the same social behaviour is apparent in chimpanzees, it's likely to have been present in our common ancestor, and therefore evolutionarily ancient. Indeed, forced copulation is common throughout the animal kingdom, a fact which is yet further evidence against the feminist notion that rape is because of 'patriarchy' (Archer & Vaughan, 2001).

Sometimes raids would be concerted, and whole communities destroyed, with adult males killed and females absorbed into the community of the raiders. A woman's new situation as the wife of a raider was likely to be, in biological fitness terms, not a disaster but an improvement. The man who coerced her into partnership is likely to be of higher rather than lower status, because he was sufficiently able and confident to launch an attack and to abduct her from the males of her own community, and may even have been a leader of his village. With the quality of the gene complement from this man with which to produce offspring, it may well be that compared to how she was placed in this respect in her life up until this point, her position had improved.

The woman's problem was how to react to the situation in both the short and the medium term. She had little option but to acquiesce to becoming the wife of a man in another community, who was probably prepared to use force to ensure sexual consummation there and then if she resisted capture. She also has to cope with the sudden transition from attachment to her community and significant individuals within it, to a community of strangers in which rapidly she will have to find others who will accept her. Both require her to be able to shut out the immediate extreme emotional reaction to what is going on, and to be swept along with events rather than be hopelessly crushed in denying and obstructing them. It seems likely that there will have evolved a mechanism universal to women to do this non-consciously.

We know that women are prepared in other ways for this possible eventuality. Human communities are male 'philopatric' or 'patrilocal'; that is, men tend to stay within their natal community, whereas women tend to go to live permanently in another community through marriage—'female exogamy'. There are three important human female behaviours that relate to this. First, with a sense of 'in-group' applied to their whole sex; unlike men, women are prepared for networking with all women everywhere. Second, females sexually favour strange males because they smell differently to males with which they grew up (owing to novel 'major histocompatibility complexes'—the chemicals involved with the immune response). Third, women are most fertile mid-cycle, just before ovulation, and this coincides with a peak in oestrogen levels. At this time, women become most receptive not to sex with their long-term partner but with strange males, on condition that they are of a higher status than their long-term partners. The point at which a woman has reached in her hormonal cycle can be predicted by the proportion of exposed flesh; this being a 'come on' signal to strange males. We know from the Family Planning Association's research that it's at this time that women are particularly reckless regarding contraception and behaviour in general. So nature conspires to skew the chances of conception to be considerably higher outside of the long-term partnership.

The reason women behave in these seemingly strange ways today is thought to be because of their evolved strategy to circumvent any compromise they made in acquiring a long-term partner, when they may have traded off the male's status for reliability. Extra-pair sex is only ever with males of higher status (or at least potentially so) than the long-term partner, and any resulting offspring can then be passed off as that of the long-term partner, who, none the wiser, will continue to be reliable. Obviously, if the husband found out, then he would probably desert the wife on the grounds that he would not want to raise children that were not his. Male jealousy has evolved expressly to sharpen male wariness for this behaviour in women, and to try to head off this scenario.

Now, it would be hard to achieve secret extra-pair mating within the very non-private, tightly-knit, small extended-family-based communities in which our ancestors lived. The male partner ran the risk of being killed if found out. Instead, just as women today go out to an anonymous nightclub in a micro-skirt, ancestral woman could walk to places away from the village near the territorial boundary with neighbouring communities, where she may encounter a lone male stranger.

This raised a new scenario, of an encounter with a foreign male that did not result in capture, but just sex. The woman returned to her natal community, where she ran the risk that her adultery had been witnessed or is detected. What then? Her best weapon was to try to deflect her husband's jealous rage on to the foreign cuckolder, taking advantage of the volatile ambivalence her husband would be feeling, and the inhibition men have towards being violent to women. The more she could convince the husband that any sex was not of her initiation or complicity, then the more the husband's ambivalence about her behaviour would precipitate as anger towards the cuckolder, and not against her.

The woman therefore pretends, very plausibly, that she was not having extra-pair sex, but was being attacked by a man and managed to thwart abduction. Over evolutionary time, such a strategy could be selected for, and made more reliably evoked by being rendered non-conscious.

A non-conscious coping mechanism would serve here, just as one does if a woman had a sexually coercive encounter with a foreign male which ended with abduction. So the coerced sex and/or abduction, and voluntary extra-pair sex situations are very similar; and an adaptation that was an integrated response to both is likely. The cognitive shut-down mode of dealing with forced sex would be an excellent tool for non-conscious

False rape and the rape fantasy in literature

The 'rape fantasy' is at the heart of the most famous 'false rape' portrayed artistically: the centrepiece of E.M.Forster's book, *A Passage To India*. (Harper Lee's *To Kill A Mockingbird*, in common with Forster's book escaped feminist censure because the victim was non-white and the offence was taken to be racism by the community.) Twenty years ago Forster's masterpiece was made into an exceptional film.

The story centres on a naïve young woman, Adela, who had only recently arrived in India to join the man to whom she was engaged to be married, Ronny; but Adela was now vacillating as to whether or not to marry him. A group excursion is arranged to the remote countryside by Aziz, an attractive Indian doctor. Through a chain of events Adela ends up alone with Aziz. In a scene reminiscent of *Picnic At Hanging Rock*, for reasons never explored Adela is emotionally overcome and rushes down the mountainside through thorn bushes that tear her clothes and skin. It is not clear as to whether she has had a delusion of sexual assault or that this is simply inferred by the authorities.

Part of the power of the film is that the central mystery is never explained. For all we are told Adela could just have a strong touch of the sun, but the film cleverly suggests that in some way the episode and its aftermath is a cover for a disturbing wish to 'be taken' by a man she finds more alluring than her fiancé.

At the heart of the story is the psychological insight that there may be a relatively benign origin of 'false rape'. It would seem that Adela's trepidation about her forthcoming marriage together with the unacknowledged possibility of a sexual liaison with someone else, brought to a head the tension in her mind between her anxiety at the prospect of the marriage bed and whether she had made a good choice. At the same time Aziz awakens her sexuality. The unconscious pitting of her options of choosing one man against the other seems to have been expressed as an hysterical imagining akin to a rape fantasy, where being carried off by the stranger would free her from her impending cocooning. Not cognizant of the huge damage to others she was causing until she started to come to her senses in Aziz's trial, Adela was 'frozen in the headlights'. She was procrastinating between the two female mating strategies, and the motivational importance of the situation was such that her mind blotted out all else. She experienced an emotionally-charged realisation of the conflict between two romantic ideals, though even at this sanitised level she could barely articulate it. It seems that Adela may have been unconsciously accessing a 'dissociated' mental state that women have evolved to enter should they find themselves in the scenario of being 'taken' by a stranger.

Is E.M Forster's A Passage to India *a classic rape fantasy?*

David Lean's film was made in 1984, before the furore over date rape, so it escaped feminist ire.

deception, both of the self and of others — the most reliable way to deceive others being to deceive yourself, of course.

An intriguing reflection of the ancestral world where this evolved is seen in the delusions psychiatric patients experience. Regardless of psychiatric diagnosis or cultural background, they are all similar in being usually of some kind of threat from other people. Just as dreams are now thought by some psychologists to be at root rehearsal of responses to typical problem situations in our evolutionary past (Franklin & Zyphur, 2005), so these waking dreams of the insane seem to be exaggerations of evolved mechanisms for 'social threat recognition'. Men's delusions feature groups of unfriendly male strangers, which is what you would expect, given that the principal danger to men in the past was raiding parties from neighbouring communities. In complete contrast, the delusions of women are paranoia regarding people — other women — familiar to them. This again is what you would expect, given the main acute social problems women would have faced: of covering up extra-pair sex in their natal community, or trying to fit into a whole new peer group as a new bride but otherwise an alien in the community of the raider who had captured her. What is most striking, though, is that very few women patients have delusions about being sexually coerced (Zolotova & Brune, 2005; Walston, David & Charlton, 1998). Evidently this was not a prominent ancestral fear, implying that, paradoxically, what sexual coercion there was, must have been more apparent than real.

Only with the study of the position of women in the evolutionary past, can several of the phenomena surrounding rape make sense. Not least the astonishingly high prevalence of fabricated rape complaints, which is now revealed as likely to be at least in part an evolved self-deception. There is also the difficulty in explaining the non-resistance that is reported by women when they are subjected to 'stranger rape', and which is reported by rapists themselves as the briefest of resistance before victims freeze and become 'gentle as lambs'. Most interesting of all is the archetypal 'rape fantasy' that women so often attest to, that I describe and explain in the chapter on pornography. Why would women fantasise about something they clearly do not want? Rape is self-evidently not something women want in the normal sense of a desire in the circumstances at the time. On a deeper level, in terms of an adaptation to increase fitness (and how this appears to shine through unconsciously in the romantic ideal), then it could well be paradoxically what women want. (This sort of disparity is hardly unusual. Childbirth similarly is an event that of itself most women could hardly be said to want. And beyond the episode itself, women often don't want children until they have their own and have to be mothers; only then finding that they wanted children all along.) There is no need for us to be directly motivated by what is important for us to achieve: merely the facility to respond when key triggers arise is all that is necessary.

Man as ubiquitous 'oppressor': all sex is now illegal unless proved otherwise

The defining down of rape to the point that all sex is deemed to be forced, would make all sex by default illegal and all men by default criminals subject to arbitrary trial and imprisonment. This was achieved in Britain with the 2003 Sexual Offences Act, which introduced three astonishing innovations.

Before having sex, a man now must 'take all reasonable steps in the circumstances to ascertain true agreement'; the legislation outlining 'a non-exhaustive list of examples' with which he is expected to be familiar. This means that all sex between any parties is potentially subject to arbitrary selection for a show trial where the defendant has to prove that he complied with the law. The Crown does not have to prove anything. That the burden of proof has shifted from the prosecution to the defence, is an entirely new development in English law. Sex, which is *the* essential behaviour, and the expression of which is the most fundamental civil and human right, is now by default an illegal activity.

The new law also overturns the second great principle of law: that nobody should be charged for an offence merely because of a risk that he might commit some other offence in the future. Based on research showing that some rapists had previously been voyeurs or 'flashers', the new law lays down ridiculously heavy sentences for both of these minor offences — as well as for bestiality and 'sexual interference with human remains'. There has been no causal link demonstrated between such low-level sexual perversion and serious sex crime, and therefore there is not even the risk of future serious offending, as disingenuously claimed.

The third unprecedented illiberal innovation in the new law is that it prosecutes individuals for a different offence to the one it purports to. The fundamental basis of rape being a crime of greater seriousness than other forms of assault is that it can lead to pregnancy, and that women react with distress for this very reason. Yet the new law expressly dispenses with the need for a vagina to be involved. Even the mouth, let alone the anus, becomes a sexual orifice fully equivalent to the vagina. Not only are acts which do not involve the insertion of the penis into the vagina clearly not rape, but they are not experienced as rape by victims. We know that most girls will concur with Bill Clinton that fellatio is not tantamount to sex, even though it is actually the more intimate act. Clearly, there is something very different about (genital) sex itself.

Rape cases usually depend on one person's word against another's. Juries are openly invited to be swayed by the demeanour of the putative victim. This is to tear up the criminal law standard of proof 'beyond reasonable doubt' — or, as it has now been weakened: 'to be sure' — and not even to substitute the civil law standard, which is 'on the balance of probability'. One person's word against another's necessarily is evidence that can only balance 50/50. Nowhere else in law (other than regarding the not-dissimilar crime of male 'oppression': domestic violence) can anybody be convicted without a weight of evidence against them.

To further the idea that man is the 'oppressor' of woman, the government has stopped believing that it's better to let ten guilty men go free than have one innocent man in jail. It's now considered acceptable to set the bar so low that ten innocent men are jailed to then get the one actual rapist. Even further injustice is planned. Before the new legislation had bedded down, the Home Office began talking of a 'justice gap' to justify even further measures.

The law on rape is a wonderful window on a prejudice against men that is so deep and pervasive that it is 'second nature', as they say. In fact not 'second' but first.

Summary

That rape is supposedly the main way that men 'oppress' women depends upon rape being on a sizeable scale, but it isn't. The real problem is the huge scale of bogus allegations—a spiral that is undeterred and is fuelled by men being routinely charged on the basis of no evidence and convicted on the basis of no proof.

The enormity of this problem is revealed by analysis of police data from both sides of the Atlantic. It may well be that an actual or even a large majority of complaints are bogus. Research by rape investigators themselves reveals a collection of reasons why women behave in this way, and none is any way a response to supposed male 'oppression'.

If rape is the main way that men supposedly oppress women, then the impact of rape must be serious, but research shows that generally it's not. Typically there may be some mild depression, but not usually lasting beyond four months. The most recent overview of studies was over twenty years ago, and it showed a range of effects so wide and bound up with pre-existing conditions, that the research was worthless.

The idea that rape is the quintessential form of 'oppression' of women is denied by the fact that men rape men. This is on such a scale in US prisons that there is much more male rape in the USA than rape of women. What's more, it's for sex, not to express 'power'.

To support the notion that supposedly rape is about systematic 'oppression', there has been a political imperative to misrepresent rape as a crime committed not by men who can't get access to sex, but by men gratuitously inflicting violence on women. Study of rapists and the profile of victims and perpetrators refutes this. Rape is about sex, and violence is almost always much less than you would imagine to be necessary, if indeed there is any at all.

Rape is the ultimate tactical subversion of the male DH, and the ultimate reason for 'policing' the male DH. With males never indispensable and females the 'limiting factor' in reproduction, there is a clear biological reason for the prejudice that the murder of a man is not seen as being as serious as the mere rape of a woman.

Rape is largely a misnomer in that much or most rape appears not to be forced sex. Several phenomena concerning rape, not least 'rape fantasy' and the seeming ready capitulation of women to an attack, can only be explained from an evolutionary perspective. Women may non-consciously desire sex with rapists because in the evolutionary past this was likely to result in offspring bearing the genes of high-status men.

The ultimate in the prejudice that anti-male conceptualisations of rape can produce has now come to pass. By a legal insistence that 'all reasonable steps' are taken to establish consent, the sex act has become by default illegal.

Chapter 12

Who's Exploiting Who?

Prostitution defrocked

A t first glance, prostitution is how the sexes get along when all is laid bare. Sex swapped, supposedly, for resources. It's not. Or, rather, at root—at least for the classic professional prostitute—it's not. With money being proxy for status, women in general are open to the possibility of sex—even sex behind the back of a long-term partner—with a man they judge to be high status by virtue of the money he has. This is not having sex for money though. The money a man provides through presents and picking up the tab for a woman during courtship is not payment either, but tokens of status or reliability to persuade her to be a long-term partner. A fee to a professional prostitute, from a biological perspective, is akin to this.

Yet long-term partnership is not, of course, the object of prostitution, so prostitution is more than a short-circuit of courtship. It's a distortion of it. For some reason, women are here exploiting the natural male desire for novel sex with a variety of partners. Most women would never prostitute themselves, except in an extreme situation of need. When women are starving they will willingly offer sex in exchange for food, but otherwise few women are prepared to 'sell' themselves. Why any women would want to do so is the interesting question.

The answer to the other question here, of why men pay for sex, is also more complicated than you'd think. There is the joke that men don't pay for the sex so much as for the woman to go away afterwards. There is truth in this. Prostitution turns out to be another window on how the separate worlds of the sexes actually come together, rather than how we mistakenly imagine they do.

* * *

A now mainstream view has arisen by the default of nobody bothering to challenge it, that the forfeit of resources by men in exchange for sex, somehow is men exercising 'power' over women. Handing over money is reckoned to be either in itself somehow hurtful to women, or to insufficiently offset some other hurt that attends the transaction. How this may be hurt-

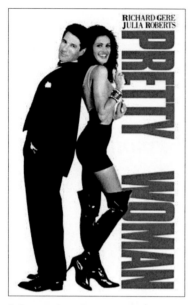

Hollywood is so frightened of prostitution that it's never actually portrayed. The lead characters in Klute, Pretty Woman *and* Indecent Proposal, *are in ostensible prostitute–client relationships which turn out not to be prostitution at all.*

ful or what kind or hurt it might be, is never ventured. Prostitution is regarded as both a different kind of sex and, at the same time, just the most blatant form of sex, and as intrinsically oppressive to women. This is at root a denial of the acceptability or even the existence of natural male sexual behaviour. Simple prejudice towards men.

This attitude has currency in part because it taps into conservative popular opinion. Ordinary people also mostly think prostitution is distinct from other sex, but not because they think it's coercive. They instinctively know that the female is the 'limiting factor' in reproduction: that this is how it is, and also how it should be. Prostitution they view as undermining the normal situation of sex being in short supply. They see something wrong with both the woman in offering and the man in taking advantage. Hence public opinion that the female 'supply' side as well as the male 'demand' side is culpable. The authorities meanwhile, being a locus of political correctness, stamp down hard on the male 'demand' side only (in complete contrast to the policy on drug abuse). The media sucks up to both views, the PC one particularly; unrelenting in an extreme negative portrayal of prostitution and male clients, whilst over-sympathising with prostitutes. Every false stereotype has been exaggerated, as in the TV series *Vice* and *Band of Gold*, and in the film, *Stella Does Tricks*. Hollywood is so frightened of the subject that it's never actually portrayed. The lead characters in *Klute, Pretty Woman* and *Indecent Proposal*, are in ostensible prostitute-client relationships which turn out not to be prostitution at all. At last, in 2007, a TV series *The Secret Diary of a Call Girl*, starring Billie Piper, depicted prostitution in a non-political manner.

Why it makes sense for men to pay for sex and for some women to provide it

The answer to the question 'why do men pay for sex?' would seem banal, but the joke about actually paying for the woman to go away afterwards reveals something that's not entirely obvious. Sex is in very short supply because women are interested only in higher- rather than lower-status men (this being relative, of course, to their own level of 'mate value'). Consequently, most men can get sex more easily through long-term partnership, because here a woman will tend to trade off status for reliability. Even so—at least until the recent attempt of the feminist-inspired ladette culture to overturn biologically-grounded morality—men are unlikely to get any sex in the early stages of courtship, whilst their prospective mates are still assessing indicators of status and reliability. Men get feigned brush-offs to test their ardour and commitment before full-blown courtship, which takes a prodigious investment of time and money. It's a delayed and expensive way to get sex and, anyway, male ardour declines as familiarity with a partner's body grows.

Getting the variety of novel sexual partners that men so crave is still harder, and this craving is in no way diminished by having a long-term partner, other than that overall libido declines (though it's not clear if this is because of over-familiarity with the long-term partner or general sexual satiation). Men could to some extent get round the problem of supply by searching out relatively unattractive women, given that such women will tend to settle for lower-status men, even for extra-pair sex. But, self-evidently, men much prefer attractive to unattractive partners, however brief the encounter. What's more, a relatively unattractive woman will be more likely not to be in a long-term partnership, and so will be seeking one. Whilst a man is thinking only in terms of a brief sexual partnership, the woman may be in courting mode, as it were; in which case she won't take kindly to what she would perceive as being dumped.

This is dangerous for a man who already has a long-term partner. Hoping that she can engender the man's long-term interest out of a short-term fling, the woman may be in no mind to allow him to peacefully return to his lover. She could threaten to expose his extra-pair sex to a wife or girlfriend, or to make a nuisance of herself in other ways. Casual sex which is not strictly a string of one-night stands risks the female partner thinking she is now in an exclusive duo. She is then shocked to find that the man is sleeping around, oblivious to the possibility that the rules of engagement were ever otherwise.

The interestingly fraught communication between the sexes means that even when it's agreed on both sides that the relationship is only casual, complications quite usually ensue. Under the influence of their different respective motivations (that beget wishful thinking), the sexes make dif-

As Dan (Michael Douglas) discovered to his cost in the film Fatal Attraction, *what was for him a casual weekend affair was anything but to his partner Alex (Glenn Close)*

ferent assumptions about the state of a relationship as it progresses. Casual sex is not subject to a contract, laying out ground rules. A female casual sex partner may feel every right to demand commitment and to impose on the man her own interpretation of what the rules should be. With their penchant for 'relational aggression', a woman may indulge in casual sex to arouse the latent jealousy of a former partner, with a view to re-establishing the relationship. She may even deliberately incite an ex to violence against her casual sex partner. There is much scope for her casual sex partner to lose his long-term mate, either directly or indirectly through the woman's machinations.

To preclude these various possibilities, it would make good sense for most men to pay for sex. The intrinsically anonymous sex of prostitution is outside the man's social life, so carries little if any risk either of being discovered, or of a party to it discovering something about the other that can (and that they would want to) be used against them. There is still a stigma, should a man be found out to be paying for sex, but the jealousy of a long-term partner is far less likely to be aroused by the one kind of sexual encounter that carries no possibility of blooming into a fully-fledged affair. For the man, paying for sex is the most straightforward and honest—and the cheapest—way to acquire extra-pair sex.

Still more interesting than looking at the 'demand' side of prostitution, is to ask why women should want to be on the 'supply' side. It's not that a prostitute is simply atomising a long-term partnership into a series of discrete encounters which, if you tot them all up, she gets as much out of as a single relationship. With the female being the 'limiting factor' in reproduction, few women cannot secure a long-term partner, and any who can't are not left without an income on which to at least survive. Unlike men, women do not need income as status to project so as to attract the opposite sex, and therefore having an income significantly above a basic one is, from an evolutionary perspective, unnecessary. There are exceptions to this, such as those who have a drug habit. There are also those at the other extreme, who merely dabble occasionally in prostitution, just when they need a little extra on top of benefits, student allowance, or a low-paid or part-time job. Excepting these women, what about those who are prostitutes by profession and earn accordingly? Why would any woman turn to prostitution to earn an income for which she has no biological need?

The answer, from the perspective of this book, is the same as may be apparent generally in the world of work. Whereas men, through the motivation of status-seeking, propel themselves up the corporate ladder; those relatively few women who do likewise, are not doing so to acquire status per se. For some or many of them, presumably it is for the weaker, different reason of placing themselves in the path of high-status men. Now, if a woman doesn't have the ability or inclination to follow a career but is nonetheless sufficiently motivated to adopt a similar trajectory, then what can she do? Well, with money, she can spend her way into the paths of high-status men. The problem is that without a career or an inheritance, women have no way to acquire money on any scale, given that they are not motivated in the direct way that men are to put any great effort into simply earning money. The beauty of prostitution is that it requires low effort and little use of time to accrue the high income to enable women to move in the circles of higher-status men; or to give themselves the delusion that they do — which itself can be motivating. If a prostitute is young and attractive enough to command high fees, then in a real sense she really does move in such circles, given that only such men can afford to visit her. 'Low-end' prostitutes, for whom the state is their de facto long-term partner; have clients inevitably of a higher status than the men they see in their ordinary lives. In effect then, the sex they have with clients is akin to the extra-pair sex women are normally disposed to.

It may be objected that this is an explanation too far, in that money and the things it can buy can become their own reward as our instrumental subsidiary motivation to behave in this way becomes a positive feedback loop short-circuiting underlying motivation. This is indeed what must happen in many cases. The question is whether this was what was going on from the outset or that it became so.

* * *

The common attitude towards prostitution is easy enough to understand in terms of what I've explained of male reproductive skew and its consequences for men in society. The sex of prostitution seems to us a case of men 'cheating' the system. The potential for a man to illicitly spread his genes — especially if they are 'duff' genes, so to speak — worries society far more than a few women as prostitutes 'letting the side down'; albeit that many women are in a rage with this minority of women for the consequent devaluation of the scarce resource of female fertility. The real problem is seen to be men 'out of control'.

Yet 'out of control' is here certainly not a case of men exercising 'power'. Men resort to prostitution despite the costs of possible detection by their partners, the all-too-common occurrence of crime (robbery, assault) by the prostitute and/or her accomplice, punitive action by law-enforcement agencies, the possible cost of further loss of social esteem should their visiting of prostitutes be found out, and the direct transfer of resources. To characterise this as abuse of 'power' is grasping the wrong end of the stick. Men who use prostitutes are demonstrating their power*less*ness. What bothers people here is a low-status man acting apparently above his station.

If the man was behaving promiscuously but without having to exchange money for his extra-pair sexual encounters, then people would tend to regard him in an entirely different light. This is because to be able to pull this off he would have to be a higher-status male, and people are predisposed to excuse certain behaviours of such individuals — extra-pair sex being specifically excusable in a higher-status male. Our psychological 'cheater detection' mechanisms are not engaged. It's the paying for it that suggests to everyone that the male is more likely to be of lower status, and so the social excusability is reversed to become opprobrium, because of the social-psychological mechanism that generally lowers people's estimation of males they perceive to be of low status. Notwithstanding that a man would have to be reasonably well-off to afford the regular use of prostitutes, and that the evidence shows that men who go to prostitutes are a cross-section of the population; the public perception that he is typically low-life is unshakeable.

We can see that this is an anti-male prejudice by comparing attitudes when the sexes in the prostitute–client relationship are reversed. In places such as the Gambia, Cuba and Turkey, there is a small but growing 'sex tourism' industry for women whose middle-age has denuded them of sexual power. They pay not for sex per se, but for a romantic experience of which sex is a part. Here the providers are seen as beach predators, and the consumers as Shirley Valentines. When a woman brings her provider to Britain to live, the newspapers and her friends all infer that the much older woman has been conned by a man, and ask 'why can't she see?' It is, of course, they who can't see: for their anti-male prejudice.

Is anyone using anyone else more than in other relationships?

As to the question of who is using whom: is prostitution actually much different to other human relationships? Are not men and women in prostitution using *each other*? What interaction between people is not reducible to some mutual using — marriage, most certainly, included? Not just marriage, but same-sex friendships are really mutual using arrangements, or at least this is how they seem to be when they unravel. As men regularly experience (though few will so analyse), the main threat to a male–male friendship is if one party begins to perceive that the other is of markedly lower status than first realised, or if the other's status has for some reason fallen substantially since the friendship was cemented. At some point, the perceived imbalance in relative status will prompt the one who is the higher status of the two to apply judgement based on a 'cheater- detection' mechanism, and this will test the friendship to destruction, or provide the excuse to dissolve it. A friendship starts over some mutual interest and/or through shared social space. It's coalition building in embryo. Men want to get together to form groups to contest other groups, or to form alliances to help to climb within the group. In picking someone as a friend, a man is not going to select someone noticeably weaker than himself, but someone who is either stronger, or who has something to offer that he himself or other group members need: especially social connections to help with further alliance building. At the very least they will be 'equals'. A friendship is an instrumental relationship.

The point is that if our more stable bonds, whether sexual or not, are mutual using-arrangements; then why would it be a worry that a fleeting sexual encounter was of the same ilk? Feminists have argued that there is an inherent lack of respect, but this is a loaded argument, being circular reasoning based on the assumption that men always oppress women, and therefore will exploit them at any opportunity. The money exchange in the opposite direction rather kills this argument. Doesn't the prostitute–client encounter more resemble a contractual relationship like in business? The most common greeting from a street girl to a man walking nearby is: 'do you want business?' This precisely describes what in essence it is; albeit complicated in the way that I've explained.

There are arguments that prostitution undermines the family or even the inclination to date, in that sex is made available for which otherwise men would have to compete and to trade their provider role. But this does not square with the historical evidence (see panel on page 217) and with what we know about the customers of prostitutes — that they are a complete cross-section of the male population — nor with the nature of male sexuality. Most use of prostitutes is by men who either have long-term partners or various sexual liaisons other than with other prostitutes. Users of prostitutes often have high numbers of sexual partners other than prostitutes. These men simply need either a parallel existence of casual sex with novel partners to their role as long-term partner, or still greater variety of sexual partnering than they already enjoy. Most men certainly prefer neither a regular prostitute, nor the thrill of picking up different girls, to a loving relationship. Not if it's an either/or choice. But it's never either/or. Ideally men would like both a regular partner and *at the same time* the variety of a series of sexual encounters with novel females. For all sorts of reasons, for some men this is more of an imperative than for others, and many or most men may well never be sufficiently disinhibited to act on the inclination. For many though, recourse to prostitutes is more honest and less disruptive to a man's long-term relationship than the alternative of affairs or one-night stands. It's a responsible and considerate course.

All in all, prostitution is sex that is very much of a piece with sex experienced in other, more usual contexts, and actually complementary to it. It's also in line with all the other kinds of relationships people have. It's normal behaviour.

The reality of prostitution

The ubiquity of prostitution as a natural social phenomenon is evident looking around the world. There are more prostitutes in China than in the whole of the rest of the world: at least four times as many sex workers per head as the world average. This is despite not having any sort of mass tourism. In Thailand, the local use of prostitutes massively outstrips the 'sex tourism' scene. All young men are first initiated into sex by visiting a prostitute, and it's thought that at least half a million prostitute–client transactions are made daily. Clearly, prostitution is in no way an import from a culturally-aberrant developed world. We in the West are aberrant in a very different way. In most cultures (including our own until Victorian times) there is no shame attached to sex, and this is not at all in conflict with strict natural morals regarding courtship. There is no political mileage in the supposed oppression of prostitutes, even when they are young girls, because usually life is hard, and the corresponding lot of boys and young men is far harsher. In China, India, Egypt and many other countries, boys are used by others as beggars; often deliberately mutilated so as to attract sympathy money. Bleach is injected into a joint which then becomes gangrenous, forcing amputation by hospital casualty staff. Alternatively, limbs are repeatedly broken, or twisted by the constant use of tourniquets. Other boys are forced by modern day Fagans to rob. In Africa, the age-old problem of slavery is a mass phenomenon mainly afflicting males. In India, there are estimated to be tens of millions of child slave labourers, the vast majority of whom are boys, some as young as six. 'Employment' is spread throughout the economy, including those occupations dangerous even for adults. Few girls and young women suffer in these ways because they are more valuable as prostitutes.

Here in Britain, as an indication of the insatiable desire of men for variety of sexual partners, the numbers of men seeking prostitutes continues to grow rapidly—actually doubling between 1990 and 2000: to one in ten of the male population. There are a number of reasons, and these have been identified by a recent survey (Ward, 2005). The fact that there are more men with money, the rising divorce rates, the internet, international

The 'oldest profession' — a potted history

At the high point of the Victorian family, there could have been 55,000 prostitutes in London (O'Daniel, 1859) — those known to the police (8,600) being only the most open: 'Were there any possibility of reckoning all those in London who would come within the definition of prostitutes, I am inclined to think that the estimates of the boldest who preceded me would be thrown into the shade' (William Acton, 1870).

This was hardly a diminution of activity from the century before, which remains the sexually bawdiest in Britain, with prostitution so open that a bestseller of its day (250,000 copies from 1757 to 1795) was the amazingly explicit *Harris's List of Covent Garden Ladies*. The thousand plus women listed were mostly praised, but readers were warned of some, such as the 'contaminated carcase' of Miss Young of the Turk's Head Bagnio; Pol Forrester's 'breath worse than a Welch bagpipe', and Lucy Peterson, who was 'as lewd as goats and monkies — a vile bitch'. Jack Harris, self-proclaimed 'Pimp General of All England', was landlord of the Rose (the scene for Hogarth's engraving below), where naked women graced tabletops.

Patrick Colquhoun, in his *Treatise on the Police of the Metropolis*, estimated in 1797 that there were 50,000 prostitutes (10% of all females) in London. The trade was the biggest employer bar service, and girls thronged the streets in groups. Much of Georgian London was built with money from the upper end of the trade, and not a few women (both prostitutes and proprietors) were made wealthy and respectable. 'Courtesans' actually set the fashions, and because they could become so themselves, were not distinguished from the kept mistresses of the wealthiest in the land. The 'higher end' was portrayed in the first erotic novel, *Fanny Hill* (1749). This entry from *Harris's List* is for Miss B____rn of No.18 Old Compton Street, Soho:

This accomplished nymph has just attained her eighteenth year, and fraught with every perfection, enters a volunteer in the field of Venus. She plays on the pianoforte, sings, dances, and is mistress of every Maneuver in the amorous contest that can enhance the coming pleasure; her price two pounds.

William Hogarth, A Rake's Progress

travel, and the increasingly liberal attitude to and availability of commercial sex. There is much less embarrassment and coyness about sex even compared to twenty years ago, and (within certain bounds) the casualisation of sex by women is now normal, or at least not abnormal. There are now not only more men with both the inclination and the means, but also more women inclined to provide the service. Numbers of prostitutes on the streets had quadrupled between 1980 and 1990, and the ever-thriving 'massage parlours' were joined in the 1990s by an explosion of girls working from a phone number advertising in newspapers, and more recently on the internet, which has also spawned a great increase in 'escort agencies'.

The internet has fuelled the boom because photos of girls with their full details are here both accessible yet not fully public, in that material only emerges if you go looking for it. It's the perfect means of targeted advertisement without the drawback of attracting complaints. The internet is also used for message boards where men can exchange recommendations and tales of woe, though such 'field reports' are often placed by the girls themselves or their employers, masquerading as their 'punters'. These boards are usually tied in some way to the provider side of the industry, and are consequently unreliable, and often no refuge from the usual prejudices against men who use prostitutes. Nevertheless, the internet serves to disinhibit men from using prostitutes through the removal of the fear of venturing into the complete unknown. And the usually bigoted picture of prostitution in the media is exposed as fiction.

The emergence above ground of the whole 'scene' has taken away some of the stigma, and now some men are up-front as users of prostitutes. Sebastian Horsley for a time wrote from the client's perspective as a sort of style guru for the Observer, claiming that we are all prostitutes selling something; whether it's our souls, our minds, or our bodies:

> "The great thing about sex with whores is the excitement and variety. If you say you're enjoying sex with the same person after a couple of years you're either a liar or on something....What I hate are meaningless and heartless one-night stands where you tell all sorts of lies to get into bed with a woman you don't care for....The prostitute and the client, like the addict and the dealer, is the most successfully exploitative relationship of all. And the most pure. It is free of ulterior motives. There is no squalid power game. The man is not taking and the woman is not giving....Why pay for it? The problem is that the modern woman is a prostitute who doesn't deliver the goods. Teasers are never pleasers; they greedily accept presents to seal a contract and then break it. At least the whore pays the flesh that's haggled for. The big difference between sex for money and sex for free is that sex for money usually costs a lot less....Some men proudly proclaim that they have never paid for it. Are they saying that money is more sacred than sex? (Horsley, 2004).

The cost of paid sex has been falling in absolute let alone real terms (at one time the price of a 'trick' was reckoned to be between a third and a half of a week's wage for the lowest paid). This is especially so on the street, which has become much more the refuge of the drug addict, whose chaotic life is incompatible with work in any other part of the 'sex industry'. With the street perceived as very much the bottom of the market, the safe and congenial 'massage parlours' thrived and multiplied, and competition set in to reduce prices here too, and also raised the quality of the service to the point that the street could no longer seriously compete. Establishments routinely advertise 'gfe' — 'girlfriend experience' — puncturing the lie that there are fault lines between sex and prostitution: purported in the film *Pretty Woman* to be kissing on the mouth.

The mushrooming of paid sex is cited as evidence of more women being faced with fewer options and entering prostitution by default, yet the trend through the previous decade was markedly the opposite: there were between one and two million more jobs in the economy as we approached the millennium, about half of which were filled by women. Becoming a prostitute became a more favoured real choice. It should be borne in mind that involvement in prostitution can vary enormously. To call a woman a prostitute or 'sex worker' is often something of a misnomer, in that the hours she needs to work typically are so low it would barely qualify as 'part-time', and many are in any case claiming state benefits, so are actually benefit fraudsters rather than workers. Studies have shown that some women take to the street or get some shifts in a 'parlour' for as little as two or three weeks in a year — just to pay winter fuel bills and to buy Christmas presents. The labels 'prostitute' or 'sex worker' also tends both to deny that the ordinary woman also is, and to imply exploitation. The PC term 'sex care worker' has little currency because it turned out highly un-PC in making the clients sound decidedly cuddly and the profession positively legitimate.

Towards criminalising the male purchaser:
The prejudicial crackdown on the male 'demand' side only

The government ignores reality and insists that prostitution in any form is a problem that should be and can be eradicated, yet conspicuously fails to tackle actually problematic aspects, thereby betraying deep prejudice towards men. With a mushrooming of the scale of prostitution, and with extreme feminist bigotry rife in government, so it was that yet another proposed 'crackdown' on prostitution wielding the stick to men but offering the carrot to women was announced by the government (Home Office, 2006). The Home Office minister then in charge, Fiona MacTaggart, has since revealed the underlying intention by advocating the criminalisation of men who pay for sex. Trailing the policy to the BBC, she described men who pay for sex as 'child abusers'.

This is fiction. The only sector of prostitution where there is any risk of encountering an under-age girl is the street scene, which has shrunk to now being a small fraction of prostitution overall. Under-sixteens trying to work the street have long been subject to immediate pick-up by the police, and this now applies to under-eighteens, given the recent law raising the minimum age for working in the 'sex industry' — itself partly explaining MacTaggart's silly jibe about 'child abuse'. Inadvertent sex with anyone under sixteen is now a rare risk for kerb crawlers. Needless to say, men would respond to girls under eighteen who solicit them, because men are hardly able to tell whether a girl is lying about her age, especially in the dark in the fraught situation of a 'red light area'; and many or most girls in their early teens can easily pass themselves off as eighteen. This would be entrapment, not 'child abuse'. Even regarding the small number of girls who dabble in the trade before their sixteenth birthday, a tiny fraction of the activity over their career would be when under-age. Most prostitutes don't begin work in earnest until adulthood, with the great bulk of prosti-tution working indoors in 'massage parlours', or as 'escorts' supplied by agencies, or — now increasingly — independently. This much more visible part of the 'scene' takes seriously the minimum age obligation, as there is close monitoring by police.

The emphasis of the Home Office proposals ostensibly is on dealing with the outdoor prostitution market, whilst liberalising the law regard-ing the indoor part of the 'industry'. All effort is to be put into punishing kerb crawlers, whereas street girls are to be offered help to leave prostitu-tion on the grounds that supposedly they are all victims: allegedly not of MacTaggart's supposed 'child abuse', but of their own drug addiction. This is another fiction, as Ana Lopez, president of the sex workers branch of the GMB union very strongly objected (GMB, 2006). Undoubtedly there has been a big increase in drug-addicted prostitutes on the street, but this in no way means that most (supposedly 95%) prostitutes are drug addicts. Even the claim for the street is based on faulty sampling. Most street pros-titutes spend little time in the role, and their presence is unlikely to be picked up in a survey. The minority of those with out-of-control drug hab-its, on the other hand, need to be out often and for long periods to earn large sums, not least because they have to wait much longer for clients who are looking for healthier, more attractive girls. The 'druggies' are therefore overwhelmingly more visible in surveys.

Prostitutes who seriously abuse drugs, either were users before they took to prostitution, or with the money prostitution provides are able to progress from flirting with drugs to a habit. Rarely is there the supposed classic pimp trick to train the girl up with her habit to prostitute herself. Pimps are little in evidence, because the prostitute and the drug dealer have a relationship that is a particularly virtuous circle. Pimping would be superfluous and counter-productive. Indeed, the argument about the sup-posed exploitation of girls by dealers would be better put the other way round: the girls earn money with (relative) ease and low risk, in order to commission the procurement of drugs by men who take high risks in obtaining and selling them. Likewise, girls in children's homes, in return for sex, commission boys to shoplift to order—so as to pay for drugs. The prejudicial view is to cite the males as agentic and ultimately responsible for the crime, whereas actually it's a female propensity to hide behind apparent male culpability when a female is herself the agent.

The Home Office views prostitutes as suffering from 'false consciousness', but this insulting misrepresentation was certainly not apparent the last time prostitution underwent a major review, back in 1957. Lord Wolfenden was under no illusions, concluding that the 'great majority of prostitutes...choose this life because they find in it a style of living which is to them easier, freer and more profitable than would be provided by any other occupation.' There is no reason to think that the human nature this reflects has fundamentally changed in the intervening forty years, and this is confirmed in surveys by the English Prostitutes Collective and the Edinburgh SHIVA project.

The current government line is based on the rationale that women who take up prostitution of their own volition cannot be admitted to the ideal world of female emancipation imagined by extreme feminists, so the corollary is that their existence must be denied. Just as mass unemployment could never be admitted by so-called communist states, extreme feminists cannot stomach legalising prostitution or even decriminalising it, because the 'free contract' between the punter and the hooker can't be free if, as they claim, men and women are unequal.

Although the mis-labelling of prostitutes generally as either the victims of 'child abuse' or drug addiction does not wash, two stock arguments that prostitution is an undesirable phenomenon remain, but neither of these stand up either. One is the notion that this is where STI (sexually transmitted infection) epidemics arise. This is easily refuted. There is strong evidence that 'commercial' sex is actually safer than 'non-commercial' sex (Ward & Robinson, 2004). The incidence of STI found to be associated with prostitution is lower than expected given the proportion this represents of all casual sex encounters with novel partners. The rate is lower than in the general population of comparably sexually-active people. With the ongoing trend in the casualisation of sex and shunning of condom use amongst young people, and the focus of prostitution in clean, controlled off-street venues; the relative rate of STI infection through prostitution compared to ordinary consensual sex is falling. What's more, any incidence that there is, represents cases that are quickly detected and treated, because prostitutes are targeted for regular sexual health screening.

The other common argument against prostitution is that more street girls means more sex crimes. 'Commodifying' sex is thought to give men the idea that all women are potentially easily persuadable to have sex, which makes men oblivious to any resistance and liable to use force.

Against this is the so-called 'hydraulic' model, that men seeking prostitutes are finding an outlet they are unlikely otherwise to find unless they commit a sex crime. Prostitution thereby leads not to a rise but a fall in sex crimes. There are too many factors to fathom, but the widespread action against kerb crawlers has coincided with a rise in recorded sex crimes.

* * *

The Home Office's line that prostitution is 'not inevitable' is a position not so much uncompromising as totally unrealistic. However, the policy appears not to be seriously motivated by any attempt to deal with the problem as such, but instead, along with much of the thrust of Home Office policy, is more of a vehicle of hatred towards men. From the Home Office's viewpoint, realism is beside the point. With lack of realism the basis of policy, then initiatives that could really help to solve problems — such as the cause of most complaints: street activity in residential areas — can be dropped. Consequently, despite the enthusiasm in places like Liverpool for piloting 'tolerance zones' in *non*-residential areas, where the safety of both girls and clients can be improved; 'zero tolerance' against men as pioneered in Middlesborough's red-light area is favoured.

It's for the very reason of evidence of some success of 'tolerance zones' abroad, that the Home Office is not allowing experimenting here. The fear is that 'tolerance zones' will work only too well. This would 'send out the wrong signal' that prostitution is thereby acceptable, the Home Office disingenuously insists — given that it has given a very loud and clear statement that prostitutes are not to be punished.

The proposed measures will lead to not fewer but more street prostitutes, a bigger problem in residential areas, and also to more crime surrounding street prostitution, in that criminally-inclined women will feel still freer to 'clip' their clients, who are even less able than they already were to complain to police. ('Clipping' is taking payment but then not providing the service; so ubiquitous that it merits this slang term.) The Home Office intends to give us the worst of all possible street prostitution worlds.

Matters will be made still worse — given the other part of the proposals to tackle those behind 'massage parlours' — on the incorrect assumption that owners are usually male. At the same time, the law against more than one girl working at an address is to be axed; instead allowing a pair of girls and a 'maid'. This is a cynical move of not wanting to be seen to be closing off the alternative to street working; nevertheless this will be the impact. 'Massage parlours' appeal to those girls who are incapable of running the business side themselves, or don't want to. Girls can move into and out of such establishments with ease. The sort of prostitutes who set up their own concerns are mostly not the kind of girls who work on the street, whose lives tend to be chaotic, and who are anything but business minded.

The proposals fly in the face of the evidence presented to the Home Office, both by prostitutes' collectives and organisations working to help girls exit the trade. These argue that, as in Sweden (Clausen, 2007; Working Group, 2004; Ostergren, nd), the increased nervousness of clients will make the street scene more dangerous, because negotiations will be more hurried and fraught, leaving girls with less to go on in making a decision of whether or not to go with a particular man. Then, in order to escape the attentions of the police, the places where contact is made with clients, and where sex is performed, will be further removed from patches which are familiar and where there are other girls nearby.

The Home Office is, in effect, confirming that it does not care about the welfare of prostitutes: its concern regarding women is that they cannot be prostitutes in reality because the reality is that they are not traders but victims. According to this reasoning, if more women get hurt as the result of the policy, then it's of little consequence given that the women are being hurt anyway, and they are exhibiting their continued 'false consciousness' in continuing to work. In any case, this will help to bolster the idea that the legislation is needed.

As for the kerb crawlers, they are to be made to attend 're-education' courses and to pay for them, despite pilots showing that such schemes don't work (Taylor, 2006). West Yorkshire Police ran one a decade ago and abandoned it because it made no impact. Charities working to get women to exit the trade relayed what the girls said: that it did not stop clients from continuing to see them. The measure is a corresponding attitude to 'punters' of the attitude that prostitutes must have 'false consciousness'. It's a similar insult and abuse; much worse when you consider who are the actual crime victims here. The large number of clients are individually a very fleeting presence, and as victims of robbery, assault, etc, what they suffer is invisible, and out of all proportion to any suffered by prostitutes. The crime of 'clipping' is so rife that the wonder is how little retaliatory assault there is against street prostitutes.

The far greater numbers of clients or potential clients, compared to the number of prostitutes, points up a very simple aspect of the problem that the government is not addressing: that there is always a bottleneck on the supply side. If the intent was to curb prostitution rather than to practice hatred towards men, then resources would be used to tackle the supply side—the prostitutes themselves. Yet kerb crawling is an arrestable offence, whereas for the girls, empty warnings replaced fines when it became politically unacceptable to jail women for repeated non-payment.

Of the proposed legislation, the anti-kerb-crawlers part was enacted in 2007, but, at the time of writing—with MacTaggart now sidelined on the back benches—more 'consultation' is being sought regarding girls working indoors. Of course, neither the anti-kerb-crawling nor any other part of the original proposals will/would work; not least because of the lack of enthusiasm by police and local authorities, who are more in touch with the situation on the ground than is the feminist 'think-tank' within the Home Office. What will win through is the natural ingenuity of people to get round inflexible obstacles to their persistent and endlessly flexible and very human behaviour. It's a retrograde step on the way to criminalising all paid sex for the male buyer, whilst giving legal immunity to the female seller. There is even less excuse for moving in this direction given the Swedish experience of similar measures. There, the buying and selling has simply intensified indoors and on the internet, leaving the girls who still work the streets more vulnerable, as I mentioned. Disingenuously, it was the Swedish experience that MacTaggart cited in support of her advocacy of criminalising men.

In late 2007 there was a new tack to underpin the goal of criminalising the male purchaser. The government put out the blatantly false claim that 85% of women working in brothels were from outside the EU, many of them 'trafficked'. In fact, the great majority of women in brothels are native British, and of those who aren't, nearly all are from the EU: notably from the nations that acceded in 2004, such as Lithuania. It's another question whether any of the very small remainder have been 'trafficked', and this is a further fraud as I will now outline.

The usual suspects were cited as 'sympathetic' (that's news-speak for originators) to the idea — the attorney general Patricia Scotland; the solicitor general Vera Baird; 'Hopeless Hattie' Harman — but also the home secretary Jacqui Smith. And, of course, MacTaggart, who suggested that an amendment could be added to a new criminal justice bill then about to be debated. The Home Office denied that there were any plans to criminalise payment for sex, but it was clear that informal discussions aimed at long-term change were afoot.

The myth of the 'white slave trade'

The line that men are the sole guilty party, and that women cannot, by definition, make a voluntary choice to become a prostitute, has been resurrected as the old myth of 'the white slave trade'. And this went up a couple of gears with a clutch of lead news stories in 2005 about alleged 'trafficking' of women from Eastern Europe. The phrase 'white slave trade' was first used in the early nineteenth century to describe (supposedly) forced prostitution. Though foreigners were demonised as slavers, it was mainly making a parallel with the sugar plantation slave trade that was finally abolished at this time. It was a moral panic that exactly parallels what is happening today. According to the leading scholar on this topic, Jo Doezema:

> The mythical nature of this paradigm of the 'white slave' has been demonstrated by historians. Similarly, recent research indicates that today's stereo-

Raid on Birmingham's Cuddles massage parlour in 2005 when supposedly nineteen 'trafficked' women were 'rescued'. In fact thirteen were here legally and working voluntarily and the other six were also working voluntarily but illegal immigrants.

typical 'trafficking victim' bears as little resemblance to women migrating for work in the sex industry as did her historical counterpart, the 'white slave'. The majority of 'trafficking victims' are aware that the jobs offered them are in the sex industry, but are lied to about the conditions they will work under....Contemporary historians are nearly unanimous in seeing the actual number of cases of 'white slavery', as defined above, as very few. (Doezema 2000)

A spate of high-profile 'anti-trafficking' operations in 2005 netted prostitutes working in 'massage parlours' in Birmingham, Sheffield, Leeds, and other cities. Many women were arrested but both the police and the immigration service were very quiet afterwards about their 'rescue'. Local shopkeepers who knew the girls told reporters how relaxed the girls were and very happy with the money they were making. It emerged that not one of the girls in any of the raids had been 'trafficked', but instead were all voluntary immigrants, either legal or illegal. The same had been the case in 2001 when raids netted sixty women in Soho, all of whom said they were working voluntarily. Prostitutes' groups actually picketed the Home Office in February 2001 to protest on their behalf. This mirrors the outcome of raids in other countries, such as one in Toronto that netted two dozen Thai and Malaysian prostitutes the local media described as 'sex slaves', until it emerged that there were wire taps of them boasting about the amount of money they were earning. They had all willingly come to Canada to ply their trade. Ironically, given the Home Office's pro-immigration and pro-woman PR angles on 'trafficking'—to try to make out that the women immigrants were victims, and the culprits were British men—it was only when the police secured a conviction of an Albanian gang themselves here illegally, that they got any 'result' re 'trafficking'. Here, just two women were deemed to have been 'trafficked', but the police picked out of the air a large number they thought must have passed through their hands. In another case, of a pair of Albanians described as 'traffickers', again only two girls were implicated: two legal Lithuanians who worked at a fully above-board 'massage parlour' in Sheffield, coming and going of their own accord and never giving any inkling to the woman manager of anything amiss. Their supposed 'traffickers' appear to have been their pimps; and pimps of a quite 'hands off' variety at that, likely their boyfriends.

It's not that there are no 'trafficked' women at all, but that the numbers are tiny. The World Cup in Germany was heralded as a magnet for 'trafficking' women, and huge resources were deployed to combat it. Just five 'trafficked' women were found. Even the Global Alliance Against Trafficking in Women, in a major report (GAATW, 1994) that trawled indirectly for all known 'victims' through their support organisations – which had a vested interest in inflating the picture – had to conclude that abduction in connection with 'trafficking' was actually very rare. Just as Doezema found, the only problems were the working conditions the women discovered, not the work itself. The Foundation for Women in Thailand found that sex workers who went to Japan knew what they were letting themselves in for. In the late 1990s, there was research in every continent, in places like Ghana, Hungary and the Caribbean: all threw up the same finding, that women were not being duped (eg; PROS, 1995). Researchers even went to the lengths of working as bar girls themselves to find out what was really going on (Watenabe, 1998).

It's a measure then of the extreme feminist takeover of the UN that that organisation – which commissioned some of the major research showing that there was no significant problem – cites an unreferenced estimate of one to two million annually of 'trafficked' women. As the GAATW notes, figures are often simply the number of prostitutes who cross a border, and not the sub-group of prostitutes allegedly 'trafficked'. Sometimes this is confusion by wilfully lax journalists or others who have been given figures for sharp increases in numbers of prostitutes and argue that 'trafficking' *may* be the explanation, and present it in such a way that 'trafficking' appears to account for all of the rise. Figures for the movement of women, or even for resident totals, are wildly variant. Confusion or deliberate lie: those who proselytise the view that all prostitutes are by definition slaves, don't care. Any movement by women across borders to work in the sex trade is taken to be an infringement of human rights.

All in all, the conclusion regarding both the nineteenth-century 'white slave' trade and the current moral panic, is that they were dreamed up to create political pressure to repress prostitution (Irwin, 1996; Walkowitz, 1980; Gibson, 1986; Corbin, 1990; Grittner, 1990; Billington-Grieg, 1913). The 'fallen woman' idea could not wash with the Victorian public because there was simply far too much prostitution in evidence. Too many women were involved for them all to be 'fallen', and so women were blamed for their own 'moral depravity'. Street girls and their liaisons with even well-to-do men were so unremarked upon that Gladstone when prime minister could regularly wander down to Piccadilly to pick one up and take back to Downing Street. To secure action on prostitution, blame had to be shifted away from the women themselves. Moral outrage was renewed by widening the scope in public imagination of the women 'at risk', to alarm the ascendant middle classes that it could be their own daughters next. This came with William Stead's famous 1885 article, *The Maiden Tribute of Modern Babylon*, in which he told how he bought a young girl. He succeeded more than he could have anticipated — being himself jailed — enabling reformers to focus away from the women: first on to the supposed buyers, next on to the clients, and then on to men as an entire sex.

The reality about prostitution in Victorian times, as now, is that it's the chosen economic exploitation *by women of men*. Then, it was a rational choice from the limited opportunities available (Walkowitz, 1980), just as it is nowadays.

To get at the true reality of the sex worker, you have to compare her with the male alternative. I don't mean the male *sex* worker, who for obvious and several reasons is thin on the ground; but the lowly male worker, who has poorer opportunities in an equivalent position of very restricted employment and social options — just as I did above regarding the Third World. Any woman who cannot find (or opts out of) both marriage and employment, can massively boost her benefits income by even just occasional prostitution, and be in a far better position than a man at the foot of the corresponding male social world. He suffers the double problem of *needing* more than subsistence income, *and* having no means other than very low-paid 'black economy' work or criminal acts with far more severe sanction than for soliciting for prostitution. The 'bottom rungs' of society here are entirely different according to whether you are male or female — indeed, it's arguable if there is any such thing as a bottom rung for a woman.

Who is the prostitute: the female whore or the male wage-slave? The word 'prostitute' means 'to expose publicly, to offer for sale'. Described this way, men generically are prostitutes in having no option but to offer themselves to the highest bidder in exchange for their labour; whereas almost all women are, at least for a major portion of their lives, supported economically without any need to bargain, as a by-product of granting exclusive sexual access. We are supposed to pity the prostitute as the ultimate economic victim, despite the musky aroma of the 'fallen woman' resuscitated from her Victorian grave. She is not a victim, being merely manufactured as such. As usual, this is to try to perpetuate the lie that woman is man's victim, in the service of gaining yet more unwarranted privilege for over-privileged womankind.

Summary

How the sexes get on with each other would seem to be laid bare in prostitution, but this is an illusion. Below the surface women are not just exchanging sex for money, and it's not as simple as it seems for men either.

For men, the extra-pair sex that provides the variety of partners they have evolved to crave is in especially short supply, and it often comes with hidden strings attached. This is why circumventing normal social interaction in sex is for men good sense. For women, prostitution makes sense as a very easy means of earning money – not, at root, for its own sake (although it can become so) but to be used to place them in the path of high-status men. So prostitution is a mutual 'using' scenario where the prize for both parties is sex, either directly or indirectly; now or in the future.

An indication that prostitution is not exploitative is a comparison with other relationships, which all turn out to be mutual 'using' scenarios; not least simple friendship. Prostitution does not undermine other relationships: merely fulfilling male needs and female wants, that no other interaction easily can.

Far from being some cultural aberration, prostitution is ubiquitous and ever growing all around the world, and not at all a Western export. In Britain, it's clear that more women are prepared to exploit the demand for prostitution, as is shown by the falling price of paid sex and the widening of forms of provision, despite the improved general employment situation.

Treating prostitutes as victims and their clients as exploiters, is the way that the Home Office tries to deal with prostitution, but this fails because the supply side is where the number of individuals is small enough to be tackled. Consequently, the street scene remains vibrant and the indoor scene to which the girls could migrate is hampered because of controls through the misapprehension that men control this trade. The usual reasons why prostitution is bad – that it is the source of STI epidemics and leads to an increase in sex crimes – are both the opposite of the truth.

The perpetuation of the notion that prostitution is female victimisation, manifests in the resurrection of the nineteenth-century myth of women being bought and/or shipped abroad. The contemporary version is based on classing all cross-border movement of prostitutes as 'trafficking'. The vast majority move voluntarily to countries where earnings are higher.

Chapter 13

Proscribing Male Thought

Erotica as 'pornography'

Just as with prostitution, attitudes to 'pornography' reveal deep-seated natural prejudice against men, based on the perception that men are 'breaking the rules' of the male hierarchy. In prostitution, low-status men are seen as illicitly obtaining sex with someone other than their regular partner. The same social psychology is behind how 'pornography' is viewed, even though there is no interactive sex by a consumer of 'pornography'. No matter: men masturbating to mere images of women is regarded as tantamount to having sex with them.

'Pornography' derives from the Greek root *porneia* referring to acts of prostitution. The distinction between 'pornography' and erotic art is derived from the commercial aspect of the act of prostitution, a difference echoed, for example, by the distinguished curators of the Barbican exhibition *Seduced: Art and Sex From Antiquity to Now* (Wallace, Kemp and Bernstein, 2007). But this is a dubious argument: 'even the greatest art involves at least one commercial transaction, between artist and patron; it is simply more obvious in pornography' (Smith, 2007). The difference between an artist's model and a Page Three 'stunna' is primarily that the latter is better paid, so one is forced to conclude that 'erotica' is little more than 'pornography' for posh people.

'Pornography' is a pejorative word that didn't exist until mid-Victorian times. The Obscene Publications Act (1857) followed, with its definition of 'the tendency to deprave and corrupt'. In all ancient civilisations, and in England in the Middle Ages (not least within the church), and certainly in the eighteenth century, a bawdy sexuality was the healthy and wholesome norm. What we refer to as 'pornography' should be thought of as simply erotica (hence my use of scare quotes): artefacts that sexually arouse. Erotica is not restricted in its appeal to men. As I explain in this chapter, romance fiction—which threatens to outsell the whole of the rest of the fiction market—is women's erotica (Salmon & Symons, 2001). Nobody has ever suggested legal controls here.

*François Boucher,
Leda and the
Swan (c.1740).
Fine art, erotica or
'pornography'?
The rape-fantasy
myth of Leda and
Zeus disguised as a
swan has been
depicted by
numerous artists
including da Vinci,
Rubens, Boucher
and Dali.*

One of the (supposed) objections to erotica targeted at males is that it 'objectifies' a whole sex, but if this was a valid criticism then it could be levelled with more justification at romance fiction. Invariably, the heroes in fiction specifically written for women are portrayed in terms of their status (worldly success, height and build, etc), just as 'girly' magazines/DVDs invariably feature women according to their fertility (beauty and youth). Those men who are successful are ascribed positive personality characteristics to go with their success, whereas other male characters are in some way presented as cheats (a classic case being the contrast between Darcy and Wickham in *Pride and Prejudice*). This does not have a parallel in (male) 'pornography'. Men don't think that a woman is more trustworthy or has a nicer personality the more physically attractive she is—if anything they fear the reverse (and perhaps not un-objectively). 'Objectifying' men in female erotica clearly has worse effects than does 'objectifying' women in male erotica.

Wendy McElroy (1997) takes issue with the 'sex object' argument:

> What is wrong with this? Women are as much their bodies as they are their minds or souls. No one gets upset if you present women as 'brains' or as spiritual beings. If I concentrated on a woman's sense of humour to the exclusion of her other characteristics, is this degrading? Why is it degrading to focus on her sexuality?

Another (supposed) objection to male erotica is that it's akin to prostitution; that it lies on the same continuum. It does so only in that both involve the exploitation of men by women for money—and in the former case a woman has only to provide images of herself, not her body 'in the flesh'. The flimsiness of this argument exposes the fear underlying it. Just as prostitution is seen to cheapen sex and thereby skew the market for it (which would otherwise be loaded even more in favour of the sex that is the 'limiting factor' in reproduction), so 'pornography' is equally detested.

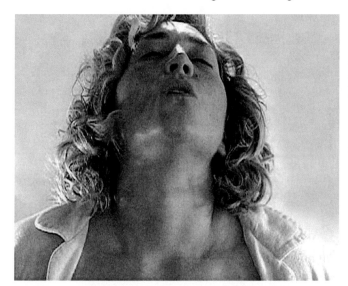

K.R. Buxey's Requiem *featured the artist as performer — so that's all right then, as no 'objectification' was involved*

That this is indeed the common view is pointed up by the reaction to 'pornography' regardless of whether any sex act is involved. Almost all the sex entailed in 'soft' 'pornography' — all that used to be available legally — is masturbation by the consumers. All that is depicted is nudity. By definition, 'soft-core' features no interactive sex.

Extreme feminists try to connect the two industries of 'pornography' and prostitution in claiming that many of the participants are in effect prostitutes, but the women involved are now very well surveyed and are unanimously vocal in upholding their free choice to financially exploit their voyeurs and to take glory in displaying themselves. So acceptable has this become to the public, that Carol Shaya of the NYPD claimed that she was helping to make the force appear with a more human face by posing for *Playboy.* Indeed some feminist artists and film-makers proffer a similar argument in order to distinguish their own work from the 'exploitation' of women by male artists. K.R. Buxey claims that *Requiem*, her homage to Andy Warhol's *Blowjob*, did not 'objectify' women, as the artist and the 'performer' were one and the same person — ie. the artist *chose* to film herself enjoying cunnilingus. Needless to say this fine distinction would be entirely lost on her audience; there is a clear parallel here to the absolute (and spurious) feminist distinction between date-rape and consensual sex examined on page 185, above.

What happens by contrast when the artist and 'performer' is male was shown when 'the naked rambler' Steve Gough and his girlfriend Melanie Roberts did their 'freedom to be yourself' walk from Lands End to John O'Groats in 2005. Steve — but not Melanie — was repeatedly imprisoned. It would seem that the authorities took something like Buxey's line regarding Melanie, or even that her nudity was as 'empowering' as the couple claimed; but when it came to Steve, apparently in their eyes he assumed the guise of an agent of oppression. (It is for just this reason that recently in Sweden there were demands that in public toilet facilities men must sit rather than stand to urinate. A man standing was deemed to be 'triumphing in his masculinity' and thereby 'degrading' women.)

Women who have sex on screen are much more likely than prostitutes to declare their liking for sex. Indeed, rather more than with prostitution, it's held to be impossible to succeed in 'hard-core' 'pornography' without liking the sex, because anything other than an honest enjoyment will not wash on screen. In any case, the rewards for performing a recorded sex act are considerably larger than in the one-to-one transaction of prostitution; and plenty of women volunteer their preference for prostitution over other work on a simple cost–benefit equation.

The arguments about 'objectification', and erotica being akin to prostitution, are merely attempts to justify prejudice: political red herrings.

Erotica is the only way to satiate male desire for endless novel sexual partners

There is little attempt to know what it is about erotica that appeals to men, let alone to understand why. It's very easily revealed that it's the sheer variety of women depicted that interests men. It's about novelty. Experiments show arousal to be significantly less when looking at images that have been seen before, even if just once; and it falls rapidly with successive exposures on subsequent occasions. This occurs even if the images are of very different sexual acts. The problem is that they are performed by the same women. This shows that it really is the novelty of the individual women that counts (Kelly & Musialowski, 1986). So the main impact of erotica is that it gets boring and quickly so. Erotica generically has to remain fresh. This is just as with actual sex. Erotica, in the form of an endless supply of images of different women, remains a potent source of arousal regardless, within reason, of how much a man consumes. There isn't the inevitable collapse of ardour as in actual sex with the same partner, however much the sex is varied.

This is why the 'sex industry' is such a goldmine, and why outlets offer a 'buy and then swap' kind of sales–lease service. It also explains why unexpectedly the best selling magazines have always been 'soft-core' titles like *Fiesta*: a magazine of not very revealing snap shots of (supposedly) readers' wives in all their real life variation and inexhaustible number. Conventional models and their standard poses have a more interchangeable beauty, so that the novelty value of the different girl on the next page is diminished, even if the images are 'hard core'. This explains the popularity of what is generically known as 'the girl next door'.

The reason that men consume 'pornography' in this way is because it taps into their drive for extra-pair sex—for an endless sequence of novel partners, just as prostitution does. Masturbating to images of different girls is the way they can satiate this natural drive, albeit as a far less-rounded experience than actual sex. The upside is that it's far cheaper, and the girls are more attractive and more numerous than in prostitution. If wives and girlfriends understood this, then they may not feel so negative when they discover a man's 'porn' stash! Would they rather their men seek one-night stands that might evolve into affairs? Or that they go to prostitutes? If men are consuming 'pornography', shouldn't it provide reassurance to wives or girlfriends that they are less likely to be finding satisfaction in extra-pair sex? Of course, but that is not the issue. What upsets women is that their partner looking at erotica is itself tantamount to his having extra-pair sex. Women never understand that for a man, having sex with a regular partner is a completely different scenario from having a string of brief casual sex encounters with a range of other partners. In a man's mind they are completely independent. Being satiated in respect of sex with a long-term partner does not mean being satiated regarding extra-pair sex, and vice versa. It's being of the sex that is the 'limiting factor' in reproduction that prevents women from ever empathising with men in this regard.

Erotica does not damage

The principal attempt to disguise prejudice against male consumption of erotica is to attack it as somehow predisposing men to commit sex crimes. This is contrary to all the evidence. Experiments show that 'pornography' has no effect at all on sexual behaviour outside the laboratory where the repeated exposure is conducted (Julien & Over, 1984). In places where there is more explicit depiction of sex, the incidence of sex crime is low; and after the legalisation of 'hard core', sex crimes actually show a significant *decrease*, and this may be more than an unexplained correlation (Green, 1985; Kutchinsky, 1985). The late, eminent sex criminologist, John Money, found that sex offenders had had *less* access to 'pornography' than their peers, had come across it later in life, and had been raised with more sexually-repressive attitudes. The leading researcher, Edward Donnerstein, has conducted an overview of hundreds of studies and writes: 'A good amount of research strongly supports the position that exposure to erotica can reduce aggressive responses in people who are predisposed to aggress.' Criminologist Bill Thompson, also looked at all the studies and concluded that: 'they prove that "soft core" is good for you, because it lowers your aggression level'. Even studies with 'pro-censorship' conclusions, like the Meese Commission Report, emphasise that there is no reliable link between 'pornography' and violence. Research by the feminist Thelma McCormick also found no connection between 'pornography' and sex crimes (and for this reason her data was suppressed, then doctored by a 'pro-censorship' advocate before publication). Pre-exposure to 'pornography' has been shown even to make men more willing to come to the aid of a woman who is hurt.

The next line of attack is to claim that harm arises from a subset of erotica: depiction or suggestion of coercion or violence (though this is for some critics a catch-all, in that all sex is seen as coercive). Yet depictions of forced sex seriously dampens male arousal, usually making penetration impossible (Barbaree & Marshall, 1991). Watching a man aggress against a woman presumably activates men's adrenaline stress response system in readiness for physical defence/attack, and this immediately shuts any process that is not survival-critical: notably the sexual response. This is because within the 'in-group' a man instinctively protects women and aggresses against men who breach social codes. In Japan there is readily available and in massive quantities 'pornography' depicting graphic violence. Exactly which quality of this material circumvents this normal male response is unclear, but Japan has a very low incidence of sex crime.

A weaker version of the argument would be to claim that erotica depicts women as always available, and that this can lead to a greater expectation in men that women will succumb to sexual advances, thus possibly lowering the threshold of what men interpret as 'come on' signals. But equally, erotica could instil within a man a sense of his own sexual inadequacy. Male 'porn' stars are physically impressive, with large and perennially erect penises. And far from increasing the chance of a man trying 'date-rape', the contrast between the relatively coy or unresponsive flesh-and-blood woman before him compared to the remembered image of yielding flesh on screen, is likely to make a man doubt that his date has anything more than a platonic interest in him. It is in any case absurd to think that men do not make a clear separation between fantasy and reality. Just as young boys universally manage this in their play with weapons, so men surely do regarding sex. There is plenty of extreme social sanction if they don't.

'Thought crime'

On the face of it, public opinion has moved very fast in favour of a relaxed view of 'hard-core' 'pornography'. Despite backing from the then Home Secretary, Jack Straw, The British Board of Film Censorship (BBFC) had been forced by the courts to allow a few 'hard-core' titles for sale in licensed sex shops (an unforseen consequence of the 1998 Human Rights Act). To avoid more fruitless legal defence, it then had no choice but to relax the rules. The BBFC subsequently ran a survey of the public, presumably expecting that such an extreme liberality would be shown to be out on a limb; only to find that, of all organisations, the Mothers' Union felt that adults have the right to see explicit sex if they want to. All kinds of public bodies and individuals were included, and the great majority expressed a similarly relaxed attitude. The National Centre for Social Research's survey in 2000 on the portrayal of sex on adult subscription channels, video and the cinema, showed that attitudes were considerably more permissive than only five years before. However, this is in line with the distinction found in surveys generally between tolerance and personal values. Most people are far from *endorsing* explicit sex on screen. They simply uphold the right of others to do what they like, as long as it's in the privacy of their own home, or at the very least where all children and very young adults are excluded if it's in public. The arguments of John Stuart Mill appear to have won the day.

Prejudice has shifted its locus to the age of those being depicted. Given the key preference of men for youthful women, the easiest way to attack male consumption of erotica is to raise the minimum age of the women whose images are captured, and to call any female below this age a child. Falsely eliding adult erotica with actual 'child pornography' creates public hysteria by massively inflating the size of what is in fact a minuscule paraphiliac minority. Here, the Children Act (1989) comes to the assistance with its definition of the age of consent for any involvement in what could, however loosely, be regarded as 'the sex industry', as two years over the normal age of consent: eighteen in place of sixteen. Of course, this would redefine most men on the planet as paedophiles — not that sixteen doesn't; by proper definition a child is a person below the age of puberty, which on average is at the age of eleven. All men are naturally attracted to girls above this age, albeit usually not to the very youngest of them; but not many girls aged fourteen or fifteen are considered unattractive by men (or at least those who are prepared to be honest).

The law is self-evidently bizarre. Whilst any couple can legally have sex at sixteen, they cannot photograph each other in any stage of undress until two years later. There is nothing in the least aberrant about a girl of, say, seventeen years and eleven months, having sexual intercourse — not excluding if she pulls a face to, say, feign consternation at the supposed size of her sexual partner's penis. Yet images of this for their own private use would be classed as the most serious 'paedophile porn' — the so-called 'level 4' and 'level 5'; respectively, depictions of sexual intercourse and 'sadism', of the kind that the TV actor Chris Langham was famously convicted of viewing in 2007. In his case, some of the images were of pre-pubescent children, but inexplicably the age of children is not a factor in the classification of images — and neither is the reality of the image, since 'pseudo-photographs' (photo-montage or computer morphing) are explicitly caught by the law. The Department for Justice is even considering laws to outlaw sites where users create images from scratch; that is, where there is nothing of a real child pictured at all, and instead there are lifelike animations completely computer generated.

That the law is in confusion and with highly disturbing results was shown some years ago when the newsreader Julia Somerville sent the holiday snaps of her children for developing. Being very young children on a beach, then naturally they were unclothed in some of the shots, but staff at her local film processing shop alerted police. This vividly confirms that crimes regarding 'child pornography' are deemed ultimately to reside purely in the mind of the viewer, having nothing to do with what is being viewed. 'Child pornography' is therefore a 'thought crime'. Fully confirming this, an art exhibit by the famous photographer, Nan Goldin (belonging to Elton John) was declared *non*-pornographic by the CPS in October 2007 after police removed it from a gallery in Gateshead at the instigation of staff. *Klara and Edda dancing* is a snap of two young children, one of whom is fully naked with her vaginal opening showing. It was placed on several discussion websites, but when 'hits' massively increased, site owners thought the worse of why so many were viewing it, and censored the image to obscure the vagina.

Orwellian Ore

A further dimension of governmental abuse is opened up in trawling for suspects by identifying men from the credit card numbers used to access websites. What will go down in history as a case study of a digital-age Orwellian nightmare—that at the last count had claimed thirty-three mostly entirely innocent lives—is the absurd and bungled Operation Ore. This sought to prosecute large numbers of men who had accessed by credit card the Landslide Productions website, which was simply a payment system for a vast array of 'adult' websites, none of which contained any 'child pornography'. The only way to view 'child pornography' via Landslide was through pop-ups and advertisements which not only were beyond the control of Landslide, but could download themselves as a 'cookie' on to the user's computer without his knowledge. (A cookie is defined by Microsoft as 'A very small text file placed on your hard drive by a web page server'.). There was not even any way of telling from the credit card details that were seized if the user had accessed any kind of 'pornography'—legal or 'child'—let alone that he had downloaded any. This has been argued successfully in court by an expert witness, Duncan Campbell, who damned the entire operation as: 'systematic injustice [for] many people and their families [who] are the victims of a combination of technical naivety and fear, fed by a media circus, a twenty-first-century witch-hunt'.

One victim of Operation Ore was Paul Reeve, who had been the head of PE at a school in King's Lynn, despite—so it emerged in 2006—being on the sex offender's register. This led to a furore and calls for the head to roll of the then education secretary, Ruth Kelly. She cowardly agreed to hold an enquiry and tighten up procedures, even though the decision had been taken before her watch by a junior education minister, Kim Howells, who stood by his decision that Reeve posed no danger to children. Reeve's photograph was regularly shown on TV news, as was his new place of abode with his parents, yet he had merely been cautioned as the result of Ore, so he was not even convicted of any crime.

Many men accepted cautions rather than contesting and facing impossible odds in going to court, in the same manner as plea bargains and signed confessions to avoid a death sentence if convicted, are used to force co-operation against the interests of those accused in the USA and Thailand respectively. All the media were resolute that Reeve's acceptance of a caution meant that he was guilty. Reeve has always insisted that he has never even viewed let alone downloaded any 'child pornography'. Police had checked his computer and found no evidence of downloading. The evidence that he used his credit card only regarding a payment system for adult pornography sites did not sway them.

In all of the furore, there was little if any discussion about the problem of placing names inappropriately on the sex offenders' register (the register includes everyone from murderers like Ian Huntley to innocent victims like Paul Reeve and many men who have been caught short and urinated against a wall for want of a public convenience—a nuance that is not respected by the likes of the *News of the World*). No mention was made of the evidence that even someone who had a paedophile sexual orientation was no more likely to act out his sexuality after viewing such images.

'Violent' porn is proscribed so as to attack erotica generally

Amazing though it is, the government has now compounded the absurdity of the law on 'pornography' by introducing a new offence of simple possession of images that are 'sexually explicit and which contain serious violence'. As with the law on 'child pornography', it is merely assumed that the image is of a crime being committed, even though there cannot be such a claim based on the default assumption that there can't be consent (as when children are involved). There is no pretence of being unaware of the potential for injustice: 'We intend to capture those scenes which appear to be real and are convincing, but which may be acted'. This is a stage beyond the madness of the law regarding 'child pornography' images, because it's not merely that adult participants *may* be merely actors, but that they are *likely* to be—and almost certainly will be. They are to be regarded as victims, 'whether or not they notionally or genuinely consent to taking part'.

'Notional' is a weasel word government is using to deprive people of their liberty; and to then condemn them to ostracism and reprisal by placement on the sex offenders register. What it means is that as far as the government is concerned, as a participant in filmed consensual sex activity it's

Rembrandt, Jupiter and Antiope *(1659). Other depictions of rape fantasy include Fragonard's* The Beautiful Servant: Pointless Resistance, *Boucher's* Leda and the Swan *and Picasso's* La Douleur.

deemed that in reality you were coerced, even if you protest to the contrary. In other words, the government has donned the Emperor's New Clothes of the extreme feminists and is actually saying that if you believe you consented, then you have 'false consciousness'. Anyone who gets hold of the film by any means will then by a false extension of responsibility be committing at the very least 'thought crime'. We have arrived back at Orwell.

Not only has no crime worth the label been committed in the film being viewed, but it's almost inconceivable that there was even any thought by the viewer of doing anyone any harm, however indirectly. At worst, the viewer would be suspending disbelief so that he could view the film as if he was viewing an actual act. This is no different to the behaviour of adults and children every day in watching all kinds of (fictional) acts that are criminal and more serious than rape, but the entire population is not as a consequence under threat of arrest for 'thought crime'.

Female erotica and rape fantasy

I want now to look more closely at female erotica and what underlies it. Although romance fiction, when compared to male erotica, is more focused on the context than the sex itself, the former has a more sexual core, that requires explanation in the context of evolutionary time.

So-called 'rape fantasies' (Hazen, 1983) are experienced by such vast numbers of women that they are regarded as the most common female fantasy. Wendy McElroy explains them as fantasies of 'being taken'. She cautions:

> The first thing to understand is that a rape fantasy does not represent a desire for the real thing. Why would a healthy woman daydream about being raped? Perhaps by losing control, she also sheds all sense of responsibility for and guilt over sex. Perhaps it is the exact opposite of the polite, gentle sex she has now. Perhaps it is flattering to imagine a particular man being so overwhelmed by her that he must have her. Perhaps she is curious. Perhaps she has some masochistic feelings that are vented through the fantasy.

Her last question seems to answer her first: women daydream (and indeed have unconscious dreams in their sleep) to satiate some kind of masochistic fantasy. It's the theory that feminists most deplore: that women have a desire to 'be taken', ostensibly against their will. The resistance must be false or ambiguous, otherwise how else can the fantasy be explained? And if the volition in the dream is not about the real thing, then what on earth is it about?

I think there is quite a simple but profound answer to this, that I have already outlined from the perspective of rape (see chapter eleven); but it bears reprising from this different angle. Rape fantasy harks back in evolutionary time to when women (and indeed, pre-human hominid females) lived with the real possibility of being abducted in a raid by males from a neighbouring group. This would hardly seem a welcome possibility in any circumstances, though certainly in the grand scheme of things it would be preferable to the alternative fate in a raid suffered by her male counterparts: murder. It may be that the outcome for her would be actually an improvement in terms of the 'mate value' of her new spouse (as I previously explained). So she somehow manages to accept it, though she certainly does not need to be *conscious* of the need to radically re-orientate in order to survive emotional trauma: survival-critical psychology and behaviour is seldom conscious. Far from a full awareness, what is needed instead is to shut down intrusive conscious consideration. So there is no suggestion that rape in itself was something a woman ever *wanted*. It sufficed not to resist in a way that might sustain serious injury, and to emotionally block the trauma of the death of her loved ones.

A powerful emotional wrapping is provided to negate the unpleasantness of the sex, not to mention the shock and mourning for the death of male loved ones. This is very much the feel of the 'swept off her feet' kernel of romantic fiction. You could see as a similar evolutionary 'strategy' the placidly euphoric and analgesic glow provided by the hormone oxytocin, nature's way of overcoming all of the pain and trouble associated with childbirth. Indeed, it may well be that oxytocin is the mediating hormone in being 'swept off her feet'.

Paradoxically, there is a real sense in which rape in this context is woman's exclusive sexual power. Simply by being female she has warded off the murder that would have been her fate had she been a man, and then in effect divested a man of control of himself. She is in a deeper sense neither subjugated by him nor does she surrender to him. The surrender is a joint one to the higher imperative—the maximisation of gene replication that stands outside and above both of them. The counter-intuitive power of the woman victim over her rapist is hinted at by McElroy: 'Perhaps it is flattering to imagine a particular man being so overwhelmed by her that he must have her.' The motivations would seem to be deep-seated psychological modules that evolved to meet a recurring scenario in human life,

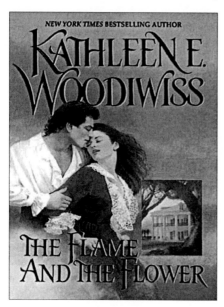

Is female romantic fiction little more than sublimated rape fantasy?

and understanding this scenario is the only way to make sense of women's behaviour.

The 'rape fantasy' is woman's 'pornography', diluted to social acceptability in the vast market for female romantic fiction. There is such insatiable demand for Mills & Boon and its ilk (much of it far more sophisticated and updated than the derided stereotype) that it does not merely rival but is every bit the true equivalent of the vast male market for what we choose to call 'pornography' proper. That in itself tells us that something psychologically profound must be at the root of romantic fiction. We will never, in some more 'liberal' future, get graphic rape scene magazines aimed at satisfying a female market.

Just as dreams are now thought by some to be rehearsal for important behaviour, the 'rape fantasy' appears to be a reprise of a primeval behavioural routine (or pre-emptive cognitive defence). Being raped and carried off into a new life is something more done to a woman than anything actively performed by her, so it requires a psychological re-orientation, rather than new behaviour routines. Just as with ubiquitous dreams of falling—the main danger for a pre-hominid primate more at home on the grassland but who takes to the trees for refuge from nocturnal predators—these sequences presumably are deeply seated in our brains, and so phylogenetically archetypal that they must be genetically and not culturally based.

As I concluded in chapter eleven, it seems that in evolutionary psychology terms, a 'coping with rape' module in women is a profound way to understand the whole phenomenon of rape. And note that *there is nothing to suggest that women do anything to precipitate sex in this situation, nor that even in a passive way is there a conscious welcome*. What a woman does appear to have is an unconscious psychological mechanism that prepares her to 'be taken' (to use Wendy McElroy's phrase) and to reconcile herself to it and not to fruitlessly resist.

This resolves, or rather blasts a hole through, the hopelessly contradictory but simultaneously-held polarisation between an 'all men are rapists' position—where rape is seen as natural male behaviour in that it's an expression of a universal 'patriarchy'—and the other position which claims conversely that rape is *un*natural, and that there can be no excuse for individual men who rape. These are actually very similar notions, both invoking a theory of 'patriarchy'; the former that it's an anachronism but somehow inherently ineradicable in all men, and the latter that the anachronism is of an era that is passing and that therefore can be socially reconstructed out of the way. The difference is simply between whether or not the future is seen in terms of a social order that sidelines men as the embodiment of an ineradicable anachronism, or one where this is undermined and men and women enter a 'post-patriarchal' age. Both theories simultaneously blame not individual men but 'patriarchy' (though then spin back to blame individual men anyway). Both theories are nonsense because the notion of psychological 'patriarchy' is equally absurd. Men do not rape because of 'patriarchy'. Within normal society (that is, within the 'in-group'), no men rape (by the generally-accepted definition), apart from those with certain psychological impairments (as in the sociopathic failure to emotionally empathise with others). It's only when there is a catastrophic social breakdown into warring 'in-group'/'out-group' elements that normal men might rape. So men may well rape in war, where there is a clear-cut 'in-group'/'out-group' contest.

The 'rape fantasy' as a foundation of romantic fiction, though more about emotional reaction and relatively divorced from the sex act, has the same function of concentrating and repeating the essence of what is arousing for the consuming sex. When translated into the concrete form of a romance novel, then 'rape fantasy' is no less 'pornography' than is the male equivalent.

There are those who find the notion of 'pornography' distasteful, warranting a pejorative label rather than the more neutral tag of 'erotica'. To quote Nadine Strossen (from her book, *Defending Pornography*): 'people use the word "pornography" to define any sexual explicitness they don't like. This is as good and concise a definition of 'pornography' as we are ever going to get.

Summary

'Pornography', or rather, erotica, no more 'objectifies' women than it does men. Only erotica that appeals to men is disapproved of. This is at root a natural prejudice that men are breaking the rules of the male hierarchy. As with prostitution, it's the outrage that low-status men are somehow illicitly obtaining extra-pair sex, albeit here merely symbolically.

The male desire for a variety of novel sexual partners is insatiable, and for almost all men this cannot be met by actual sex. Masturbation to endlessly varying images of women is the harmless solution (now that we know it doesn't make us blind).

The basic fear about 'pornography' is that it 'depraves and corrupts' to the point of encouraging sex crime, but in fact it produces the opposite effect. Conversely, dangerous sex criminals are found to have been exposed to little if any erotica, and generally to have had a sheltered existence regarding sex.

Anti-male prejudice is especially apparent in that the law increasingly targets not offences per se but the mere thought of actions that would be offences only if actually carried out. Fantasy short-circuits the desire to act out. The law against 'child pornography' is used against men who have in no way, however indirectly, harmed a child; and this betrays that the law is really about the hatred of male sexuality.

A notorious police trawling exercise has persecuted very many entirely innocent men in the supposedly 'anti child-pornography' police witch hunt code-named Ore. Men have been convicted, forced to accept cautions or committed suicide as a result of persecution for having merely accessed a pay portal to adult erotica.

The new law on 'violent' images further exemplifies anti-male prejudice. It's really a general 'anti-pornography' measure, because there is no actual violence readily available as 'pornography', and by feminist definition there is no sexual act that cannot be categorised as violent.

For women, erotica is the romance novel, and the core of this is fantasy about sex that ostensibly is against the woman's will but which nonconsciously she desires. This is the 'rape fantasy', which has real evolutionary roots.

Chapter 14

Excluding the Family

The state as the real absent father

The separate worlds of men and women are starkly apparent in so many ways, but nowhere more so than in the determination to keep men out of the family. Here follows an astounding tale of intransigence and deception that is impossible to explain without what we know of the evolved differences between the sexes and what they entail. More superficially, sense can be made of this only in terms of an entirely woman-centred, anti-male and anti-family politics that stems from 'cultural Marxism' underpinned by evolved 'folk prejudice' against (lower-status) men.

The family and the domestic sphere around it is regarded as being firmly within woman's separate world, even more — much more — strongly than the workplace is regarded as the separate world of men. Of all the rights abuses systematically directed against men, the worst is the unwarranted obstruction from playing their natural part in the lives of their biological children, by denying the basic human and civil right to contact (apart for the barest minimum). This is at root justified through refusing to recognise that men have a strong affiliation to and bond with their own children which a step-father does not have. This most blatant denial of human nature lasts only until the issue of money arises. Entirely regardless of circumstances, it's the biological father and not the 'social' male parent who must support the child financially.

Imposed on men are non-negotiable and often unreasonable financial demands for child support, even in respect of a child that resulted from a one-night-stand when, more than ever, fertility is controlled by women. (The man very likely will have no knowledge of the woman's contraceptive use, and may well not be told the truth if he asks; and the passion of the encounter is likely to mean that the issue of condom use is waived or not even broached.) There is also the unfairness to men of divorce settlements, and the policies of the government that actively encourage the dissolution of relationships. This is in not so much by financially penalising couples as encouraging single parenthood with huge subsidies.

Guy Harrison, a member of the Fathers 4 Justice group, climbs up on the roof of Westminster Hall to display a banner reading 'Does Blair Care?'

This is all in the face of overwhelming evidence of the positive social outcomes of marriage for children and the negative outcomes on average for any other arrangement, with a single-parent household shown to be the worst possible milieu of all for a child to start in life (even controlling for income and other variables concerned with disadvantage). The evidence for this is so readily available that it is unnecessary for me to set it out here, though I will be dealing with an aspect that has had little discussion. Despite repeated requests to various government departments and agencies for any research to show that a non-shared parenting model is in any way preferable, none has ever been forthcoming. This is because there isn't any. Sometimes it's claimed that marriage merely correlates with positive outcomes—ignoring the fact that other variables that could have produced positive outcomes have been controlled for.

As much as destroying the family is central to PC politics, it will never succeed because the family is the natural social unit we have evolved to live within. Three in four children remain in intact families even today.

The same legal abuses regarding contact with children are evident across the developed world, yet there has been no serious attempt at reform, or even to recognise that there is a grave injustice. This is despite the millions of people devastated by it, and some of the most effective news-grabbing stunts in pressure-group campaigning history by Fathers 4 Justice (such as the prime minister's question time and Buckingham Palace stunts). The very different reaction to this campaign by ordinary people, compared with how most of the media and the political classes saw it, yet again shows a yawning reality gap. Even celebrity endorsement was ineffective: witness the revelations in 2003 by Bob Geldof of the ridiculous obstacles in his custody battles against an obviously unsuitable mother in the form of Paula Yates. Although Saint Bob received a sympathetic portrayal and huge publicity, the revelations in no sense heralded a sea change in opinion within the political classes.

Bribing couples to split up

There is no longer any dispute that Britain is the lone-parent capital of the world, partly — if not largely — because of government bribes for women to eschew having a partner. With a *six-fold* multiplier of effective net earnings to £30 an hour, the sums at stake are so huge that this anti-social engineering must be a main or *the* main factor in the decision not to start or to continue living together for hundreds of thousands of people. Single parenthood is now a major career option for *any* woman, let alone just for the underclass.

The issue of heavy financial discrimination against fathers and the two-parent family was put into stark relief by a 2007 report by the former Labour minister for welfare reform, Frank Field. He did the following calculations: In 2007, a single parent with two children under eleven, working part-time (sixteen hours a week) on the minimum wage, receives in total after tax credits, £487 per week net. For this same single parent to re-couple or revert to the status quo ante and have a man living with her, she and her man between them would have to work 116 hours a week to achieve the same income. That is the equivalent of both of them working a full-time job plus more than three days a week of a second job. This is not only impossible but illegal under the working time directive.

This tax-credit subsidy of single parenthood was introduced in 1998, making a single parent who had never worked as well-off, to the nearest pound per person, as married or co-habiting couples on average earnings (as was pointed out in the Centre for Policy Studies report, *The Price of Parenting*). Tax credits are massive welfare benefits in disguise, and the very reverse of Bill Clinton's reforms of time-limiting benefits that have so successfully cut US welfare dependency (literally in half).

Leaving aside the cost to the taxpayer of such overwhelming financial support, there is a clear effect of paying benefits to single parents. Looking across all countries across Europe, for every thousand Euros increase in annual benefits, the number of single parents rises two percent. No government has ever tried to argue that changes in tax rates don't affect behaviour. Financial support, even at the high levels single parents now enjoy, is of course not always a sufficient spur to family breakdown; but it's a necessary one. When support is not there, then the problem tends to disappear fast, as has now been found in the USA.

The mess we are in arises from a wilful blindness to the most basic reality that it takes both a mother and a father to raise children; and not just the one to provide most of the care, the other most of the resources. Both are needed to provide complementary, but very different parenting to produce a well-adjusted child who will grow into a responsible adult with a window on the separate worlds of the sexes. A father is the conduit to the wider world, and the domain of men, and of how reliable it is. Without a father, the government has to step in to pay enormous sums to deal with the long-term consequences (children growing into dysfunctional adults), but more immediately to pay benefits and/or tax credits. All out of the pockets primarily of the fathers who properly planned to provide for their own children through households supported by working (not to mention all of the men who would like to start a family but don't earn enough).

A woman now has the choice of not bothering with any kind of relationship, and moving straight into lone motherhood. Or she can establish a relationship and bear a child and then, for no particular reason, simply walk out on — or throw out (using an 'ouster' order) — the man who has been providing for her. If the partnership had progressed to marriage, then she can abuse her former partner by imposing on him for maintenance, as well as imposing on the rest of the working population. Divorce is overwhelmingly female initiated, and not because women fare worse than men in marriage: quite the reverse. Marriage is a trap for the male, albeit a benign one in many ways. A man is far more likely to be obliged to be the main or sole provider, to be 'controlled' by his partner, and the victim of domestic violence (see chapter ten), albeit that marriage generally 'protects' partners from this. Research shows that marriage is a cultural codification not of a supposed male monopolisation of female reproduction but of a sexual division of labour whereby paternal investment ensures that the female need for reliable support for her children and herself is met (Winking, 2007). Men enter marriage because they can secure a more attractive partner by offering reliability; women trading this off against male status. But as a marriage progresses, the wife's 'mate value' falls — precipitously so — whereas the husband's rises. So it is usually the wife's position in a marriage more than a husband's that is precarious, and her comparative lack of 'worth' that may turn the marriage into a sham. The wife has the choice of either continuing under the husband's protective umbrella or to 'cash in her chips', as it were — though 'the chips' are very much her husband's. She wins either way.

The ideology leading to this feat of social engineering is that somehow children are a *collective* social asset, yet having children is the natural, but perfectly selfish, desire of most women. In important ways this corresponds to the desire in men — equally natural, but perfectly selfish — to have sex with an endless stream of different partners. Societies try to stop the latter, but now not only allow the former, but encourage it through payment extracted from others: mainly men.

The one thing the world does not lack is people. Women need no encouragement to have children, and the less encouragement they're given then the more likely are the children they have to be wanted, loved, and well-adjusted as adults — so that they are not actually deleterious to society. Population, even leaving out the consequences of direct immigration, is still increasing: the supposed decline in birth rate is an illusion caused by the ongoing shift to later childbearing by an entire age cohort of women. Using the measure of 'cohort fertility', fertility in the UK is at near replacement level. Population decline would be of enormous benefit to all those millions who are currently deprived of work merely because they are over-fifty or even over-forty, and would make it easier to force into work the large numbers of idle younger people. The children of single parents — as research overwhelmingly demonstrates — are much more likely to be social problems and cost the taxpayer further expense; not least when they perpetuate the cycle and become single mothers or feckless fathers who in turn themselves become strangers to their own children.

Why continue to pay women to create social breakdown? It makes less sense than it would to pay men to visit prostitutes to further their corresponding natural inclinations. Nobody in their right mind would suggest such a thing, of course; but the social implications would be incomparably more benign than subsidising women to have children.

Having children is the most obvious personal asset anyone could have; and those who are childless, and especially those who are single and who may be unable to form a partnership, are the truly disadvantaged in any society. The principal attraction that women feel for men is status, and this most easily translates into earnings. Men who earn so little that they are unattractive to most or to nearly all women, form the most disadvantaged subgroup in our own, as in any, society. Yet as a proportion of their income, they more than anyone are forced to pay to provide for single parenthood. They are literally bankrolling a lifestyle for the very women who would not have them in the first place.

The answer to this problem is simple and twofold: require single parents to meet the same conditions as unemployed people, and revoke no-fault divorce and place all of the financial obligation on a parent who simply walks out, or invents a reason to throw out the other. This is the policy put forward by the think-tank CIVITAS and some new small parties across the political spectrum. The long-converged consensus of the main political parties (always fearful of the floating voter), is the direct opposite of what needs to be done.

Exposing the pro-wife bias of family courts

In his ground-breaking 2005 book, *Institutional Injustice*, Martin Mears, former president of the Law Society, criticised in the strongest terms the family courts regarding child contact and divorce cases. He sees prejudice and unfairness as so routine and entrenched that it's an institutional making of legislation by the back door, according to the 'meal-ticket-for-life' principle for mothers and (ex-)wives. (Supposed) equality and non-discrimination are guiding principles, despite their being nowhere in the legislation, yet the application of justice 'would not be recognisable as such to anyone else'. In his summary Mears particularly points up the problem of divorce settlements:

> There is a deep pro-wife bias, with every single presumption in her favour—the most egregious being that every wife's contribution to the marriage is deemed to be equal to that of the husband even when plainly the contrary is true. This means that a party who has repudiated all the obligations of the marriage can claim the financial benefits accruing from it to the same extent as if he or she had behaved impeccably.

Mears makes four recommendations for reform: fully binding pre- and post-nuptial agreements (which the courts already uphold but only when they feel like it); leaving out assets owned before the marriage; disallowing maintenance to any party whose conduct has effectively repudiated the marriage; and recognising in fact as well as in principle the right of a child to maintain maximum contact with both parents.

Taking part in a discussion on BBC *Woman's Hour*, in January 2006, the first point Mears made was a pre-emptive one to head off the usual line that all is in the interests of the child. It's not just fathers and (ex-)husbands who had a serious grievance, Mears insisted, but 'children get an extremely raw deal as well'. A deputy district judge participating in the discussion threw in the standard challenge that the unfairness was only to a minority and the rich, but Mears was having none of it. The rich were privileged in being able to press their claims as far as the Court of Appeal, giving them ostensibly the chance of justice that to most people was firmly denied; but endless court action in any case nearly always denied it. Mears put out a challenge: 'You'd have great difficulty in finding any lay person who's been through the divorce courts praising the system....The whole system is characterised by folly, bias, expense and injustice.' He laid into the family court judiciary for ignoring the law and making it up as they went along, abusing their wide leeway for discretion. Most tellingly, he cited the best known family judge, Lord Justice Thorpe, who:

> said that he required authority for the proposition that a child had the right to maximum contact with both parents. Now that is an extraordinary thing, the most senior judge regarding that as a contentious point, and that's an excellent example of the attitude of the courts.

How we got here, Mears suggests, is not a little to do with the privileged upbringing of most judges, where children were more or less entirely in the mother's domain, and were hardly seen by the father once they were sent to public school. A once-a-fortnight contact arrangement can appear appropriate to someone with this odd background. At the same time, judges take fully on board new nostrums—no matter how stupid—because the nature of the establishment as with any social group is solidarity; conforming to whatever prevails. It's no contradiction for a judge to hold both old elitist views alongside the products of 'cultural Marxism'. The partiality of (male) judges in favour of women should also be seen in the context of the natural, biologically-derived, male chivalry towards the 'gentle' sex.

There is a combination of appalling delays and

> the court's failure to get to grips with the mother's groundless allegations (and) defiance of its orders, and the court's failure to ensure its own orders. …A flabby judicial response encourages the defaulting parents to believe that court orders can be ignored with impunity.

It seems that there is always flight from awkward conflict: 'the characteristic judicial response when difficulties with contact emerged: reduce the amount of contact and replace unsupervised with supervised contact'. In other words, the mother is rewarded for her obstruction. This frequently, indeed normally, results in such a derisory award of contact that: 'It is hard to see the value of 'contact' of this kind either to the parent or the child. It is more reminiscent of visiting time at the local hospital or prison.'

A major strand through Mears' book is the myth of the interests of the *child:*

> Time and again the courts have emphasised that their overriding concern is for the welfare of the child; the interests of the parents being a peripheral factor (if indeed it is a factor at all). They have also declared repeatedly that parental contact is the child's right. If anyone doubted it, the emigration cases provide overwhelming evidence that what courts actually do is very different from what they say. Where there is a conflict between the interests of the child and those of the mother, the reality is that it is those of the mother which nearly always prevail.

Such a conflict of interest exists whenever the mother wants it to be, so in practice the court always accedes to whatever the mother demands, entirely regardless of any other considerations. Anything the father requests, no matter how much this may be in the interests of the child, will often be considered essentially the opposite of what is in the interests of the mother, so may actually serve to worsen the outcome for the father! The predictable outcome is very low or effectively nil contact awarded to the father, in particular where the mother has found a new partner.

The emigration cases Mears points to are a series of Court of Appeal decisions allowing mothers to move abroad with their children in almost any circumstances. He sees the interests of the child being an 'afterthought'; that it was tacitly assumed that the child 'somehow belonged' to the custodial parent, and had no say, on the assumption that children take readily to a new step-parent. A fundamental fallacy of the system is that it insists that there is no essential difference between a biological and a step-parent, when of course there is no comparison. Given the invariable siding with the mother, then the step-father is favoured by the court as being the male the mother has decided currently to be with. Mears cites cases where the mother is allowed to emigrate even though the Court Welfare Officer had reported that likely emotional damage to a child would ensue from being uprooted from a stable environment and/or losing contact with the father. Mothers have threatened to leave the children behind — thereby demonstrating that they care less about their children than their new boy-friends — and still their wishes have been granted. In the judgement of Payne–v–Payne (2001) it is stated that 'the move would be in the child's best interests because it would make her mother happy'.

Confirming the judiciary's position, the president (at that time) of the Family Division, Elizabeth Butler-Sloss, actually stated in a 2001 conference speech that to put the mother's interests first is to put the child's interests first: 'the protection of the primary carer for the benefit of the child is of primary importance.'

Only female bad behaviour is irrelevant in divorce

If the family court makes an unholy mess of child contact, Mears argues that it makes at least as big a mess of conduct in divorce cases. The case of Clark–v–Clark 1999 was an extreme but classic example of not taking the wife's conduct into account. The marriage had never been consummated and clearly Mrs Clark had married an old man for his fortune. She had stopped any pretence from the start of the reception, banishing her husband from the home, virtually imprisoning him, fleecing him of hundreds of thousands of pounds — some of it to spend on the younger man she took as a lover. Finally, she put her husband in a geriatric home and then contested a generous financial settlement. The judge concluded: 'however much the wife can be criticised, it would be harsh in the extreme to leave her with nothing.' The legal profession tries to make out that such absurdity occurs only in big money cases, but Mears squashes this:

> It must not be thought that *Clark* was a maverick case. On the contrary, it was merely one in a long and continuing series of imbecilities. The excesses were not inevitable. The jurisdiction of the courts is derived from Section 25 of the Matrimonial Causes Act 1973....(but) judges like Lord Denning have regarded Section 25 as giving the courts an almost unlimited discretion, though plainly this was not Parliament's intention.

In the very year the Act came into being, there was consternation over a comment by Denning (in the case of Wachtel):

> [T]he court should not reduce its order for financial provision merely because of what was formerly regarded as guilt or blame. To do so would be to impose a fine for supposed misbehaviour in the course of an unhappy married life.

Mears takes the word 'supposed' here to imply that there could be no such behaviour that was real and caused the breakdown. Despite subsequent cases that contradicted Denning, this became the orthodox position, and public outrage led in 1984 to a conduct provision being inserted into the 1973 act, and also a provision for 'clean break' settlements wherever possible, but this made not the slightest difference. The president of the Family

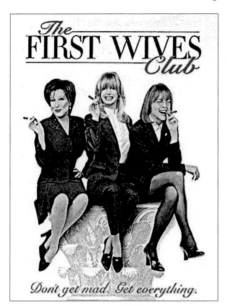

Don't get mad. Get Everything.
Bette Midler, Goldie Hawn and Diane
Keaton in The First Wives Club
(1996)

Division insisted that the law was already being implemented in the way that parliament had intended. This focused the problem because, as Mears emphasises: 'A claim for *continuing* support is an entirely different matter. In that case behaviour ought to have the highest relevance.'

Even the most appalling, indeed seriously criminal, behaviour does not lead to the termination of maintenance. Famously, in Hall–v–Hall (1984) a wife actually stabbed her estranged husband in the stomach and was convicted of assault, but this led only to a reduction in maintenance, upheld in the Court of Appeal! It's by no means clear that even if she had killed him, that maintenance would have been ended. Lord Justice Balcombe, in dismissing an appeal by a woman who had actually hired a hit man to kill her ex-husband, said that: 'It is not every homicide or attempted homicide, by a wife of a husband which necessarily involves a financial penalty.'

The absurdity of all this is made much worse when you consider the argument the other way round: what if the husband is claiming against the wife? The law is quite clear that either party has a right to claim from the other. It should not surprise you that, yes indeed, the issue of conduct *does* apply in cases where maintenance from a wife to a husband is at issue. And here 'conduct' goes way beyond any possible rational conception. In Kay–v–Kay (1990) an unemployed man was refused maintenance from his well-salaried wife because, despite an accepted diagnosis of a personality disorder as the reason he was out of work, the judge said that this had been 'brought about to an extent by his own conduct'. The judge taking an inappropriate moral position on male unemployment is one thing; but all this concerned his worklessness, and had nothing whatsoever to do with his conduct within the marriage!

Another man found himself in a similar situation (Whiting–v–Whiting, 1988), except that he had been made redundant and was applying to have his maintenance obligation discharged. The court was having none of it:

> It cannot be assumed that the wife's independence will necessarily continue indefinitely. Everything turns on her good health and employment. If redundancy or bad health were to intervene, her present good earnings might cease prematurely.

This was precisely what had happened to the applicant, but no man is ever discharged from payment on such grounds. This thinking continues the meal-ticket-for-life unfairness that was never intended by parliament in the 1973 act, and was expressly addressed in the 1984 amendment. Even after a long separation and when the woman is in secure cohabitation, maintenance cannot be ended (eg, Hepburn–v–Hepburn, 1989, where the judge reasoned that he should not 'pressurise an ex-wife to regularise her position with the other man so that he would assume a husband's obligation to her'.)

The prize for most astounding injustice in this context goes to Lord Justice Nourse, who actually increased maintenance in respect of a child an ex-wife conceived with another man. It's hard to decide who was the more audacious: the woman for having the cheek to apply to the court, or the numbskull judge. The judge in this case (Fisher–v–Fisher, 1989) actually stated that the 'general proposition' that this was unjust was not sustainable! It is to be feared just what principle of justice *is* sustainable in UK law.

There is an underlying assumption that somehow a wife automatically makes a contribution to the marriage on a par with that of the husband, yet there is no feasible case that a wife fulfilling her natural desire to have a child and therefore acquiring a benefit, in any way corresponds to a husband's contribution of going out to work and therefore sustaining a cost. (A woman's lifestyle today as mother/home-maker is essentially a natural one and as it has always been, whereas men's world of work is completely removed from their natural role as hunters as it was in hunter-gatherer societies, being far more time-consuming, regimented, alienating and in most ways more onerous — even compared to male life in agricultural societies.) In the high-profile cases that hit the news, the divorcing couple are usually so wealthy that the wife had never had to do any housework and was relieved of any childcare she did not actively want to perform. So in terms of a contribution that incurred any cost, hers was nil. Mears explains:

> Section 25 itself requires the court to take into account the wife's contribution 'by looking after the home or caring for the family'. No-one has ever argued that this contribution should be minimised. But neither should it be maximised to the extent that *in itself* it would justify an equal division of assets.

There is an entirely novel notion nowhere present in law of 'legitimate expectation', and family courts detest the raising of misconduct issues regarding the wife that would undermine this. Yet reliance is placed on a husband's alleged misconduct to support claims for inflated awards. For the non-rich, the impact of this bizarre turn of the law is the unfairness over the disposal of the matrimonial home. Following the 1984 amendments, it did become usual for those husbands without the income to provide significant continuing maintenance to be allowed a clean break, but only by forfeiting most of the equity in the matrimonial home. And this despite a continuing maintenance order in respect of children.

At the end of his persistent tirade, the former president of the Law Society is not hopeful of any swift change that will reinstate justice:

> It is the culture which needs changing. That takes time, although eventually the wheel will turn — particularly under the impact of sustained and vigorous criticism. Even very senior judges now pay lip-service to the right of a child to maintain close contact with its father (although, as the emigration cases show, it *is* only lip-service). This unfortunately is an area of law where legislative intervention by Parliament can have only a limited role.

How parliament was undermined:
The disaster of the Child Support Act

Shared parenting (i.e., not what the family court dispenses) was the express intention of parliament when the Children Act was passed in 1989. Supposedly, out went the notion of 'custody' with one parent, and in came the 'parental responsibility' of both; promoted through 'residence orders' to get rid of the assumption that only the mother was fit, good, and responsible. It was to mimic, we were told, the success of 'joint custody' schemes in California, New Zealand and Australia. These schemes turned out to have a common flaw in being open to hijacking by those politically motivated to bring about the reverse of what was intended; not least governments, which have a major fiscal reason to insist that shared/equal parenting should *not* be the norm. In the UK version, it was all for nothing in any case, because the Act contained fatal internal contradictions that actually made matters worse in forcing former partners apart by calling one the 'parent with care' and the other the 'absent parent', thereby destroying the child's right to two parents. This was in order to suit the purposes of the Child Support Agency (CSA). The collection of money from fathers, to offset the rapidly-escalating costs to the state of single parenthood, would have been hindered if it wasn't easy to distinguish between the cash cow and the cow, as it were.

So the Children Act, in being made to fit the purposes of not just the family court but also the CSA, was a hopeless compromise (ditto the subsequent 1991 Child Support Act). The entire purpose of the Act was then comprehensively undermined by the legislation's 'guidance notes'. As at other government departments, officers at the CSA consult day-to-day not the legislation, but the notes produced to interpret it. One sentence proved key: 'It is not expected that (a residence order) will become a common form of order because most children will need the stability of a single home.'

This one line meant that men were once again relegated from the status of parent to visitor; the very state of affairs that the Children Act was passed in order to counter. The intention may well have been merely to clarify that a 50/50 sharing of residence was not an objective but a symbolic starting point. But it was a Trojan horse that allowed an interpretation that was the very opposite of the thinking behind the Act: that any sort of significant residence with the father was to be rare. At one stroke the Children Act turned into an instrument to deprive fathers, on any pretext or none, of the bulk of contact they would normally enjoy with their own children whenever a dispute over contact arose.

For a long time everyone thought that the 1989 Children Act was fine, and it was regularly cited as what everyone should be reminded of to counter the increasing bias against fathers. Without being able to see the guidance notes, people missed that the Act had been retrospectively nobbled. The penny had still to drop outside fathers' activist groups, and was only dawning on sections of the government itself in late 2005, as I will explain. People also still didn't see that the Children Act was the basis of the CSA as well as contact disputes.

The CSA has had an enormous impact on the outcomes of separation, effectively setting the parameters of the family court. Before the Children Act and the CSA, separating married partners took their particular circumstances to court, but après CSA, the ordinary courts have proved powerless. Judgements made by courts in the past—'clean break' settlements, even legally drawn and witnessed statements of intent made before marriage—are retrospectively declared void. The CSA can cancel court orders without even being required to tell the father or the court. Detachment of earnings orders are made over which magistrates have no jurisdiction at all. Maintenance payments can be massive and can last until the youngest child is nineteen.

* * *

It's worth going back a decade and examining the CSA and how it operated, because the CSA being bound up with the family court means that only by viewing the two as part of the same government project can the debacle as a whole be explained.

The abolition of the CSA was announced in 2006, but this is merely the body, not the principles. The principles remain in the 'Child Maintenance and Enforcement Commission' that will replace it, eventually. Of course, the never-ending poor performance in not getting support payments to mothers was and is always in the news; never the greater injustice of a high volume of unreasonable, inflexible, unjustifiable or mistaken payment demands to men, who are at the same time being denied any meaningful contact with the very children the CSA demands that they pay for. If the issue of child contact does surface in the news, then it's often one of the ten percent of cases where the mother is the 'absent parent'.

The appalling impact of the CSA was brought to light in 1996 by Professor Jonathan Bradshaw, director of social policy research at the University of York. The Act betrays a straight absence of morality, as Bradshaw protested to the Commons all-party select committee on the Child Support Act:

> The attempt in the Act to separate the whole issue of contact from that of financial support is doomed to failure. Fathers just cannot understand why one agency of government insists that they pay child support when another agency of government fails to protect their rights to have contact with their children.

This is of course a core reason why millions of fathers are angry. Second:

> While (fathers) agree that they have a financial obligation to their children, their understanding of fairness leaves them outraged at the spousal (carer's) element in the formula, particularly if they think that the caring parent was responsible for the breakdown of the relationship.

Even more fundamentally there was:

> an increasing proportion of fathers who had never been in a 'living together relationship' when they conceived a child. Some of these relationships were very casual, or at least tenuous. The obligation of fatherhood in these circumstances is, to say the least, contentious. The assertion of biological liability in the Child Support Act, in the absence of any social relationship, has created some fundamental problems that we are only beginning to consider. Getting a girl pregnant can now be a form of entrapment.

Clear cases of entrapment are now showing up, so that in the USA there is a major political movement concerning 'paternity fraud', and a battle between an intransigent Supreme Court and state jurisdictions. Bradshaw's conclusion is that, as with its sisters across the world that have superseded a system of decision between ex-partners at some form of adjudication, the Act is literally unenforceable. Like the poll tax, it jeopardises the consent people give to be ruled.

It's hard to imagine how a report could be more critical of government legislation. Any one of Bradshaw's three moral objections was by itself an infringement of men's basic civil rights. Taken together they are almost incredible. Of course, apart from those men who become an actual CSA case, all men are at risk of becoming subject to the CSA. The legislation is an immoral interference with men's right to pursue happiness and to enjoy family life, by usurping it in favour of forcing his support of what could not be considered any kind of intention to begin family life.

'Getting a girl pregnant can now be a form of entrapment', Professor Jonathan Bradshaw, director of social policy research at the University of York.

The problem created by ignoring the casualness of a relationship is the most insidious, and Bradshaw draws particular attention to it.

> Young men are, as ever, becoming fathers without their knowledge and — if they did know — without any rights to influence whether a pregnancy is aborted. Many very young men are being locked into a financial relationship, often without any prospect of a social one, for up to 16 years — 16 years during which they might otherwise have become effective social and biological fathers; socially useful rather than disenfranchised and bloody-minded men....The behavioural consequences of the act have been quite extraordinary: fewer fathers in employment, many more 'absent and untraceable', fewer in contact with their children, less informal financial support of children, fewer taking on new partners, more new partnerships breaking down, and so on.

The CSA provoked massive hostility from fathers, who typically were paying out 40% of their net income, with low earners paying more like 75%. Many were reduced to below dole levels, making honest work impossible; driving men instead to claim benefits. Sequestration at this level made a nonsense of the notion that the CSA was about child support: it was really about offsetting the cost to the state of the single-parent households it had itself been instrumental in creating; most of the cost of which is in respect of not the child but the mother. Astonishingly, reduced allowances punished men if they went on to try to support another woman (and her children) by effectively *raising* his maintenance payments. The clear presumption was that the father was the guilty party in the splitting of the family, and that any subsequent life is somehow the spoils of this (despite 80-90% of divorces being initiated by wives).

An artificial polarisation was caused by the CSA's insistence on dealing only with the 'parent with care', despite the courts having previously often awarded joint custody. Then there was the unjust rule that the father, stigmatised as the 'absent parent', could get no reduction in maintenance unless his children stayed over more than 103 nights per year. This is of course a key basis for the risibly-low contact awarded. It ensures that in only a small minority of cases does the Treasury get less than the full amount from fathers to offset benefits payments.

The in-trays of MPs were full of fathers' complaints and the CSA back-logs became unmanageable, so the Treasury stepped in to try to increase revenue by simplifying assessment to a formula that took into account no individual circumstances at all. The result was that from 2002 the situation for those on low incomes actually got worse. The move bought off the articulate, vociferous and organised middle-class activists, who then focused on the still greater injustice of the prevention of contact.

The CSA was the means by which fathers were made to pay for their own oppression (reminding one of the Chinese government policy of charging the families of executed prisoners for the cost of the bullet), but the family courts were the main locus of that oppression. This was shown in stark relief when in 2003, to enforce new anti-truancy measures, judges found no difficulty in jailing mothers who repeatedly failed to ensure that their children attended school. Yet it's the impact of depriving children of their mothers that is cited as the reason why mothers who flouted contact orders could not be jailed.

Reproductive rights only when its not through sex: prejudice exposed by crazy law

A man's liability to pay child support is always assumed, because the woman who claims a man is a father is always believed. If he contests, he is made to pay for a DNA test, and the guilt of men who refuse a DNA test is assumed on the basis of the hearsay evidence of a woman or simply by adverse inference. As an example of the clearly unjust imposition of this ruling, there was a case of a 'Mr F' who had had a drunken office frolic with a married women. The defence offered was that since the woman was married at the time, then there was a presumption that the husband was the father and not 'Mr F'. Clear evidence was therefore required to rebut this, but the judge relied on the 1993 Children (Admissibility of Hearsay Evidence) Order.

The ludicrous line that men must carry the financial burden entirely regardless of the circumstances, even runs to compassionate sperm dona-tion, as Andy Bathie (and some years before, a Manchester man) found out when he helped a lesbian couple he knew to start a family. Presumably, the same would apply to a man who visits a prostitute, in the event of the prostitute deciding to conceive and have his baby. Even though the very purpose of prostitution is explicitly to substitute payment for any subse-quent liability, the state, in cahoots with the prostitute, could exact ongo-ing payment through entrapping a client. It's only a matter of time before a case arises.

Of those men who take a CSA DNA test, one in six are found not to be the father (on figures up to 2005). This is most probably the tip of the iceberg, because most men who had suspicions will have already tested their child privately, and a result proving non-paternity would enable them to confront the mother, who would then not have the option of subsequently naming him to the CSA. Also, most of those women whose paternity fraud was still unknown to their ex-partner would not name them to the CSA, because this would reveal the secret and entail loss of any informal support they could otherwise expect. CSA rules make it easy for a woman to avoid naming a father in such circumstances; by simply falsely citing threat of violence. Couples with any sense make private arrangements and avoid entanglement with the CSA. This is not least because women are often better off accepting informal support from their ex-partners than receiving CSA payment, only for it to be offset against benefits.

Women trick men into becoming fathers all the time. A 2004 poll for *That's Life!* magazine showed that 42% of women say they would lie about contraception so as to get pregnant, no matter what they knew their partner would feel; and US research estimates that a million American men annually are saddled with fathering babies they did not want. In 1972, Elliott Philip looked at several hundred families in South-East England and concluded that a staggering 30% of the children could not have been fathered by the mother's husband. British medical students are taught that the 'non-paternity' rate is 10–15%. The Family Planning Association and others have researched the deliberate (or absent-mindedly unconsciously-on-purpose) ineffective use of contraception — colloquially known as 'oopsing' — and shown that women use contraceptives less reliably the more casual the sexual encounter (Eisenman, 2003). This is through an unconscious psychology to try to conceive in those circumstances rather than in the context of the stable relationship (for the reasons explained in chapter eleven). There are also the very many cases where women have intentionally deceived.

'Paternity fraud' has become a hot topic in the US, where court cases have been hitting the news for several years. The 'best interests of the child' test was still resulting in men being told by judges they must continue to pay child support, even in the most bizarre cases. The classic paternity-fraud case is that of a woman taking the semen from a condom a man used for sex with her, and then inserting it into herself to get pregnant. Far from an 'urban myth', this is an actual scenario that has faced US courts, and the men have lost! There has even been a case where the condom used for impregnation was from sex between the man and *another* woman. Women who conceal pregnancy to deny paternal rights and then sue for child support a decade later, or women who statutorily rape boys, or women who con their husbands that a baby is his when it is not: all real cases where child support was determined still to be payable. So men are replying by suing, and in 2005 courts began to allow men to do this and to appeal against previously-lost cases.

Gary Robinson in Florida is suing his former employer, Jackie Gallagher-Smith, who had seduced him and got pregnant. He knew she was married and had not considered the possibility that a married woman would want to have his child, but her husband was infertile. Robinson objects to being 'an unwitting sperm donor', claiming fraud and intentional infliction of emotional distress. Richard Phillips in Illinois is suing Sharon Irons for secretly keeping his semen after having oral sex and then using it to get pregnant. He only found out two years later when Irons went to court for child support. In 2005, an appeal court ruled that Irons 'deceitfully engaged in sexual acts, which no reasonable person would expect could result in pregnancy', but also pointed out that the sperm was a gift, and as such Phillips had relinquished control of it. This is clearly in error because in fellatio the woman takes the man's sperm: it was theft. Whatever the outcome of this case, it must only be a matter of time before the absurdity of 'sperm theft' is stamped upon. The position at the moment is that of a dam held back by 'the best interests of the child' concept, which is proxy for 'the best interests of the state' in not paying child support. It only takes one case to successfully assert the rights of the deceived man for the dam wall to break.

* * *

Everything changes when in place of natural sex, conception is by artificial means. In IVF, the law states that a man's written consent is required for a woman to use his sperm for procreation. The same applies to the implantation of stored embryos. Two cases came to appeal courts in 2003, brought by women who wished to use the frozen embryos they had conceived with their former partners' sperm before receiving treatment for cancer which would render them infertile. They argued that following their treatment this was the only chance they had to become mothers, and that the law as it stood infringed their rights. These men argued that they no longer wished to be fathers now that their relationships with the women had ended. The court sided with the men and upheld the law.

After a concerted media campaign, the law had been waived for Diane Blood when she argued that her deceased husband, Steven, had said in front of witnesses that he wished to become a father posthumously; albeit he had not written anything down. In the wake of this, there was another attempt by women with embryos in storage that had been fertilised by ex-partners no longer willing to have a child. Lots of sympathy from the media, with the pleas of these women widely aired. Nevertheless, explicitly, by virtue of the legal framework of necessary mutual agreement to have the embryo unfrozen, the decision to donate was not a decision to conceive. The judiciary and medical ethics experts remained correctly un-budged in insisting that men could not be co-opted against their will to set up a family. This was upheld in early 2006 when the European Court of

Human Rights declined to back Natalie Evans after she failed to get the House of Lords to hear her case. Most but by no means all of the commentariat supported the decision. Several maintained that what was the woman's last chance to have a natural child trumped all other considerations, and that the law should be changed to make donation of sperm an irrevocable commitment to fertilisation, irrespective of changing circumstances and consequences. However, not a few pointed out that supporting the woman would invite a corresponding right of men to have a say in abortion—and, I would add, invites a comparison to the consent of women in sex regarding the rape law. This, and not men's rights, is at the bottom of why the law was upheld.

It's a mockery that the law should be so rigorous in these contexts but so startlingly absent in the everyday world where millions of men are daily deprived of the right to withhold consent to starting a family. Normally, a man has no 'right to choose' in any sense whatsoever; having no legal right even to know, let alone be consulted, that he is or is about to be a father or the co-producer of a foetus that has been or is soon to be wilfully destroyed, with or without any good reason. Only if sex is reduced to masturbation into donor name-tagged sperm vials for a registered fertility clinic does a man have a legal 'right to choose', and the woman forfeits her privilege of telling him any story, true or false, about contraception she is/isn't using, the abortion she is/isn't having or would/wouldn't have; and that there is/isn't another man who is/isn't the real father.

A man does not necessarily even have the right to know if he is the father of any child that his partner claims is his. Helena Kennedy, chair of the Human Genetics Commission, had recommended a change in the law so that a man would not be able to take a mouth swab of his own (putative) child's DNA unless he got the mother's permission! This is the most amazing example of the 'best interests of the child' principle clearly masquerading as the best interests of the mother. The law that came into effect in September 2006 does not go as far as Kennedy wanted, and allows either parent to take a sample for DNA testing. But, crucially, this excludes any putative father who does not have parental rights, so there is still a major civil-rights abuse. Often the genetic father will not have parental rights yet the step-father will have.

Issues over testing will soon be rendered history by proper male contraception; surrounding which are politics that reveal the root of all of the bizarre law and practice to do with parenting. There is real hostility to males taking control of their own fertility. Gynaecology professor Elsimar Coutinho relates:

> some years ago I presented a paper on the male pill at a world conference. Afterwards, women, mainly feminists, came up and said they were against me. They protested that they had won the battle to decide when they got pregnant and I was handing that over to men.

With widespread use of sophisticated male contraceptives, the presumption of paternity in court could no longer stand up, and men would be free of the risk of CSA intervention following extra-pair sex or sex with a regular partner ahead of an unanticipated break-up. Any freeing of the male from the constraints of his sex role is seen as a 'disempowerment' of the female, instead of the belated gift of control to men over the consequences of their natural sexuality.

Failed attempts to reform the administration of the family courts

I've looked at how over-chivalrous judges, compliant with the dominant PC culture, have utilised or inserted holes in the law behind the back of parliament; but a real core of the problem is with those who write the ill-considered reports on which the judges act. An attempt was made to reform the Family Courts Service by reorganisation as CAFCASS, the Family Court Advisory Service, but it has proved worse than futile in the face of comprehensively incompetent, deliberately obstructive and extreme-feminist Child Welfare Reporters. Most of these are ex-probation officers (or ex-social workers) with no training of any kind (just one in seven get any training, and that is for a mere two days). Their union, NAPO, takes an extreme prejudiced stance on the issue of domestic violence, loosely defining it as 'physical, sexual, emotional, mental or economic abuse'; and actively 'challenges the assumptions that after separation or divorce, contact with the perpetrator is beneficial to children'. This is the classic defining down of a phenomenon so that it falsely applies to almost everyone, in the service of the bigotry that domestic violence is ubiquitous male behaviour; that it's a major reason for relationship breakdown; and that men generically are fundamentally bad parents (just as men are supposedly bad people by virtue of their being the supposed oppressive side of 'patriarchy'). This is made possible by the facility in the Child Support Act for women to claim 'harm or undue distress', giving carte blanche to cite anything as 'domestic violence' — not least any manifestation of the mother's emotional feelings attending her malicious denial to a father his basic civil and human right of being involved in the life of his child. What compounds this is the attitude, as enshrined in the CSA guidance, that 'the "parent with care" should be believed'. Nothing has to be proved according to any standard of proof in the enforced secrecy of the family courts. All men are deemed to commit domestic violence by default simply by being a family member. This removes any need to make plausible, let alone prove, that in any individual case domestic violence has been perpetrated. It's a truly evil tyranny, and all is now encapsulated by CAFCASS itself in 2005, in its published *Domestic Violence Assessment Policy*.

The serious problems with CAFCASS have been evident for years. Its chairman, Anthony Hewson, finding obstruction at every turn, resigned in 2003, not long after being appointed. This prompted the then minister for constitutional affairs, Lord Falconer, and Margaret Hodge, the then (beleaguered) minister for children, both to call for the resignation of the entire CAFCASS board. What is needed, of course, is the complete dismantling of the current system; the dismissal of the entire management for serious misconduct, the banishment of NAPO from the workplace on the grounds of demonstrable hatred towards men, and all staff required to re-apply for position. A training manual — which CAFCASS was supposed to have produced but had failed to do so — needs to be compiled urgently and to include a zero tolerance attitude not to mythical notions about domestic violence, but to sex hate towards men. Recruitment should be aimed at the wider community and not at those from the legal arena such as probation officers (who would bring an inappropriate adversarial stance), nor from the realm of social work, which would bring an unacceptable extreme feminist perspective.

To try to combat CAFCASS, a consortium has been formed: the Coalition of Equal Parenting headed by the Equal Parenting Council. Its president, Tony Coe, delivered a damning appraisal of CAFCASS to the parliamentary select committee investigating it in 2003, in the wake of the condemnatory report by the Lord Chancellor, *Making Contact Work*. Coe reiterated that CAFCASS officers routinely discriminate against non-resident parents, and aid and abet hostile resident parents. The very concept of shared parenting was 'foreign thinking' to most of them, he claims. Yet family court judges rely heavily on their recommendations:

> They are not experts. It is impossible to discern in most cases any sound methodology or knowledge base by reference to which officers have arrived at their conclusions. This is because they have no methodology or training in the role they are supposed to be fulfilling; nor are they required to support their recommendations by reference to any research data. Even their factual findings are frequently wrong or loaded in favour of one parent....On the whole they merely report what children told them at a particular point in time in a given set of circumstances. Worse, they do not have a clue when to involve an external expert.

With less training than traffic wardens, Coe likened the belief of CAFCASS officers that their role was merely to write reports and not to do anything to support contact, to that of a fire brigade that turned up only to write a report of how the building was being consumed by fire. There is no evaluation of outcomes, by any measure; not even seeking feedback from parents about what they thought of the service:

> Their conclusions are based on nothing more than their personal biases. In our experience, perversely, many CAFCASS officers believe that a non-resident parent can only continue as a parent if the resident parent is prepared to co-operate....Many have never once made a recommendation for a shared residence order. Many do not even know what the term means.

CAFCASS merely pretended to go through consultation. When he met Hewson, Coe found him dismayed that all the consultation documents presaging the formation of CAFCASS had never reached him. And still the submissions made by stakeholders before CAFCASS came into existence remain not only unanswered but unread, having been blocked by senior officers intent on maintaining the status quo. The rot of the previous regime remained in the new organisation from top to bottom. Hewson was shocked to find out from Coe that the promised complaints procedure was never installed by his own senior officers. Complaints are still: 'fobbed off, usually on the basis that you can only raise them in court…(but) family court judges have made plain that they are not interested in entertaining complaints against CAFCASS'.

The Equal Parenting Council's policy statement calls for a legal pre-sumption of shared parenting, so that parenting is divided between fit parents on an equitable (not necessarily equal) basis. To decide that one parent was unfit, the burden of proof must be on others, including the other parent, to prove why contact should be restricted. The policy state-ment notes the failure of government to explain why it opposes this posi-tion, despite the strong all-party support for legal shared parenting; and tackles head-on the main excuse for the status quo:

> It is argued that shared parenting cannot work when parents are in conflict. But conflict can be easily created by one parent being unreasonable. It takes two people to reach agreement, but only one to be unreasonable. Our sys-tem's current approach means that one parent can deny shared parenting simply by creating conflict. But rewarding conflict is not in the best interests of children who need both their parents.…Our family justice system must be made to face up to the fact that there are parents who are hell-bent on exclud-ing the other parent from their children's lives.

The problem of the degree of contact is not so much with the small per-centage of fathers who are denied contact completely. This is how CAFCASS and the Department for Constitutional Affairs like misrepre-senting the problem. Though this is in itself a major human rights issue and affects many fathers who have done nothing to deserve such appall-ing treatment, it's the overwhelmingly greater number of fathers who for no reason have all but nominal contact withheld from them that is the main issue. The very small minority affected by total denial of contact is an obfuscatory line that the DCA and CAFCASS took via the report by the House of Commons constitutional affairs committee on family courts in March 2005. They cited that the grounds for complete denial of contact was usually domestic violence — though of course CAFCASS does not go into what was done if anything to establish the veracity of any such accu-sations, nor of the mildness or severity of the supposed violence, whether or not it was reciprocal, or if actually the violence was from the mother with the father being the victim. The report did not even address the great bulk of the problem — that is the systematic restriction of contact to the point where it's so small that it's neither reasonable nor meaningful, and as good as complete denial. And this is just an aspect of a range of abuse by family courts. As Coe complains:

> Courts all too often fail to make any contact order — or they make it too late....or they order it to be supervised (or subject to unnatural conditions) — or they water down the ordered contact instead of requiring the blocking parent to comply!

A frequent decision by the family court — to allow just two hours contact a fortnight — is tantamount to zero access. Neither reasonable nor meaningful, it's a compact by family court staff with mothers to alienate fathers from their own children. Sometimes defended as reducing the complication of life after the end of a relationship, there is no thought to the damage done to the children, and instead merely the exercise of a nasty selfishness. There is no real prospect of an enduring father–child relationship on such nominal time together. A family court contact order of this kind is transparently a punishment and an invitation to regard it as a provocation. Sure enough, as soon as a father acts on this, a pretext can be found to further restrict or even deny any contact. If, on the other hand, a father tries to get the court to increase his contact time, not only can years of action be fruitless, but the very act of insisting on rights can be deemed the sort of unreasonable behaviour on which courts decide to further restrict father–child contact. The courts are not interested in upholding the father's rights; only what is 'in the best interests of the child', narrowly conceived to exclude even the general evidence that children thrive and avoid damage when they have two natural parents instead of just one. Though this evidence is no longer in any dispute, it's not provided in even the most rudimentary education of the judiciary and CAFCASS staff. Evidence is only admissible if it's in respect of the particular case, and the father is left with the impossible burden of trying to prove that the individual circumstances of himself and his child could be changed to the benefit of the child. As Lord (Freddy) Howe explained in the House of Lords, this is a reversal of the burden of proof and an impossible burden to shoulder.

The problem is that the father should need to show any reason to have proper contact with his child, when 'reasonable' or 'meaningful' contact was intended in the Children Act. Just as it was rescinded by a government circular, it can be reversed back again without primary legislation. Case law cannot be relied upon, because all this says is merely that there should not be no contact at all (without good reason); but this means that *almost all* contact can be stopped without any good reason whatsoever. A further problem is that there is no overall view except case by case. 'Every case is different' is the mantra from the family courts behind which unfairness hides through illogically taking this to mean that there cannot be any presumption of entitlement to reasonable contact.

The killing of children in the family is more by mothers

Another bogus argument that is used to try to bolster the travesty of negligible contact for fathers, is that children are somehow uniquely at risk from them, when in fact natural fathers are the very people children have least to fear—less in fact than their own mothers. Women's Aid published a report in 2005 supposedly looking into child deaths at the hands of their fathers who had been given contact orders, and the equally misandrist NSPCC used this to run anti-male advertisements.

In the decade 1994 to 2004, supposedly twenty-nine children met their deaths in these circumstances, but after several attempts to get the NSPCC to reveal their source, the charity finally admitted that there were in fact five. We know (from Home Office figures in 2002) that there are between fifty and fifty-five child deaths at the hands of biological parents annually, so child deaths in the context of contact situations are under one percent, which is less than the proportion of biological fathers who have contact arrangements.

On the face of it, culpability for murder of their own children is roughly the same by biological fathers and mothers (55% and 45% respectively) but this does not take account of 'sudden infant deaths' (SIDs), which total almost as many as murders by both parents combined, of which conservatively 10% are regarded as 'covert homicides', and almost all these are attributed to mothers. There is a further under-count of 'covert homicides' that are not registered as SIDS; covert methods being the usual mode of women. So in total, mothers are actually considerably *more* culpable than are fathers.

The danger from male figures is mostly in the form of *step*-fathers. Large-scale research projects have shown a 50 to 100 times greater likelihood of child murder by a step-father than a genetic father. This is nothing to do with an inherent problem of child homicide in men, but because by far the most common step-parent is male—women are the resident parent in nine out of ten times after a break-up.

This greatly increased risk of child death is actually caused by the very failure of the family courts system to abide by the natural justice of equal parenting, and the entire thrust of government policy that encourages and facilitates family breakdown. These same failures have also not a little to do with the much rarer deaths of children at the hands of despairing, access-denied biological fathers (where, typically, such fathers also kill themselves). Mothers are more culpable, and single mothers are proportionately considerably greater killers of their own children than are married or even cohabiting mothers, as reflected in the six-fold preponderance of single over married mothers in the SIDs figures.

Government deliberately cocks up and covers up

The government's subterfuge was found out in November 2005. The Bill to introduce the Child (Contact) and Adoption Act — the act that was supposed to begin sorting out the mess — was revealed as a complete farce during its first reading. The Department for Education and Science (DfES — for some bizarre reason the implementing department) seemingly had only just realised that there was no presumption of 'reasonable' and/or 'meaningful' contact. The DfES seemingly had not bothered to check. Without this underpinning, none of the provisions of the new bill would be operable. The government is culpable at a high level. The ministerial-authored foreword to the green paper begins:

> The current way in which the Courts intervene in contact disputes does not work well. This is the opinion of both Government and the senior judiciary....After separation, both parents should have responsibility for, and a meaningful relationship with, their children, so long as it is safe. This is the view of most people in our society. And it is the current legal position.

The Labour peer, Lord Adonis, speaking in the Lords declared:

> We fully support the position established in case law that children normally benefit from a meaningful relationship with both parents following separation, so long as it is safe and in the child's best interests.

This would be news to everyone involved in the family courts, and everyone who has ever enquired about this.

Lord (Freddy) Howe performed a brilliant forensic dissection in the House of Lords, pointing out that there is no case law regarding a presumptive entitlement to 'reasonable' or 'meaningful' contact. Rather, case law is in respect of merely 'contact'. The only principle established by case law is that there has to be good reason for a complete absence of contact. Irrespective of this, it's held that every case is different, and so case law cannot be applicable. The impact of this is a de facto reversal of the burden of proof. Therefore there needs to be inserted into the Children Act the word 'reasonable'.

The government's apparent mistake in not being aware of the absence of any stipulation of 'reasonable' or 'meaningful' contact in law, meant that two years of work by civil servants had been an utter waste of time. However, the remedy was simple enough, as Lord Howe clearly explained. The opposition parties were amused to oblige by tabling amendments to insert the simple words 'reasonable' and/or 'meaningful' into the new bill. But the government actually attacked the proposed amendments. It didn't want the law changed after all. This remained the position when the bill was fully debated in June 2006.

Baroness Ashton of the Department for Constitutional Affairs (DCA) was now agitating that the Children Act is, or should be, based on *no* presumption of contact at all. The DCA is where the bill originated but the

DfES was where it was torpedoed, just as had been an earlier project based on 'reasonable contact' for compulsory mediation called 'Early Interventions'. The DfES has been the Government's clandestine executioner of moves that would remedy the scandal regarding contact it feels obliged to table but essential to kill off.

The government in the guise of the Treasury may well imagine it has potentially much to lose by anything that moves towards shared parenting; so concepts of 'reasonable' contact and compulsory mediation had to be negated. It's one thing having a huge and growing population of indolent single parents, the vast cost of which to the taxpayer is only partly offset by payments from fathers. But what if overnight a law was passed that could potentially double the single parent population, through enabling and fuelling a trend quite independent of the rapid growth of single parenthood already underway? This is what could happen by fathers also becoming single parents through shared parenting. Just as mostly female single parents are now supported in all sorts of ways, the taxpayer would be faced with dealing with their male partners on an equal footing. This is the government's nightmare. Instead of one ex-partner dependent on the state and the other contributing taxes, it can be envisaged that in its place would be two dependents on the state and nobody contributing anything.

This is why it has taken until only very recently for the jobseekers' allowance rules to be successfully challenged over the payment of single-person supplements to a man who parents 50% of the time. On 21 December 2004, Eugen Hockenjos won his seven-year battle with a House of Lords ruling that as a parent with a joint residence order, he was entitled to jobseeker's dependants' allowances for the children; notwithstanding that the mother had the child benefit payments and that he cared for the children less than 50% of the time. (The government had refused to split child benefit payments between parents on the flimsy argument that the antiquated computer system couldn't handle it.) The government's argument that sex discrimination could be justified was summed up by Lord Justice Ward as 'grotesque'.

Of course, most men would not give up work and nor would most restrict work to just sixteen hours to take advantage of the tax credit rules. Most men do not want to share parenting 50/50. Most will want to continue working full-time. The government's fears are explicable though by its believing its own rhetoric about the supposed essential similarity of the sexes. The sexes are not similar, and the fears of the government are grossly exaggerated.

The government may also fear linking parental responsibility in the form of paying child support benefits with parental rights in the form of actually having proper contact with the children, in respect of which child support is being paid. Making explicit the injustice that exists may well lead to many more angry fathers refusing to pay their child support, but this would be a prelude to sorting out the whole mess that would then remove the excuses or good reason to withhold child support payment. The government might then also make some real effort to sort out the ridiculous incompetence of the child support system, instead of the cosmetic exercise of abolishing the CSA and getting heavy on the collection side. Without looking into the inflexibility and injustices to fathers, this serves to compound still further the sense of grievance that fathers have, so it will be counter-productive insofar as it will spur efforts to avoid not only paying but co-operation in the first place.

Parts of government are intent on frustrating contact through the ruse of exploiting its conditionality: 'as long as it is *safe* and in the *best interest of the child*' through an almost default assumption of male domestic violence. With the widening of definitions of DV—even extending to mere witnessing of argument—and the failure to test the veracity of accusations; then any change in the Children's Act alone will not change the current state of affairs. So even if the other problems—mothers not complying with contact orders, and the family court refusing to enforce its own orders—are addressed; there would still be a hurdle to vault even if the new bill had been passed in any meaningful form. All this will achieve is the ever-brighter illumination of the hatred towards men that underlies the impasse that can run its course only for so long.

The joint residence principle

That sex discrimination was being systematically applied against men was thrown into sharp relief in 2005, with the milestone case of a lesbian couple. Based on the past and current performance of the family courts, it's clear that they are guided by the principle not only that one parent has exclusive residence with the child; but also that that parent must be female. What then, if both parties are female?

A lesbian non-resident parent was awarded shared parental rights with her lesbian ex. With no male in the scenario, the default asserted itself that the female was the deserving party, irrespective of her circumstances or her conduct. Women are regarded as by definition fully-fit parents, so when two female parents are at odds in a family court, then the decision is to exactly divide residency without any examination of the worthiness of either. In total contrast, men are by default considered unfit parents unless it can be shown otherwise. Nowhere is the hatred of men in the family court seen as starkly, albeit indirectly, as in this lesbian case.

The issue is whether all couples should be treated as the lesbian couple was. Split-down-the-middle parenting would usually be impractical; inconsistent with the fact that women as mothers naturally are and want to be the primary carers of children. A father provides a necessary complementary role that is quite different, and bound up with his providing for

Michael Cox was jailed in 2007 for refusing 'absent parent' status (he divides parenting 50/50 with his former wife.

both mother and child that takes up much of his time, precluding his availability for parenting to the same extent as the mother. A 50/50 divide of residence must be the *starting point* of discussion, but the ratio can then slide, usually towards the mother, according to what is practically possible given the work commitments of both parties. There has to be default equitability given that some mothers are clearly unfit parents, and currently a significant proportion—one in ten—single parents are men. Many men are marginalised at work and could sensibly take on a large share of parenting time; but the male ex-spouse needs to earn a surplus income if he is to attract a new partner. Men usually are trapped into working full-time.

The man from a broken family is faced with working full-time to provide himself with little more than a subsistence income, despite the fact that in the great majority of cases the broken family is not of his making. Why should he work for the woman who broke up his family? It might well be a rational choice to give up full-time work to mix part-time work and parenting and claim tax credits. But he's not offered the choice. Even after the recent landmark case of a successful challenge to the DWP to pay single-parent supplements just mentioned, the government has gone to the Lords to try to get it reversed. The government's contemptible attitude is exemplified by the jailing in 2007 of Michael Cox, who refuses to pay child support on the grounds that he is in no way an 'absent parent', dividing, as he does, parenting of his children exactly 50/50 with his ex-wife. When she pleaded with the court that the children needed her ex-husband to care for them whilst she was at work, Cox was freed, pending a judicial review.

The fair situation would be just as the Coxes have worked out: that both parents work part-time and split the parenting. Although this goes against the natural differences between mothers and fathers, increasingly such an arrangement will appeal to men on low incomes, given the financial cushion of tax credits and the increasingly unfulfilling nature of the work that for most is all that is available. Not only should men have this option as a right, but correspondingly, women should have the *obligation* to pull their weight financially, with the same rules regarding benefits as all other unemployed. Research has shown that childcare is not an obstacle to part-time working, even for a mother with pre-school-age children. If the father is mixing working and childcare, and thereby relieving the mother of up to half the burden of childcare, then why should the mother be exempted from having to work?

Clearly, the state has a fiscal objection to any notion of shared parenting, because it would take the focus of fathers away from total work commit-ment, and threaten its tax base. Even if the time freed up for the mother was taken up with work, two people working part-time doesn't usually add up to anywhere near the tax take from one person working full-time. This is a short-sighted view by the Treasury though; as well as serious dis-crimination against men. In the longer term it would serve to dissuade women from dissolving relationships, and most men in any case would not avail themselves of the option—especially the higher earners, who provide the bulk of taxes. The overall problem of broken families would recede still more if this approach was widened to take out the pernicious complication of incentives at the time that divorce and custody arrange-ments are being settled. It's because there are significant things to contend that often there is rancour—avoiding this appears to be part of the think-ing behind the default assumption of sole custody. But the territory for acrimony merely shifts to the issue of dividing assets, so a similar unfair-ness has to rule here too: a default assumption that the carer gets the house plus half of everything.

Men have been prevented from effectively challenging this by the soli-darity of lawyers in persuading their male clients that it's pointless to fight. But the logic is now unravelling. There is acrimony from both sides: from the men because of the breathtaking unfairness, and from the women to try to ensure that the unfairness is maintained in their favour. So there is now a pandemic of women making false allegations of domestic violence, actively encouraged by CAFCASS and Women's Aid staff. This under-mines the argument that trying to make the process fairer will lead to more acrimony. On the contrary, if everyone knows that there are fair rules and that not playing fair will probably be found out by testing claims to a proper standard of proof, and false allegations will be severely punished; then the incentives to behave acrimoniously will be removed. In time everyone will be keen to avoid going to court at all.

The problem then shifts back to the divorce itself. Given that in effect no real fault has to be shown to initiate separation—the concept of fault is in name only and serves only to provide a procedural delay—then to get the lion's share of the subsequent proceeds, a fault can be merely invented. Nothing so serious as abuse need be falsely accused, but this sets the stage.

Abuse allegations may then be asserted, first to try to skew the dividing of assets, and then in a contact dispute. But what if instead of a de facto no-fault assumption, the very cause of the separation had to be determined? What if one of the parties is more culpable, and this had a direct bearing on subsequent division of spoils and custody issues? Fairly quickly, the level of relationship breakdown would reduce as people try harder to keep their marriages and cohabitations together, because no party is going to gain much from pushing for separation unless he or she is genuinely aggrieved.

Although thoroughgoing no-fault divorce was to have been brought in with an act in 1996, these provisions have never been activated because pilot studies found them to be unworkable. Nevertheless, divorce is effectively no-fault because of the grounds of 'unreasonable conduct', which can mean anything. Conduct then plays a part in unfairness in divorce settlements. According to section 25 of the 1973 Matrimonial Causes Act, the judge can indeed take conduct into account, but case law has evolved to the point that rarely is it considered. When it is, it's usually financial misconduct: nearly always deemed to be the husband unreasonably (but understandably) disposing of assets. As Mears highlights, conduct by the wife, no matter how bad, is almost never considered.

Divorce settlements are supposedly to provide for the children of the marriage, and only to this end is accommodation and caretaking income provided for the ex-wife. Supposedly. Actually, there is no practical means of separating provision for children from that for the wife. The notion of continuing for the children the lifestyle enjoyed during the married years exacerbated this. Over time, the pretence was more or less dropped, but then in effect resurrected when the Lords judgment in White–v–White set the precedent of the wife's entitlement to 50% of everything, including even the future earned income of the ex-husband and any inheritance. With the situation still that pre-nuptial agreements are not enforceable in British courts, this makes the situation for men impossible.

* * *

Delving into the recent history of the debacle over contact and child support, does not on its own — without understanding the separate worlds of the sexes and the disadvantage of most men inherent in all societies — tell us why the most basic rights have disappeared. What on earth has happened legally to the right of men to father their own children? What has happened to the right of children to be parented by both their biological parents? And what has happened to the right of people generally to live a family life, unhindered by the state? All this despite a long list of relevant European conventions and laws to which Britain is signatory.

There is no legal origin of where/when/why all of this started. It's a warning for all time of what can happen when a prejudice propels enough people into positions where they can exercise it, and they disregard the spirit and bend the letter of the law until it bears no resemblance at all to what most of those who made the law thought they had enacted. It's also a warning that worthy, abstract principles written down as rights offer no protection for citizens from the most unimaginable abuses against them by and through their own government. Professor Jonathan Bradshaw in talking about the CSA warned a decade ago that government: 'has jeopardised the consent to be ruled of a very large number of people.' With government determined *not* to fix a problem of this magnitude, and instead to continue to make it ever worse… sooner or later there will be true hell to pay.

Summary

That the domestic domain is part of the separate world of women and not men, is shown by the systematic obstruction of men from playing their natural part in the lives of their own children through derisory contact orders. This is a failure to recognise that men have a strong bond with their own children, which a step-father does not have. The reality is not ignored when it comes to child support payments. The only sense that can be made of this is an entirely anti-family, and more fundamentally anti-male, politics.

Women as single parents are very much financially better off than many households that include a full-time worker. This huge distortion has been engineered by big increases in benefit payments masquerading as tax credits. This is the major driver of the rapidly increased prevalence of single parenting.

In both divorce and contact, the judiciary act not according to the law but according to their own natural pro-female prejudice, mutually reinforced by the new establishment of militant PC. This has become standard practice and yields a limitless absurdity of judgements, which are transparently anti-male when cases come to light where the scenario is the same but the sexes are reversed. The 'best interests of the child' mantra is a fig-leaf to hide what is actually the 'best interests of the mother', as revealed in emigration cases.

There is no limit to the bad conduct of women – even attempted murder of the ex-husband – that will still result in an unfair financial settlement imposed by the court on the husband. The high-profile cases are not special but typical of the reality at all financial levels: a 50/50 division of assets despite no such principle in statute law. Women in the breadwinner role are not imposed on, yet when male breadwinners experience financial hardship, then no allowance is made. The attitudes are so entrenched that changes in the law will not remedy the injustice.

The intentions of politicians to address the problem of fathers being squeezed out of their own families by a perversion of the law, was sabotaged by guidance notes that overturned the legislation. Then the Treasury imperative of distinguishing between a financial provider and a receiver, led to the abandonment of any idea of joint parenting in favour of polarisation between the 'parent with care' and the 'absent parent'.

The root of this manifest injustice in prejudice is readily seen when you contrast the complete absence of reproductive rights in natural sex, that are asserted with the full weight of the law when conception is unnatural, as in IVF or embryo implantation.

Apart from the judiciary, the other reservoir of attitudinal problems is in those who prepare the reports on which family-court judges act. So deep-seated is anti-male prejudice here, that any attempt at reform has been blatantly obstructed from within. In particular, this is where the notion of all men being domestically violent manifests, as a basis for denial of all but the bare minimum of contact to men generally, irrespective of any accusation against them.

To support the political abuse of fathers, the myth has emerged that fathers are mostly responsible for what murders there are in families, but data strongly suggests that not only are mothers more responsible, but where males are responsible they are far more likely to be step-fathers: the very males brought into the family to replace the biological fathers. This would be obvious to anyone not blinded by polemic: people care for their genetic children, and those of others far less; and mothers are the people who spend most time with their children.

Pretending not to know that it was the absence of the word 'reasonable' in the law regarding contact that allowed the wholesale circumvention of the law, the government deliberately orchestrated a useless bill to become law. The Children and Adoption Act fails to address any substantive problems.

That a profound discrimination against men is in operation is crystal clear in cases where, instead of a woman and a man, two women are the parties. Now the law suddenly becomes all too equitable. In a custody dispute between lesbians, uniquely-shared parenting is the outcome. Yet the principle of joint residence should not mean an invariable 50/50 split; just the assumption at the outset which can then be skewed according to arguments made by both parties and practical exigencies.

Seeing the Game

The phenomenon I've been outlining – in its varying manifestations – in this book is the privilege afforded universally and unconditionally to women. There is nothing corresponding for men, who have to meet certain criteria even to be given basic consideration. This scenario I've provocatively dubbed 'the woman racket'.

The phrase is not mine. I stole it from the late Norman Mailer, who came out with it on one of those late-night 'talking heads' TV shows you could still catch a decade ago. I clearly recall him quipping:

'The woman racket is the McCarthyism of the 1990s.'

'That's my title!' I immediately knew. (The book has been a decade in gestation and has mutated into a much more hopeful monster after such a protracted labour!)

Viewers knew what he was talking about. He didn't have to spell it out. His tone was gently sardonic. Evidently he thought this racket to be a political obscenity, but one he expected to be merely an interlude, a short blip in time. In the particular manifestation we currently see, it likely is. And a 'racket' benefiting women in the more literal sense of the word, is certainly evident in many aspects of society today. But it was ever thus and always will be, albeit that in our own times it has run away with itself. Particular cultural factors, a changing ideological landscape, philosophical backdrop and changing social and working practices have come together to spin our evolved social psychology off at the tangent we see it travelling along today. But however it fetches up, this prejudice will *always* be with us: the over-privileging of the female along with unwarranted contempt for the male.

Such a counter-intuitive truth is hard to get a handle on, let alone to become conscious of in our own lives, to the degree required to avoid social breakdown, let alone create a truly equitable society. But that's the test we're facing. Although a biological or evolutionary psychology perspective is often accused of failing the naturalistic fallacy by confusing 'ought' with 'is', the truth is very different. A truly 'progressive' political project requires us first of all to acknowledge the evolved psychology of

It would take a skyhook of miraculous power to enable us to transcend our genes.

the human creature, warts and all. And before we can do that we need to demolish one of the prevailing myths of our age—'patriarchy'—and expose its harmful consequences.

As these biologically-rooted prejudices are so strongly ingrained, can we ever...how can we say...get round, or transcend them? As Daniel Dennett might put it: how big a skyhook[1] would be required? (I would agree with Dennett that this would require a miracle. Or more than a miracle, as philosopher John Gray points out: Dawkins and Dennett still cling to the residue of Christian thought in the idea that there is something within us that is apart from nature, when in fact we don't and can't ever transcend it (Gray, 2007). It is absurd to imagine that we can transcend ourselves, but that's for another book). And if our anti-male/pro-female prejudices are 'built-in' rather than optional extras, then individually should we even want to? Politically one thing that the twentieth century has demonstrated conclusively is the tragic folly of utopian attempts to re-engineer societies by ignoring or denying the evolved nature of the creatures that make them up.

Even if, in the end, there's not much we can do about it, we do at least need to be *aware* of how we 'do down' males and 'big up' females. There really is no point complaining about, for example, what it is in men that attracts women. That would be like Naomi Wolf pointlessly ranting on about 'the beauty myth', as if men are going to start wanting women for some completely different quality dreamed up by a bunch of Women's Studies lecturers. None of us will ever stop competing with those of our own sex and judging the relative suitability of those of the opposite sex as potential sexual partners. And we will continue to do so essentially

---

[1] A source of design complexity that does not build on lower, simpler layers—in simple terms, a miracle..

according to the same criteria as always. This is the core of our social lives and our raison d'etre. Get used to it.

The reason we need to be aware of anti-male prejudice and pro-female privilege, is not so as to change this, or even, necessarily, to significantly ameliorate it. It's to stop compounding what is reality with the *truly* unfair practice of mistakenly identifying men as an 'oppressor' class; and of viewing the majority of men as various kinds of failures for not conforming to artificially-constructed ideals. You can regard this as a corrective to a recent political mistake, or as advance notice of a social paradigm shift. What it is *not* is special pleading — we've had quite enough of that already.

We just need to see life as the game that it is and that we all play — just like at school, the game is compulsory. We need to play by the rules we have inherited. We can better organise our societies to be congruent with this, so that we improve equitability; but we can't just make up the rules as we go along or rewrite the rule-book to suit the fads and intellectual prejudices of the time.

Bibliography

Acton, William (1870) *Prostitution, Considered in its Moral, Social and Sanitary Aspects in London and Other Large Cities and Garrison Towns, with Proposals for the Control and Prevention of its Attendant Evils.* 2nd edition. J Churchill, London.

Adler, Patricia A & Peter (1998) *Peer Power: Preadolescent Culture and Identity.* Rutgers University Press.

Adolphs, Ralph (1999). Social cognition and the human brain. *Trends in Cognitive Sciences* 3.

Agrawal, Aneil F (2006) Evolution of sex: Why do organisms shuffle their genotypes? *Current Biology* 16.

Anzenberger, Gustl (1992) Monogamous social system and paternity in primates in *Paternity in primates: genetic tests and theories* ed. Basel, Karger.

Anzenberger, Gustl (1993) Social conflict in two monogamous New World primates: Pairs and rivals in *Primate Social Conflict* W.A. Mason; S.P. Mendoza (ed).

Archer, John A (2000) Sex differences in aggression between heterosexual partners: A meta-analytic review *Psychological Bulletin* 126.

Archer, John A (2001) Partner aggression: Is mate-guarding too narrow a perspective? *Conference presentation Human Behaviour & Evolution Society.*

Archer, John A & Vaughan, Elaine (2001) Evolutionary theories of rape. *Sexualities. Evolution & Gender* v3n1.

Archer, John A (2005) Personal communication.

Atkinson, Gerald L (2004) *Radical Feminism and 'Political Correctness'.* Chapter 5 in Lind (ed) *'Political Correctness': A Short History of an Ideology.* Free Congress Foundation.

Atmar, Wirt (1991) On the role of males. *Animal Behaviour* 41.

Barbaree, Howard E & Marshall, William L (1991) The role of male sexual arousal in rape: Six models. *Journal of Consulting and Clinical Psychology* 59.

Baron-Cohen, Simon (2003) *The Essential Difference: Men, Women and the Extreme Male Brain.* Allen Lane.

Bateau, Helen S; Booth, Alan; Shirtcliff, Elizabeth A & Granger, Douglas A (2002) Testosterone, cortisol, and women's competition. *Evolution and Human Behavior* v23 n3.

Bateup, Helen S; Booth, Alan; Shirtcliff, Elizabeth A & Granger, Douglas A (2002) Testosterone, cortisol, and women's competition. *Evolution and Human Behavior* 23

Baumeister, Roy (2007) Is *There Anything Good About Men?* Invited address to the American Psychological Association.

Bayard, Kimberley et al (2003) New evidence on sex segregation and sex differences in wages from matched employee-employer data. *Journal of Labor Economics* 21(4).

Benenson, Joyce F (1993) Greater preference among females than males for dyadic interaction in early childhood. *Child Development* 64.

Berg, Nathan & Lien, Donald (2002) Measuring the effect of sexual orientation on income: evidence of discrimination? *Contemporary Economic Policy* v20 n4.

Bernstein, Irwin S; Judge, Peter G & Ruehlmann, Thomas E (1993) Sex differences in adolescent rhesus monkey (*Macaca mulatta*) behavior. *American Journal of Primatology* 31.

Bernstein, Richard (1994) *The Dictatorship of Virtue: Multiculturalism and the Battle for America's Future.* Knopf.

Billington-Grieg, Teresa (1913) The truth about white slavery. *English Review* June 1913.

Birky jr, C William (1999) An even broader perspective on sex and recombination. *Journal of Evolutionary Biology* 12.

Blackstone, Sir William (1769) *Commentaries on the Laws of England* (1765-1769) Open access internet edition 2005: http://www.lonang.com/exlibris/blackstone/bla-000.htm.

Blair, Ian (1985) *Investigating Rape: A New Approach for Police*. Police Foundation.

Blossfeld, Hans-Peter (1987) Labor market entry and the sexual segregation of careers in the Federal Republic of Germany. *American Journal of Sociology* 93.

Böheim, René & Taylor, Mark P (2001) Option or obligation? The determinants of labour supply preferences in Britain. *The Institute for Social and Economic Research*.

Boniface, Borne J (1994) Ruining a good boy for the sake of a bad girl: False accusation theory in sexual offences. *Current Issues in Criminal Justice* V 6, N 1.

Booth, Alan; Granger, Douglas A; Mazur, Allan & Kivlighan, Katie T (2006) Testosterone and Social Behavior. *Social Forces* v85n1.

Bosanquet, Nicholas & Sikora, Karol (2006) *The Economics of Cancer Care*. Cambridge University Press.

Bose, Christine (1985) *Jobs and Gender: Sex and Occupational Prestige*. Praeger Publishing, New York.

Bourgeois, Martin & Perkins, James (2003) A test of evolutionary and socio-cultural explanations of reactions to sexual harassment. *Sex Roles: A Journal of Research*.

Bradshaw, Jonathan R (1996) The Child Support Act: Talk to the All-Party Commons Committee. *NACSA News* March/April (Network Against the Child Support Agency).

Brewer, Sarah (2001) *A Child's World: A Unique Insight into How Children Think*. Headline Book Publishing. Channel 4 TV series.

Bribiescas, Richard G (2006) *Men: Evolutionary and Life History*. Harvard University Press

British Crime Survey (1996) Supplement. *Home Office*.

Brown, Bradford B & Klute, Christa (2003) Cliques, crowds, and friendships. In Adams & Berzonsky (Eds) *Handbook of Adolescent Development*. Blackwell, London.

Brown, Callum (2000), The Death of Christian Britain (London: Routledge).

Browne, Anthony (2006) *The Retreat of Reason: Political Correctness and the Corruption of Public Debate in Modern Britain*. Civitas, London.

Burmeister, Sabrina S (2005) Rapid behavioral and genomic responses to social opportunity. *Public Library of Science*.

Burston, Daniel (1991) *The Legacy of Erich Fromm*. Cambridge: Harvard University Press.

Buss, David M (2003) *The Evolution of Desire*. Basic Books, New York.

Byrne, Donn & Kelley, Catherine (1986) Psychological Research & Public Policy: Taking a Long hard look Before we Leap. A review of behavioral and social science research. Paper presented at the U.S. Justice Department Hearings, Houston.

Carpenter, Christopher S (2005) Self-reported sexual orientation and earnings: evidence from California. *Industrial & Labor Relations Review* v58 n2.

Cerullo, Margaret (1979), Marcuse and Feminism, *New German Critique*, No.18, Autumn, 1979, pp. 21-23.

Chagnon, Napoleon (1979) Mate competition, favoring close kin, and village fissioning among the Yanomamo Indians. *Evolutionary biology and human social behaviour: An anthropological perspective* (ed Chagnon & William Irons).

Chandola, Tarana; Kuper, Hannah; Singh-Manoux, Archana; Bartley, Mel & Marmot, Michael (2004) The effect of control at home on CHD events in the Whitehall II study: Gender differences in psychosocial domestic pathways to social inequalities in CHD. *Social Science & Medicine* v58n8.

Children and Family Court Advisory and Support Service (CAFCASS) (2005) Domestic Violence Assessment Policy. CAFCASS.

Clausen, Vincent (2007) An assessment of Gunilla Ekberg's account of Swedish prostitution policy. Online article.

Cohen, Yinon & Yitchak, Haberfeld (1991) Why do married men earn more than unmarried men? *Social Science Research* 20.

Colarelli, Stephen M; Spranger, Jennifer L & Hechanova, Regina (2006) Women, power, and sex composition in small groups: An evolutionary perspective. *Journal of Organizational Behavior* v27n2.

Connellan, Jennifer; Baron-Cohen, Simon; Wheelwright, Sally; Batki, Anna & Ahluwalia, Jag (2001) Sex differences in human neonatal social perception. *Infant Behavior and Development* 23.

Corbin, Alain (1990) *Women for Hire: Prostitution and Sexuality in France after 1850.* Harvard University Press.

Cosmides, Leda (1989) The logic of social exchange: Has natural selection shaped how humans reason? Studies with the Wason selection task. *Cognition* 31.

Cowlishaw, Guy & Dunbar, Robin IM (1991) Dominance rank and mating success in male primates. *Animal Behavior* 41.

Creel, Scott (2001) Social dominance and stress hormones. *Trends in Ecology and Evolution* v1 n9.

Cribb Jr, T Kenneth (2004) *'Political Correctness' in Higher Education.* Chapter 3 in Lind (ed) *'Political Correctness': A Short History of an Ideology.* Free Congress Foundation.

Cummins, Denise D (1996) Evidence for the innateness of deontic reasoning. *Mind and Language* 11.

Cummins, Denise D (1996a) Dominance hierarchies and the evolution of human reasoning. *Minds and Machines* 6, 4.

Cummins, Denise D (1996c) Evidence of deontic reasoning in 3- and 4-year-old children. *Memory & Cognition* 24, 6.

Cummins, Denise D (1998) Social norms and other minds: the evolutionary roots of higher cognition. Chapter 2 in Cummins & Allen (ed) *The Evolution of Mind.*

Cummins, Denise D & Allen, Collin (ed) (1998) *The Evolution of Mind.* Oxford University Press.

Cummins, Denise D (1999) Cheater detection is modified by social rank. *Evolution and Human Behavior* 20.

Cummins, Denise D (2000) How the social environment shaped the evolution of mind. *Synthese* v122 n1-2.

Davis, Kingsley & Van den Oever, Pietronella (1982) Demographic Foundations of New Sex Roles. *Population and Development Review* 8.

Dawkins, Richard (1976, rev ed 2006) *The Selfish Gene.* Oxford University Press.

De Castillejo, Irene Clairmont (1973, repub 1997) *Knowing Woman: A Feminine Psychology.* Shambhala US.

De Ruiter Jan R & van Hooff Jan ARAM (1993) Male dominance rank and reproductive success in primate groups *Biomedical and Life Sciences* v34n4.

De Visser, J Arjan & Elena, Santiago F (2007) The evolution of sex: empirical insights into the roles of epistasis and drift. *Nature Reviews Genetics* v8.

Deary, Ian J & Der, Geoffrey (2005) Reaction time, age, and cognitive ability: Longitudinal findings from age 16 to 63 years in representative population samples. *Aging, Neuropsychology and Cognition* 12.

Degirmencioglu, Serdar M; Urberg, Kathryn A; Tolson, Jerry M & Richard, P (1998) Adolescent friendship networks: Continuity and change over the school years. *Merrill-Palmer Quarterly* 44.

Dennett, Daniel C (1996) *Darwin's Dangerous Idea: Evolution and the meanings of Life.* Penguin.

Dennett, Daniel C (2003) *Freedom Evolves.* Allen Lane, London.

Di Fiore, Anthony (2003) Molecular genetic approaches to the study of primate behavior, social organization, and reproduction. *Yearbook Physiological Anthropology* 46.

Doezema, Jo (1998) Forced to choose: Beyond the voluntary v. forced prostitution dichotomy. In Kempadoo & Doezema (eds) *Global Sex Workers: Rights, Resistance and Redefinition.*

Doezema, Jo (2000) Loose women or lost women? The re-emergence of the myth of 'white slavery'. *Contemporary discourses of 'trafficking in women'.*

Donnerstein, Edward; Linz, Daniel & Penrod, Steven (1987) *The Question of Pornography: Research Findings and Policy Implications.* Free Press, New York.

Dumond, Robert W (1992) The sexual assault of male inmates in incarcerated settings. *International Journal of the Sociology of Law* 20.

Dunphy, Dexter (1963) The social structure of urban adolescent peer groups. *Sociometry* vol 26 no 2. Reprinted in Grinder, Robert E *Studies in Psychology* v11 1969.

Dutton, Donald & Nicholls, Tonia (2005) The gender paradigm in domestic violence research and theory. *Aggression and Violent Behaviour* v10 n6.

Eisenman, Russell (2003) Forgetting to use birth control: Unwanted pregnancies support evolutionary psychology theory. *Journal of Evolutionary Psychology* 24.

Ennis, Michael; Kelly, Kimberly S & Lambert, Paul L (2001) Sex differences in cortisol excretion during anticipation of a psychological stressor: possible support for the tend-and-befriend hypothesis. *Stress and Health* v17n4.

Etaugh, Claire & Liss, Marsha B (1992) Home, school, and playroom: Training grounds for adult gender roles. *Sex Roles* 26.

Evardone, Milagros; Alexander, Gerianne M & Morey, Leslie C (2007) Hormones and borderline personality features. *Personality and Individual Differences*

Fabes, Richard A; Martin, Carol L & Hanish, Laura D (2004) The next 50 years: Considering gender as a context for understanding young children's peer relationships *Merrill Palmer Quarterly Journal of Developmental Psychology* v50n3.

Falk, Dean; Froese, Nicholee; Sade, Donald & Dudek, Bruce (1999) Sex differences in brain/body relationships of rhesus monkeys and humans. *Journal of Human Evolution.*

Farrar (2005), False rape complaints, on David P Farrar's 'Kiwiblog'. (Wellington, NZ, August 8th. 2005).

Farrell, Warren (1994) *The Myth of Male Power*. Fourth Estate, London.

Feldman-Summers, Shirley & Palmer, Gayle C (1980) Rape as viewed by judges, prosecutors and police officers. *Criminal Justice and Behavior* 7.

Felson, Richard B & Cares, Alison C (2005) Gender and the seriousness of assaults on intimate partners and other victims. *Journal of Marriage and Family* v67 n5.

Fernald, Russell; Fox, Helen; White, Stephanie & Kao, Mimi (2002) Stress and dominance in a social fish. *Neuroscience.*

Fiddick, Laurence; Cosmides, Leda & Tooby, John (2000) No interpretation without representation: the role of domain-specific representations and inferences in the Wason selection task. *Cognition* 77.

Fiddick, Laurence & Cummins, Denise D (2001) Reciprocity in ranked relationships: Does social structure influence social reasoning? *Journal of Bioeconomics* 3.

Fiebert, Martin S (2007) References Examining Assaults by Women on their Spouses or Male Partners: an Annotated Bibliography. On-line: www.csulb.edu/~mfiebert/assault.htm

Fillingim, RB & Maixner, W (1995) Gender differences in the responses to noxious stimuli. *Pain Forum* 4.

Franklin, Michael S & Zyphur, Michael J (2005) The role of dreams in the evolution of the human mind. *Evolutionary Psychology* 3.

Franks, Susan (1999) *Having None Of It: Women, Men And The Future Of Work*. Granta.

Fromm, Erich (1941, repub 1994) *Escape from Freedom*. Owl Books.

Fukuyama, Francis (1999) *The Great Disruption: Human Nature and the Reconstitution of Social Order*. Profile, London.

GAATW (1994) A proposal to replace the Convention for the Suppression of the Traffic in Persons and of the Exploitation of the Prostitution of Others. Utrecht GAATW.

Geary, David (1998) *Male, Female: The Evolution Of Human Sex Differences*. American Psychological Association.

George, Malcolm J (1994) Riding the donkey backwards: Men as the unacceptable victims of marital violence. *Journal of Men's Studies* 3.

George, Malcolm J (2002) Skimmington revisited. *Journal of Men's Studies* 10 n2.

George, Malcolm J (2003) Invisible touch. *Aggression & Violent Behaviour* 8.

George, Malcolm J & Yarwood, David J (2004) Male domestic violence victims survey 2001. www.dewar4research.org/downloads.htm

Giallombardo, Rose (1966) *Society of Women: a Study of Women's Prison*. John Wiley & Sons, New York.

Gibson, Mary (1986) *Prostitution and the State in Italy, 1860-1915*. Rutgers University Press.

Gintzler, Alan R & Liu, Nai-Jiang (2000) Ovarian sex steroids activate antinociceptive systems and reveal gender-specific mechanisms. In Fillingim (ed) *Sex, Gender, and Pain. Progress in Pain Research and Management* v17 IASP Press, Seattle.

GMB (2006) Ana Lopez quoted in: GMB reaction to Government white paper on prostitution *Labournet UK*.

Gneezy, Uri; Niederle, Muriel & Rustichini, Aldo (2003) Performance in competitive environments: Gender Differences. *Quarterly Journal of Economics*.

Gneezy, Uri & Rustichini, Aldo (2004) Gender and competition at a young age. *American Economic Review Papers and Proceedings*.

Goodwin, Stephanie & Rudman, Lawrie (2004) Gender differences in automatic in-group bias: Why do women like women more than men like men? *Social Psychology 87(4)*.

Graham-Kevan, Nicola & Archer, John A (2005) Investigating four explanations of women's relationship aggression. *Psychology of Women Quarterly* 29.

Graham-Kevan, Nicola (2007) Power and control in relationship aggression. In Hamel, John & Nicholls, Tonia L (ed) *Family Interventions in Domestic Violence*. Springer Publishing, New York.

Graham-Kevan, Nicola (2007) Partner violence typologies. In Hamel, John & Nicholls, Tonia L (ed) *Family Interventions in Domestic Violence*. Springer Publishing, New York.

Gray, John (2007) *Black Mass: Apocalyptic Religion and the Death of Utopia*. Allen Lane, London.

Green, David G (2006) *We're (Nearly) All Victims Now: How Political Correctness is Undermining our Liberal Culture*. Civitas, London.

Green, Richard (1987) Exposure to explicit sexual materials and sexual assault: A Review of Behavioral and Social Science Research. In Walsh (ed) *The Psychology of Women, Ongoing Debates. Yale* University Press

Gregory, Stanford W; Webster, Stephen & Huang, G (1993) Voice pitch and amplitude convergence as a metric of quality in dyadic interviews. *Language & Communication* 13.

Gregory, Stanford W & Webster, Stephen (1996) A nonverbal signal in voices of interview partners effectively predicts communication accommodation and social status perceptions. *Journal of Personal Social Psychology* 70(6).

Gregory, Stanford W; Dagan, K & Webster, S (1997) Evaluating the relation of vocal accommodation in conversation of partner's fundamental frequencies to perceptions of communication quality. *Journal of Nonverbal Behavior* 21.

Gregory, Stanford W & Gallagher, Timothy J (2002) Spectral analysis of candidates' nonverbal vocal communication: Predicting U.S. presidential election outcomes. *Social Psychology Quarterly* v65 n3.

Gregory, Stanford W (2005) Analysis of fundamental frequency reveals covariation in interview partners' speech. *Journal of nonverbal behavior* v14 n4.

Grittner, Frederick K (1990) *White Slavery: Myth, Ideology and American Law*. Taylor & Francis.

Grogan, Sarah, Conner, Mark, and Smithson, Helen (2006), Sexuality and Exercise Motivations: Are Gay Men and Heterosexual Women Most Likely to be Motivated by Concern About Weight and Appearance? *Sex Roles*, 55 (7-8).

Guisinger, Shan (2003). Adapted to flee famine: adding an evolutionary perspective on anorexia nervosa. *Psychological Review*, 110, pp. 745–761.

Haier, Richard J; Jung, Rex E; Yeo, Roland A; Head, Kevin & Alkire, Michael T (2005) The neuroanatomy of general intelligence: sex matters. *Neuroimage* v25 n1.

Hakim, Catherine (2004) *Key Issues In Women's Work (second edition)*. Glasshouse, London.

Hakim, Catherine (2003) *Models of the Family in Modern Societies: Ideals and Realities*. Ashgate.

Hakim, Catherine (2000) *Work-lifestyle Choices in the 21st Century: Preference theory*. Oxford University Press.

Hall, D. (2006), Spears' Space: The Play of Innocence and Experience in the Bare-Midriff Fashion, *Journal of Popular Culture*, 39 (6), 1025–1034.

Harkness, Susan & Waldfogel, Jane (1999) The family gap in pay: Evidence from seven industrialised countries. CASEpaper 30 LSE.

Harris, Judith Rich (1998) *The Nurture Assumption*. Bloomsbury, London.

Hazen, Helen (1983) *Endless Rapture: Rape, Romance and the Female Imagination*. Charles Scribners, New York.

Hecker, Daniel (1998) How hours of work affect occupational earnings. *Monthly Labor Review* v121n10.

Hoffmann, Melissa L & Powlishta, Kimberly K (2001) Gender segregation in childhood: a test of the interaction style theory. *Journal of Genetic Psychology* 162.

Home Office (1999) Research Study 196. A question of evidence? Investigating and prosecuting rape in the 1990s, by Jessica Harris and Sharon Grace.

Home Office (1999) Research Study 191.

Home Office (2005) Research Study 293 Kelly, Liz; Lovett, Jo & Regan, Linda (2005) A gap or a chasm? Attrition in reported rape cases. Child and Woman Abuse Studies Unit, London Metropolitan University.

Home Office (2006) A coordinated prostitution strategy.

Horsley, Sebastian (2004) The brothel creeper. *Observer* September 19.

House of Commons Constitutional Affairs Committee (2005) Report on Family Courts.

Hughes, Hywel; Peters, Rachael; Davies, Gareth & Griffiths, Keith (2007) A study of patients presenting to an emergency department having had a "spiked drink". *Emergency Medicine Journal* 24.

Hunter, Michael et al (2005) Male and female voices activate distinct regions in the male brain. *Neuroimage v27n3*.

Hurley, S.L. (n.d.), *Feminism and Evolutionary Psychology: Can They be Reconciled?*, www.warwick.ac.uk/staff/S.L.Hurley/papers/fep.pdf

Ingo, K.M., Mize, K.D., & Pratarelli, M.E. (2007) Female Intrasexual Competition: Toward an Evolutionary Feminist Theory, *Theory and Science*.

Ireland, Jane L (1999) Bullying behaviors amongst male and female prisoners: A study of young offenders and adults. *Aggressive Behavior* 25.

Irwin, Mary Anne (1996) 'White slavery' as metaphor: Anatomy of a moral panic. *The History Journal V*.

Irwing, Paul & Lynn, Richard (2005) Sex differences in means and variability on the progressive matrices in university students: A meta-analysis. *British Journal of Psychology*.

Jaffe, Klaus (2002) On the adaptive value of Sex. *Proceedings of the Fourth International Conference on Complex Systems*.

Jaffe, Klaus (2004) Sex promotes gamete selection: a quantitative comparative study of features favoring the evolution of sex. *Complexity v9 n6*.

Jay, Martin (1973) *The Dialectical Imagination: A History of the Frankfurt School and the Institute of Social Research, 1923-1950*. University of California Press.

Jensen, Arthur R (2006) *Clocking the mind: Mental chronometry and individual differences*. Elsevier, Oxford.

Johnson, Helen Kendrick (1913) *A Survey of the Woman Suffrage Movement in the United States and a Discussion of the Claims and Arguments of Its Foremost Advocates*. (Full text: http://womenshistory.about.com/library/etext/bl_watr_1.htm)

Johnson, Michael P (1995) Patriarchal terrorism and common couple violence: Two forms of violence against women *Journal of Marriage and the Family* v57n2.

Johnson, Michael P (2005) Domestic violence: It's not about gender—Or is it? *Journal of Marriage and Family* 67.

Johnson, Michael P (2006) Conflict and control: Symmetry and asymmetry in domestic violence *Violence Against Women* v12n11.

Julien, Elise & Over, Ray (1984) Male sexual arousal with repeated exposure to erotic stimuli. *Archives of sexual behavior* v13n3.

Kalma, Akko (1991) Hierarchisation & dominance at first glance. *European Journal of Social Psychology*, v21n2.

Kappeler, Peter M (1993) Female dominance in primates and other mammals. In *Perspectives in Ethology*. Vol. 10. *Behavior and Evolution* (ed Bateson PPG, Klopfer PH, & Thompson NS).

Katz, Leonard D. (2000), *Evolutionary Origins of Morality: Cross-disciplinary perspectives* (Exeter: Imprint Academic).

Kaufman, Daniel; Smith, Eric LP; Gohil, Baiju C; Banerji, MaryAnn; Coplan, Jeremy D; Kral, John G & Rosenblum, Leonard A (2005) Early appearance of the metabolic syndrome in socially reared bonnet macaques. *Journal of Clinical Endocrinology & Metabolism* v90n1.

Keller, Laurent (ed) (1999) *Levels of selection in evolution.* Princeton University Press.

Kellner, Douglas (nd), Erich Fromm, Feminism, and the Frankfurt School, *Illuminations: The Critical Theory Website.* www.uta.edu/huma/illuminations/kell8.htm

Kelly, Kathryn & Musialowski, Donna (1986) Repeated exposure to sexually explicit stimuli: Novelty, sex, and sexual attitudes. *Archives of sexual behaviour* v15n6.

Kimchi, Tali; Xu, Jennings & Dulac, Catherine (2007) A functional circuit underlying male sexual behaviour in the female mouse brain. *Nature advance online publication.*

King, Michael & Mezey, Gillian (1987) Male victims of sexual assault *Medicine, Science & the Law* v27n2.

King, Michael & Mezey, Gillian (1989) The effects of sexual assault on men: a survey of 22 victims. *Psychological Medicine v*19n1.

Kirby, Jill (2005) *The Price of Parenting.* Centre for Policy Studies.

Kirschbaum, Clemens; Wust, Stefan & Hellhammer, Dirk (1992) Consistent sex differences in cortisol responses to psychological stress. *Psychosomatic Medicine* 54.

Klinkova, Ekaterina; Hodges, J Keith; Fuhrmann, Kerstin; de Jong, Tom & Heistermann, Michael (2005) Male dominance rank, female mate choice and male mating and reproductive success in captive chimpanzees *International Journal of Primatology* v26n2.

Komisaruk, Barry R & Whipple, Beverly (2000) How does vaginal stimulation produce pleasure, pain, and analgesia? In Fillingim (ed) *Sex, Gender, and Pain. Progress in Pain Research and Management* v17 IASP Press, Seattle.

Kodric-Brown, Astrid & Brown, James H (1987) Anisogamy, sexual selection, and the evolution and maintenance of sex. *Evolutionary Ecology* v1n2.

Kors, Alan Charles & Silvergate, Harvey A (1999) *The Shadow University: The Betrayal Of Liberty On America's Campuses.* Harper.

Krauthammer, Charles (1993) Defining deviancy up: The new assault on bourgeois life. *The New Republic* November 22.

Khrushchev, Nikita (1956) Secret speech delivered by First Party Secretary at the Twentieth Party Congress of the Communist Party of the Soviet Union, February 25, 1956. From *the Congressional Record: Proceedings and Debates* of *the 84th Congress, 2nd Session* (May 22, 1956-June 11, 1956), C11, Part 7 (June 4, 1956). Full text on-line at the Modern History Sourcebook.

Kutchinsky, Berl (1985) Pornography and its effects in Denmark and the United States: A rejoinder and beyond. *Comparative Social Research* 8.

Larson, Christine Lia (2005) When Girls Stop Competing Against Boys: An Experimental Analysis of the Competitive Behaviour of Young Children. (Harvard Honors Thesis).

Lenormand, Thomas & Dutheil Julien (2005) Recombination difference between sexes: A role for haploid selection. *Public Library of Science Biology* 3(3).

Levinson, Richard M (1975) Sex discrimination and employment practices: An experiment with unconventional job inquiries. *Social Problems* 22.

Lewis, Ann & Sarantakos, Sotiris (2001) Domestic violence and the male victim. *Nuance* 3.

Leys, Ruth (2000) *Trauma: A Genealogy.* University of Chicago Press, Chicago & London.

Lind, William S (1997) *What is 'Political Correctness'? Essays on our Times.* Free Congress Foundation.

Lind, William S (2004) *'Political Correctness': A Short History of an Ideology.* Chapter 1 in Lind (ed) *'Political Correctness': A Short History of an Ideology.* Free Congress Foundation.

Lind, William S (2004) *Further Reading on the Frankfurt School.* Chapter 6 in Lind (ed) *'Political Correctness': A Short History of an Ideology.* Free Congress Foundation. *http://www.anu.edu.au/polsci/marx/classics/manifesto.html*

Loftus, Elizabeth F., and Ketcham, Katherine (1994), *The Myth of Repressed Memory.* St. Martin's Press.

Lord Chancellor's Department (2005) Making Contact Work
    http://www.dca.gov.uk/family/abfla/mcwrep.htm

Lowenstein, Ludwig F (2000a) The obsessive-compulsive rapist. *Justice of the Peace* v164n25.

Lutchmaya, Svetlana; Baron-Cohen, Simon & Raggett, Peter (2002) Foetal testosterone and
    eye contact in 12 month old infants. *Infant Behavior and Development* 25.

Maccoby, Eleanor E & Jacklin, Carol N (1987) Gender segregation in childhood. In Reese
    (ed) *Advances in Child Development and Behavior v20*. Academic Press, New York.

MacDonald, Ian (1998) *Revolution in the Head: The "Beatles" Records and the Sixties*. Pimlico.

Maddox, William & Brewer, Marilynn (2005) Gender differences in the relational and
    collective bases for trust. *Group Processes Intergroup Relations* 8(2).

Malloy, Kim (2001) *Are men or women more committed to organizations?* International Survey
    Research Corporation (ISR), Chicago.

Marcuse, Herbert (1955, repub 1992) *Eros and Civilization: A Philosophical Inquiry into Freud*.
    Beacon Press.

Marmot, Michael G; Smith, GD; Stansfeld, S; Patel, C; North, F; Head, J; White, I; Brunner,
    E & Feeney, A (1991) Health inequalities among British civil servants: the Whitehall II
    study. *The Lancet* 337.

Marmot, Sir Michael G (2004) *Status Syndrome: How Social Standing Affects our Health and
    Longevity*. Bloomsbury.

Marx, Karl & Engel, Friedrich (1848) *Manifesto of the Communist Party*.

Mavin, Sharon & Bryans, P (2003) Women's place in organization: the role of female
    misogyny. Paper presented at the *Third International Gender, Work and Organization
    Conference*, Keele, UK.

Mavin, Sandra & Lockwood, A (2004) Sisterhood and solidarity vs queen bees and female
    misogyny: A future for women in management? *British Academy of management
    Conference, 2004, St Andrews*.

Mazur, Allan; Susman, Elizabeth J & Edelbrock, Sandy (1997) Sex difference in testosterone
    response to a video game competition. *Evolution and Human Behavior* 18.

McCormick, Thelma (1983) Report for the Metropolitan Toronto Task Force on Violence
    Against Women. (unpublished: suppressed).

McDonald, Jamie (2004) *'Political Correctness' Deconstruction and Literature*. Chapter 4 in
    Lind (ed) *'Political Correctness': A Short History of an Ideology*. Free Congress Foundation.

McDowell, Charles (1985) The FBI Behavioural Science Unit's Behaviour Manual on
    Recognizing False Allegations.

McDowell, Charles (1985) False Allegations. *Forensic Science Digest* v11n4.

McElroy, Wendy (1997) A Feminist Defense of Pornography. *Free Inquiry* v17n4.

McLaughlin, Ken (2004) PC or not PC? *Spiked! 18 February*.
    http://www.spiked-online.com/Articles/0000000CA405.htm

McLaughlin, Neil (1999) Origin Myths in the Social Sciences: Fromm, the Frankfurt School
    and the Emergence of Critical Theory. *Canadian Journal of Sociology* v24n1

Mealey, Linda; Daood, Christopher & Krage, Michael (1996) Enhanced memory for faces of
    cheaters. *Ethological Sociobiology* 17.

Mealey, Linda (2000) *Sex Differences: Developmental and Evolutionary Strategies*. Academic
    Press.

Mears, Martin (2005) *Institutional Injustice*. Civitas, London.

Messer-Davidow, Ellen (1993) Manufacturing the Attack on Liberalized Higher Education,
    Social Text, 36.

Mezey, Gillian (1985) Rape — victimological and psychiatric aspects. *The Journal of Hospital
    Medicine*.

Misevic, Dusan; Ofria, Charles & Lenski, Richard E (2005) Sexual reproduction reshapes
    the genetic architecture of digital organisms. *Proceedings of the Royal Society: Biological
    Sciences*. Published online.

Moir, Anne & Bill (1998) *Why Men Don't Iron: The Real Science Of Gender Studies*.
    HarperCollins, London.

Molm, Linda D (1986) Gender, power, and legitimation: A test of three theories. *American
    Journal of Sociology* v91n6.

Moser, Kath; Pugh, Helena & Goldblatt, Peter (1988) Inequalities in women's health in England and Wales: mortality among married women according to social circumstances, employment characteristics and life cycle stage. Subsequently pub in *Genus v* XLVI 1990.

Moxon, Steven P. (2007) Dominance hierarchy as integral to reproductive suppression; an adaptation consequent to the evolution of the male mating type. See: http://imprint-academic.com/dh.html

Muehnenhard, Charlene L & Hollabaugh, Lisa C (1988) Do women sometimes say no when they mean yes? The prevalence and correlates of women's token resistance to sex. *Journal of Personality and Social Psychology 54.*

Niederle, Muriel & Vesterlund, Lise (2005) Do women shy away from competition? Do men compete too much? *NBER Working Paper n11474.*

Nunney, Leonard (1999) Lineage selection: natural selection for long-term benefit. In Keller L (ed) *Levels of selection in evolution* (1999) Princeton University Press.

Oda, Ryo (1997) Biased face recognition in the prisoner's dilemma games. *Evolution and Human Behavior* 18.

O'Daniel, William (1859) *Ins and Outs of London.* SC Lamb.

Ochoa, Gabriela & Jaffe, Klaus (2006) Assortative mating drastically alters the magnitude of error thresholds. (Refereed conference contribution) http://metronum.inria.fr/html/Papers/files/pdf

Okami, Paul & Shackelford, Todd K (2001) Human sex differences in sexual psychology and behavior. *Annual Review of Sex Research* 12.

Omark, D Ronald; Omark, Monica V & Edelman, Murray S (1975) Formation of dominance hierarchies in young children: Action and perception. In Williams, TR (ed) *Psychological anthropology* Mouton Publishers, Paris.

Onojeharho, J E & Bloom, L (1986) Inmate subculture in a Nigerian prison. *The Newspaper of Psychology* v120n5.

Östergren, Petra (nd) Sexworkers Critique of Swedish Prostitution Policy. On-line article.

Otto, Sarah P & Gerstein, Aleeza C (2006) Why have sex? The population genetics of sex and recombination. *Biochemical Society Transactions* v34part 4.

Paland, Susanne & Lynch, Michael (2006) Transitions to asexuality result in excess amino acid substitutions. *Science* v311n5763.

Parker, GA; Baker, RR & Smith VGF (1972) The origin and evolution of gamete dimorphism and the male-female phenomenon. *Journal of Theoretical Biology* 36.

Pelling, Henry (1967) *The Social Geography of British Elections 1885-1910* Macmillan, London.

Pickard, Tom (2000) *Rough Music* (Ruff Muzhik), extract 'A Work Conchy ' in *The Chicago Review* 46.

Pinker, Steven (1998) *How the Mind Works.* Allen Lane, London.

Pinker, Steven (2002) *The Blank Slate.* Penguin

Plomin, Robert & Daniels, Denise (1987) Why are children in the same family so different from one another? *Behavioral and Brain Sciences* 10.

Prigatano, George & Schacter, Daniel L (eds) (1991) *Awareness of Deficit After Brain Injury: Clinical and Theoretical Issues.* Oxford University Press.

Prostitutes Rights Organisation for Sex Workers (PROS) et al (1995) Alleged trafficking of Asian sex workers in Australia, Sydney. Discussion paper for Beijing.

Pugh, Martin (1978) *Electoral Reform in War and Peace 1906-18.* Routledge & Kegan Paul, London & Boston.

Pugh, Martin (2002) *March of the Women: A Revisionist Analysis of the Campaign for Women's Suffrage, 1866-1914.* Oxford university Press.

Radespiel, Ute & Zimmerman, E (2001) Female dominance in captive gray mouse lemurs (Microcebus murinus). *American Journal of Primatology* 54 (4).

Raehn, Raymond V (1996) *Critical Theory: A Special Research Report.*

Raehn, Raymond V (1997) *The Historical Roots of 'Political Correctness'.* Free Congress Foundation n44.

Raehn, Raymond V (2004) *The Historical Roots of 'Political Correctness'.* Chapter 2 in Lind (ed) *'Political Correctness': A Short History of an Ideology.* Free Congress Foundation.

Ramachandran, V.S., and Hirstein, William (1999), The Science of Art: A Neurological Theory of Aesthetic Experience, *Journal of Consciousness Studies*, 6 (6-7), pp. 15-51.

Reed, Edward; Vernon, Phillip & Johnson, Andrew (2004) Confirmation of correlation between brain nerve conduction velocity and intelligence level in normal adults. *Intelligence* v32n6.

Reich, Wilhelm (1933 repub 1980) *The Mass Psychology of Fascism*. Farrar, Straus and Giroux

Riach, Peter A & Rich, Judith (2006) An experimental investigation of sexual discrimination in hiring in the English labour market. *Advances in Economic Analysis & Policy* v6n2.

Ridley, Matt (1997) *The Origins of Virtue*. Penguin.

Ridley, Matt (2003) *Nature via Nurture*. Fourth Estate, London.

Riley, JL; Robinson, ME; Wise, EA; Myers, CD & Fillingim, RB (1998) Sex differences in the perception of noxious experimental stimuli: a meta-analysis. *Pain 74*.

Roiphe, Katie 1994 *The Morning After: Sex, Fear and Feminism*. Back Bay.

Rubin, Kenneth H & Coplan, Robert J (1993) Peer relationships in childhood. In M. Bornstein and M. Lamb (eds) *Developmental psychology: an advanced textbook*.

Russell, Andrew F; Clutton-Brock, Tim H; Brotherton, Peter N M; Sharpe, Lynda L; McIlrath, Grant M; Dalerum, Fredrik D; Cameron, EZ & Barnard, JA (2002) Factors affecting pup growth and survival in cooperatively breeding meerkats. *Journal of Animal Ecology 7*.

Sacker, Amanda; Firth, David; Fitzpatrick, Ray; Lynch, Kevin & Bartley, Mel (2000) Comparing health inequality in men and women: prospective study of mortality 1986-96. BMJ.

Salmon, Catherine & Symons, Donald (2001) *Warrior Lovers: Erotic fiction, Evolution and Female Sexuality*. Weidenfeld & Nicolson, London.

Sapolsky, Robert M (2004) Social status and health in humans and other animals. *Annual Review of Anthropology* v33.

Sapolsky, Robert M (2005) The influence of social hierarchy on health. *Science* 308.

Sarantakos, Sotirios 2004 Deconstructing self-defense in wife-to-husband violence. *Journal of men's studies* v12.

Scatamburlo, Valerie L. (1998) Soldiers of Misfortune: The New Right's Culture War and the Politics of Political Correctness. in Kincheloe & Steinberg (ed) *Studies in the Postmodern Theory of Education* (Peter Lang, New York).

Schultz, Debra L. (1993) *To Reclaim a Legacy of Diversity: Analyzing the 'Political Correctness' Debates in Higher Education* (National Council for Research on Women).

Scott-Ham, Michael & Burton, Fiona C (2003) Boundaries of Drug-assisted Rape. *Journal of Clinical Forensic Medicines*.

Scriven, John (1896, 2000) *A Practical Treatise on Copyhold Tenure: and of the other tenures (customary & freehold) of lands within manors: with the law of manors and manorial customs generally, and the rules of evidence applicable thereto: including the law of commons or waste lands, and also the jurisdiction of the various manorial courts. 7th edition*. Archibald Brown, Florida.

Segal, Marilyn; Peck, Johanne; Vega-Lahr, Nitza & Field, Tiffany M (1987) A medieval kingdom: leader-follower styles of preschool play. *Journal of Applied Developmental Psychology* 8.

Seymour, Charles (1915) *Electoral Reform in England & Wales: the Development and Operation of the Parliamentary Franchise 1832-1885*. Yale University Press, New Haven.

Shackelford, Todd K; Schmitt, David P & Buss, David M (2005) Universal dimensions of human mate preferences. *Personality and Individual Differences* 39.

Sharp, Evelyn (1933) *Unfinished Adventure: selected reminiscences from an Englishwoman's life*. John Lane/The Bodley Head, London.

Silverman, Irwin & Eals, Marion (1994) The hunter-gatherer theory of spatial sex differences: Proximate factors mediating the female advantage in recall of object arrays. *Ethology & Sociobiology* v15.

Silverman, Irwin W (2006) Sex differences in simple visual reaction times: A historical meta-analysis. *Sex Roles 54*.

Smith, Joan (2007), Sex Lies and Videotape, *New Statesman*, 15 October 2007, pp. 38-40.

Soothill, Ken & Piggott, Linda (1999) False accusations of rape. *Police Journal*.

Soothill, Keith (2004) quoted in *The Guardian*, February 7, in a piece titled: An Unshakeable Delusion, by Dea Birkett.

Sorenson, Richard C & Amick, Nancy J (2005) Factors influencing women's perceptions of a sexually hostile workplace. In Geffner, Robert (ed) *Aggression in Organizations Violence, Abuse, and Harassment at Work and in Schools*.

Spant, Sara & Gonas, Lena (2002) National report on gender pay gap — the Swedish case. Department of Working Life Science, University of Karlstad.

Stead, William (1885) The Maiden Tribute of Modern Babylon. *The Pall Mall Gazette*.

Stets, Jan E & Straus, Murray A (1990) Gender differences in reporting of marital violence and its medical and psychological consequences. In Straus & Gelles (eds) *Physical violence in American families*.

Stets, Jan E & Straus, Murray A (1992) Gender differences in reporting marital violence. In Straus & Gelles (eds) *Physical violence in American families*.

Stone, Valerie E; Cosmides, Leda; Tooby, John; Kroll, Neal & Knight, Robert T (2002) Selective impairment of reasoning about social exchange in a patient with bilateral limbic system damage. *Proceedings of the National Academy of Sciences* 99.

Stowers, Lisa; Holy, Timothy E; Meister, Markus; Dulac, Catherine & Koentges, Georgy (2002) Loss of sex discrimination and male-male aggression in mice deficient for TRP2. *Science* v295n559.

Straus, Murray A (1999) The controversy over domestic violence by women: A methodological, theoretical and sociology of science analysis. In Arriaga, Ximena B & Oskamp, Stuart *Violence in Intimate Relationships*.

Strossen, Nadine (1996) *Defending Pornography: Free Speech, Sex and the Fight for Women's Rights*. Anchor.

Stroud, Laura R; Salovey, Peter & Epel, Elissa S (2002) Sex differences in adrenocortical responses to achievement and interpersonal stress. *Biological Psychiatry* v52n318.

Sugiyama, Lawrence S; Tooby, John & Cosmides, Leda (2002) Cross-cultural evidence of cognitive adaptations for social exchange among the Shiwiar of Ecuadorian Amazonia. *Proceedings of the National Academy of Sciences* 99.

Summers, Christina Hoff (1995) *Who Stole Feminism? How women have betrayed women*. Simon & Schuster.

Swami, Viren, and Tovée, Martin J. (2007), The relative contribution of profile body shape and weight to judgements of women's physical attractiveness in Britain and Malaysia. *Body Image*, 4 (4), 391-396.

Taylor, Diane 2006 The deadly effect of zero tolerance. *Guardian* January 18, 2006. (Taylor is the editor of Mainliners, a magazine for a charity that works with drug users and sex workers. She reports that prostitutes themselves report that 're-education' courses for kerb-crawlers did not stop clients returning to them. West Yorkshire Police ran one in 1998/9 and abandoned it, reporting that: "There does not appear to have been any noticeable reduction in the number of kerb crawlers since the scheme was introduced.")

Temkin, Jennifer (1997) Plus ça change: Reporting rape in the 1990s. *British Journal of Criminology* v37n4.

Thompson, Bill (1994) *Softcore: Moral Crusades Against Pornography in Britain and America*. Cassell.

Tilbrook, AJ; Turner, AI & Clarke, IJ (2000) Effects of stress on reproduction in non-rodent mammals: the role of glucocorticoids and sex differences. *Reviews of Reproduction* (2000) 5.

Turkheimer, Eric (2000) Three laws of behavior genetics and what they mean. *Current Directions in Psychological Science* 9.

Turkheimer, Eric & Waldron, Mary C (2000) Non-shared environment: A theoretical, methodological, and quantitative review. *Psychological Bulletin* 126.

Tyree, A & Hicks, R (1998) Sex and the second moment of prestige distributions. *Social Forces* v66n4.

United States General Accounting Office 2002 re CDC (US Centers for Disease Control and Prevention), stated on May 2002: "CDC reported that, while additional research is needed in this area, current study findings suggest that for most abused women, the risk of physical violence does not seem to increase during pregnancy. Moreover, some women who previously experienced violence do not experience violence during their pregnancies".

Urberg, Kathryn A (1992) Locus of peer influence: Social crowd and best friend. *Journal of Youth and Adolescence* 21.

Urberg, Kathryn A; Degirmencioglu, Serdar M; Tolson, Jerry M & Halliday-Scher, Kathy D (1995) The structure. of adolescent peer networks. *Developmental Psychology* 31.

Urberg, Kathryn A; Degirmencioglu, Serdar M; Tolson, Jerry M & Halliday-Scher, Kathy D (2000) Adolescent social crowds: Measurement and relationship to friendships. *Journal of Adolescent Research* 15.

Valsiner J ,& van der Veer R (2000) *The Social Mind: Construction of the Idea* (New York: Cambridge University Press).

Vogel, David; Murphy, Megan et al (2007) Sex differences in the use of demand and withdraw behavior in marriage. *Journal of Counseling Psychology* v54n2.

Vuilleumier, Patrik (2004) Anosognosia: The neurology of beliefs & uncertainties. *Cortex* 40.

Walkowitz, Judith R (1980) *Prostitution and Victorian Society: Women, Class and the State.* Cambridge University Press.

Wallace, Marina, Kemp, Martin, and Bernstein, Joanne (2007) *Seduced: Art and Sex From Antiquity to Now* (Merrell Publishers).

Walston, Florence; David, Anthony S & Charlton, Bruce G (1998) Sex differences in the content of persecutory delusions: a reflection of hostile threats in the ancestral environment? *Evolution and Human Behaviour* 19.

Ward, David A & Kassebaum, Gene G (1965) *Women's Prison: Sex and Social Structure.* Aldine Publishing Co, Chicago.

Ward, Helen & Robinson, Angela (2004) Response to Paying the Price, Home Office consultation on prostitution. *British Association for Sexual Health and HIV .*

Ward, Helen; Mercer, CH; Wellings, K; Fenton, K; Erens, B; Copas, A & Johnson, AM (2005) Who pays for sex? An analysis of the increasing prevalence of female commercial sex contacts among men in Britain. *Sexually Transmitted Infections* 81.

Watenabe, Satoko (1998) From Thailand to Japan: Migrant sex workers as autonomous subjects. in Kempadoo, Kamala & Doezema, Jo (eds) *Global Sex Workers: Rights, Resistance and Redefinition.*

Webb, Sidney & Beatrice (1963 edition) *English Local Government Vols I-X (1906 through 1929).* Routledge.

Wegner, Daniel (2003), *The Illusion of Conscious Will,* Cambridge, MA: MIT Press.

West, Stuart A; Lively, Curt M & Read, Andrew F (1999) A pluralist approach to sex and recombination. *Journal of Evolutionary Biology* 12.

Whitehall I study (1967-): UCL Department of Epidemiology & Public Health http://www.workhealth.org/projects/pwhitew.html.

Whitehall II study (1985-) UCL Department of Epidemiology & Public Health www.ucl.ac.uk/whitehallII

Wilkinson, Richard (2000) *Mind the Gap: Hierarchies, Health and Human Evolution* Weidenfeld & Nicolson.

Wilson, John K. (1995) *The Myth of Political Correctness: The Conservative Attack on Higher Education* (Durham and London: Duke University Press).

Winking, Jeffrey; Kaplan, Hillard; Gurven, Michael & Rucas, Stacey (2007) Why do men marry and why do they stray? *Proceedings of the Royal Society B (Biological Sciences)* v274n1618.

Working Group (2004) *Purchasing Sexual Services in Sweden and the Netherlands: Local regulation and experiences.* Norwegian Ministry of Justice and Police Affairs.

Wright, Danaya C (1999) De Manneville v. De Manneville: Rethinking the birth of custody law under patriarchy. *Law and History Review* 17.

Yamagishi, Toshio; Tanida, Shigehito; Mashima, Rie; Shimoma, Eri & Kanazawa, Satoshi (2003) You can judge a book by its cover: Evidence that cheaters may look different from co-operators. *Evolution and Human Behavior* 24.

Zolotova, Julia & Brune, Martin (2005) Persecutory delusions: reminiscence of ancestral hostile threats? *Human Behavior & Evolution Society.*

Index